BERLITZ®

DISCOVER
PORTUGAL

Editor: Donald Greig

Typeset and designed by
D & N Publishing,
Ramsbury, Wiltshire.

All cartography by Hardlines, Charlbury, Oxfordshire, except the maps on pages 92 and 94 by Visual Image, Street, Somerset.

Thanks to: the Portuguese National Tourist Office and Pousadas de Portugal for their assistance in the preparation of this book.

Although we have made every effort to ensure the accuracy of all the information in this book, changes do occur. We cannot therefore take responsibility for facts, addresses and circumstances in general which are constantly subject to alteration.

If you have any new information, suggestions or corrections to contribute to this guide, we would like to hear from you. Please write to Berlitz Publishing at one of the above addresses.

Photographic Acknowledgements

All photographs by Claude Huber and © Berlitz Publishing Company Ltd. except for the following: Hulton Deutsch Collection Limited 242, 244; Mary Evans Picture Library 239, 241; Paul Murphy, © Berlitz Publishing Company Ltd. 1, 9, 25, 44, 51 (upper), 59, 284, 293, 294, 295, 303, 307, 324, back cover.

Front cover: Castelo dos Mouros, Sintra

Back cover: Sardine Dock, Portimão, Algarve

Photograph previous page: Serra de Monchique, Algarve

 The Berlitz tick is used to indicate places or events of particular interest.

Phototypeset, originated and printed by C.S. Graphics, Singapore.

BERLITZ®

DISCOVER
PORTUGAL

Martin Gostelow

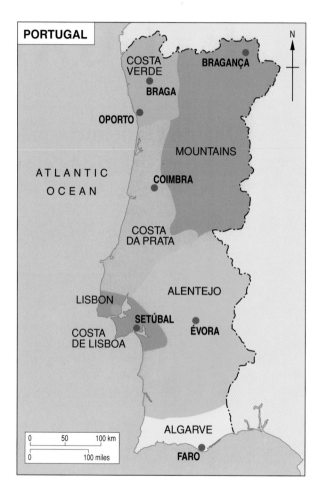

PORTUGAL

N

COSTA VERDE

BRAGANÇA

BRAGA

OPORTO

MOUNTAINS

ATLANTIC
OCEAN

COIMBRA

COSTA
DA PRATA

ALENTEJO

LISBON

SETÚBAL

ÉVORA

COSTA
DE LISBOA

ALGARVE

0   50   100 km

0   100 miles

FARO

Contents

Practical Information to Help You on Your Way

Friendly, accessible and not too big, Portugal is one of the easiest of countries to visit. However, it has its own ways of doing things, from odd opening hours to variable driving habits, and the choice of accommodation in particular can seem confusing. We offer this section of information and advice to smooth your path.

This book covers all of Portugal's regions and their most important towns. For the sake of simplicity we have divided the country into the same seven areas, and used the same names, as the national tourism organization. Each is given a chapter, beginning with **Lisbon** and then moving roughly clockwise. After Lisbon, we look at the **Costa de Lisboa**, near the capital to the north and south. ('Costa' here means not only the coast but inland areas too.) Then come the **Costa da Prata** ('Silver Coast'); **Costa Verde** ('Green Coast'), including the city of Oporto; the **Mountains** of the north-east; the **Alentejo** or Plains; and finally the **Algarve**, the south coast.

Some of the gentler pleasures of southern Portugal, a land of whitewashed churches and belltowers, old stone walls and gardens shaded by a profusion of shrubs. The cockerel on the windvane is a national symbol.

REMEMBER TO TAKE ...
Sun glasses.
Sun screen, even in winter. Use one with a high protection factor in summer.
Mosquito repellent.
Folding umbrella.
Comfortable walking shoes.
Binoculars, for bird-watching and looking at inaccessible architectural details.
Torch/flashlight.
Photocopies of essential documents.

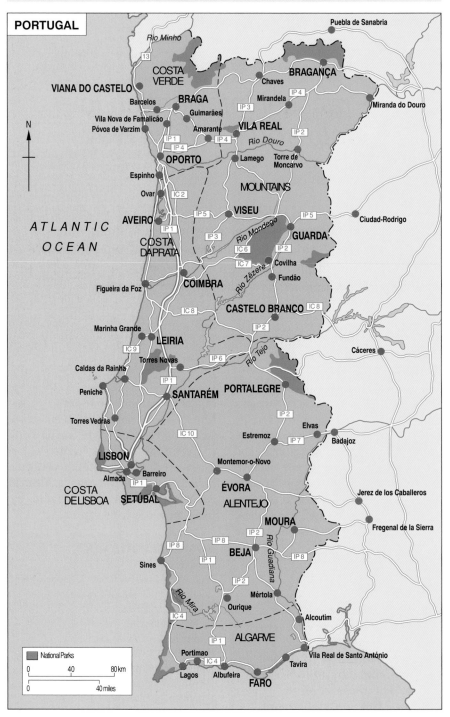

PORTUGAL

Puebla de Sanabria

Rio Minho

13

COSTA VERDE

BRAGANÇA

Chaves

VIANA DO CASTELO

Barcelos

BRAGA

Mirandela

IP 4

Miranda do Douro

IP 3

Guimarães

Vila Nova de Famalicão

Póvoa de Varzim

Amarante

VILA REAL

IP 2

IP 1

IP 4

Rio Douro

IP 4

OPORTO

Lamego

Torre de Moncarvo

Espinho

Ovar

IC 2

MOUNTAINS

ATLANTIC OCEAN

AVEIRO

IP 5

VISEU

IP 5

Ciudad-Rodrigo

IP 1

IP 3

Rio Mondego

GUARDA

COSTA DAPRATA

IC 6

IP 2

IC 7

Rio Zêzere

Covilha

Figueira da Foz

COIMBRA

Fundão

IC 8

CASTELO BRANCO

IC 8

Marinha Grande

LEIRIA

IP 2

IC 9

Cáceres

Torres Novas

IP 6

Rio Tejo

Caldas da Rainha

IP 1

Peniche

SANTARÉM

PORTALEGRE

Torres Vedras

IP 2

IC 10

Estremoz

Elvas

IP 7

Badajoz

LISBON

Montemor-o-Novo

Almada

Barreiro

IP 1

ÉVORA

Jerez de los Caballeros

COSTA DE LISBOA

SETÚBAL

ALENTEJO

MOURA

IP 2

Rio Guadiana

Fregenal de la Sierra

IP 8

IP 8

IP 2

BEJA

IP 8

Sines

IP 1

IP 2

Rio Mira

Mértola

Ourique

IC 4

Alcoutim

IP 1

ALGARVE

National Parks

Portimao

IC 4

Vila Real de Santo António

0   40   80 km

Tavira

Lagos   Albufeira

FARO

0   40 miles

N

8

When to Go and What to Wear

Portugal has hot, dry summers and mild winters when there's a good chance of rain (and even snow in the northern mountains). On the coast the temperature rarely dips below freezing. The peak months of the tourist season are July and August, so think about visiting in spring or autumn if you are not looking for the maximum of sunshine. You'll avoid some of the crowds, the weather is relatively balmy, hotels are less busy and prices are a lot lower at the resorts. You probably won't need anything heavier than a sweater in the daytime. Summer days can be hot, but pack a wrap for the cooler and windy evenings. Outside the summer months, rainwear is recommended.

Spring flowers are at their best from February to April; September and even October can be quite hot and the sea temperature on the Algarve will still be comfortable. Winter there has its special appeal, with frequent warm sunny days. Even if you aren't tempted to swim, the weather can be perfect for tennis or golf.

Portugal used to be quite formal, and businessmen still stick to their suits and ties. For anyone on holiday, though, things have changed drastically. Virtually no establishment requires men to wear a tie, but many people still like to 'dress up'.

A typical sandy beach with strange rocks on the western Algarve. This one near Armação de Pera isn't always so empty.

AVERAGE DAYTIME TEMPERATURES							
		Jan	Mar	May	July	Sept	Nov
Lisbon	°F	53	57	63	70	70	59
	°C	12	14	17	21	21	15
Oporto	°F	49	53	59	67	65	53
	°C	9	12	15	19	18	12
Coimbra	°F	50	56	60	67	67	56
	°C	10	13	16	19	19	13
Faro	°F	54	57	65	75	72	60
	°C	12	14	18	24	22	16

Time Differences

After years of coinciding with the UK and Ireland, Portugal now keeps the same time as Spain, France and most of the rest of the EU. Thus the time is GMT + 1 except from the last Sunday in March to the last Sunday in September, when it's GMT + 2, as follows:

New York	6am
London (GMT + 1)	11am
Lisbon	**noon**
Paris	noon
Johannesburg	noon
Sydney	8pm
Auckland	10pm

Getting to Portugal

By Air

Lisbon is on several intercontinental routes, mainly from North and South America and southern Africa. There are direct scheduled flights (more in summer than winter) from New York, Boston, Los Angeles, Montreal and Toronto. From elsewhere in the US and Canada, you'll need to connect with one of those departure points. Fares may be lower for short stays or if you fly mid-week.

Most European capitals have direct flights to Lisbon, some also to Oporto and Faro (see Airports below). London and Manchester have frequent flights to all three. If you book in advance and are able to stick to the dates, remarkably low-cost fares may be available on these routes, especially outside the peak holiday months of June-August. If you are 26, 25 or under (the small print varies), always ask about youth and student fares, whatever the route. Some surprising savings are possible.

Portugal is a popular **package tour** destination, using both charter flights and scheduled services, with all-inclusive and self-catering holidays as well as fly/drive and flight-only arrangements. From the UK and Ireland, flights are available from both London and provincial airports. From North America, tours are available in combination with Spanish or other European destinations. For tours to Portugal only, you can either make independent air, transfer and hotel (plus car rental) arrangements, or alternatively you can book a fly/drive combination.

Because fares and conditions change frequently and last-minute bargains are sometimes available, it is always advisable to consult a good travel agent for the latest information.

Airports (*aeroporto*)
Lisbon: The Aeroporto de Lisboa (also known as Portela, the northern suburb where it's located) is only 15 minutes from Lisbon centre if traffic is light, but allow at least twice as long at rush hour. Facilities include a bank, car-rental desks and a tourist office as well as porters and free baggage trolleys. Departing passengers can shop at souvenir stands and the duty-free shop. There are also bars and a restaurant.

Besides taxis, which are plentiful (see Transport on page 17), frequent buses (44

Old Oporto, where houses cluster on a slope facing the River Douro. Little restaurants line the quayside and steep, narrow streets climb towards the landmark Torre dos Clérigos.

and 45) leave for the Cais do Sodré station (abbreviated 'C. Sodré'). They pass through the city centre, including the Rossio. From the Cais do Sodré station, buses to the airport are marked 'Moscavide' (44) and 'Prior Velho' (45). Green buses (*Linha Verde*) link the airport with Santa Apolónia railway station.

For information on flight times, tel. (01) 80 20 60; the main airport number is (01) 848 11 01.

Oporto: The modern Francisco Sá Carneiro airport lies a 15-minute drive north of the city. It has car-rental desks, money exchange facilities, a tourist information office (not 24-hour), bar and snack bar. Baggage trolleys are free. Departing passengers will find a good duty-free shop. For information tel. (02) 948 2141.

Faro: The big building is certainly needed at busy holiday times. It has plenty of car rental desks, and other operators send representatives holding placards or wearing signs. There's a post office, bar, restaurant, money exchange, tourist information office (not 24-hour) and a duty-free shop for departing passengers. For further information, tel. (089) 818 281.

Where do I get the bus to the airport/to the centre of the city?	**Onde posso apanhar o autocarro para aeroporto/paro centro da cidade?**

By Rail
There are two main routes to Lisbon via Paris (a journey of about 24 hours): to Hendaye (south-west France) via Fuentes de Onoro/Vilar Formoso (Spanish/Portuguese frontier points), or via Madrid and Valencia de Alcántara (frontier point). From the UK, both routes offer a choice of sea crossings. You can also take advantage of the new Channel Tunnel crossing via Paris.

Both Inter-Rail and Rail Europ Senior tickets are valid in Portugal, as is the Eurailpass for non-European residents (sign up before you leave home).

By Car
The main access road to Lisbon from France through Spain is at the western end of the Pyrenees. A motorway (expressway) runs from Biarritz (France) to Burgos. From there, take either the N1 to Madrid and continue on E4 via Badajoz and Setúbal to Lisbon, or the N620 and then the E3 via Valladolid, Salamanca, Guarda and Coimbra. Driving distances from the UK are reduced by taking one of the long-distance car-ferry services to northern Spain: Plymouth or Portsmouth to Santander, and Portsmouth to Bilbao.

Ferry sailings are more frequent in summer but you're strongly advised to reserve early for holiday periods, especially if you plan to take a car.

By Sea
Some cruise ships include Lisbon and occasionally Oporto in their itineraries. Check with your travel agent.

Customs and Entry Regulations
Citizens of a long list of countries including the USA, Canada, Australia, New Zealand and South Africa, need only a valid passport to enter Portugal. No visa is required. For citizens of European Union (EU) and some other west European countries, a national identity card is sufficient. UK citizens can use a passport or visitor's passport. The length of stay allowed for tourists in Portugal is 90 days (60 days for US citizens).

Hotels almost invariably ask for your passport when you check in, and some may also request that they retain it overnight for the first night of your stay. Traffic police may also demand it from a driver, so you'll save time and trouble by having yours available when checking in or driving.

If you are arriving with a car, bring the registration document, insurance certificate valid for Portugal (generally the Green Card issued by your insurance company) and your driving licence. The car should have a nationality plate or sticker, and you must have a red warning triangle ready for use. If you are likely to be driving in Spain at all, you must also obtain a 'bail bond' from the insurance company.

Duty Free Goods

As Portugal is part of the EU, free exchange of **non-duty free** goods for personal use is permitted between Portugal and other EU countries. The allowance of duty-free goods which you can carry into the country is: 200 cigarettes **or** 50 cigars **or** 250g of tobacco; 1 litre of spirits (liquor), **or** 2 litres of liqueurs **or** fortified wines below 22% alcohol, **or** 2 litres of sparkling wine; **and** 2 litres of wine.

For residents of non-EU countries, restrictions on returning to your own country apply as follows: **Australia**: 250 cigarettes **or** 250g tobacco; 1l alcohol; **Canada**: 200 cigarettes **and** 50 cigars **and** 400g tobacco; 1.1l spirits **or** wine **or** 8.5l beer; **New Zealand**: 200 cigarettes **or** 50 cigars **or** 250g tobacco; 4.5l wine **or** beer **and** 1.1l spirits; **South Africa**: 400 cigarettes **and** 50 cigars **and** 250g tobacco; 2l wine **and** 1l spirits; **USA**: 200 cigarettes **and** 100 cigars or a 'reasonable amount' of tobacco.

Money Matters

Currency (*moeda*). The $ sign in Portugal means *escudo* (abbreviated esc. or PTE); the sign normally replaces the decimal point (thus 5.000 $ 00 means 5,000 escudos). The escudo is nominally divided into 100 *centavos*, although you aren't likely to see centavo coins these days. There are coins for 1, 2.5, 5, 10, 20, 50, 100 and 200 escudos. Banknotes come in denominations of 500, 1,000 (equalling one *conto*), 5,000 and 10,000 escudos.

Banks and Currency Exchange (*banco*; *câmbio*). Normal banking hours are Mon-Fri 8.30am-2.30/2.45pm. Some branches close for lunch from 11.45am to 1pm. In tourist areas some banks remain open later and on weekends to change money.

Ask about commission rates and avoid changing small amounts where there's a fixed minimum commission. An even larger flat rate fee is charged for changing traveller's cheques, and you will need to show your passport. You can use the automatic teller machines outside many banks to get cash with a Visa or Mastercard credit card provided you know the personal identification number (P.I.N.). Check with the card-issuing bank before leaving on your trip. Outside some banks in central Lisbon, machines change certain foreign currency notes (bills), including US dollars but not pounds sterling.

I want to change some pounds/ dollars.	**Queria trocar libras/dólares**
Can you cash a traveller's cheque?	**Pode pagar um cheque de viagem?**

Credit Cards (*cartão de crédito*). 'Plastic' in the form of major international

13

credit cards is accepted in most hotels, restaurants and tourist-oriented enterprises such as car rental agencies. Many petrol (gas) stations accept cards, but add a 100 esc. tax if you pay that way. If you're touring well off the beaten track, don't automatically expect to be able to use a credit card. To cancel a credit card, telephone UNICRE, tel. (01) 53 35 60.

To cash Eurocheques, you'll need a Eurocheque encashment card.

Can I pay with this credit card?	**Posso pagar com cartão de crédito?**

Getting Around

By Car

Many new roads have recently been built, and others greatly improved. When you see those that haven't – narrow, twisting and consisting entirely of patches and potholes – you'll appreciate the difference. Traffic has increased enormously too, especially in and near the big cities and towns and along the Algarve.

Away from the cities and off the major highways, roads can be pleasantly uncrowded, but watch out for wandering farm animals, dogs and unlit carts at night – driving in the dark is something to be avoided where possible.

Local standards of driving have somewhat improved in recent years, influenced by high insurance rates and a reluctance to risk the precious family car. Nonetheless, they can still be erratic, notably during city rush hours and in rural areas where drivers tend not to use direction signals. Where there's a hard shoulder, it's quite normal to find an oncoming vehicle on your side of the road, expecting you to veer off onto it.

Speed limits are widely ignored and you'll see some hair-raising examples of passing on blind bends. It makes sense to adopt a defensive strategy, but not to go *too* slowly, which will only provoke frustrated followers into even more crackbrained exploits.

Driving conditions: If you are not used to driving on the right, you'll soon become ac-

Symbol of a rapidly improving road system, a new bridge soars over the Guadiana River, the border between the Algarve and southern Spain.

customed. Stay alert, though: it's too easy to set off on the wrong side after making a stop, especially first thing in the morning.

The rules of the road are the same as in most western European countries. At roundabouts (traffic circles) the vehicle in the circle has priority unless road markings or lights indicate otherwise. In the towns, pedestrians nominally have priority at zebra-crossings – but if you're on foot, don't bank on it!

All but the most minor roads are numbered. 'A' roads are *Auto-estradas* (motorways) with restricted access. Tolls are charged for most sections. 'IP' roads are fast, new or upgraded roads. Practically all other roads have an 'N' number: the fewer digits, the more important the road. 'E' numbers refer to a pan-European system, only in token use so far.

Speed limits are 60kph (37mph) in built-up areas and 90kph (56mph) on the open road, unless signs indicate otherwise. On the stretches of motorway (freeway), the speed limit is 120kph (75mph). Minimum speeds are posted (in blue) for some lanes of *Auto-estradas* (motorways) and other fast roads, as well as for the suspension bridge across the Tagus. Cars towing caravans (trailers) are restricted to 50kph (31mph) in towns and 70kph (43mph) on the open road and motorways (*portagem*).

Front seat belts must be worn. Dipped headlights are required at night in built up areas. You can be fined on the spot for traffic offences. If this happens, be sure to get a receipt. The laws regarding alcohol levels and driving are strict but not uniformly enforced. However, only a couple of drinks could put you over the limit of 0.05% as assessed by breath or blood tests. Jail or heavy fines and the loss of your licence can result.

Parking: You have to park facing in the same direction as the flow of traffic on that side of the road. Unless there's an indication to the contrary, you can park for as long as you wish. If marked, a sign will specify the maximum time you can stay. Check the local regulations before parking. Some towns have meters; in others you buy a pay-and-display ticket. Increased car ownership has made parking spots hard to find in the towns and cities.

Repairs: Car rental companies will give you details of what to do if the car breaks down. Be sure to carry them in the vehicle. If you have your own car and belong to a motoring organization affiliated to the Automóvel Clube de Portugal, tel. (01) 56 39 31, you can make use of their emergency and repair services free of charge. Otherwise, most garages in Portugal can handle all the usual driving problems. (See also Emergencies on p. 39)

Road signs: The standard international pictograms are used in Portugal, but you'll also encounter some of the following:

Alto	*Halt*
Cruzamento	*Crossroads*
Curva perigosa	*Dangerous bend (curve)*
Descida ingreme	*Steep hill*
Desvio	*Diversion (detour)*
Encruzilhada	*Crossroads*
Estacionamento permitido	*Parking allowed*
Estacionamento proíbido	*No parking*
Guiar com cuidado	*Drive with care*
Obras/Fim de obras	*Road works (men working)/ end of road works*
Paragem de autocarro	*Bus stop*

Pare	Stop
Passagem proibida	No entry
Pedestres, peões	Pedestrians
Perigo	Danger
Proibida a entrada	No entry
Seguir pela direita/esquerda	Keep right/left
Sem saída	No through road
Sentido proibido	No entry
Sentido único	One-way street
Silêncio	Silence zone
Trânsito proibido	No through traffic
Velocidade máxima	Maximum speed
Are we on the right road for ...?	É esta a estrada para ...?
Check the oil/ tires/battery.	Verifique o óleo/os pneus/a bateria, se faz favor.
I've had a breakdown.	O meu carro está avariado.
There's been an accident.	Houve um acidente.

Car Rental (carros de aluguer)

Many local and international companies have offices at the airports and in the big cities and major tourist areas. Rates are comparable with the UK, and high by US standards. They're usually less outside the peak summer months and if you reserve a car in advance, especially as part of a fly-drive or sail-drive package. A local com-pany may have lower rates but might make a 'drop-off' charge for leaving the car elsewhere. Per kilometre or unlimited distance rates are both available.

You must have your national licence and be over 21 (25 for some companies; others require the licence to have been held for two years). If you don't have a major credit card, a large deposit will be required. If the car is provided with a full fuel tank, you may be asked for a small deposit or a signed credit card voucher, returnable if you bring back the car equally full. Third-party insurance is included but a collision-damage waiver and personal accident policy may be added. If you are thinking of taking the car into Spain, say so. There may be insurance restrictions or an extra charge.

I'd like to hire a car today/ tomorrow.	Queria alugar um carro para hoje/ amanhã.
for one day/a week	por um dia/uma semana
Please include full insurance.	Que inclua um seguro contra todosos riscos, por favor.

Fuel: All types of fuel are widely available. If you hire a car, make sure you know which grade of petrol it uses. Stations can be far apart in rural areas and may open only for limited hours, especially out of season.

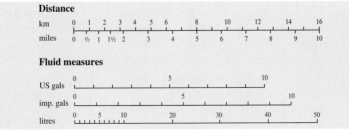

Distance

| km | 0 | 1 | 2 | 3 | 4 | 5 | 6 | | 8 | | 10 | | 12 | | 14 | | 16 |
| miles | 0 | ½ | 1 | 1½ | 2 | | 3 | | 4 | | 5 | | 6 | 7 | | 8 | | 9 | 10 |

Fluid measures

US gals	0		5		10
imp. gals	0		5		10
litres	0	5	10	20	30	40	50

Public Transport

Buses

Buses are frequent and usually quick, and fares are reasonable. Tourist information offices will advise you about routes, and you will find other passengers willing to help. Tell them where you want to go and they'll tell you what bus to take. Once aboard, ask them to tell you where to get off!

In Lisbon, **trams** offer local colour, and the **Metro** (underground/subway) system is modern and fast. Most public transport operates 6 or 7am-midnight or 1am.

Inter-city buses

In Lisbon and Oporto a number of terminals serve different parts of the country. The easiest thing is to ask where buses leave from at the tourist office in each city. Elsewhere, ask at the bus station or the local *Turismo*. Buses are good and prices are reasonable; you tend to see more of the country than if you go by train. Two sample journeys are as follows: Lisbon to Castelo Branco, roughly 260km, takes about 4 hours; Lisbon to Coimbra, around 200km, takes 3.5 hours.

Trains (comboio)

All trains are operated by *CP* (*Caminhos de Ferro Portugueses*), the national railway corporation, and although there have been many line closures in recent years, most cities and towns are still linked by a good service. *Regional* trains stop at most stations; *Intercidade* trains cost more and make few stops; and *Rápido* trains link Lisbon and Oporto non-stop at high speed and even greater expense. More of these links are planned.

In the major stations, first- and second-

*T*he journey is part of the fun when you take one of Lisbon's antique trams, still climbing some of the city's steep hills almost a century after they were built.

class tickets are sold at separate windows. A first-class carriage usually has a yellow stripe above the windows and the number '1' near the doors. If you have a Eurailpass or InterRailpass, it's valid here, but extra charges are made for the premium services.

Lisbon has four principal railway stations scattered around the city. International services and trains for northern Portugal start from **Santa Apolónia** station. Commuter trains for the western suburbs and Estoril and Cascais leave from **Cais do Sodré**. Trains for Sintra and the west depart from **Rossio** station. The fourth busy station, called **Sul e Sueste** (South and South-east) has ferryboats which cross the Tagus to meet the trains that go on as far as the Algarve. The price of the ticket includes the ferry link.

How much is the fare to ...?	**Quanto custa o bilhete para ...?**
Will you tell me when to get off?	**Pode dizer-me quando devo descer?**
Where's the nearest bus/tram stop?	**Onde fica a mais próxima paragem dos autocarros/ eléctricos?**

Taxis (*táxi*)

Most taxis are black with a green roof and a sign reading 'Taxi'. In rural areas similar cars marked 'A' (meaning *aluguer –* for hire) perform the taxi function.

Big city taxis have meters. See that it's running to avoid doubts about the bill. Drivers add 20 percent at night and an extra charge if you have more than 30kg (66lb) of baggage. A tip of 10 percent would be appropriate.

Taxis without meters are supposed to apply standard fares – ask what the charge is likely to be before setting off.

Some taxis cruise the streets looking for business, but most wait at taxi stands, stations, airports and big hotels. Your best bet is to go to a stand, or telephone for a radio-controlled taxi.

Where can I get a taxi?	**Onde posso encontrar um táxi?**
Taxi!	**Táxi!**
What's the fare to ...?	**Quanto custa o percurso até ...?**

Domestic Flights

You probably won't have any need to fly from city to city within Portugal. If you need them, however, TAP (Air Portugal) operates flights between several of the major cities, the frequency varying with the importance of the destination.

Bicycle Rental

Bikes are quite widely available for rent at holiday centres, and some resort hotels have their own. Check up on the insurance position and make sure a good lock is supplied as well.

Take to the Water

Yachts, windsurfers and other craft can be hired at coastal resorts and on some reservoirs, lagoons and rivers. If you want someone else to do the work, consider taking one of the harbour or river cruises on offer in dozens of places.

Hitchhiking

You'll see a lot of people, including single women, standing by the road waiting for a ride, but most of them are locals. They'll know the drivers who are likely to come by, and the drivers will know them and where they want to get to. It isn't the same for a stranger, so apply the usual common sense rules. Portugal is safer than most places, but women travelling alone are strongly advised not to hitch. In rural areas, you may face a long wait in the heat – or perhaps the rain.

Guides and Tours

At some palaces and monasteries, you have to go round with a guide, but this can be part of the pleasure as some are well informed and tell entertaining stories. Otherwise, tourist offices can find guides for you, but with all the literature that's available, they're hardly necessary. All guides must belong to the professional association of guides and meet their standards. A guide or interpreter can be hired directly through them in Lisbon at Rua do Telhal 4, 3°, tel. 346 71 70, 9am-1pm and 2.30-6pm.

Check with the tourist office or a travel agent for information on half- or full-day city tours.

Bus tours lasting from half a day to a week or more cover all the well-known destinations. You'll be relieved of all the trouble of planning, navigating and finding accommodation, and you'll certainly see the country through the windows, but you won't get off the beaten path. If you take a tour, try to arrange a schedule that gives you some free days as well.

We'd like an **Queremos um**
English-speaking **guia que fale inglês.**
guide.

Tourist Information Offices (*Turismo*)

The Portuguese government maintains tourist offices in more than a dozen foreign cities. Here are some addresses:

British Isles: Portuguese National Tourist Office, 22/25a Sackville St, London W1X 1DE; tel. (0171) 494-1441.

Canada: Portuguese National Tourist Office, Suite 1005, 60 Bloor Street West, Toronto, Ont. M4W 3B8; tel. (416) 921 7376.

Japan: Portuguese National Tourist Office, Regency Shinsaka 101, 8-5-8 Akasaka, Minato-ku, Tokyo 107; tel. (3) 5474 4400.

USA: Portuguese National Tourist Office, 590 Fifth Ave, New York 10036; tel. (212) 354-4403.

In Lisbon, the national tourist office (*Direcção-Geral do Turismo*) is located at: Av. António Augusto de Aguiar, 86, 1000-Lisboa; tel. 315 50 91. More convenient to the city centre is the information office in Palácio Foz, on Praça dos Restauradores, tel. 346 36 43.

The Lisbon tourist office (*Posto de Turismo da Camara Municipal de Lisboa*) is at the Amoreiras shopping centre, tel. 65 74 86. There is a special number for information in English, tel. 70 63 41.

All over Portugal, every town of any consequence has a local tourist information office, called the *Turismo*. Most are staffed by enthusiastic people, who are often excellent linguists, ready to provide you with information on accommodation and facilities, maps and leaflets and help of all kinds. If you need somewhere to stay, they will often be willing to telephone around for you until they find a suitable room. You'll also find offices at all the main arrival ports and airports. From the outskirts and within each town, the road sign *i* (large *italic*) points you in the direction of the tourist office. The only problem is that the office itself is often not marked, so you can easily go past it.

Maps

Tourist information offices usually have free or low cost maps of their immediate areas. Car hire companies may provide a road map but you'll need one for advance planning. Several publishers produce useful road maps to a scale of 1:300,000 (about 1 inch to 5 miles). Bookstores and news-stands sell a variety of maps by domestic and foreign publishers.

If you're walking or cycling, or driving on the back roads, you will want a more detailed map. It is advisable to purchase one before leaving home as they can be hard to find in Portugal.

a street map of Lisbon	**uma planta de Lisboa**
a road map of Portugal	**um mapa das estradas de Portugal**

Travellers with Disabilities

In general, many hotels and restaurants are paying closer attention to wheelchair travellers and others with special needs, but there is still much more that could be done. Not all tourist sites are accessible to wheelchairs and the terrain means that some never will be. Special toilet facilities are being provided but they are still far from universal.

Lisbon is not an easy city to negotiate at the best of times: hills are steep and much of the road surface poor. In addition, the public transport system is far from being modern enough to consider the needs of disabled travellers: buses are old and trams ancient.

The National Rehabilitation Secretariat, Avenida Conde Valbom 63, 1000 Lisbon, publishes a guide to transport facilities (in Portuguese only) and an *Access Guide to Lisbon* with symbols explained in English. The Portuguese National Tourist Office can provide a list of hotels with few barriers to wheelchair users.

If travelling from the UK, before you go contact the Holiday Care Service, who are experts in the field of holidays for disabled people and will try to answer specific enquiries; tel (01293) 774535.

Health and Medical Care

Your travel insurance policy ought to include medical expenses, although residents of European Union countries are entitled to free medical treatment in Portugal. (There is a charge for medicines.) They should bring the E111 social security form. Make it clear to the doctor that you wish to be treated in accordance with EU regulations.

No vaccinations are required for entering Portugal, unless you are arriving from a known infected area, but check with your travel agent before departure.

Farmácias (chemists' shops or drugstores) are open during normal business hours. At other times one shop in each neighbourhood is on duty round the clock. Addresses are listed in the newspapers and on the door of every other chemist's shop.

a doctor	**um médico**
a dentist	**um dentista**
an ambulance	**uma ambulância**
hospital	**hospital**
an upset stomach	**mal de estômago**
sunstroke	**uma insolação**
a fever	**febre**

Embassies and Consulates
(consulado; embaixada)

You'll find a list of all diplomatic representatives in Lisbon, and the consuls with offices in Oporto and other regional cities, in local telephone books (under *Consulado* or *Embaixada*).

Australia (Embassy): Av. da Liberdade 244, 4°, Lisbon; tel. 52 33 50.

Canada (Embassy/Consulate): Av. da Liberdade 144, 3°, Lisbon; tel. 347 48 92; (Consulate): 1.1° E Fr Lourç Santa Maria, Faro; tel. 80 37 57.

Republic of Ireland (Embassy/Consulate): Rua da Impresa a Estrela 1, 4°, Lisbon; tel. 396 15 69.

Japan (Embassy): Rua Mouzinho da Silveira, 11, Lisbon; tel. 352 34 85.

South Africa (Embassy): Av. Luis Bivar 10/10 A, Lisbon; tel. 53 50 41.

United Kingdom (Embassy): Rua S Domingos-Lapa 37, Lisbon; tel. 396 11 91; (Consulate): 7.1° Largo Francisco A Maurício, Portimão; tel 41 78 00; (Consulate): 3072 Avenida Boavista, Oporto; tel. 618 47 89.

USA (Embassy/Consulate): Av Forças Armadas 16, Lisbon; tel. 726 66 00.

Most embassies and consulates are open Mon-Fri 9 or 10am-5pm, with a 1 to 2.5 hour break in the middle of the day.

Where's the British/American embassy?	**Onde é a embaixada inglesa/americana?**
It's very urgent.	**E muito urgente.**

Accommodation

(See also Camping on p.24, Youth Hostels on p.25 and the selection of Recommended Hotels starting on p.326.)

The choice is vast, and made confusing by the many and varied names given to different sorts of establishment. Wherever you stay you are generally going to get value for money, thanks to official inspection and the Portuguese people's instinctive hospitality.

Hotels are graded from 2-star to 5-star deluxe. Less elaborate sorts of hostelry – an *estalagem* or inn, or a *pensão* (rooms with meals also available) or *residencial* (rooms, generally without meals) – are graded on a separate scale from 1-star to 3-star. Maximum permitted prices are fixed for each grade. Luxury-class hotels have their own restaurants, swimming pools, saunas, etc, but at the other end of the scale you can have a double room with bath in a *pensão* for a fraction of the cost. Villas and apartments (with cooking facilities) are also graded, from 1-star to 3-star. They're usully reserved well in advance for July and August, but may be a bargain at other times. The government-run *Pousadas* (see below) have their own system of grading.

If you arrive somewhere without a reservation at a busy time – summer at the beaches, or festive days – you may have a problem. Try the local *turismo* (tourist information office) to see what's available.

When you check in at your hotel or other accommodation, you'll usually be asked for your passport (which may be retained overnight and returned the next day) and to sign a form which sets out the conditions, prices and room number. Continental breakfast (or sometimes a full breakfast) is included in the cost of a room.

21

In a land of many small, traditional farms, early spring turns the stone-walled fields into a sea of wild flowers.

Portugal's **Pousadas** are a remarkable group of hotels operated by ENATUR, the national tourism organization. When they began in the 1940s, the idea was to fill a need for good accommodation in out-of-the-way areas and near historic sites. The first *Pousadas* were specially built, using as far as possible the architecture and handicrafts of the region. Renovated and expanded, they are similar to mountain chalets, hunting lodges or inns. More re-

a double/single	**um quarto**
room with/	**duplo/simples**
without bath	**com/sem banho**

cent *Pousadas* have been installed in restored castles such as at Óbidos, palaces such as at Estremoz, or convents, including the stunning Santa Marinha da Costa at Guimarães. Each is unique. The most opulent are the equivalent to 5-star hotels; others are much simpler and less expensive and winter rates everywhere are greatly reduced. They all have restaurants, from good to excellent, with quite ambitious menus which concentrate on local dishes and wines. Ask at tourist offices for the detailed list.

Bed and Breakfast

'Quartos/Rooms/Chambres/Zimmer' – the signs are common in the holiday areas, less frequent across the rest of the country,

V̄ines provide shade as well as grapes. Here in northern Portugal you can find many houses with rooms to let, from country mansions to little cottages.

found outside houses in towns and villages. The best are as comfortable as a hotel, at much less cost. Rooms and standards vary, so it's a good idea to take a look and ask the price before making a decision to stay. In holiday areas, people with rooms sometimes send young family members to stand outside the tourist office and drum up business: 'You want a room?'

Camping and Caravanning

Sites range from a farmer's field to leisure parks with hot showers, shops and sports facilities. Portugal has over 70 official camping sites, mostly near beaches or historic monuments. Facilities at the most elaborate can include swimming pools, tennis courts, and even bars and restaurants.

To stay in the organized camping spots you must show your passport and in certain sites you must have an official card identifying you as a member of a national or international camping association. Outside recognized sites you must not camp within city limits or on beaches and other public places, nor light fires in forests. You should leave your site clean by taking away or burying any litter.

Information on camping can be obtained from tourist offices, which have an excellent brochure, or the Federação Portuguesa de Campismo, Rua Voz do Operário, 1, 1000-Lisboa; tel. 886 23 50.

May we camp here?	**Podemos acampar aqui?**
We have a caravan (trailer).	**Nós temos uma roulotte.**

Youth Hostels
(pousadas de juventude)

Young visitors from the age of 14 up can stay in dormitories at very low rates if they're members of a national or international youth hostel association. Membership of the Portuguese Youth Hostel Association is open to 'juniors' (aged 14 to 21) and 'seniors' (22 to 40). Parents with children younger than 14 may, in certain cases, stay in these hostels if there is room, but preference is given to those within the set age brackets. You can get in touch with the Associação Portuguesa de Pousadas de Juventude at Av. Duque de Ávila, 137, 1000 Lisbon; tel. 355 90 81.

Eating Out

Hearty food for hearty appetites, that's the Portuguese way. At first you may be daunted by the size of the portions and the number of courses you are expected to get through – soups and appetizers can be meals in themselves. Fresh fish and shellfish are the staple of many menus, and not only on the coast: nowhere is far from the sea and distribution is efficient. Meat-eaters can find a wide choice of pork and lamb dishes, as well as some pretty good steaks. Then there's the pure pleasure of freshly picked fruit and vegetables, juicy tomatoes, and intensely scented herbs such as coriander and oregano. To wash it all down, the wines are always reliable and sometimes superb.

Where to Eat

In the big cities and the holiday resorts the choice of eating establishments is vast. Some streets consist entirely of competing

The walls of some Lisbon restaurants are covered with azulejos, the decorative ceramic tiles which are a particularly Portuguese art form.

restaurants and there's always a cluster next to markets and fishing harbours. Many move into the open air in summer, the tables of one cafe or restaurant merging with the next.

Government inspectors rate restaurants as *de luxo* (luxury), *de primeira, de segunda* and *de terceira classe* (first, second and third class), more on the basis of facilities and ambience than the cooking. The higher the rating the more the restaurant is permitted to charge. A sign announcing the class is normally posted outside, and menus displayed in the window or at the door let you know what to expect in variety and price. A *tasca* is a small informal restaurant, like a bistro. A *marisqueiria* specializes in seafood and a *churrasqueiria* serves mainly char-grilled meats. A *cervejaria* ('beerhouse') will serve snacks and may have a restaurant section as well. In some small towns, it may be the only place to eat.

Some of this variety of choice is more apparent than real. Most of the restaurants serve Portuguese food, and that is what they're best at, not French, nouvelle cuisine or 'international'. You'll find favourite national dishes on menus right across the price spectrum.

Prices normally include taxes and a service charge, but you can leave an additional 5 to 10 percent tip for excellent service, or a coin or two on the table in an informal place. Practically everywhere, the service will be quick (sometimes *too* quick) and friendly, except perhaps from harassed waiters at crowded beach cafés.

When to Eat

Breakfast (*o pequeno almoço*), whether a light affair of juice, coffee, rolls and jam, or a full scale buffet, runs from 7am until around 10am. Lunch (*o almoço*) is served from shortly after noon until 3pm. Dinner (*o jantar*) runs from about 7.30 to 9.30pm, though later in a *casa de fado*. Between-meal snacks may be found at a *pastelaria* (pastry and cake shop), *salão de chá* (tea shop), or *snack-bar*.

What to Eat

Soups

On the menu at both lunch and dinner, these can be so substantial you'll hardly want a main course. *Caldo verde* (green soup) is the most distinctive Portuguese soup – a thick broth of potato purée and finely-shredded cabbage or kale, sometimes with pieces of sausage. *Sopa à Portuguesa* is similar, but with added beans, broccoli, carrots, turnips and anything else that happens to be on hand. *Sopa de cozido*, a rich meat broth

---

WORDS OF WARNING

Many restaurants and cafés offer an *ementa turística*, literally 'tourist menu', but not just for tourists. It's an economically priced set meal, typically bread, butter, soup, main course (perhaps a choice of two) and dessert. Beware, though: if you deviate even slightly from it you may be charged à la carte prices for each item. Likewise, posted prices outside some cafés can be a 'come-on', only applying if you stand up at the bar. Sit down and you'll pay the higher prices quoted on the regular menu.

Note also that nothing comes free. Generous appetizers are often scattered on your table, ranging from tasty fish pastes, mini-cheeses, and *chouriço* (delicious aromatic smoked sausage) to olives and different breads. What you eat you pay for. Also, in restaurants where some seafoods are charged by weight, portions may keep coming and if you don't say stop soon enough, the bill can be a shock.

---

with cabbage and perhaps macaroni, might be followed in a traditional meal by *cozido* – a huge serving of all the things that were boiled to create the broth, including beef, pork, chicken, sausages, potatoes, cabbage and carrots. *Sopa de grão* is based on chick-peas, but the similar sounding *sopa de agrião* is cream of watercress.

Fish and Shellfish

The best advertisement for seafood is in the window of a restaurant – a refrigerated display case full of prawns and crabs, oysters and mussels, sea bass and sole. Seafood restaurants generally sell shellfish by weight, giving the price in escudos per kilo. Fresh fish is usually served grilled, either whole or filleted, or as steaks such as *atum* (tuna) and *espadarte* (swordfish). The smell of fresh sardines (*sardinhas*) grilling in the open air pervades city streets and sunbaked beaches from June to September (the sardine season fortunately coincides with summer).

There should be no difficulty in finding plenty of fresh local foods and good, reliable wines.

ACQUIRED TASTE

Dried salt cod – *bacalhau* – is practically the national dish, which may seem odd when some of the best fresh fish in the world is landed every day all along the coast. Portuguese palates are attuned to the strong flavour of the preserved version and every grocery shop and tiny village store has a pile of grey, stiff, pungent-smelling sheets of it, and a guillotine for cutting them up. There's said to be a different way of preparing *bacalhau* for each day of the year, and you'll find it in any restaurant which aspires to the label of *tipico* (meaning it serves traditional Portuguese food). That includes the most expensive places, where this one-time staple of peasant diets can paradoxically be the priciest dish on the menu. If you plan to try it, go for one of the recipes with plenty of flavourful herbs and other ingredients. Beer goes well with it, or even better, the frothy and acidic *vinho verde tinto*.

Most ways of cooking bacalhau begin by soaking it for at least 24 hours, changing the water several times to reduce the saltiness and leathery texture. In *Bacalhau a Moda de Estremoz* the cod is finely flaked with garlic in a creamy sauce and baked with spinach. *Bacalhau à Gomes de Sá* consists of flaky chunks, baked with parsley, potatoes, onion and olives and garnished with grated hard-boiled egg.

Améijoas na cataplana is an Algarve speciality named after the steamer in which it's cooked and served, like a wok with a hinged cover. *Améijoas* are clams: other ingredients can vary but normally include bits of sausage or ham, white wine, tomato, onion and herbs. Look out too for *Açorda de marisco*, a spicy, garlic-scented bread-soup full of seafood bits; raw eggs are folded into the mixture at the table. *Lulas recheadas* are tender squid stuffed with rice, olives, herbs, onion and tomato.

A seasonal speciality is *Lampreia à Minho*, the eel-like lamprey fished from the northern rivers in the winter months and served with a red wine sauce on a bed of rice. Also in the north, and all year round, try the local trout (*truta*) stuffed with *presunto*, the excellent air-dried ham of the region.

Meat

The Portuguese are not squeamish. All sorts of offal, pigs' heads, tails, testicles and other bits and pieces hang in butchers' shops for customers to inspect. Liver (*fígado*) is a Lisbon favourite, while Oporto is famous for tripe (*tripas*). *Cabrito assado* is baked kid (young goat). Like many meat courses, it is usually served with both potatoes *and* rice.

Carne de porco à Alentejana, like the cataplana dishes, combines both meat and seafood (in this case pork and clams) with paprika and garlic. *Feijoada*, a less elaborate version of Brazil's national dish, is a filling stew of pigs' trotters and sausage, white beans and cabbage. *Bife na frigideira* is not what you may think. *Frigideira* means frying pan, and this dish is a beef-steak in a wine sauce. *Bife à Portuguesa* is a steak fried with onions and served in a casserole, with the option of a fried egg on top. (Note: *bife* doesn't always mean beef: *bife de salmão* is a salmon steak.)

If you find the portions – soup, fish or meat – too large, ask if you can share one between two, or if you can have a half portion (*uma meia dose*). Most restaurants will be happy to oblige. Another thing, you'll often find no salt or pepper on the table, but you can have them for the asking – '*sal e pimenta, por favor*' – and the chef won't be offended.

Poultry and Game

Shoppers in the produce markets don't hesitate to squeeze the live rabbits, ducks, hens, geese and guinea fowl to check for plumpness before buying. Chicken – *frango* – is popular cooked in many ways: stewed in wine sauce, fried, roast or barbecued. *Frango na Púcara* consists of chicken cooked in a clay pot with vegetables and spices.

Some restaurants specialize in *caça* (game), with varying seasonal choices of *codorniz* (quail), *perdiz* (partridge), *lebre* (hare), *veado* (venison) and *javali* (wild boar). Rabbit (*coelho*) is less expensive and often the basis of a delicious stew.

Dessert

'*Sobremesa*', the waiter will say as soon as you have finished your filling main course. It's a statement, not a question. Even so, the national sweet tooth may be too much for your taste. Fanciful names for the variations tell you very little, but many of them are based on eggs, almonds and lashings of sugar, like *Ovos moles de Aveiro*, made of beaten egg yolks cooked in syrup. Some of the pastries are feather light and delicious, others solid and heavy. All the items on a restaurant dessert trolley can be a uniform golden brown! You may be able to persuade the waiter to find some fresh fruit, but he'll think you rather eccentric. Among the standard offerings:

Pudim flã – sometimes written *flam* or *flan* or *flão* – is a sweet caramel custard.
Arroz doce: rice pudding with a dash of cinnamon.
Maçã assada: sugary baked apple.
Pudim Molotov: nobody's certain about the derivation of the name, but it's a soft meringue with caramel or apricot sauce.
Mel e Noz: 'honey and nuts', and semi-crystallized Elvas plums with the coffee keep up the sugar level to the end.

Cheeses

Most mainland Portuguese cheeses are made from ewes' or goats' milk, or a mixture of the two. *Queijo da serra* is cured ewes' milk cheese from the mountains, the most esteemed variety being *Serra da Estrêla*. A similar one comes from Serpa in the Alentejo. *Flamengo* is a solid, plain cheese like Edam. The soft white *queijo fresco* may turn up on your table as an appetizer, or your may be offered small, round and hard cheeses which have been cured by drying or kept in brine. It's a tradition in the mountain areas to serve cheese with *marmelada*, a tangy preserve made not from oranges, but quinces.

Ethnic Diversity

Portugal's imperial past explains the number of African, Indian and Chinese restaurants you'll find, especially in Lisbon. The former colony of Goa accounts for the local popularity of *caril* (curry) and other Indian-style dishes. A typical Goan delicacy, less pungent than some Indian food, is *xacuti* (pronounced and sometimes spelled *chacuti*). It's simply chunks of fried chicken in a sauce of pepper, coriander, cumin, cloves, cinnamon, anise, saffron and coconut milk, served with steamed rice.

Mozambique's favourite spice, *piri piri*, is made from hot chilies and added to sauces or sprinkled on chicken or prawns before grilling. The link with the territory of Macau means you can find Chinese (generally Cantonese) food in most of the larger towns. Other choices are few and far between, unless you count British fish-and-chips and German *wurst* in the Algarve resorts.

Vegetarians, unless they permit themselves fish, have had a difficult time in Portugal in the past. Even innocent-sounding vegetable soups often have a bit of sausage or ham thrown in and are probably made with a meat stock. Recently, though, a few restaurants have begun to feature specifically vegetarian dishes.

Wines

To order a drinkable wine to go with your dinner, all you really need to tell the waiter is *tinto* (red) or *branco* (white), *séco* (dry) or *doce* (sweet). The house wines in any restaurant are likely to be reliable, and some are admirable. When you want to try something a bit special, you'll find that wine lists almost always offer only Portuguese wines, and why not? The choice is so varied there's no need for imports. They also tend to concentrate on the wines of the local region, and waiters will usually know most about these and be happy to recommend them.

Other Drinks

Portuguese beers are good, and not expensive. Light or dark, they are served chilled, bottled or straight from the tap. *Aguardente* is the local brandy – a veritable firewater.

You can find various brands of mineral water in small or large bottles, bubbly or still. The fresh fruit juices which you'll come across can be delicious, and well-known soft drinks are also available.

THE WINE LIST

Certain wine-producing regions are demarcated by law, although they are not the only areas to make good wines. The names you are most likely to meet are:

Vinho verde ('green wine') from the fertile north-west is green only in the sense of being youthful. Most of it is white, slightly sparkling and refreshing. By growing the vines up trees and fences, the grapes are kept cooler so they and the wine retain a freshness and pleasant acidity. Less well known is the fizzy red wine from the same region, with the unlikely name of *vinho verde tinto* ('green red wine'). The rosé is slightly bubbly too – some widely sold brands are artificially carbonated – and may be either sweet or very dry. The skilfully marketed Mateus Rosé and its competitors imitate the *vinho verde* style, blending wines from several regions to create a mass production brand tailored to a wide range of tastes.

Dão, to the south and east of Viseu in northern Portugal, produces reliable but rarely exciting reds for drinking between three and five years old. Dão Reservas, 10 to 15 years old, develop a gentle smoothness. Dão whites are refreshing and fragrant but should be drunk when young.

Bairrada wines, long-lasting reds and whites, come from the hills north of Coimbra. Always appreciated in the region, their fame has spread further afield in recent years.

Borba, in the eastern Alentejo near Estremoz, produces good dry reds and whites, frequently served as the house wines in hotels and restaurants.

Algarve wines are made along most of the south coast, the better examples coming from near Lagoa and Tavira. Drinkable rather than great, they're mainly for local consumption.

Setúbal, from the Arrábida peninsula south of Lisbon, is a mellow, sweet white wine made from the scented Muscat grape, slightly fortified (much less than Port). The Arrábida peninsula also makes good dry table wines, including the soft red *Periquita*, and a number of fine estate wines (see below). *Bucelas* (labels use the old spelling, *Bucellas*) is a light, fresh, slightly oaky white wine, from a small region just north of Lisbon.

Colares, a traditional red wine from the sandy soils west of Sintra, is deep in colour and needs years to mature. Little is produced now.

Carcavelos, a sweet, amber-coloured dessert wine, originally came from the epnoymous village on the Estoril coast. A few vineyards remain in the area just inland.

Garrafeira is not a region at all, but a word meaning 'selected old wine'. It was a habit in the past to blend wines from different parts of the country and keep them for a long time as *Reservas*, to reduce the high levels of tannin which traditional methods gave the wine. The best of the *Reservas* were known as *Garrafeiras* and the name continues to be used for some of the best quality wines.

Vinho espumante is sparkling wine usually packaged to look like Champagne. Most are sweetish but there are also quite dry versions.

Keeping up with a New World trend, producers and merchants are marketing wines from individual **estates** (*quintas*). One of the first and best is Barca Velha, from the region which normally concentrates on Port. Look out also for *Quinta da Lagoalva*, *Quinta do Carmo* and *Quinta da Pedralvites* from Bairrada. Another fashion is to make **varietals**, wines from a single species of grape, although names such as Maria Gomes and Bical don't ring as many bells as Cabernet Sauvignon.

Finally, of course, there is **Port** (see p.193), the fortified wine of the upper Douro. The sweeter reds constitute the time-honoured way of finishing a dinner, but dry or extra-dry white Ports served chilled make a fine apéritif. So too does a dry **Madeira,** a *Sercial* or *Verdelho*. After dinner, try a sweeter Madeira, a *Boal* (Bual) or *Malvasia* (Malmsey).

Coffee and Tea

At the end of lunch or dinner, most people order a *bica*, a small cup of black espresso coffee. Curiously, a diluted black coffee is called a *carioca* – even though the Cariocas (the inhabitants of Rio de Janeiro) drink theirs infinitely stronger. Cafés also serve white coffee; in a tall glass it's called a *galão*, in a small one, a *garoto* ('little boy'). Tea (*chá*) is very popular – after all, the Portuguese explorers introduced it to the Western world.

To Help You Order ...

Could we have a table?	**Queríamos uma mesa.**
Do you have a set-price menu?	**Tem uma ementa turística?**
I'd like a/an/ some ...	**Queria ...**
beer	**uma cerveja**
bill	**conta**
bread	**pão**
butter	**manteiga**
coffee	**um café**
dessert	**uma sobremesa**
fish	**peixe**
fruit	**fruta**
ice-cream	**um gelado**
meat	**carne**
menu	**a ementa**
milk	**leite**
mineral water	**água mineral**
napkin	**um guardanapo**
pepper	**pimenta**
potatoes	**batatas**
rice	**arroz**
salad	**uma salada**
salt	**sal**
sandwich	**uma sanduíche**
soup	**uma sopa**
sugar	**açúcar**
tea	**chá**
wine	**vinho**

... and Read the Menu

alho	*garlic*
almôndegas	*meatballs*
alperces	*apricots*
ameijoas	*baby clams*
ananaz	*pineapple*
arroz	*rice*
assado	*roast*
atum	*tuna*
azeitonas	*olives*
bacalhau	*codfish*
banana	*banana*
besugo	*sea bream*
bife (vaca)	*beef steak*
biscoitos/	*biscuits/*
bolachas	*cookies*
bolo	*cake*
borrego	*lamb*
cabrito	*kid*
caracóis	*snails*
caranguejo	*crab*
cavala	*mackerel*
cebola	*onion*
chouriço	*a spicy sausage*
coelho	*rabbit*
cogumelos	*mushrooms*
costeletas	*chops*
couve	*cabbage*
dobrada	*tripe*
dourada	*sea-bass*
enguias	*eel*
ervilhas	*peas*
filete	*fillet of fish*
flã	*caramel mould*
framboesas	*raspberries*
frango	*chicken*
frito	*fried*
gambas	*prawns (shrimp)*
gelado	*ice-cream*
guisado	*stew*
lagosta	*spiny lobster*
laranja	*orange*
legumes	*vegetables*
limão	*lemon*

linguado	*sole*
lombo	*fillet*
lulas	*squid*
(à sevilhana)	*(deep-fried)*
maçã	*apple*
mariscos	*shellfish*
melancia	*watermelon*
mexilhões	*mussels*
molho	*sauce*
morangos	*strawberries*
omelete	*omelette*
ostras	*oysters*
ovo	*egg*
peixe	*fish*
pescada	*hake*
pescadinha	*whiting*
pêssego	*peach*
pimento	*green pepper*
polvos pequenos	*baby octopus*
porco	*pork*
presunto	*ham*
queijo	*smoked cheese*
salmonete	*red mullet*
salsichão	*salami*
sardinhas	*sardines*
sobremesa	*dessert*
torrada	*toast*
truta	*trout*
uvas	*grapes*
vitela	*veal*

* For more information on wining and dining in Portugal, consult the Berlitz EUROPEAN MENU READER.

Hairdressers
(*cabeleireiros*);
Barbers (*barbeiros*)

Every sizeable town has its unisex salon as well as traditional ladies' and old style gentlemen's hairdressers. Take advice, and take a look, if you want to get an idea of how up-to-date they are. Prices are far less in neighbourhood salons than in the most chic establishments. You should tip the hairdresser about 10 percent.

The following expressions may help:

haircut	**corte**
blow-dry *(brushing)*	**brushing**
permanent wave	**permanente**
a colour chart	**um mostruário de cores**
a colour rinse	**uma rinsage**
manicure	**manicura**
shampoo and set	**lavar e mise**
razor cut	**corte à navalha**
shave	**barba**
Not too much off *(here)*.	**Não corte muito (aqui).**
A little more off *(here)*.	**Corte mais um pouco (aqui).**

Laundry and
Dry Cleaning
(*lavandaria; tinturaria*)

The bigger hotels offer these services, at a price. There are also self-service launderettes (laundromats) in and around the big cities; you can find them listed under *Lavandarias e Tinturarias* in the yellow pages phone book. Their hours are often limited; generally 9am-1pm, 3-7pm weekdays, 9am-noon Saturday.

Most dry cleaners take three or four days, although a few in city shopping centres will do urgent work for the next day.

When will it be ready?	**Quando estará pronto?**
I must have this for tomorrow morning.	**Preciso disto para amanhã de manhã.**

Photography (*fotografia*) and Video

Well-known brands of film in all popular sizes are widely available. Colour film is processed in two to three days; rapid processing (in one hour) of colour prints can be done in big cities and holiday centres. Transparencies (slides) will take longer – in most cases it's worth taking films home.

Apart from possible military secrets, there are no restrictions on what you may film in Portugal.

Standard and camcorder videotape is available, but European tapes and US equipment are not compatible, and vice-versa.

I'd like a film for this camera.	**Quero um rolo para esta máquina.**
a black-and-white film	**um rolo a preto e branco**
a colour film	**um rolo a cores**
a colour-slide film	**um rolo de diapositivos a cores**
35-mm film	**um rolo de trinta e cinco milímetros**
How long will it take to develop this film?	**Quanto tempo leva a revelar este filme?**

May I take a picture?	**Posso tirar uma fotografia?**

Electric Current

The standard supply is 220-230V, 50Hz, with European plugs. Most hotels provide a 110V shaver outlet, but otherwise, US-made equipment will need both an adaptor and transformer.

Water

Unless there is a sign to the contrary, it is safe to drink the tap water in Portugal, but it may taste metallic or chlorinated. Many people prefer to drink one of the various bottled mineral waters, fizzy or still.

a bottle of mineral water	**uma garrafa de água mineral**
carbonated/non-carbonated	**com/sem gás**

Weights and Measures

The metric system is used in Portugal.

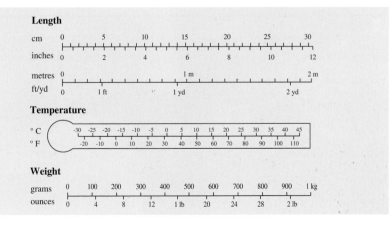

33

Communications

Post (*correios*)

The Portuguese mail service is quite efficient. Most mailboxes on the street follow the British pillar-box design and are painted bright red, too. A few are larger and more elaborate.

Local post offices are open Mon-Fri 9am-7pm. Major branch offices also operate on Saturday morning until noon. Round-the-clock service for the public can be found at the airport. Lisbon's main post office is situated in Praça dos Restauradores (opposite the tourist office) and is open daily 8am-midnight. Small shops which sell stamps (and often postcards) also display a sign which says '*Correio de Portugal - Selos*'.

If you don't know where you'll be staying you can have mail sent to you poste restante (general delivery) at the main post office in any town. In Lisbon you could have mail addressed to:

Jane Jones
Posta Restante
Praça dos Restauradores 58
1200 Lisboa, Portugal

Take your passport to pick up mail at the poste restante window. You will be charged a small handling fee.

Have you received any mail for ...?	**Tem correio para ...?**
A stamp for this letter/postcard, please.	**Um selo para esta carta/este postal, por favor.**
express (special delivery)	**expresso**
airmail	**via aérea**
registered	**registado**
poste restante (general delivery)	**posta restante**

*T*ime for a snooze in the shade... Lace, embroidery, and a British-style post box.

Telephone (telefone)

Direct dialling is now virtually universal. Automatic street telephones are usually found in British-style phone boxes (booths). Coin boxes take 50, 20 and 10 esc. coins; unused ones can be retrieved. **Card phones** ('Credifone') are at least as common as the coin-operated ones: cards are sold in the main post offices and telecommunications centres, in denominations of 750 and 1,800 esc. Unfortunately, more than one phone company operates in Portugal and their cards are not interchangeable.

You can dial most of the world direct on card or coin phones, or make calls through the clerk at larger post offices or hotels. For international direct dialling, use 00 (both Europe and overseas, e.g. UK 0044, USA 001), followed by the area code (without the initial '0', where there is one) and subscriber's number. Dial 099 for the international operator for Europe, 098 for the rest of the world.

To call Portugal from another country, dial the international access code, then 351, followed by the area code (omitting the initial zero) and number.

reverse-charge call	**paga pelo destinatário**
person-to-person call	**com préaviso**
Can you get me this number in ...?	**Pode ligar-me para este número em ...?**

Telegrams, Telex and Fax

Post offices handle long-distance telephone, telegraph and telex traffic. In Lisbon the Marconi Company at Rua S. Julião 131 operates a 24-hour international service. Larger hotels and business services can send faxes for you. Telex is increasingly being replaced by fax.

Media

Newspapers and Magazines (jornal; revista)

Europe's principal newspapers, including most British dailies and the *International Herald Tribune*, edited in Paris, are regularly available on the day of publication at many news-stands and hotels. Popular foreign magazines are also sold at the same stands. For both cinema and theatre programmes, check in one of the local Portuguese-language dailies; the most complete listings are in *Diário de Notícias*. The weekly *Se7e* (a play on the word for seven) has details of a wide range of Lisbon events. Other cities and towns, especially holiday centres, have their own guides.

Have you any English-language newspapers?	**Tem jornais em inglês?**

Radio and TV

Portugal has two government-run and two other **TV** channels. Imported programmes are usually dubbed, but films are often shown with subtitles. Spanish channels can be picked up in much of Portugal.

Many larger hotels offer a selection of satellite or cable channels.

The government operates four **radio** channels. Programme Two consists almost entirely of classical music, Programme Four mostly of pop music.

Travel suggestions in English for tourists are broadcast every morning on Programme Two (755 kHz MW, 94.3 MHz FM) at 8.15am. The Voice of America, BBC World Service, Radio Canada International and other foreign stations can be picked up on shortwave at certain times, usually early morning and night.

Religion

Most Portuguese are Roman Catholic, and church attendance is high, although less diligent than it was. Mass is held for English-speaking Catholics on Sunday at the Dominican Church of Corpo Santo, Travessa do Corpo Santo 32, Lisbon.

Anglican services are conducted in English on Sunday at St George's Church in the Estrela district of Lisbon, and at St Paul's, which is at Avenida Bombeiros Voluntarios 1 c, Estoril.

For the services of other denominations and in other cities and towns, ask at the local tourist information offices or the concierges at the bigger hotels.

Etiquette

People are punctual for appointments and social events. It's usual to shake hands on meeting and taking leave, and for business people to exchange cards. Business dress is quite formal, but if you're on holiday you can be as casual as you like. Even in formal restaurants it is rare for men to be asked to wear a jacket and tie, but T-shirts or beach wear would certainly be out of place.

Although quite reserved, the Portuguese are friendly and helpful. Young people, as everywhere, are more spontaneous and outgoing than the older generation. Don't be startled if somebody taps you firmly on the arm to attract your attention. It's the Portuguese way. Also, if people, especially villagers in the more remote areas (notably in the north), seem to be staring at you, it's only unaffected curiosity.

One problem is how to catch the eye of a waiter. The Portuguese have no equivalent for 'Waiter!' but say *Faz favor* (please!). (See also Language on p.37)

Opening Hours
(*horas de abertura*)

Most banks open Mon-Fri 8.30am-2.30 or 2.45pm. Some take lunch 11.45am-1pm. Offices and businesses usually operate Mon-Fri 9am-1pm and 3pm-7pm. Shops keep similar hours, plus 9am-1pm on Saturday. The large shopping centres open through the midday break and may also stay open until late in the evening.

Public Holidays

1 January	*Ano Novo*
	New Year's Day
25 April	*Dia de Portugal*
	National Day
1 May	*Dia do Trabalho*
	Labour Day
10 June	*Dia de Camões*
	Camoens' Day
15 August	*Assunçao*
	Assumption
5 October	*Dia da Republica*
	Republic Day
1 November	*Todos-os-Santos*
	All Saints' Day
1 December	*Restauração*
	Restoration Day (of Independence)
8 December	*Imaculada Conceição*
	Immaculate Conception
25 December	*Natal*
	Christmas Day

Movable dates:

Sexta-feira Santa
Good Friday
Corpo de Deus
Corpus Christi

In some towns everything closes for the local saint's day.

Language

Portuguese, a derivative of Latin, may look like Spanish (a help in reading menus and signs) but certainly doesn't sound like it, and although almost all Portuguese understand it, some may resent being addressed in Spanish. Many speak French, having worked in France. Portuguese schoolchildren are taught both French and English, taking up one language at the age of ten and the other at 13.

The Berlitz PORTUGUESE PHRASEBOOK AND DICTIONARY FOR TRAVELLERS covers practically all the situations you're likely to encounter. Also useful is the Berlitz Portuguese-English/English-Portuguese pocket dictionary, which has a menu-reader supplement.

Good morning	**Bom dia**
	(bawng **dee**er)
Good evening	**Boa noite**
	(boaer **nawng**ter)
Thank you	**Obrigado** (women say **obrigada**)
Please	**Por favor**
	(poor fer **voar**)
Goodbye	**Adeus** (erdheh**o**osh)

Some Useful Expressions

yes/no	**sim/não**
excuse me/you're welcome	**perdão/de nada**
where/when/how	**onde/quando/como**
how long/how far	**quanto tempo/a que distância**
yesterday/today/ tomorrow	**ontem/hoje/amanh**
day/week/month/ year	**dia/semana/mês/ano**
left/right	**esquerdo/direito**
good/bad	**bom/mau**

big/small	**grande/pequeno**
cheap/expensive	**barato/caro**
hot/cold	**quente/frio**
old/new	**velho/novo**
open/closed	**aberto/fechado**
Does anyone here speak English?	**Alguém fala inglês?**
I don't understand.	**Não compreendo.**
Please write it down.	**Escreva-mo, por favor.**
What does this mean?	**Que quer dizer isto?**
Help me, please.	**Ajude-me, por favor.**
Get a doctor quickly.	**Chame um médico, depressa.**
What time is it?	**Que horas são?**
How much is that?	**Quanto custa isto?**
I'd like ...	**Queria/Quero ...**
Just a minute.	**Um momento.**
Waiter!/Waitress!	**Faz favor!**
What day is it today?	**Que dia é hoje?**

DAYS

Sunday	**domingo**
Monday	**segunda-feira**
Tuesday	**terça-feira**
Wednesday	**quarta-feira**
Thursday	**quinta-feira**
Friday	**sexta-feira**
Saturday	**sábado**

Smoking

Major international and local brands are available. In general, smoking is commoner than in the US or UK but it is banned in theatres, cinemas, local buses, trams and the Lisbon Metro. Some hotels and restaurants have non-smoking areas but the atmosphere in busy bars can be torture for sensitive eyes and noses.

Tipping

Hotel bills include a service charge. So do most restaurants, but an additional gratuity is expected. In informal eating places you may like to leave a coin or two on the table. The total on credit cards may be left open in restaurants: before adding a tip, find out whether service has already been included.

Hotel porters will expect something for carrying cases and other services.

The following are suggestions.

Hairdresser/Barber	**10%**
Hotel maid, per week	**500 esc**
Lavatory attendant	**25-50 esc**
Hotel porter, per bag	**100 esc**
Taxi driver	**10%**
Tour Guide	**10-15% of excursion fare**
Waiter	**5-10% of cheque**

Toilets
(lavabos/sanitarios/ toiletes)

Most towns have public toilets; as do many tourist sites. They are better kept than in some other countries but there may be no paper. They are also provided in the larger hotels, the cafés and bars – if you go in to use them it would be polite to buy a coffee or a drink.

Lost Property
(objectos perdidos)

After checking with the hotel housekeeper or front desk, public transport authorities or other obvious leads, contact the local police station for information and advice.

In Lisbon, the police have a special lost property telephone number, tel. 346 61 41. If you've lost something in a Lisbon bus or tram, go to the public transport lost-and-found department at the base of the Santa Justa lift near the Rossio station, or tel. 347 08 77.

I've lost my wallet/ purse/passport. **Perdi a minha mala/passaporte.**

Complaints
(reclamação)

By far the best policy is to sort out any difficulty on the spot, in a friendly way if possible, with the shop or hotel manager or other responsible person. Writing a letter afterwards won't solve the problem when it matters most. In cases where accommodation isn't up to standard and the management won't rectify the problem right away, you could try going to the local tourist office. In Lisbon contact the head office of the department of tourism at Av. António Augusto de Aguiar 86, 1100 Lisbon, tel. 57 52 86. Bring documents along to support your claim where possible, and keep them in case you want to raise the matter with your travel agent later. Hotels and restaurants are required to keep a complaints book: merely asking to use it may encourage a positive response to your complaint.

Crime and Theft

It's always wise to keep your valuables in the hotel safe. Report any theft to the hotel receptionist, the nearest police station or the local tourist office. Portugal is still a law-abiding country but sadly, as in most of the world, big city street crime and thefts from (and of) cars are on the increase, especially in Lisbon and along the Algarve. Don't leave anything attractive on view in your car, either in towns or rural areas. Avoid parking in dark and unfrequented places and don't carry lots of cash or valuables. Bag-snatching has become more frequent, so carry your handbag firmly under your arm, on the side away from the street. Beware of pickpockets in crowded places, especially public transport, markets and sports events. Also watch out when boarding a bus or tram; you can be jostled and robbed at the same time.

I want to report a   **Quero participar**
theft.   **um roubo.**

Police

The state police (PSP) take care of routine police matters and traffic control in towns. They tend to be friendly and helpful, although you should not expect fluency in your own language. The Guarda Nacional Republicana (GNR) is a more military organization, one of its duties being to patrol highways. In holiday resorts, police wearing armbands marked CD (*Corpo Distrital* – local corps) are assigned to assist visitors and normally speak a foreign language. The correct way to address any policeman is *Senhor Guarda*.

Emergencies (*urgência*)

For Police, Fire or Ambulance services, the telephone number everywhere is 115. Calls are free.

For emergency road service there are SOS telephones every 3km (2 miles) on main roads. (See also p.14)

Although you can call the police from any one of the blue boxes in the street marked *polícia*, it's unlikely you'll get anyone on the other end who speaks anything but Portuguese. (See also Health and Medical Care on p.20)

Calendar of Events

Nearly every town has its **market day**, held once or twice a week or once a month. Some of the biggest are: São Pedro de Sintra (2nd and 4th Sunday of each month); Barcelos (Thursday); Estremoz (Saturday); Lamego (Wednesday); and Loulé (Saturday).

The annual celebration of a local **saint's day** can be a low key affair or a full-scale *festa* (festival) on the eve and the day itself. The list below includes these, and other, celebrations. Events marked with an * are tied to the church calendar and can move from year to year. As you plan your excursions, it is worth checking with tourist information offices, which carry a timetable of **festivals** and **fairs** (*feiras*) around the country.

January
Vila Nova de Gaia: Festival of St Gonçalo and St Cristovão.

February-March
*Carnival (Mardi Gras) processions and fireworks in many towns.

March-April
* Holy Week: Palm Sunday, Good Friday and Easter Day (Sunday) services and processions, notably at *Braga* and other northern cities.

April
Alter do Chão: Annual horse sales.

*F*olk dances and colourful costumes are a feature of traditional festivals throughout Portugal.

May
Sesimbra: Festival of Senhor das Chagas (3-5 May).
Barcelos: Festival of the Crosses, processions, fair.
Fátima: Pilgrimage (days leading up to 13 May).
Coimbra: Queima das Fitas, celebrating the end of the university year.
May-June
Algarve Music Festival: concerts in several Algarve towns.
June
Lisbon: Festival of music, dance and theatre. Concerts and performances.
Amarante: Festival of São Gonçalo, processions (1st weekend).
Coimbra: Festival of Rainha Santa Isabel,

the city's patron saint.
Santarém: National Agricultural Fair, with bullfights and a folk festival.
Lisbon and many other places: fairs and festivities for the 'People's Saints': Santo António (St Anthony) on 13 June; São João (St John) 24 June – notably in *Oporto*, *Braga* and *Évora*; and *São Pedro* (St Peter) 29 June.
July
Sintra: Music Festival, performances in the palaces and gardens.
Guimarães: Pilgrimage to church of São Torcato.
Vila Franca de Xira, north of Lisbon on the Tagus: running of bulls in the streets (first and second Sundays).
July-August
Estoril and *Cascais*: Estoril International Music Festival.
Estoril: Crafts Fair, every evening, open air.
Setúbal: Festival of Santiago, fair and exhibition (last week July, first week August).
Vila do Conde: craft fair

40

August

Peniche: Festival of Nossa Senhora da Boa Viagem (Our Lady of the Good Voyage) in early August.

Vila Viçosa: Horse Fair.

Viana do Castelo: Festival of Nossa Senhora da Agonia, including processions over carpets of flowers, parades, fireworks (weekend nearest to 20 August).

August-September

Lamego: Pilgrimage to shrine of Nossa Senhora dos Remédios, including processions, and fair.

Viseu: Festival of São Mateus, agricultural fair, bullfights.

September

Estoril: Portuguese Grand Prix, Formula One motor race.

Palmela Wine Festival: parades, tastings and fireworks (mid-month).

Nazaré: Festival of Nossa Senhora de Nazaré (second week in September).

Ponte de Lima: *Feiras Novas*, huge festival and market (mid-September).

Algarve: Folk Music and Dance Festival staged in Praia da Rocha and other Algarve towns.

Cabo Espichel, near Sesimbra: Festival of Nossa Senhora do Cabo (Our Lady of the Cape) on the last Sunday.

October

Vila Franca de Xira (see July): fair, running of bulls in the streets (first Sunday) and bullfights.

Fátima: pilgrimage (takes place on the days leading up to 13 October).

Óbidos: Early Music Festival (during the 2nd week).

October-November

Santarém: National Gastronomy Festival.

November

Golega: National Horse Show and São Martinho Fair (also held in a number of other towns).

READING THE SIGNS

anta	*Portuguese for dolmen (qv)*
azulejo	*painted ceramic tile*
barragem	*dam*
capela	*chapel*
capela môr	*chancel, sanctuary*
castelo	*castle*
castro	*pre-Roman hilltop fort*
chafariz	*fountain*
citánia	*pre-Roman hilltop town*
claustro	*cloister*
convento	*convent/monastery*
dolmen	*group of standing stones with a cap stone (prehistoric tomb)*
fortaleza	*fortress*
igreja	*church*
igreja matriz	*'mother church' (i.e. parish church)*
janela	*window*
judiaria	*old Jewish quarter of a town*
largo	*town square*
Manueline	*highly decorative architecture from early 16th century*
menhir	*prehistoric standing stone*
mercado	*market*
miradouro	*viewpoint*
mosteiro	*monastery*
mouraria	*old Moorish quarter of town*
mozárab (moçárabe)	*Christian living under Moslem rule*
mudéjar	*Moor living under Christian rule, generally 'converted'*
nascente	*east*
paço, palácio	*palace*
pelourinho	*pillory, tall column and emblem of a town*
poente	*west*
ponte	*bridge*
praça	*square*
praia	*beach*
quinta	*farm or estate, or an estate's main house*
sé	*cathedral*
torre	*tower*
torre de menagem	*keep of a castle*

Good Things Come in
Small Packages

Newcomers soon feel at home in Portugal, for this is an accessible country. The musical sounding Portuguese language may be impossible to decipher, but most people speak some English or French. The food and customs are different, but not impossibly strange. There is plenty to keep you amused here: the beaches are justly famous; golfers can play all year round on the growing number of Algarve courses; and lovers of romantic castles can find a lifetime supply. With improved roads making it much easier to get around, you will find more variety in this compact country than in most others many times its size.

Who are the Portuguese and where did they come from? Waves of invaders and immigrants arrived by land and sea: Celts and Carthaginians, Romans and Germanic tribes, Moors from North Africa, Jews and Spanish and north Europeans, including quite a few British, from foot soldiers to royalty – Prince Henry the Navigator's mother was English. All must have contributed something to the make-up of a people that could only be Portuguese.

High days and holidays... Earlier generations used to keep much of the family wealth in the form of gold chains and filigree work. It was only brought out for festive occasions.

There is a north-south variation in this, as in many other things. North of Lisbon, you'll see some taller and fairer individuals, maybe with more Germanic and north European ancestors. South of Lisbon, the stereotype is short of stature, wiry, dark-haired and dark-eyed, perhaps descended from the Celts, Iberians and Moors. Lisbon itself over the centuries has been a magnet for the whole country, and more recently for the inhabitants of the former empire – the shanty towns of Cape Verde islanders look like African villages.

The Portuguese character is completely individual. People are patient, tolerant and exceptionally courteous. They're not usually the ones to make the first move, but are nonetheless friendly and helpful when approached. Giving assistance when it's requested is second nature: there's a word in the language for it, *cunha*. Ask for directions and you're quite likely to find someone accompanying you at least part of the way to make sure you don't go wrong. There's no resentment of the odd ways of foreigners. If heads turn to stare at you in the remote country areas, it's only natural curiosity – they don't see many strangers. Other Latin people tend to make fun of the rather quieter and more modest Portuguese, the only ones who don't use extravagant hand gestures.

Cut off from the rest of Europe by her big and often hostile neighbour, Spain, Portugal naturally turned to her other frontier, the sea. Her navigators pioneered the routes to India, the East Indies and Japan in the 15th and 16th centuries and were the first to sail round the world. The first colonial empire of modern times was created (it was also the last to be dissolved), and it had to be peopled and defended. Emigration became a way of life, which may partly account for the supposed national

mood of *saudade*, a blend of longing, fatalism and nostalgia, felt by those who were leaving as well as the ones they left behind. The same emotions are expressed in the *fado*, wailing songs on the themes of tragedy and regret. Although these may have been derived from the laments of African slaves or perhaps from Arabic music, *fado* is quintessentially Portuguese.

Even in the recent past, almost everyone depended on farming and fishing, the land and the sea. Now only 12% of the labour force works on the land, compared with 25% in 1980, and fewer still are involved in the fishing industry. Rural unemployment has rocketed, and the young continue to migrate to the cities; but the boom of the 1980s is over and jobs are scarce there too. Even the traditional escape valve of emigration to work in France or Germany has almost been closed. Many of the older generation of emigrants are coming home from those equally recession-hit countries.

The simple life is changing fast, but the old ways survive. Traditional fairs and markets have roots in ancient, maybe Celtic, origins and are flourishing still – they are certainly not staged for tourists. When the harvest has been gathered, people really celebrate. Festivals often seem as much a tribute to a pre-Christian Earth Goddess in the guise of Mother Nature as to the Virgin Mary. Most people are Catholic but the influence of the church is less than all-pervasive, although it is far greater in the more conservative north than the left-wing south.

It sometimes seems as if most Portuguese are country dwellers at heart. They turn the cities into villages, balconies into flower gardens and laundries. In narrow streets, wet shirts and sheets and intimate underwear flap overhead while birds sing from their hanging cages. Town houses often present closed doors and shutters to the street (although rarely reinforced with forbidding iron bars). Concealed behind them might be a charming courtyard filled with flowers and shaded by orange trees and grapevines. This is a country of constant surprises. Inside the walls of an imposing fortress, you could easily stumble across a whole quaint village where the livestock wanders in the street and nothing seems to have changed since the Middle Ages.

The Portuguese ranged the world during the Age of Discoveries and brought home untold riches. Today visitors can make their own voyages of discovery through

To be seen on most beaches throughout the year – the never-ending task of untangling and repairing the fishing nets and long plastic lines.

Portugal. Most of the country sees comparatively few foreign visitors, and rarely enough of them to distort the local way of life. Lisbon is one exception, but this is a city with such a strong character of its own that outside influences are easily absorbed. The Algarve is in the business of mass tourism, but even there, when the summer is over traditional patterns reassert themselves. A fast growing new trend is for local travel. There was a time when a few of the rich went to a spa, and no-one else could afford to go anywhere. Now people flock to the coast in their millions, but others are exploring the interior for the first time. You'll sometimes be competing with them for accommodation.

A glance at the map shows Portugal as a rough rectangle in the south-west corner of the Iberian peninsula, minuscule compared with the Spanish share. It might be expected that the two would be quite similar. Emphatically they are not. The Portuguese landscape is far gentler and greener. Forests of pine and eucalyptus dress the mountain slopes; cork oak trees with their oddly blackened trunks are scattered across the plains; and deep river valleys give shelter to orchards and terraced vineyards. The fertile north-west is divided into little family farms, often enclosed by stone walls and a curtain of vines trained up trees and high fences, while the rolling southern plain of the Alentejo has been a land of vast estates since Roman times: the wheatfields can stretch from horizon to horizon. Here and in the granite uplands of the north-east it can be oven-hot in summer, bitterly cold in winter. Everywhere else the Atlantic Ocean tempers the climate. Its waves pound the cliffs and beaches of the west coast while the Algarve in the south is more sheltered, with an almost Mediterranean feel to it.

Valley slopes painstakingly carved into terraces by hand centuries ago are planted with almond and olive trees, vines and vegetables. Spring covers the hillsides in a veil of green.

GEOGRAPHY

Forming the western extremity of mainland Europe, Portugal runs about 560km (350 miles) from north to south and no more than 220km (140 miles) from east to west. The only land border is with Spain, to the north and east. The south and west are bounded by the Atlantic in which lie the Portuguese islands of Madeira and the Azores.

Apart from a narrow coastal plain, the northern half is quite mountainous, although nowhere reaching higher than Torre, at 1,993m (6,538 ft). It is cut through from east to west by the valleys of great rivers: the Minho (the border with Spain), Lima, Douro and Mondego. The flat flood plain of the Tagus (*Tejo*) cuts inland north-east from Lisbon. Most of the southern half of the country is a vast rolling prairie, the Alentejo, growing grain and cork trees. An east-west range of hills cuts off the southern coastal strip, the Algarve.

Population: 12 million

Capital: Lisbon (pop. 1.4 million; greater Lisbon 2.5 million).

Main cities: Oporto (450,000), Coimbra (90,000), Braga (80,000), Évora (40,000), Faro (40,000), Guimarães(30,000).

Government: An independent republic and parliamentary democracy; the elected president's role is largely ceremonial. Portugal is a full member of the European Union.

History

Flint axes and blades scattered over Portugal's southern plains show that Stone Age hunter-gatherers lived here tens of thousands of years ago. A few cave paintings dating from perhaps 16,000 BC give clues to their way of life and you can see some of their tools on display in the Museum of Archaeology in Belém, in Lisbon (see p.107). They probably lived and hunted in family units, but by 4,000 BC there is evidence of larger,

organized communities. Here as in France, Britain and Ireland, they built megalithic monuments – standing stones, passage graves and dolmens (groups of stones supporting a heavy capstone), which can still be seen in many parts of Portugal today. They carved designs on the rocks, as at Outeiro Machado near Chaves (see p.235). Later in the Neolithic era, troubled times led to the building of fortified villages, some on hilltop sites which were taken over at a later date by successive waves of invaders.

On the coast, the earliest inhabitants lived on the abundant shellfish, their descendants learning to fish from the shore and then from boats. By 1,200 BC, Phoenician ships from the far-off eastern Mediterranean had begun to explore beyond the Straits of Gibraltar in search of trade. They sailed along the south and west coasts of today's Portugal, establishing settlements at sheltered rivermouths. One such settlement was to develop into Lisbon, while further north, the fisherfolk of Nazaré and Aveiro claim descent from the Phoenicians.

Around 700 BC, Celtic tribes moved into northern and central Portugal, occupying earlier settlements and building their own hilltop strongholds. Many sites are doubtless buried beneath today's towns and cities; others such as that of Citânia de Briteiros (see p. 214) have been excavated and can be visited. At the same time, Iberians, perhaps originating from North Africa, were living in the inland areas to the south. The coastal settlements became part of the seafaring empire of Carthage, a former Phoenician colony on the North African coast.

Roman Province

The rise of a new power in the Mediterranean, Rome, soon led to conflict with Carthage. Eventually victorious at the end of the Second Punic War (218-201 BC), the Romans claimed their defeated rival's possessions. In the Iberian peninsula, it took them most of the next two centuries

to turn that claim into reality. The Celts put up a fierce resistance, particularly the Lusitani in the north. One of their leaders, Viriatus, inflicted a succession of stunning reverses on the Romans until in 139 BC, unable to match him in battle, they bribed some traitors to assassinate him. Even then, Rome's best legions and generals were incapable of capturing all the Celts' mountain strongholds.

Julius Caesar, based at Lisbon in 60 BC and again between 49 and 45 BC, pacified the Alentejo area and much of the north. Finally, by 25 BC, under Augustus, resistance was crushed and the remnants of the hill tribes were forcibly resettled in the plains. The Romans now marked off a new province called Lusitania, comprising most of today's Portugal and some of neighbouring Spain. Rome introduced the growing of wheat, olives and grapes, built roads and bridges and bequeathed to the nation the basis of the Portuguese language.

As in the rest of the empire, the spread of Christianity began slowly but gathered pace in the 3rd century, despite – or perhaps because of – vicious persecution. With Constantine's Edict of Toleration (306) and then its adoption as the official religion of the empire, the Christian faith was triumphant. All the while, however, Roman power was declining, until the 5th century saw the Iberian peninsula overrun by Vandals, Alani and Suevi, Germanic 'barbarians'

The mosaic floors of dozens of Roman villas and palaces have been unearthed in many parts of Portugal and are often of extravagant or intricate designs. This one is near Vilamoura in the Algarve.

Early azulejos, *painted and glazed ceramic tiles, used geometric designs, but by the 17th century, complex pictures were being produced such as this of St John the Baptist.*

the Moslem religion. More than 500 years were to pass before the Moors were forced out of their last possessions in the Algarve. The imprint of their rule is still evident today, in the layout of towns, architecture, design (they introduced the art of the ceramic tile or *azulejo*), agriculture, place names and many words in the language.

The Christians had kept a precarious but significant foothold in northern Portugal, which became a springboard for attempts to reclaim the rest of the country. Oporto was soon captured, and lost again, changing hands frequently over the centuries, until in 1092 the Christian forces took it and stayed. It gave its name to Portucale, a county ruled by Henry of Burgundy, owing allegiance to the Spanish King of León and Castile whose daughter Teresa he had married. She took over when Henry died, until independence-minded barons persuaded her 17-year-old son, Afonso Henriques, to seize control and he swiftly defeated his mother's supporters. After a victory over Moorish forces in 1139 at the Battle of Ourique (now believed to have been a fairly small skirmish near Santarém), he declared himself King Afonso I of Portugal and moved his capital from Guimarães to Coimbra. Lisbon eluded his grasp for another eight years, however; the Moors were too securely entrenched.

swarming in across the Pyrenees. Lisbon fell at the beginning of this century and a succession of migrating tribes occupied Portugal until the arrival in the 6th century of the more disciplined, mostly Christian, Visigoths, who provided a period of peace. As admirers of Roman civilization, they adopted the Latin spoken in the peninsula instead of imposing their own language.

Moorish Conquest and Christian Revival

The year 711 AD saw a formidable invasion fleet from North Africa cross the Strait of Gibraltar. This army of Arabs and their allies, known to the Christians as Moors, had in fact been invited by one warring faction to help against another, although there's little doubt they would have come anyway, so powerful was the impetus of expansionary Islam. Within a few years, almost all of Iberia had been conquered in the name of

The castle at Guimarães is thought to have been the birthplace of Afonso Henriques, the first King of Portugal.

In 1147 the king recruited a volunteer force of thousands of Norman, Flemish, German and English crusaders who were passing through on their way to the Holy Land. He convinced them to stay long enough to strike a blow against the Moslems and, just as tempting, collect the booty of Lisbon. The combined forces, Portuguese and crusaders, besieged the fortress for four months. At last the walls were breached, and the surviving defenders asked for a truce. An orderly handover was agreed, but the Crusaders ignored the terms and set about looting the city and murdering Moslems and *mozárab* Christians alike. The Moors were slowly driven south until fresh forces from North Africa, the fanatical Almohads, staged a revival, recapturing almost all the land south of the River Tagus by 1171. It was not to last. In 1249, Afonso III completed the reconquest of his country by taking their last stronghold, Faro in the Algarve. Soon afterwards he moved the national capital again, from Coimbra to Lisbon.

His successor, Dinis (1279-1325), then set about consolidating the kingdom and fending off Castilian claims with a twin-track policy combining dynastic marriages and castle-building. A university was founded at Lisbon in 1290 and moved to Coimbra in 1308.

The Avis Dynasty

In 1383 the last king in the Burgundian line, Fernando I, died, leaving only a young daughter, Beatriz. He had promised her to various suitors, including an English lord, the son of the Earl of Cambridge. The earl failed to supply the promised army for an attack on Castile, however, so in a sudden reversal of policy, Beatriz was married to Juan I, the king of that powerful neighbour. When it became clear that Juan had plans to combine the kingdoms (an old Castilian ambition), Portugal rose in revolt. João of Avis, the illegitimate son of Pedro I of Portugal, had been acting as regent: now he was acclaimed king by the people of Lisbon. In the same year, 1385, the Castilian army was decisively beaten at Aljubarrota, 100km (60 miles) north of the capital. As it happened, John of Gaunt, Duke of Lancaster was pursuing a tenuous

*P*igeons perch on the Lisbon statue of King João I, whose marriage to Philippa of Lancaster affirmed his new alliance with England.

*T*heir son Prince Henry 'the Navigator' set in motion the explorations that marked the start of the Portuguese empire.

claim to the throne of Castile at the time (like the Earl of Cambridge, he had married a previous king's daughter), and English archers played their part in the victory. Portuguese independence was assured, and João of Avis was crowned King João I in the cathedral at Coimbra.

The alliance between Portugal and England was cemented in the 1386 Treaty of Windsor, which called for eternal and true friendship. A year later João I married John of Gaunt's daughter, Philippa of Lancaster. Their third surviving son, the Duke of Viseu, changed the map of the world. We know him better as Henry the Navigator.

Age of Discoveries

The war with Castile dragged on until peace was patched up in 1411. Perhaps to keep his army busy or to gain credit for a crusade, João sent an expedition to capture the Moslem stronghold of Ceuta on the coast of Morocco in 1415. The 21-year-old Henry was one of its leaders and in celebration for their victory, João appointed him Master of the Order of Christ, the fighting monks who were successors to the Knights Templar in Portugal (see p. 161). Henry rarely went travelling again, but instead retired to the 'end-of-the-world', Sagres peninsula, to establish a school of navigation. There he assembled astronomers, map-makers and other experts who helped him to organize expeditions that pushed back the horizon. During his lifetime Portuguese caravels sailed beyond the westernmost point of Africa, Madeira and the Azores were colonized, and the foundations of the future Portuguese empire were laid.

The king who ruled over Portugal's golden age of exploration was Manuel I (1495-1521). Discoveries made during his reign helped to make him one of Europe's richest rulers. The style of architecture of the period, an intermission between the Gothic and the Renaissance, bears his name. Whimsical decorative touches, especially references to the sea, and an exotic mixture of disparate elements are the trademarks of Manueline art, as exemplified by the Tower of Belém (see p.107) and the nearby Jerónimos Monastery (see p.106), the unfinished chapels at Batalha (see p.155) and the Convent of Christ at Tomar (see p.160).

The most significant expedition under Manuel's flag was Vasco da Gama's sea voyage of 1497-98. Rounding what is now called the Cape of Good Hope, he opened up East Africa and India to Portuguese trade. A colony was established at Goa in India in 1510 and at Malacca on the coast of Malaya in 1511. The sea route was open to the spice islands of the East.

In 1500 the Portuguese explorer Pedro Álvares Cabral had shown the way to vast new territories with his accidental discovery of Brazil. Perhaps it was more than coincidence (had sailors long known of Brazil?) that the Treaty of Tordesillas signed with Spain in 1494 had *already* allocated any land to be found in those longitudes to Portugal.

Times of Trial

In the meantime, neighbouring Spain had managed to complete the reconquest of its territory from the Moors. This was followed by the expulsion of the large Jewish population, perhaps numbering half a million, with a minority accepting the alternative of conversion to Christianity. Some moved into Portugal, especially the northern mountains, but under pressure from Spain the Jews of Portugal were also forced to convert or emigrate.

The 16th-century Inquisition which racked Spain spread to Portugal, but its application there was much more moderate and haphazard. The round-up of heretics never really attained major proportions, although many thousands of the 'New Christians' (converted Jews) were investigated and hundreds burned at the stake.

The overseas territories were proving a mixed blessing: the manpower needed to exploit them was a drain on a small nation; the rich pickings were encouraging decadence and laziness at home; and the need to defend their new empires was forcing Portugal into alliance with Spain. As a country with only two frontiers – the sea and the Spanish border – Portugal has always kept a wary eye on its bigger neighbour. The worst happened in 1580 when the king (and cardinal), Dom Henrique, died leaving no heir. Spain's King Philip II claimed the throne as Dom Filipe I of Portugal and his troops invaded the country to enforce a union of the two crowns.

It took 60 years for local forces to organize a successful uprising against the hated occupation. On 1 December 1640 (still celebrated as Portugal's Restoration Day) Spanish rule was finally overthrown. The Duke of Bragança was crowned King João IV in Lisbon's riverfront square, the Terreiro do Paço. Only Spain's problems elsewhere prevented an all-out assault to crush the revolt, but frontier wars continued for years, draining Portuguese resources. To help secure independence, the old alliance with England was reaffirmed, and strengthened when Charles II of England married João's daughter, Catherine, in 1662.

QUEEN OF QUEENS

On St Catherine's Day, 25 November 1638, in the palace at Vila Viçosa (see p.264), a daughter was born to the Duke and Duchess of Bragança. She was baptized Catherine. Two years later, her father became King João IV of Portugal, ending a 60-year spell of Spanish domination. His reign was a constant struggle to retain that independence. Royal marriages and the dowries that went with them were the agent that held alliances together, and Catherine's was an obvious bargaining counter for the future. Before João died in 1656, a marriage with Louis XIV of France had been mooted, but the complexities of Franco-Spanish relations ruled it out.

When Charles II was restored to the throne of England after the death of Cromwell (who had executed his father), he suddenly became one of the most eligible bachelors in Europe. The Portuguese ambassador in London was instructed to suggest that 'there was a princess who would suit his needs, given her beauty, her character and good nature'. The marriage suited both parties. Portugal gained a strong ally; Charles acquired the greatest dowry ever recorded: £500,000 in cash (equivalent to £50 million in today's money), free trade with all Portuguese possessions, and the ports of Tangier and Bombay. This last gift marked the beginning of the British Empire in India.

In 1662 a British fleet arrived at Lisbon to collect the princess, and after a spectacular farewell with bullfights, processions and fireworks, she sailed for England. A secret Catholic wedding ceremony was held at Portsmouth, followed by a public Anglican service. Writing to his Lord Chancellor, Charles tells of his reaction to his bride:

It was happy for the honour of the nation that I was not put to the consummation of the marriage last night for I was too sleepy by haveing slept but two houers in my journy ... I can only now give you an account of what I have seene abed, which in shorte is, her face is not so exact as to be caled a beuty though her eyes are excelent good and not anything in her face that in the least degree can shoque one ... and if I have any skill in visiognimy which I think I have she must be as good a woman as ever was borne.

In spite of his notorious infidelities, numerous mistresses and illegitimate offspring, and her inability to conceive an heir, their relations remained good to the end of his life in 1685. She wanted to return to Portugal then, but diplomacy prevented it until 1692. Thirty years after her grand departure, more fireworks, bullfights and crowds greeted her return. She died in 1705 and is buried in the Church of São Vicente de Fora in Lisbon (see p.97).

Catherine has a special place in the history of New York City. When it was taken from the Dutch in 1664, one borough (now Brooklyn) was called King's County in her husband's honour. Queen's County, named for Catherine, has more or less kept its name – the Borough of Queens.

During the long reign of João V (1706-50), the finances of Portugal were transformed as gold poured in from new discoveries in Brazil. Emulating his contemporary, Louis XIV of France, the king spent it on lavish monuments and public works, such as the University Library at Coimbra (see p.170) and the colossal palace and monastery at Mafra (see p. 137). In another effort to enhance the grandeur of his court and country, the king convinced the pope to promote the see of Lisbon to a patriarchate. Religious passion permeated João's private life as well: his most notorious habit was a penchant for nuns.

Destruction and Rebuilding

The great divide between early history and modern times in Portugal falls in the middle of the 18th century. On All Saints' Day, 1 November 1755, an earthquake devastated large parts of the country from the Algarve to the northern Alentejo. It was felt especially badly in Lisbon, where churches filled with worshippers collapsed; overturned candles and lanterns spread fires throughout the city; and then a huge tidal wave crashed ashore. The triple disaster killed between 15,000 and 60,000 people (sources differ drastically). Reminders of the nightmare are found in many parts of Portugal to this day. In Lisbon the most dramatic is the wreckage of the Carmelite church, which has been open to the sky ever since the morning the roof fell in.

Since routine problems of state were beyond the talents of the ineffectual King José I (1750-77), he could hardly be expected to cope with the challenge of post-quake recovery. The power behind the throne was in fact a tough, ambitious minister called Sebastião José de Carvalho e Melo, who was later elevated to Count of Oeiras and – the name best remembered

– the Marquês de Pombal. Taking advantage of the power vacuum, once the earth stopped shaking, Pombal mobilized all Portugal's resources for the clean-up. The survivors were fed and housed, the corpses disposed of, the ruins cleared and plans for an impressive new city laid out.

Pombal had already made enemies of the rich and powerful Jesuits. They tried to put the blame for the earthquake on his alleged godlessness but he had the last word, banning them from Portugal in 1759. For another 18 years he was the undisputed master, implementing his autocratic rule wherever he could. He revolutionized

every aspect of government, promoted industry and agriculture and regulated the port wine trade (see p.193). When King José died in 1777, however, he was instantly dismissed and banished to his estates, as the devout Maria I tried to reverse some of his anti-religious policies.

The great earthquake of 1755 devastated many parts of Portugal. Most of Lisbon was left in ruins, including the 13th-century cloisters of the cathedral.

Peninsular War and Civil War

At the beginning of the 19th century, Napoleon dragged Portugal into the heat of Europe's conflicts by demanding the impossible – that Portugal declare war on Britain. Responding to the predictable refusal, the French army marched into Por-

tugal in 1807. The royal family led by Prince João, regent for the mad Maria, fled to Rio de Janeiro – where they stayed until ten years after the crisis. General Andoche Junot, who led the invasion, had the good taste to set up his headquarters in the

pink palace at Queluz. For months the people of Lisbon had to put up with the sight of Napoleon's colours flying above the Castelo de São Jorge.

British help arrived in 1808, and Junot's army was quickly defeated. A truce was signed and the French were forced to withdraw. The following year they were back, but in engagements over the next three years they suffered a string of defeats. The success of the combined Portuguese-British forces owed much to the strategic brilliance of Sir Arthur Wellesley, the British commander, who was later to become the Duke of Wellington. After battering fruitlessly against the defensive Lines of Torres Vedras, north of Lisbon, the French began a long retreat, sacking and looting as they went. Napoleon's last outpost in Portugal was evacuated in the spring of 1811. (For more about Wellington's campaigns, see p.239.)

Only 22 years later the country was again at war – this time in its most tragic variety, brother against brother. Pedro IV, formerly emperor of Brazil (which had asserted its independence from Portugal in 1882), fought to wrest the crown from his absolutist brother, Miguel I. Pedro won the so-called War of Two Brothers, but only a few months later he died of consumption. He was just 36 years old. His adolescent daughter, Maria da Glória, assumed the throne. She married a German

*F*ocal *point of modern Lisbon, the statue of the Marquês de Pombal at the top of Avenida da Liberdade. He was the energetic dictator who organized the reconstruction of the city after the 1755 earthquake.*

nobleman, Ferdinand of Saxe-Coburg-Gotha, who built her the eccentric Pena Palace above Sintra (see p.135) and fathered her five sons and six daughters. Maria II died in childbirth at 34.

Republic and Dictatorship

Premature and tragic deaths claimed many royal Portuguese, but in all the country's history only one king was assassinated. The victim was Carlos I, the date 1 February 1908. As the royal family was riding through Lisbon's vast Terreiro do Paço (Praça do Comércio) in an open carriage, Carlos was shot in the head. A few seconds later, another conspirator fatally shot his son and heir, Prince Luís Filipe. A third bullet hit the young prince Manuel in the arm. Thus wounded and haunted, Manuel II began a brief reign as Portugal's last king. He was deposed in 1910 in a republican uprising by elements of the armed forces. The royal yacht took him to Gibraltar and later England, where he spent the rest of his life exiled in Twickenham.

The republican form of government turned out to be as unstable as it was unfamiliar. Resignations, coups and assassinations kept a merry-go-round of presidents and prime ministers whirling. In the political and economic crisis, the nation could scarcely afford the luxury of war. German threats to its African territories, among other motives, edged Portugal into World War I on the Allied side. On 24 February 1916, the Portuguese navy seized a group of German ships anchored in the River Tagus and the Kaiser replied with the expected declaration of war. A Portuguese expeditionary force sailed for France and went through the hell of the trenches.

The period after the war was more chaotic than ever, precipitating a military coup in 1926, after which General An-

tónio Óscar Carmona became president. Two years later he made his most fateful appointment, entrusting the economy to the hands of a professor named António de Oliveira Salazar. The exhausted Portuguese finances immediately perked up, and in 1932 Dr Salazar took over as prime minister. His tough authoritarian regime emphasized economic self-sufficiency. He kept Portugal neutral during World War II, though permitting the Allies to use the Azores. Unlike his fellow dictator across the border, Spain's Francisco Franco, Dr Salazar avoided a personality cult; his portrait never graced stamps or coins. Instead, his isolated country, the poorest in western Europe, was fed on a diet of past imperial glories.

Revolution and Democracy

When a massive stroke felled Salazar in 1968, the reins were handed to a former rector of the University of Lisbon, Dr Marcelo Caetano. Then in 1974 the armed forces, fed up with fighting hopeless colonial wars, overthrew the dictatorship in the dramatic but peaceful 'red carnation' revolution, so called after the flowers which the soldiers put in the barrel of their guns. Portugal rapidly disengaged from its seething African possessions and somehow managed to absorb the million or so refugees who fled the collapsed empire for a motherland most had never seen.

The nation was to go through several years of political confusion before healing its wounds and learning to live in a democracy. At elections in April 1975, the socialists under Mário Soares topped the poll, but the much smaller communist party exerted its influence through the trade union movement. Banks and many businesses were nationalized; workers' councils took over factories, universities,

hotels and even schools; and radical officers handed out guns, calling for an armed uprising of the left . The attempt began on 25 November 1975, but the extremists had overreached themselves. The insurrection was quickly put down by moderate forces including most of the army, led by General Ramalho Eanes, who was elected president the following year.

A variety of coalition and non-party governments alternated in office and the simmering cauldron gradually cooled. In 1985, a centre-right government was formed under Aníbal Cavaco Silva. Portugal had first applied to join the European Community (since become the European Union, EU) in 1977. Now democracy and economic stability were judged to be solidly established and the application was approved. With admission to membership in 1986, the pace of development suddenly quickened, helped by generous regional aid. In the 1990s the economic climate has turned harsher. The boom has evaporated and Portugal finds itself com-

A modern tribute to the explorers who expanded Portugal's horizons, the Monument to the Discoveries *at Belém.*

peting with eastern Europe for foreign investment. With increasing mechanization, many jobs in agriculture have vanished. Earnings from tourism are highly significant to the economy and a lot of effort is being put into improving facilities still further. That's good news for visitors who will find themselves more than welcome.

At Miranda do Douro, the river marking the border with Spain has been tamed by a dam. In 1813, the Duke of Wellington was hauled across the rapids here in a suspended basket (overleaf).

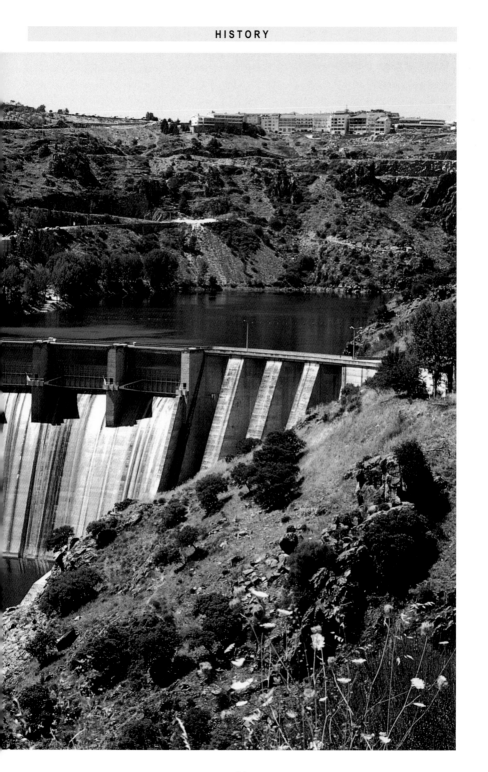

HISTORICAL LANDMARKS

c.16,000 BC	Cave paintings left by Stone Age hunters in the southern plains.
c.7000 BC	Shell-gatherers living along the coast and river estuaries.
c.4000-2000 BC	Neolithic culture including the building of megalithic monuments and fortified settlements.
c.1000 BC	Phoenicians from Eastern Mediterranean establish trading posts on the coast.
c.700 BC	Celtic tribes invade from north and dominate northern interior.
c.600 BC	Coastal settlements become part of Carthaginian trading empire.
218-201 BC	Second Punic War: Rome defeats Carthage and takes over all her possessions.
205-180 BC	Romans gain control of most of Iberian peninsula, despite resistance from the Celts.
154-139 BC	Rising of Celtic Lusitani under Viriatus, who is then assassinated.
60 BC	Julius Caesar takes Lisbon as his headquarters and expands Roman settlements in interior.
25 BC	Romans establish province of Lusitania, including most of present day Portugal and some of adjoining Spain.
3rd-4th century AD	Gradual spread of Christianity.
409 AD	A succession of barbarian invasions begins with the Germanic Suevi raiding the Iberian peninsula.
6th century AD	Visigoths, Christian converts, bring a period of stability.
711-17	Moslem Moors from North Africa cross the Strait of Gibraltar and conquer most of Iberian peninsula.
8-11th centuries	Christian recapture of north, including Oporto.
1097	Henry of Burgundy becomes Count of Portugal, ruling as far south as Coimbra.
1139	Henry's son Afonso Henriques defeats Moors at Ourique, assumes title of King of Portugal. Coimbra becomes capital.
1147	Lisbon taken from Moors by Afonso Henriques and crusaders.
1249	Reconquest of Algarve completed by Afonso III.
1256	Capital moved to Lisbon.
1369	War with Castile.
1372	Alliance with John of Gaunt, Duke of Lancaster, claimant to throne of Castile.
1385	João of Avis declared king of Portugal. Castilians defeated at Battle of Aljubarrota
1386	Treaty of Windsor affirms eternal alliance with England.
1387	Marriage of João I and Philippa of Lancaster.
15th century	Overseas discoveries inspired by Prince Henriques ('Henry the Navigator'): Madeira (1418), the Azores (1427), Cape Verde (1444).
1488	Bartolomeu Dias rounds the Cape of Good Hope.
1498	Vasco da Gama reaches India.
1500	Cabral discovers Brazil.
c.1500	Expulsion and forced conversion of Jews.
c.1550	Spanish Inquisition begins and spreads to Portugal.

1557	Colony founded at Macau, China.
1572	Camões publishes *The Lusiads*.
1580	Philip II of Spain claims throne of Portugal. Union of the two crowns.
1640	Portuguese independence restored. Duke of Bragança becomes King João IV.
1662	Catherine of Bragança marries Charles II of England. Bombay ceded to England as part of her dowry.
1703	'Port wine for wool' trade treaty with England.
1755	Earthquake, fire and tidal wave devastate Lisbon. Reconstruction begins under the Marquês de Pombal.
1777	Pombal dismissed on accession of Maria I.
1807	French troops occupy Lisbon. Portuguese court flees to Brazil.
1808	French defeated by British and Portuguese armies under Wellesley (later Duke of Wellington) and forced to withdraw.
1809	Second French invasion.
1809-11	Wellington's campaign to expel French from country.
1821	King João VI returns from Brazil.
1822	Brazil declares independence with João's son as Emperor Pedro I.
1826	Death of João VI. Dispute over succession between Pedro and his younger brother Miguel.
1832-4	War of the Two Brothers: Miguel defeated; church property confiscated and sold.
1834	Death of Pedro. His daughter Maria da Glória becomes queen.
1836	Septembrists revolt, impose liberal constitution.
1880-1910	Growth of republicanism.
1908	Assassination of Carlos I.
1910	Republican rising; Manuel II flees the country.
1916	Portugal joins Allied side in World War I.
1926	Right-wing coup. General Carmona becomes President.
1932	Dr Salazar becomes Prime Minister and virtual dictator.
1939-45	Portugal remains neutral in World War II.
1961	India seizes colony of Goa.
1968	Salazar incapacitated by stroke. Former University of Lisbon rector, Dr Marcelo Caetano becomes Prime Minister.
1970	Death of Salazar.
1974	Colonial wars lead to armed forces 'red carnation' revolution in Portugal (25 April).
1975	Democratic elections. Colonial empire dissolved. Attempted left-wing revolt fails.
1976	General Eanes elected president; Mário Soares Prime Minister.
1980	Moderate coalition elected.
1985	Aníbal Cavaco Silva heads moderate right-wing government.
1986	Portugal joins the European Community (now the European Union). Mário Soares elected president.

Meaningful Manueline

During the 1490's, an utterly original, home-grown style of architecture and stone-carving suddenly appeared in Portugal. Taking late Gothic as a base, it added decorative features, restrained at first but soon developing into an extravaganza of exotic effects. It flourished for only a few decades, more or less matching the reign of Manuel I (1495-1521), and was later given the name 'Manueline'. Nothing like it had been seen before, and the fashion spread with extraordinary speed. This was the Age of Discovery, an era of self-confidence when the money was available to indulge in ambitious building projects. The movement never caught on outside Portugal – the rest of Europe was busy embracing the quite different attractions of the Renaissance.

The first hints of what was to come appear in the Igreja de Jesus in Setúbal (see p.140), begun in 1494 under the direction of a French master of works called Boytac (Boitac or Boitaca to the Portuguese). The twisted columns dividing the three-aisle church were not a new idea, but here the stone is carved to look like three intertwined strands of clay, or even the stems of climbing plants. The ribs of the vaulting over the high altar resemble rope. Was this a conscious tribute to Portugal's navigators who were exploring the oceans of the world? Boytac's name seems to have come quickly to the king's attention. When Vasco da Gama returned from India in 1499 with a highly profitable cargo of spices and the promise of more, Dom Manuel ordered the building of a great monastery, the Mosteiro dos Jerónimos at Belém (see p.106), and the Frenchman was appointed as the first architect.

Although on a greater scale than his church at Setúbal, the Jerónimos monastery has the same fundamentally plain Gothic lines. This time the outside displays the rope motif, carved friezes and complex curvilinear frames to the windows. The great south portal was added by Boytac's successor at Belém, João de Castilho (the Portuguese name for Spanish-born Juan de Castillo). If the outside is striking, the interior is breathtaking, with pillars covered in fanciful decoration. References to the sea which began with the simple rope idea now come in rich profusion, certainly inspired by the great voyages of discovery. Stone is sculpted into imitation coral, sea creatures, nets and waves, as well as non-nautical designs of leaves and flowers.

With the chapter house of the Convento do Cristo at Tomar (see p.160), Manueline stonecarving reached a pinnacle of imaginative design. The first sight of its west front has viewers reeling, and closer study only increases the amazement. The themes of the sea and the discoveries continued to inspire the unknown sculptor (as master of works, Diogo de Arruda is sometimes wrongly given the credit). The cross of the Order of Christ is flanked by two 'armillary spheres', skeleton globes showing the equator and tropics, which were King Manuel's symbol and turn up again and again in the art of his time.

The Torre de Belém in the River Tagus is the only purely Manueline building, begun and finished while the fashion was at its height. Here Francisco de Arruda, brother of Diogo, created one of the prettiest forts ever built, able to act as a cannon platform but clearly not intended to be fired at. Mercifully, it was spared damage in a dozen wars, whether out of respect for its beauty or due to bad marksmanship. Parapets carry the same Cross of Christ as the sails of the explorers' ships, and the barbizans at each corner have the same ribbed cupolas as great mosques from Morocco to India. Stone 'rope' outlines

The Torre de Belém in the Tagus estuary was begun and completed in the Manueline style. Land reclamation has brought the shoreline right up to its walls.

each level and armillary spheres and the arms of King Manuel are emblazoned on the seaward side, which is much more decorated than the others.

Of all the major examples of Manueline design, no two are alike. It's as if there is no rule, only exceptions. Some country churches were given huge portals, like that at Golega (see p.167); others have just a modest suggestion of Manueline lines. At the Abbey of Batalha (see p.155) the arches of the cloister were filled with stone tracery like an organic growth (probably the work of Boytac). The great portal of the Unfinished Chapels (*Capelas Imperfeitas*) could have been inspired by descriptions – perhaps drawings – of Moghul buildings in India brought back after Vasco da Gama opened the sea route, and perhaps the organic detail owes something to Hindu temple architecture.

The fashion faded almost as quickly as it had begun, but the idea that it died with its great patron, King Manuel, in 1521 is not supported by the evidence. Nor is the suggestion that his successor

João III so disliked the style that he banned it. On the contrary, work continued on some projects for a few more years. In the smaller towns and villages, mansions continued to be embellished with Manueline windows and churches with doorways long after royal patronage ceased. However, nothing as ambitious as the Torre de Belém was started and the Unfinished Chapels at Batalha were left dramatically open to the skies, much as they stand today. Judging by the buttresses which stood ready to support them, the most spectacular *tour de force* had been planned for their upper storey and vaulted roof. The will to continue in the style evaporated, however, and it was evidently – and understandably – thought impossible to switch to another style in mid-flight.

By about 1540, Portugal had rejoined the rest of Europe, building in the sober Renaissance image. Almost four centuries were to pass before architects returned to such fluid forms, many of them based on living things, in the Art Nouveau movement (c.1900).

Just the Essentials

It is unlikely that you will have time to see all the highlights listed opposite, but they will provide a good starting point for whichever region(s) you are visiting.

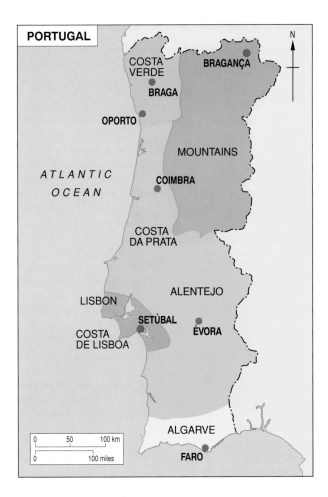

Lisbon

Waterfront, Praça do Comércio and Baixa
district
Cathedral (*Sé*)
Castelo de São Jorge and Alfama district
Museu do Azulejo
Gulbenkian Museum
Bairro Alto
Aguas Livres Aqueduct
Museu Nacional de Arte Antiga
Belém: Mosteiro dos Jerónimos and Torre
de Belém.

Costa Verde

Oporto: Old City and cathedral
Waterfront and Bridges
Igreja de São Francisco, gilded
baroque church
Vila Nova de Gaia: port shippers' lodges
Amarante: river town.
Vila do Conde and Póvoa de Varzim: old
port and resort
Viana do Castelo: historic centre
Vila Nova de Cerveira: castle and old town.
Valença: spectacular fortress
Ponte de Lima: Roman bridge and old
town on the River Lima
Braga: cathedral city
Bom Jesus: monumental staircase
Citânia de Briteiros: pre-Roman city
Guimarães: walled city and museums
Peneda-Gerês National Park: scenery and
Roman relics.

Alentejo

Castelo de Vide: ancient spa
Marvão: mountain-top fortress
Alter do Chão: 18th-century 'palace' and
stud farm for horses
Elvas: the ultimate fortress and aqueduct
Vila Viçosa: 16th-century royal retreat of
the dukes of Bragança
Estremoz: marble citadel
Évora: Roman temple
Romanesque cathedral museum
Monsaraz: border stronghold and
prehistoric monuments
Beja: Roman city and museum
Mértola: ancient town, former mosque
and museums.
West Coast: coves and beaches.

Costa de Lisboa

Estoril: royal retreat and resort
Cascais: holiday town
Queluz: rococo palace
Sintra: palaces and gardens
Mafra: convent and palace
Setúbal: Igreja de Jesus and 'Primitives'
(16th century paintings)
Sesimbra: harbour, resort and Arrábida
peninsula.

Costa da Prata

Óbidos: walled town
Alcobaça: 12th century monastery, tombs
of Pedro and Inês de Castro
Batalha: Gothic monastery, architectural
treasure
Tomar: Convento do Cristo, Templar
stronghold
Almourol: picture book castle on an island
Santarém: historic hilltop town.
Conimbriga: Roman city, mosaics.
Coimbra: university city and old capital
Aveiro: canals and mansions.

Mountains

Viseu: old town, Grão Vasco paintings
Lamego: Nossa Senhora dos Remédios,
staircase and sanctuary, and museum
Port vineyards
Vila Real: Solar de Mateus
Chaves: Roman spa, Roman bridge prehist-
oric rock carvings at Outeiro Machado
Bragança: fortress, Romanesque Domus
Miranda do Douro: historic border town,
spectacular views
Serra da Estrêla National Park: mountain
villages and scenery
Monsanto: ancient village in the rocks
Idana-a-Velha: Visigoth basilica.

Algarve

Faro: old walled town
Ria Formosa: lagoons, wetlands and
beaches on offshore islands
Loulé: lively hill town and market
Silves: the Moors' capital
Portimão: fishing port and busy town
Lagos: old town and beaches.
Sagres peninsula: 'end of the world'
Tavira: elegant town.

Going Places with Something Special in Mind

Portugal's cultural riches are scattered throughout the country and found in unexpected places. Rather than trying to visit all the castles, churches, museums, scenic mountain villages, picturesque fishing harbours and archaeological sites in a region, you may want to pursue particular interests of your own, or use a theme to structure your trip. Here are a few suggestions, some concentrated in one part of the country, others spread widely. Numbered entries correspond to the markers on the adjoining maps.

Prehistory

Stone Age people left hundreds of monuments – dolmens, menhirs and stone circles – particularly in the north and the Alentejo. Their successors, the Celts and Iberians, built hilltop *castros*, fortified villages, in the pre-Roman era. Many were later covered by buildings, but a few can be clearly seen today.

The Algarve resort of Vilamoura is the largest leisure development in Portugal and uses modern interpretations of traditional architecture. Its marina shelters hundreds of pleasure craft.

1 VIANA DO CASTELO
Celtic *citânia* on Monte de Santa Luzia.

2 CITÂNIA DE BRITEIROS
The best preserved pre-Roman town.

3 SABROSO
Overgrown *citânia* near Briteiros.

4 GUIMARÃES
Martins Sarmento Museum: extraordinary stone carvings from Citânia de Briteiros and other sites.

5 VILA REAL
Sacred site of Panóias: carved boulders.

6 MURÇA
Celtic or even older stone figure depicting a wild boar.

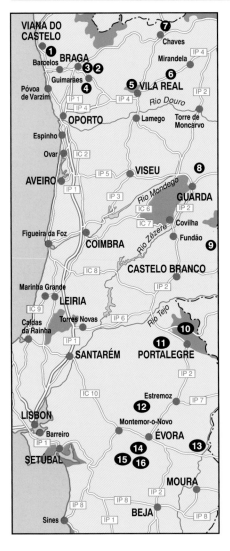

*Long time gone,
Portugal's Prehistoric monuments
bear silent witness to the events
of the distant past.*

10 CASTELO DE VIDE
Many dolmens and menhirs in the area.

11 CRATO
Perfectly preserved dolmen.

12 PAVIA
Dolmen converted to Christian chapel.

13 MONSARAZ
Large menhir surrounded by stone square formation of smaller ones; other monuments in the area.

14 ALMENDRES
Oval of 95 standing stones.

15 ZAMBUJEIRO
Tallest dolmen still standing in Portugal.

16 SÃO BRISSOS
Another dolmen with a tiny church built on.

The Romans in Portugal

7 OUTEIRO MACHADO
Massive boulder covered in mysterious carvings, near Chaves.

8 MARTIANES
Finely preserved Neolithic dolmen.

9 MONSANTO
Village in the rocks on a site which has been used since the Stone Age.

Traces of six centuries of Roman rule are found all over Portugal. Many bridges, sections of pavement and tall inscribed milestones survive from what must have been a superb road system, and vestiges of walls, temples and early churches and villas with fine mosaics have been excavated. Archaeology is in its infancy here, so it's certain that many more remain to be found.

1 TRÓIA
The site of *Cetobriga*; large fishing and fish-salting town.

2 ODRINHAS
An excavation of a large Roman villa not far from Sintra.

3 CONIMBRIGA
Portugal's most important Roman site, featuring superb mosaics.

4 COIMBRA
Massive foundations of *Aeminium*, under the museum.

5 PONTE DE LIMA
Several arches of the Roman bridge still survive here today.

6 PENEDA-GERÊS
   NATIONAL PARK
Many Roman milestones are still in place along the old road to Braga.

7 CHAVES
Roman bridge with milestones, plus Roman artefacts in museum.

8 BELMONTE
Strange three-storey tower called the *Centum Cellas*.

9 IDANHA-A-VELHA
Roman street and arch, and early Christian basilica in a quiet village.

The Romans spent six centuries in Portugal. Here are some of the best sites to see villas, mosaics, bridges, temples and other evidence of their presence.

10 ALTER DO CHÃO

The most perfectly preserved Roman bridge in Portugal, if not the empire, still in use near Vila Formosa.

11 MONFORTE

Extensive excavations of Torre de Palma villa and estate.

12 ÉVORA

Portugal's best preserved Roman temple; sculpture in the museum.

13 BEJA

Gateways; stonework in the Santo Amaro museum. Excavations at Pisões.

14 MÉRTOLA

Imaginative museum set in the Roman foundations of the Town Hall. Early Christian basilica.

15 FARO

Mosaics and busts in the museum. Excavations of *Ossonoba* at Milreu.

16 VILAMOURA

Excavations of villa, mosaics and baths at Cerro da Vila.

17 SANTIAGO DO CACEM

Excavations of *Miróbriga*; town, temple to Jupiter and baths.

Moorish Survivals

Five centuries of Muslim rule made an indelible mark on the look, life and language of Portugal. The wars of the Reconquest, fires and earthquakes have left no complete examples, but countless buildings from castles to cottages stand on Moorish foundations, and the narrow alleys and steep streets of the old quarters of many towns still show their Arab origins.

1 SINTRA

Castelo dos Mouros, standing on top of a mountain ridge.

2 LISBON

Alfama district retains the street pattern and appearance of a North African casbah. Castelo de São Jorge at the top of the city was the Moors' citadel.

3 ALCÁCER DO SAL

The walls of the citadel are substantially of Moorish construction.

4 SORTELHA

Stonework carved with Arabic script and Arabesque patterns.

5 IDANHA-A-VELHA

Mihrab (niche showing the direction of Mecca) facing Mecca in the early Christian basilica.

6 CASTELO DE VIDE

Old quarter follows the Moorish lines.

7 ÉVORA

Citadel preserves the Moorish pattern of streets, inside the older Roman wall.

8 MÉRTOLA

Columned hall and mihrab of the mosque, now the parish church.

9 SALIR

Picturesque village inside the ruins of a Moorish castle.

10 LOULÉ

Old quarter was a refuge for Moorish artisans and remains a handicraft centre.

11 PADERNE
Remains of Moorish castle situated above a river bend.

12 SILVES
Former Moorish capital of the Algarve; rebuilt citadel. An Arab well is now the centrepiece of a new museum.

The Muslims ruled Portugal for five centuries, nearly as long as the Romans. Here is a collection of what they have left behind.

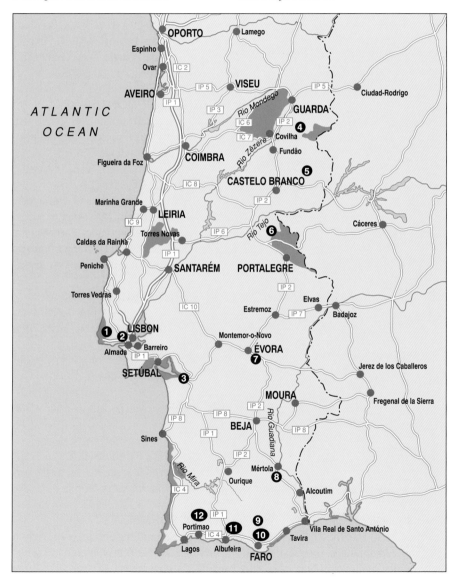

National Parks and Nature Reserves

As environmental awareness takes hold, more areas are being designated for protection: mountain wilderness, forest, river estuary, coastal, and wetland reserves. There are many opportunities for bird watching, walking and climbing.

For the naturalist and anybody keen on the wilder side of life, Portugal is a treasure trove of unspoilt wildernesses. This is a selection of the better parks and reserves.

1 SADO ESTUARY
Quiet waters, salt marshes and sand dunes. Seabirds, waders and birds of prey such as the marsh eagle.

2 SERRA DA ARRÁBIDA
Small rugged mountain range dropping to the sea. Spring wild flowers, walks.

3 TAGUS ESTUARY
The shallows, mudflats and flood plain are a haven for birds, both residents and migrants alike.

4 BERLENGA ISLANDS
Bird sanctuary with remarkable rock formations, surrounded by clear waters. A 17th-century fortress is joined by a narrow causeway to the main island.

5 BUÇACO FOREST
Planted by monks in the 17th and 18th centuries, with many exotic species grown from seeds brought from all over the world. Popular picnic area.

6 AVEIRO LAGOONS
Tranquil waters rich in fish and shellfish, home to seabirds and waders.

7 PENEDA-GERÊS
 NATIONAL PARK
Two mountain ranges on the northern border with Spain. Artificial lakes with watersports and fishing. Remote villages in the Serra da Peneda. Spas, walks and Roman relics in Serra do Gerês.

8 SERRA DE MONTESINHO
The north-eastern hills along the border with Spain where traditional life still goes on in the remote villages.

9 SERRA DA ESTRÊLA
A mountainous region and Portugal's largest national park. Wooded at lower levels. Rocky upland moors renowned for wild flowers in spring. Walking, climbing, and Portugal's only organized ski resort.

10 SERRA DE SÃO MAMEDE
Rolling hills and woods, plus wildlife and many Neolithic monuments in the area around Castelo de Vide.

11 CASTRO MARIM
Salt marshes, rest stop for migrating birds, home to many species of heron and a rare chameleon.

12 SAGRES PENINSULA
Land and seabirds cling and nest on the vertiginous cliffs. Migrants drop in for a rest.

13 RIA FORMOSA
Sand bars, mudflats and lagoons, rich in shellfish and birdlife, including avocets, stilts, flamingos.

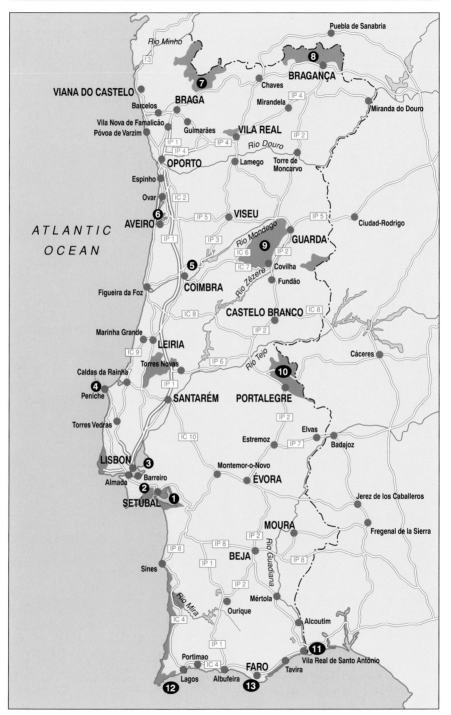

The Wine Regions

You'll see vineyards almost everywhere, from the Minho in the north right down to the Algarve. Some welcome visitors and offer tastings – local tourist information offices may be able to help. Through the *Turismo no Espaço Rural* organization (see p.23), you can stay on a few wine estates and even help with the harvest.

1 LAGOA
The Algarve's wine headquarters.

2 ARRÁBIDA PENINSULA
Huge range of wines. Tastings at the cellars of Azeitão.

3 BUCELAS
Traditional wine-growing area just north of Lisbon.

4 BAIRRADA
In the hills to the north of Coimbra. Tastings at Sangalhos.

5 VILA NOVA DE GAIA
Where the Port is stored at the shippers' lodges. Tastings and tours.

6 COSTA VERDE
Lively *vinho verde* is produced all over the region. Tastings and festivals held at Monçao and Ponte de Lima.

7 UPPER DOURO
Where Port comes from. Visit the vineyards and perhaps stay at a *quinta*.

A taste of the tipsier side of Portugal, in the form of its multitude of vineyards.

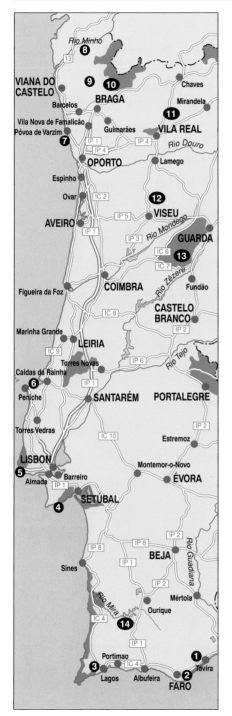

*F*ishing is a popular pastime in this country with so much coast. However, inland fishing is popular and widely available too.

8 LAMEGO
Production of sweet and sparkling wines. Visits and tastings.

9 DÃO
Vineyards are dotted all over one of Portugal's prettiest and most traditional wine-growing areas.

10 BORBA
Marble town which is also a wine centre. Tastings at the cooperative.

Fishing

It's a national industry *and* a national pastime, but that's no reason why visitors shouldn't join in. You won't be resented: the local experts will not view you as serious competition!

In the Sea
You can try your luck from beaches, rocks, small craft in sheltered estuaries and ocean-going boats. Permits are not required.

1 TAVIRA
Plaice, sole and sea bass are caught from the nearby beaches.

2 FARO
Boats will take you out through the Ria Formosa to the open Atlantic in search of swordfish and shark.

3 LAGOS and SAGRES
Deep sea and inshore boats for rental. Some of the best fishing grounds are situated off the Sagres peninsula. The locals also fish from the cliffs for sea bream: only those of you completely impervious to vertigo should try this.

4 SESIMBRA
Boats are available to take you deep sea fishing. Big swordfish and sometimes marlin or tuna are the main attraction.

5 GUINCHO
The local fishermen catch sea bass, grey mullet, sole and sea bream from the rocks. If you want to try your hand also, beware of the big waves.

6 PENICHE
Boats for sport-fishing for hire at the port.

7 PÓVOA DE VARZIM
Sea bream and sea bass are caught from the beaches. Sport-fishing boats are available for rental at the marina.

In Rivers and Lakes
Ask about permits at local *Turismo* offices. In general, they are issued by local authorities without delay.

8 RIVER MINHO
The Melgaço area is fabled for trout.

9 RIVER LIMA
Fish the upper reaches for trout.

10 GERÊS
Some fishing is permitted in the rivers and lakes of the Peneda-Gerês National Park.

11 RIVER CORGO
Trout fishing north of Vila Real.

12 RIVER VOUGA
Excellent trout fishing.

13 SERRA DA ESTRÊLA NATIONAL PARK
Trout fishing in the lakes and rivers.

14 SANTA CLARA-A-VELHA
Fishing in the reservoir below the Pousada.

Narrow-Gauge and Scenic Railways

The list is shorter these days: several branch lines have sadly been closed, and steam locomotives have been pensioned off (the sparks from their funnels caused too many forest fires). There are still a number of scenic routes to choose from, however, including narrow gauge and main lines.

1 DOURO LINE
Oporto to Livração, Peso da Régua, Pinhão and Pocinho. Views of the Douro valley and the Port vineyards which cling to its rocky slopes.

2 TÂMEGA LINE
The narrow gauge single track line from Livração follows the gorge of the Tâmega to Amarante. Buses have taken over the rest of the route into the Basto region.

3 CORGO LINE
The narrow gauge line follows the Corgo gorge from Peso da Régua to Vila Real. Buses continue the old route to Chaves.

*W*hat better way to view the countryside than from one of Portugal's railways.

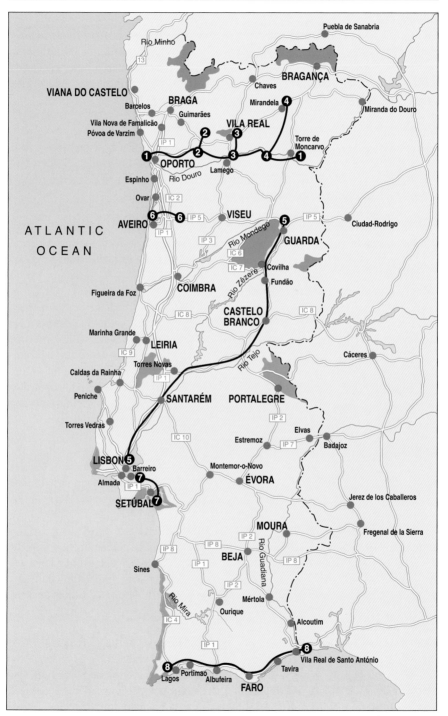

4 TUA LINE

Narrow gauge line along the picturesque rocky valley of the Tua river to Mirandela.

5 BEIRA-BAIXA LINE

The main line from Lisbon to Abrantes and Belver, Castelo Branco and Guarda runs through some spectacular scenery.

6 VOUGA LINE

Trains only run on the first section from Aveiro through farms and vineyards to Sernada do Vouga now. Buses have taken over the scenic route through the mountains to Viseu.

7 SETÚBAL LINE

Little local trains from Barreiro south of the Tagus, across the Arrábida Peninsula to Palmela and Setúbal.

8 ALGARVE LINE

Running almost the whole length of the Algarve coast, from Lagos in the west to Faro and Vila Real in the east.

Golf

Growing numbers of visitors, especially to the Algarve in spring, don't go near the castles, churches or even the beaches. They are here for the golf. Some of the most attractive courses in Europe can be found in Portugal. Here we list most of the Algarve's and a selection of other 18-hole courses around the country.

Algarve Courses

QUINTA DO LAGO

Amid the pine woods, lakes and dunes of the 800ha (2000 acre) luxury estate and sports complex, two 18-hole championship courses.

SÃO LORENZO

One of the newest and most scenic courses, already voted one of Europe's best, set in the Ria Formosa National Park, near Quinta do Lago. Dona Filipa and Penina hotel guests have priority.

VALE DO LOBO

Long established course on this big residential and holiday estate. 27 holes laid out among the pines and dunes, and next to sandstone cliffs.

VILA SOL

Challenging new championship course of narrow fairways, set amidst rolling wooded country.

VILAMOURA

Three contrasting courses: Vilamoura I is the longest established with most tree cover; Vilamoura II winds through umbrella pines before climbing into more open country; Vilamoura III is on heathland near the sea, with varied sand and water hazards.

PINE CLIFFS

Beautiful new clifftop course of 9 holes among mature umbrella pines, on the same estate as the Sheraton Algarve.

CARVOEIRO

Fast growing as a golf destination, with the lightly wooded, 18-hole Vale de Pinta and two 9-hole courses, Quinta do Gramacho and the short Vale de Milho all in the area.

ALTO

On quite open rolling ground, the last course to be planned by golf legend Sir Henry Cotton. The 604m (661yd) sixteenth may be the longest hole in Europe, but the rest are not too difficult.

PENINA

Championship course designed by Sir Henry Cotton in 1966, with two other 9-hole courses. Formerly swampy ground has been transformed into well-wooded parkland, with a profusion of streams and lakes.

PALMARES

In a varied terrain of coastal dunes and undulating hills that enjoy an outlook over the Bay of Lagos.

BUDENS

The Parque da Floresta course of 18 distinctive holes is set in the wooded hills and valleys of the western Algarve.

Elsewhere in Portugal

BELAS

The Lisbon Sports Club's championship course is set in woodland scenery, 18km (11 miles) north of the city, and was laid out in 1922.

CASCAIS

Quinta da Marinha, designed by Robert Trent Jones, is part of the club and sports resort just west of Cascais.

SINTRA

Penha Longa, another course designed by Robert Trent Jones, is set in the hills and valleys north of Estoril.

AROIEIRA

Carved out of an established forest of tall pines, easily reached just across the Tagus bridge from Lisbon.

TRÓIA

Designed by Robert Trent Jones, winding in narrow green ribbons between pine trees and sand dunes on the Tróia Peninsula south of Lisbon.

ESTELA

This narrow links course along the shore north of Póvoa de Varzim has been likened to the famous Old Course at St Andrews in Scotland.

ESPINHO

Another links course, the oldest in Portugal; it was laid out in 1890 by the Port wine shippers of Oporto.

Romanesque Architecture

The first style to be used in church building following the Reconquest survives in just a handful of great cathedrals and many parish churches – often those which were too poor to follow later fashions for remodelling.

1 LISBON

Sé (Cathedral) and cloister – in spite of earthquake damage.

2 TOMAR

The 12th-century, sixteen-sided Templar church (restored in the 16th century).

3 COIMBRA

Sé Velha (the old cathedral), dating from the 12th century.

4 OPORTO

Church of São Martinho da Cedofeita.

5 RATES

One of the best 12th-century churches in the country.

6 GUIMARÃES

Church of São Miguel, where tradition says Afonso Henriques was bapitzed.

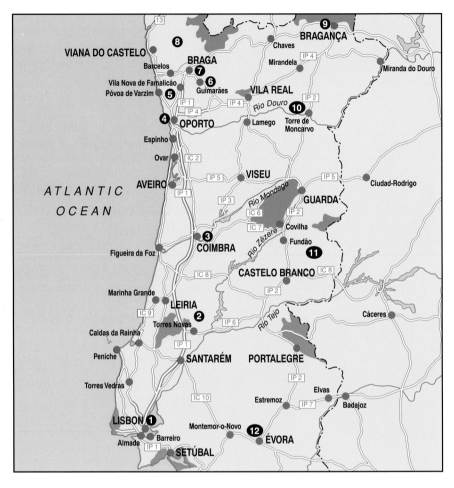

*P*ortugal has its share of Romanesque architecture, seen in its cathedrals and parish churches.

7 BRAGA
Much-altered Sé retains elements of the Romanesque original.

8 BRAVÃES
11th-century church with extraordinary carving around the west and south doors.

9 BRAGANÇA
The five-sided *Domus Municipalis* (meeting house) from the 12th century.

10 ANSIÃES
Magnificent doorway of the Church of São Salvador.

11 MONSANTO
Roofless church inside the hilltop citadel.

12 ÉVORA
The 12-13th-century Sé is one of the finest in Portugal.

Manueline Architecture

Once seen, never forgotten, and found only in Portugal, this highly individual architectural style celebrated the voyages of discovery and lasted for only three decades, at the start of the 16th century. Designs were often inspired by images related to the sea, including sails, ropes, nets and coral.

1 SETÚBAL
Igreja de Jesus, possibly the first appearance of some Manueline themes.

2 LISBON
At Belém, the Mosteiro dos Jerónimos and Torre de Belém.

3 SINTRA
Exterior and interior additions to the Palácio Nacional dating from the time of King Manuel.

4 SANTARÉM
Igreja de Marvila doorway.

5 TOMAR
The astonishing Chapter House windows on nautical themes.

6 BATALHA
The cloister and Capelas Imperfeitas (unfinished chapels), influenced by Hindu and Moghul styles seen in India.

Manueline architecture is unique to Portugal and dates from the 16th century. Don't miss it at these sites chosen from around the country.

7 COIMBRA
The Casa Sub Ripas doorway; University chapel doorway; Church of Santa Cruz.

8 VILA DO CONDE
Parish church and many houses have Manueline doorways and windows.

9 VIANA DO CASTELO
Mansions in the old centre have elaborate Manueline windows.

10 VISEU
Sé (cathedral) interior.

11 ÉVORA
Palácio de Dom Manuel.

12 VIANA DO ALENTEJO
Battlemented parish church.

13 LOULÉ
Portal of the Misericórdia church.

14 ALVOR
The parish church, with its fine west door and interior.

15 MONCHIQUE
Igreja Matriz, unique doorway with five radiating pinnacles.

Border Fortresses

From the birth of an independent Portugal in the 12th century until the Peninsular War seven hundred years later, there was the constant threat, or reality, of invasion from Spain. Castles and fortified towns were built to defend the border, and with the advent of powerful artillery, most were remodelled or given extra layers of bastions between the 16th and 18th centuries.

1 VILA NOVA DE CERVEIRA
Dom Dinis's 14th-century castle is now a Pousada. Parts of 17th-century bastions also.

2 VALENÇA DO MINHO
A whole town on the River Minho set within star-shaped 17th-century ramparts.

3 MONTALEGRE
Majestic towers on a hill, dating from the time of Dom Dinis.

4 CHAVES
Medieval keep on Roman foundations, ringed by 17th-century walls.

5 BRAGANÇA
The north-eastern outpost, a grim grey keep and citadel.

6 FREIXO DO ESPADA-À-CINTA
Majestic seven-sided tower of the 14th-century and sections of wall.

7 CASTELO RODRIGO
Ancient hilltop town, partly Moorish walls and romantic ruin of a castle.

8 ALMEIDA
Magnificent star-shaped walls enclose the town. Devastated by an explosion in 1810, during siege by French in Peninsular War.

9 MARVÃO
Dramatic 'eagle's nest' village.

10 CAMPO MAIOR
Strong walls withstood much, but the keep was razed by an explosion in 1732.

11 ELVAS
The ultimate in 'Vaubanesque': an entire town encased by infinitely complex and massive fortifications.

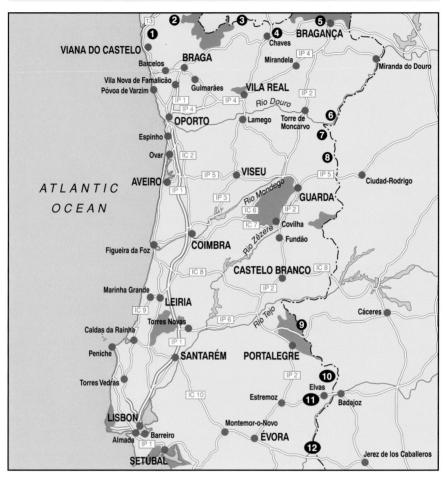

12 MONSARAZ
Beautiful hilltop citadel and village within the walls. 13th-century castle and 17th-century bastions

Early Portuguese Painting

Taking their inspiration from Flemish masters working in Portugal in the early 16th century, local artists (the so-called 'Primitives') began to produce dramatic, often vividly coloured religious paintings.

An independent nation must protect itself from its neighbours. Portugal's only neighbour was Spain, hence the string of fortresses and fortified towns along its border.

Many remain anonymous, or identified only by their styles, such as 'The Master of Setúbal'. Other names are well established, but attributions may be disputed.

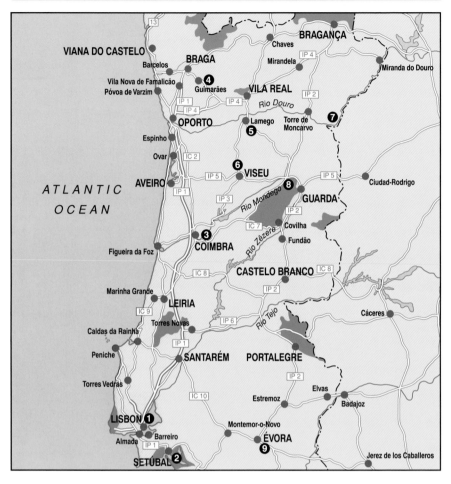

*P*ortugal's artistic heritage can be found in both churches and museums across the land. Here are a selection of the best from about the 16th century onwards.

Those working in Lisbon included Jorge Afonso, Cristóvão Figueiredo and Gregório Lopes. The important 'Viseu School' was led by Vasco Fernandes (*'O Grão Vasco'*) and Gaspar Vaz.

1 LISBON

The largest collection is in the Museu de Arte Antiga, with many works by artists of the Lisbon school, and many more anonymous examples. Don't miss the work of the 15th-century painter, Nuno Gonçalves, whose *The Adoration of St Vincent* is quite magnificent.

2 SETÚBAL
Fourteen pictures by Jorge Afonso, Gregório Lopes and followers from the altar piece of the Igreja de Jesus, and other masterpieces, in the adjoining museum. Also some earlier Flemish work.

3 COIMBRA
Sacristy of Church of Santa Cruz: Grão Vasco and Figueiredo paintings.

4 GUIMARÃES
Alberto Sampaio Museum. Paintings by António Vaz and others.

5 LAMEGO
More fine works by Grão Vasco in the excellent museum.

6 VISEU
Grão Vasco Museum: paintings from the cathedral by Vasco, Vaz and followers.

7 FREIXO DO ESPADA-À-CINTA
16 paintings attributed to Grão Vasco.

8 LINHARES
Three more possible Grão Vasco pictures are still kept in the church.

9 ÉVORA
Many works by Flemish artists working in Portugal, and a few of the 'Primitives', in the museum.

Shrines and Pilgrimages

The power of the Catholic church was greatly reduced when the monasteries were dissolved and a lot of church property seized and sold off in the 19th century. Many shrines were neglected and the

*A*s a strongly Catholic country, Portugal has a number of important shrines and places of pilgrimage.

custom of pilgrimage declined until it was actively promoted – especially to Fátima – by the Salazar regime. Today the influence of religion is much more evident in northern Portugal.

1 CABO ESPICHEL

Windswept cape with neglected, early 18th-century church of Nossa Senhora do Cabo and deserted pilgrims' quarters on the cliffs.

2 FÁTIMA

Since the famous 1917 visions, this has been one of the biggest centres of pilgrimage in the Catholic world. A whole town has grown up to cater to the pilgrims. 13 May and 13 October are the most significant dates in the calendar.

3 VIANA DO CASTELO

The sanctuary of Santa Luzia, on Monte de Santa Luzia. Nossa Senhora da Agonia processions take place through the town to the waterfront in August. The image of the saint is carried to the docks and then loaded onto a flag-festooned boat which tours the harbour.

4 BRAGA

Holy Week and Pentecost are marked by elaborate and dramatic processions. Outside Braga, Bom Jesus has a famous baroque double staircase climbing steeply to the sanctuary church.

5 SAMEIRO

A hilltop site not far from Bom Jesus, second only to Fátima in numbers of pilgrims.

6 GUIMARÃES

The sanctuary of São Torcato north east of the city is the focus of a pilgrimage in early July.

*W*ellington was here in the early 19th century waging the Peninsular War against Napoleon.

7 AMARANTE

Processions converge on the Church of São Gonçalo at the beginning of June. It.is said that spinsters who touch the tomb of the saint will find a husband.

8 LAMEGO

Double staircase and sanctuary of Nossa Senhora dos Remédios. Festival and processions in early September.

In Wellington's Footsteps

Students of military history can visit all the battlefields and other sites connected with the Peninsular War. Some have nothing to show but the often dramatic terrain or a simple memorial. Others have highly informative museums. (See also p.239, *Wellington in Portugal*.)

1 FIGUEIRA DA FOZ

Where Wellington landed in 1808: 9,000 troops brought ashore in small boats.

2 ROLIÇA

The first engagement of the War.

3 VIMEIRO

French defeat leads to truce and first withdrawal, 21 August 1808.

4 TORRES VEDRAS

The pivot of Wellington's ingenious lines of defence in 1810.

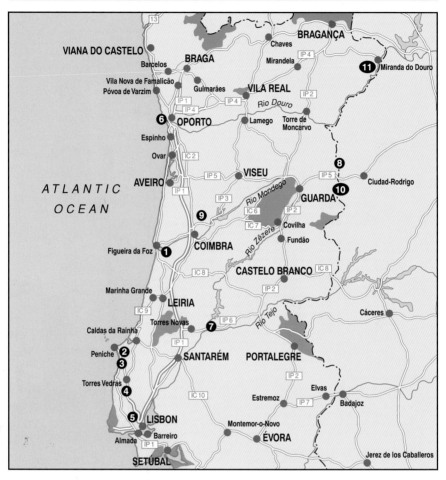

5 QUELUZ
Palace where Wellington conferred with Sir John Moore.

6 OPORTO
The 'Passage of the Douro', 12 May 1809. Second French invasion turned back.

7 ABRANTES
Wellington's headquarters before his first foray into Spain.

8 ALMEIDA
Fortress besieged and razed in explosion.

9 BUÇACO
Wellington's classic defensive victory. Convent cell where he slept on 27 September 1810; military museum.

10 FREINADA
Village with stone hall which served as Wellington's winter quarters between 1812 and 1813.

11 MIRANDA DO DOURO
Where Wellington crossed the gorge in a suspended basket and said farewell to Portugal for the last time.

A Friendly Capital with an Old World Quality

The setting is superb, on slopes facing south across the broad estuary of the River Tagus, with the sun catching wide, leafy avenues and turning the bay the golden colour that has earned it the nickname of *Mar da Palha* (Sea of Straw). Different districts, each with a special character, are strung along the river banks and over Lisbon's seven hills like adjoining villages. People from Portugal's former colonies crowd the streets, the chic and fashionable mingling with the lottery ticket sellers, shoe-shine men and beggars. Here you'll find a bit of Africa and Asia rolled in with southern Europe.

Phoenicians trading along the coast probably founded the first settlement in about 1200 BC. Later, Lisbon became an important outpost of the Roman Empire. Julius Caesar himself was based here during the campaign to pacify the interior. As the power of Rome declined in the 5th century AD, a succession of barbarian tribes moved in, culminating in the Visigoths who provided some stability. In 714 the city fell to the Moslem Moors, under whom it remained until 1147, when Afonso Henriques persuaded a group of crusaders on their way to the Holy Land to help him capture it. It fell after a four-month siege (see p.50) and the Moors were forced to retreat beyond the Tagus. By 1249 they had been driven from Portugal and Afonso III made Lisbon his capital.

The Age of Discoveries in the 15th and 16th centuries brought new wealth from the East. Lisbon and the rest of Portugal then suffered 60 years of Spanish rule, until the people of the capital rose against it in 1640, declaring a reluctant Duke of Bragança King João IV. His grandson, João V (1706-50), was able to undertake vast projects to embellish the capital, funded by seemingly limitless supplies of gold, newly discovered in Brazil. All was undone when the violent earthquake and ensuing fires and flood of 1755 devastated

Once Lisbon's largest church, the Igreja do Carmo on the hillside overlooking the Baixa district was destroyed in the earthquake of 1755.

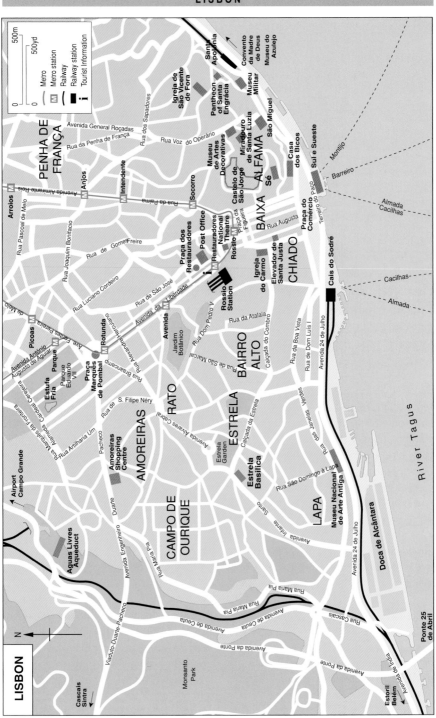

the city (see p.54). In the reconstruction, the Baixa district in particular took on an entirely new appearance.

Through the brief French occupation in 1808, the War of Two Brothers, the assassination of the king and crown prince in 1908 and republican revolution two years later, Lisbon's history was the history of Portugal. The capital's streets were the scene of celebration in 1974, with the overthrow of the right-wing dictatorship which had lasted half a century.

Getting Around

Lisbon stretches nearly 32km (20 miles) along the Tagus, and several kilometres inland, but the outstanding sights are much more concentrated. Many are within walking distance of either the river or the Avenida da Liberdade.

Public transport is efficient and cheap. The **buses** are quick and it's not difficult to learn the system. Antique **trams** (*eléctricos*) ply some routes, and **funiculars** climb a couple of the steepest hills. Lisbon's **Metro** (subway) is modern and fast, but serves only a limited area. **Taxis** are usually plentiful and not expensive.

All bus stops have signs indicating which buses stop there, and many also give details of routes. You can get a free map of the transit system at information posts of *Carris* (literally 'rails'), the local transport authority. The main one is at the base of the Santa Justa lift, near the Rossio station, where you can also buy passes and tickets in advance at a big saving.

Most buses load from the front: you pay the driver or show him your pre-paid ticket before putting it in the clipping machine. Others load from the rear – just follow the crowd. There may be a conductor

at the door who'll check your pass or sell you a ticket. Otherwise, take a seat and the collector will come to you. Keep your ticket for the whole trip in case an inspector boards the bus to double check.

Trams may be slow but they're full of character. Some in daily operation in Lisbon were built before World War I! Tram stops are indicated by large signs marked *Paragem* (stop), which often hang from the electric tram wires above the street.

Traffic jams in Lisbon are getting worse and rush hours – roughly 7.30-10am, 1-2pm and 5-7pm – are hectic. **Parking** is difficult or impossible on weekdays, so a car is generally only useful for out-of-town excursions or weekends. When you first arrive, a guided **city tour** can be a good way to grasp the layout.

We begin at the waterfront, in an elegant 18th-century square.

The Centre and Baixa District

Stately pink arcades line three sides of the **Praça do Comércio** (Commerce Square), which is also still known by its old name of Terreiro do Paço (Palace Square). The fourth side is open to the broad expanse of the river. With steps leading down to the water, seagulls screeching and bobbing boats, it's a little like Venice, but without the gondolas.

Before the 1755 earthquake, the buildings around the square were an impressive but rather incoherent mixture of styles, to judge from old prints and *azulejo* panels. In the reconstruction, the energetic Marquês de Pombal created a formal ceremonial space faced by matching palaces. Nowadays, the square is packed with parked cars and circling buses.

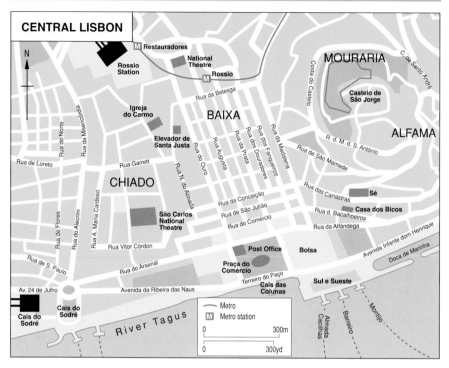

The **statue** of a man in a plumed helmet on horseback represents King José I, who reigned while Pombal ruled. A triumphal arch connects the government buildings on the north side of the square.

Through the arch, the pedestrians-only Rua Augusta is the axis of a rigidly rectangular zone of 15 streets which was also laid out after 1755. The buildings, designed to be earthquake-proof, are all similar in height and style, which can seem monotonous, although some walls are covered with *azulejos* and other decorative touches, helping to relieve the severity. The area is called the **Baixa**, or 'lowland', and is full of banks, shops, small restaurants and tea shops.

The top end of Rua Augusta runs into Lisbon's main square, the **Rossio**. In days gone by, this was the scene of witch burning and bullfights. It's still a centre of ac-

tivity today, the place to meet friends, drink coffee, window shop, watch the crowds, and listen to the incomprehensible calls of the newsboys. The statue on the tall column in this square honours Pedro IV of Portugal (1826-34), who was also the first emperor of Brazil. A persistent legend says that it's not Pedro at all, but a discarded statue of his contemporary, Emperor Maximilian of Mexico, bought on the cheap after that ruler had been shot by his ungrateful subjects. The double horseshoe doorway of the Rossio suburban railway station looks at first glance as if it leads to something much more exotic. Dating from the late 19th century, the style is called neo-Manueline. Trains to Sintra leave from here.

Confusingly, the Rossio sits side by side with another major square, the **Praça da Figueira**. This one is built around an equestrian statue of King João I, which is

94

Not the entrance to a Moorish palace, but the 19th-century railway station facing Lisbon's Rossio. Take a train from here to visit the palaces at Sintra.

usually plastered with pigeons waiting to be fed. The twin squares are the starting point of many bus routes and an important junction for many more, as well as a popular place to wait for a taxi. While you're waiting to get on board, beware of pickpockets who are active here.

Past the Teatro Nacional at the top end of the Rossio, an obelisk marks the **Praça dos Restauradores**, commemorating the overthrow of Spanish rule in 1640. The once splendid palace on the west side of the square (*Palácio Foz*) houses a **Turismo** (tourist information office) in its lower end. Right next to it, the Elevador da Glória funiciular climbs to the Bairro Alto (see p.102).

The **Avenida da Liberdade** continues uphill for 1.5km (1 mile), its central reservation laid out like a garden with fountains, statues, ponds, park benches and pavement mosaics. It ends at the traffic circle called **Praça Marquês de Pombal** (otherwise known as 'Rotunda'), which is marked by an elevated statue of the dictator, oddly accompanied by a lion. Beyond Pombal, the lawns and shrubs of **Parque Eduardo VII** continue the line of the avenue, with wooded areas and gardens on either side. The park was named after England's King Edward VII, following his visit to Lisbon in 1903, and today it is a popular place to sit and chat with friends, or just relax and watch the world go by.

Up in the north-west corner, the **Estufa Fria** ('cold greenhouse') is a tropical rainforest in the heart of a European capital. Plants and flowers from Africa, Asia and South America feel at home here in the Lisbon air, thanks to a simple system of slatted roofs and walls to filter the extremes of weather. Amid pools and waterfalls, bananas grow big enough to eat (but too high to reach). A huge standard greenhouse accommodates more delicate plants and trees, and outside in the open air there's a collection of indigenous Portuguese flora.

All sorts of tropical and exotic plants find that the microclimate in Lisbon's Estufa Fria agrees with them (overleaf).

Old Lisbon

Almost every hill in town has a *miradouro* or viewing point, but the best panorama of all belongs to the **Castelo de São Jorge** (St George's Castle), which is reached by a steep alley and steps that continue east from Rua de Santa Justa. If you feel less energetic, take a taxi or bus.

From the castle ramparts, you look out over Baixa to Bairro Alto (see p.102), along the Tagus to Belém, and across to the south bank of the river and the hills beyond. The strategic value of this promontory is obvious and it was probably fortified even before the Romans came, over two thousand years ago. The castle was the Moors' citadel from the 8th cen-tury until they were finally dislodged in 1147. The Christian conquerors expanded it and in the early years of the kingdom it served as a royal residence, before becoming a prison. By the 20th century, earthquakes and general wear and tear had left the ramparts crumbling.

T he hilltop Castelo de São Jorge offers one of the best views of the city from its ramparts, which were breached by Christian forces in 1147. The walls were shattered in the great earthquake, but have since been restored. Now they shelter a city park.

What you see today is the result of major restoration. It's pleasant to walk around the citadel and palace and clamber over the walls and towers, which are generally the domain of peacocks, pheasants, pelicans, flamingos, swans, geese and ducks. You'll also see albino birds and shiny black ravens, all looked after by the city – white and black are Lisbon's colours.

Standing out due east of the castle are the tall twin towers of the 16th-century church of **São Vicente de Fora** (St Vincent Beyond the Walls). Seen close up, the white limestone Renaissance façade seems enormous, out of scale for this part of Lisbon. The architect was an Italian, Filippo Terzi, who is said to have been inspired by the Jesuit church in Rome. The interior – a single nave and vaulted ceiling – has clean, crisp lines like a black-and-white drawing from a design manual. On the right as you face the altar, a heavy wooden door leads to the monastic cloister – and a surprise. The walls are lined with azulejos, blue-and-white glazed tiles, depicting scenes of 18th-century French life and leisure, along with the animal fables of La Fontaine. The pantheon just off the cloister contains the tombs of members of the royal Bragança family, including Catherine of Bragança, Queen of England (see p.53).

Behind the church, in the Campo de Santa Clara, a **market** (known as *Feira da Ladra*) is held on Tuesday and Saturday. On the fringes of the workaday clothing and kitchenware stalls, antique collectors may uncover a valuable old clock, or at least a rusty iron. Here, as in many places, you'll hardly believe the range of second hand items people will try to sell.

Directly downhill is the grandiose marble church of **Santa Engrácia**, topped by a tall cupola. Construction started in the 17th century but never seemed to get finished, with the result that if something is said to be like 'the works of Santa Engrácia', it is regarded as an endless task.

*L*isbon's 12th-century *Romanesque cathedral is half-hidden among the narrow streets leading up to the Castelo de São Jorge. You could easily stumble across it by accident.*

It was eventually decided to complete the building, not as a church but as a National Pantheon, and by 1966 it was ready to open. Under the sumptuous rotunda, the great men of Portuguese history – including Henry the Navigator, Vasco da Gama and Luis de Camões – are honoured by symbolic tombs (the men themselves are actually buried elsewhere). Off to the side are real tombs of presidents of the republic. You can sometimes climb to the base of the dome for a dizzying view down to the marble floor of the rotunda. Outside, a terrace looks out over rooftops and down to the river.

Unlike the cathedrals of most great cities, Lisbon's **cathedral** (*Sé*) doesn't face a broad ceremonial square, but lies on a bend in the road and appears out of nowhere (it is most easily reached from the centre by continuing east on the extension of Rua da Conceição). Begun in the 12th century, soon after the Reconquest, its towers and firing slits are still suggestive of a beleaguered fortress. Earthquakes badly damaged it in the 14th, 16th and 18th centuries, so architectural touches range from Romanesque and Gothic to baroque. An 18th-century organ is still in playing order.

Walk round inside the apse at the eastern end to see a couple of notable 14th-century **tombs**. The statue of a bearded old man, Lopo Fernandes Pacheco, lies on his sarcophagus with his hand on his sword and a favourite dog at his feet; on an adjacent stone coffin, a statue of his second wife reads her prayer book, accompanied by three dogs, two of them fighting. In the 13th-century **cloister**, which was severely damaged by the 1755 earthquake, you can view parts of pre-Roman and Roman columns, statues and inscriptions. One old

chapel has a fine wrought iron screen with Moorish and Romanesque designs. Religious statuary and vestments are displayed in the cathedral treasury.

A few steps down the hill, the church of Santo António da Sé honours Lisbon's revered native son, St Anthony of Padua (known locally as St Anthony of Lisbon), who was born here in 1195. The crypt of this church was built on the spot where, according to local lore, his house stood. Among other roles, he is the patron saint of women looking for husbands – sometimes bridal bouquets are left at the altar of St Anthony in the cathedral, with thanks for the good work.

At the eastern end of the cathedral, **Rua de São João da Praça** is where Portugal's first king, Afonso Henriques, entered Lisbon through the old Moorish wall on 25 October 1147. Between here and the waterfront, the unusual **Casa dos Bicos** (House of Facets), built in the early 16th century, is faced with stones shaped like pyramids. It belonged to a son of Afonso de Albuquerque, viceroy of Portuguese India. The street that begins here, Rua dos Bacalhoeiros (Street of the Cod Sellers), is lined with fascinating little shops. One sells nothing but corks for bottles and flasks of all sizes. Another is piled high with empty sacks, while the stock of a third consists entirely of little cans of Portuguese sardines and tuna – thousands of them – either with or without openers. Also starting near the Casa dos Bicos, Rua Alfândega (Customs House Street) leads past the fine Manueline door of the church of Nossa Senhora da Conceição Velha, back to the waterfront square, Praça do Comércio.

Alfama

South of the Castelo de São Jorge, between the cathedral and São Vicente, is Alfama. This is the oldest part of Lisbon, a labyrinth of crooked streets, stairways and alleys that go nowhere. Houses tilt at strange angles, laundry drips into the street, and apart from a few antique shops and restaurants taking advantage of the tourist traffic, you may have the feeling that nothing much has changed since the Middle Ages. Be warned, though: even if you keep your nose in a map, you will get lost – but this is half the fun. Roads go over and under each other and end in blank walls, and touring is a matter of trial and error.

No one knows why the builder of the Casa dos Bicos faced it with pointed stones, and the style didn't catch on. The upper storeys were added in modern times.

You could start walking uphill from the southern extremities of the neighbourhood – Largo do Chafariz de Dentro or Largo do Terreiro do Trigo. It's easier, though, to start from the top, and let gravity take you down towards the river. Below the castle, next to the tram tracks which climb up from the cathedral, **Largo das Portas do Sol** is like a great balcony looking out over Alfama. Before setting off down the steps here, move round to the adjoining **Miradouro de Santa Luzia** (the other side of the Decorative Arts Museum; see p.123). In the little park here, old men in black berets take the sun or play cards, oblivious to the view. Look for the two remarkable *azulejo* panels on the wall: one shows Lisbon's waterfront as it was prior to the great earthquake, the other depicts with bloodthirsty detail the expulsion of the Moors in 1147.

Alfama is a seemingly endless source of old-world delights. To make the most of the main points of interest however, you may want to (try and) pick out a route which goes past the following landmarks and sights:

Igreja de São Miguel (St Michael's Church): built in the 12th century, restored in the 18th, with a glorious ceiling of Brazilian jacaranda wood. It's dark inside, but the caretaker will turn on the lights so that you can see the rococo gilt altar screen.

Beco da Cardosa: an alley with blind-alley offshoots, the very essence of the appeal of Alfama.

Rua de São Pedro: Alfama's boisterous main shopping street, too narrow for cars. Fruit and vegetables are cheaper here than downtown; fishwives shriek, chickens and dogs get in the way, and cheerful children run wild.

Beco do Carneiro (Sheep Alley): ancient houses sag towards each other across

A more or less central landmark amid the streets of Alfama, the Church of São Miguel faces a square which is sometimes filled with market stalls.

a stepped-street just wide enough for one-and-a-half pedestrians. Look up: it's not a trick of perspective, the eaves of the buildings really do touch.

Igreja de Santo Estêvão (St Stephen's Church): with a 13th-century octagonal floor-plan, but rebuilt several times over the years. The overhanging back of the church nearly collides with the front gate of an old palace.

Largo de São Rafael: the remains of a tower, part of the Moorish defences which were finally breached in 1147.

The chances are that you will be diverted, get lost, or take a quite different path in Alfama. If so, come back another day, or in the evening to try one of the local bars or cafés. (You are recommended not to come alone, though, and to watch out for pickpockets and bag snatchers at any time.) Summer nights can turn into street festivals for saints' days and a variety of other celebrations, but even on a normal evening some little lanes are transformed into outdoor restaurants.

Bairro Alto

Lisbon spread up and over this hilltop in the 17th century to form the Bairro Alto (the name means 'high neighbourhood'). By day it's a little like Alfama, an extended village of old houses hung with bird cages and flowerpots, although here the street pattern is more logical. At night it changes character when countless restaurants, bars and *fado* nightclubs open for business. Crowds can pack the streets for most of the night, especially at weekends, when discos and *boites* stay open until 4 am.

The easiest way to reach the Bairro Alto is to board the yellow funicular, **Elevador da Glória**, at Praça dos Restauradores for the cost of a bus ticket. (The hill is walkable if you're on an emergency budget or feel in need of exercise.) The nightspots are scattered all over the district, but the greatest concentration is along Rua do Diário de Notícias – a street named after a newspaper.

At the top end of the brief funicular journey, a lookout park called the Miradouro de São Pedro de Alcântara gives a good view of the Baixa and Castelo de São Jorge across the valley. A tile orientation table, slightly out of date, helps you identify the landmarks. A little further uphill, the **Jardim Botânico** (Botanical Garden) is reached through the university gate along-

*T*he funicular trams of the Elevador da Glória will carry you up to the edge of the Bairro Alto district, focus of most of Lisbon's evening entertainment.

*E*laborate façades of some houses in the 'high neighbourhood' tell of times when it was the most elegant quarter of the city (opposite).

side the Academy of Sciences. It specializes in the scientific cultivation of unusual plants from distant climes, and is an appealing place of lush beauty and tranquillity.

Two churches in the Bairro Alto are particularly unusual. Just down the street from the top of the funicular, the **Church of São Roque** has a dull exterior – the original

16th-century façade perished in the 1755 earthquake – but inside you will find the most lavishly decorated chapels in Lisbon. The baroque **altar** of the chapel of São João Baptista (St John the Baptist), on the left, is a wealth of gold, silver, bronze, amethyst, agate, lapis lazuli, ivory and Carrara marble. In 1742 King João V of Portugal sent off an order to Rome, where teams of artists and artisans worked on this altar for five years. Then the pope gave his blessing and the altar was dismantled and shipped to the customer – an incredible prefabricated masterpiece. Next to the church, the Museu de Arte Sacra (Museum of Sacred Art) contains a collection of precious reliquaries, delicately worked jewellery and vestments.

Downhill from here, the 14th-century **Igreja do Carmo** (Carmelite Church) is rich only in memories. As you stand on the grass inside the shell of what was one of Lisbon's great churches, look up through the rebuilt arches into the blue sky and imagine the scene that day in 1755 when the roof fell in on a full congregation.

Part of the church is still roofed and houses a small archaeological museum with prehistoric pottery, Roman sculpture, early Portuguese tombs and even a few ancient mummies under glass.

The fastest way to reach the centre of town from here is by the **Elevador de Santa Justa** (often credited to Gustave

*A*nother Lisbon landmark, and an alternative way to reach the heights: the strange Elevador de Santa Justa, a lift climbing to a catwalk and the Igreja do Carmo. Dating from the turn of the century, it has recently been renovated.

Eiffel of Eiffel Tower fame, but actually designed by the French-sounding, Portuguese engineer Raoul Mesnier de Ponsard). This lift, inaugurated in 1901, was originally powered by steam. Rebuilt in 1993, it is 30m (100ft) high and a remarkable sight in itself.

The longer, slower way downhill meanders through the district known as the Chiado. For centuries these zigzagging streets were known for Lisbon's most elegant shopping – silverware, leather, fashions, books – and fine pastry and tea shops. In 1988, however, the area was devastated by a fire in which two of Europe's oldest department stores were wiped out. Reconstruction is well under way and makes quite a spectacle, with up to six storeys below street level as well as four or five above.

Belém

Some of Lisbon's most important monuments and museums are located west of the centre along the Tagus at Belém (Portuguese for Bethlehem), about 6km (4 miles) from Praça do Comércio. Land has been reclaimed from the river to provide parkland and marinas, so the shore itself is unrecognizable, but this is where many great Portuguese voyages of discovery began in the 15th and 16th centuries.

Closest to central Lisbon, the **Museu Nacional dos Coches** (National Coach Museum) is housed, aptly, in the former riding school of the Belém Royal Palace. Two great halls display dozens of horse-drawn carriages for city or ceremonial use or rugged cross-country travel, spanning four centuries of European history. The most extravagant are three sculpted, gilt carriages used by the Portuguese embassy

Stately ceremonial carriages are lined up for your inspection in the intriguing Museu Nacional dos Coches at Belém, west of Lisbon.

The convent wing was shattered in the 1755 earthquake, but the church and cloister survive as testaments to 16th-century faith and taste. The vast south façade of the church, parallel to the river, is mostly unadorned limestone, so embellishments really stand out (notice the stone 'rope'). The **south portal** is a wonder of intricate stonework. A figure of Nossa Senhora de Belém is uppermost; the lower central statue is thought to depict Henry the Navigator. Inside, columns carved in the complex style of the Manueline era (which bridged the gap between Gothic and Renaissance styles in Portugal; see p.64) contribute to a feeling of infinite height and space. The first architect in charge was a Frenchman named Boytac; he was succeeded by the Spaniard João de Castilho.

Though it's usually quite dark inside the church, you'll probably be able to pick out several royal tombs, supported by stone elephants in a tribute to the newly discovered marvels of the East. To see if you have acquired the taste for Manueline architecture, have a look at the **capela môr** at the eastern end of the church, which was completed later, in Renaissance style. If you find the sudden change to classical severity a shock, you're a convert. The irony is that King Manuel himself is interred in this cold marble mausoleum. Near the west door, under a majestic vaulted canopy are the modern tombs of two other giants of Portugal's golden age, Vasco da Gama (see p.52) and the poet Luís de Camões (see p.163).

Outside again, turn to see the fine sculptural work surrounding the **west portal**, before heading right for the cloister. This is an airy doubledecker structure with most original proportions. As you stroll round the arcades, the very dimensions of the place seem to change because of the

in Rome in the early 18th century to impress Pope Clement XI. One coach after another illustrates the painfully slow evolution of technical details, leading up to the sleek 19th-century Crown Carriage, still worthy of any royal procession. Even the regal riding accessories from stirrups to coachhorns are on show.

A short stroll westward along the Rua de Belém leads to Lisbon's most magnificent religious monument, the **Mosteiro dos Jerónimos**. This monastery was begun by Manuel I with the riches brought back by Portuguese ships from the East.

clever intersection of angles and arches. No two columns are alike. The upper storey of the cloister gives access to the upper choir of the church, from where you can enjoy new perspectives on its utterly original design.

The western part of the monastery has been restored and now houses the **Museu Nacional de Arqueologia** (National Museum of Archaeology). This is the definitive collection of ancient relics – Stone Age tools, Bronze Age jewels and, from the Roman days, excellent sculptures and mosaics (just a small part of the collection; the rest is in storage through lack of space). The neighbouring planetarium was a gift from Portugal's ubiquitous benefactor, Calouste Gulbenkian (see p.118).

In the western end of the monastery and overflowing into new buildings beyond, the **Museu da Marinha** (Naval Museum) will interest anyone who cares about history or the sea. The countless model ships of all ages are often fiendishly intricate. A huge new hall across a courtyard to the west was needed to hold the biggest exhibits, notably the actual galliot or brigantine built in 1785 to celebrate a royal marriage, with seats for 80 oarsmen.

Between the monastery and the river is a large garden with rose beds, bird-of-paradise flowers and swan ponds. The Fonte Luminosa (luminous fountain) provides a 45-minute show of changing light and colour patterns. Facing it from the west, the modern pink building like a long low fortress is the **Centro Cultural de Belém**, which was built to house European Union meetings when Portugal holds the presidency. It also serves as a fully-equipped international congress centre and even incorporates an Opera House.

The modern **Padrão dos Descobrimentos** (Monument to the Discoveries) juts from the riverbank like a caravel cresting a wave. On the prow stands Prince Henry the Navigator, shown as always in a strange round hat. The statues behind him recall the explorers, mapmakers, astronomers, chroniclers and others he mobilized in the dauntless days of discovery. For the price of a ticket, an elevator takes you part way up, then stairs lead to the top and a superb view. A compass and map of the world inlaid in the pavement below emphasize the phenomenal range of Portugal's explorations in the golden age, from the Azores and Brazil to India, Macau and Japan.

One more museum here on the waterfront, the **Museu de Arte Popular** (Popular Art Museum), surveys the folk art and customs of Portugal, region by region, with plenty of charming fabrics, furniture, embroidery, toys and dolls.

A replica of the Fairey IIIB seaplane, Santa Cruz, honours the aviators who first flew across the South Atlantic in 1922. The original aircraft itself is on display across the road in the Museu da Marinha.

Turn finally to the **Torre de Belém**, one of the jewels of Manueline architecture and an enduring symbol of both Portugal in general and Lisbon in particular. It's wonderfully graceful and imaginative, although much smaller than you may have imagined from photographs. As old prints show, it was once quite far out in the river,

T he two-storey cloisters of the 16th-century Mosteiro dos Jerónimos at Belém. The lower level, with its incredible ornamental carving, was designed by the Manueline architect João de Castilho (overleaf).

but land reclamation has brought the shoreline almost up to its walls. You can cross a wooden bridge and enter a 16th-century world, though the interior is unexpectedly austere. The most handsome aspect is the side facing the river, with a lovely loggia and lacy stone balustrade. A 19th-century Portuguese writer, Ramalho Ortigão, conceded that the tower had no importance as a military construction. He said: 'The only defensive arm the tower of Belém can use against an enemy is its beauty.'

Tagus Bridge and Statue of Christ the King

On the way to Belém, you'll pass under the **Ponte 25 de Abril** across the Tagus. This was Europe's longest suspension bridge when opened to traffic in 1966. Originally named in honour of the nation's dictator, after the revolution of 1974 the word 'Salazar' was removed and for quite a time it was just 'the bridge'. Finally it was renamed after the date of that revolution, 25 April. You can't stop on it, but the view of Lisbon *from* the bridge is as impressive as the vista from an airliner.

Just across the river, looming over the bridge's toll booths, is Lisbon's variation on Rio de Janeiro's landmark statue of **Christ the King**. Almost 30m (over 90ft) tall, it stands on a modern four-pronged pedestal. A church, the Santuário de Cristo-Rei, is housed in the base of the monument. Take the lift to the viewing terrace for the glorious 360-degree **panorama** of the whole Tagus estuary, the bridge, all Lisbon and a vast expanse of the Arrábida peninsula to the south (see p.141). To visit the statue you can drive across the bridge or take one of the **ferryboats** from Praça do Comércio to Cacilhas, and then catch a taxi or a bus marked

'Cristo-Rei'. The ferryboat is recommended as an exciting introduction to the port. The commuters may not seem to take any notice of the view, but you'll enjoy the ferry's manoeuvrings among cruise liners, freighters, tankers, warships and tugs. Merchant ships leave here destined for the old Portuguese territories – from Rio de Janeiro to Maputo – and wherever else the sea lanes lead.

Coming back from Cacilhas, there's a choice of ferries. Some head for Praça do Comércio, others for **Cais do Sodré**, a few hundred metres further west, which is worth seeing. (The railway station here is the place to catch a commuter train for Estoril and Cascais.) In this nautical neighbourhood, the stores sell full-size anchors, compasses,

*T*he Ponte 25 de Abril suspension bridge (below) clocks in at 1,013m (3,323ft). It soars over the estuary of the River Tagus and offers incredible views of Lisbon.

At its southern end, facing Lisbon, stands a tall statue of Christ the King (Cristo Rei), inspired by the similar monument in Rio de Janeiro and inaugurated in 1959.

*F*resh produce is piled high in the biggest market in the city at Cais do Sodré, just to the west of Praça do Comércio.

buoys and engine room telegraphs – all serious maritime equipment, obviously not for the Sunday sailor. Across the street under an Indian-looking dome is Lisbon's main **market**, the Mercado da Ribeira, which is the work place for more than one thousand people. Men in padded caps balance unwieldy wicker trays of fruit and vegetables on their heads and the scent of fresh coriander pervades the air. Since it's both a wholesale and retail market, something colourful is always going on from 2am to 9pm. The best time to absorb the atmo-

sphere is before lunch, when you might also pick up the makings for a great picnic, or eat at the market restaurant.

North-Western Outskirts

Uphill for about 1km (0.5 mile) from the Museu dos Coches, the **Palácio da Ajuda** is the biggest palace inside the city limits, brimming with artworks and curiosities. The Italianate building is like a smaller version of Buckingham Palace in London and is arranged in a hollow square, although the western side was gutted in a fire and only a façade remains. Portugal's King Luís I (1861-89) and his bride, Maria Pia of Savoy, became the first royal family to live there; they were responsible for the furnishings, including the Gobelin tapestries, oriental ceramics and rare old Portuguese furniture, as well as plenty of little artistic merit. Guides point out Maria Pia's sewing machine in a special rococo case and her bathroom with made-in-England wash-basins. Her papers still clutter her desk and family photos of other European royals are just where she left them.

North of the palace lies the city's biggest park, **Monsanto**. Here, eucalyptus, cypress, cedar and oak trees thrive on the rolling hillsides. In addition to calm and fresh air, the park is well supplied with amenities – sports grounds, bars and restaurants. Its municipal camping ground ranks as one of Europe's prettiest and best organized, and there are also some outstanding *miradouros* (lookout points) over Lisbon and the Tagus estuary. Two less desirable features have marred the picture in recent years: some of Lisbon's busiest commuter routes now cut through the park, jammed with cars four times a day; and you would be unwise to wander alone, even in daytime. Squatters' camps have taken over parts of the park, and some of the less law-abiding districts of Lisbon abut directly onto it.

The futuristic towers of the **Amoreiras** shopping complex stand out on the Lisbon skyline, a vision of orange, pink, blue and black. Call it 'theme park' architecture or post-modernism, the design by Tomás Taveira is an eyecatcher. A free bus shuttles shoppers here from Praça Marquês de Pombal (Rotunda), which is much better than trying to drive yourself as there can be epic traffic snarls getting into and out of the car parks.

Marching across the Alcântara valley between Amoreiras and the Monsanto Park, the soaring pointed arches of the **Aqueduct of Aguas Livres** are part of an engineering triumph 18km (11 miles) long. Inspired by ancient Roman models and examples in many other Portuguese cities, it was finished in 1748, bringing clean water to the fountains of central Lisbon. Restoration work has been going on, precluding the chance to take a walk along the top. Ask at the tourist information office in Palácio Foz to find out if it has opened again for visits.

Near the Sete Rios Metro station is Lisbon's **Jardim Zoológico**. This is an old-style zoo, with little space for the animals to move about, but at least its designers had a sense of humour: one of the big chimpanzee cages is designed as a wine store with kegs, unbreakable bottles and scales. The star of the show is a money-spinning elephant who rings a bell and blows a horn when you hand him a coin. Children are well taken care of, with their own little amusement park and a driving school with foot-powered cars. Feeding time for the animals is 4pm; for the humans there's a choice of snack bars, a restaurant, and push-carts. **Campo Grande**, between the zoo and the airport, is a popular park with local people. Palm, cedar and willow trees shade pretty walks, outdoor cafés and a small lake with rowing boats.

Estrêla

The area south of the Amoreiras centre and west of Bairro Alto sees fewer outside visitors, but is not without reasons to go exploring there. Two landmarks can give you your bearings. One is the **Parliament building** (*Palácio da Assembleia da República*) at the top of Rua de Dom Carlos I. Its classical bulk has more or less encased the old Convent of São Bento, which was taken over after the 1834 expulsion of the monastic orders. People often refer to it as the Palácio de São Bento instead of using the official name. The **Basilica da Estrêla** (Estrêla means 'star'), further uphill along Calçada da Estrêla, is still more striking: its twin belltowers and dome are visible on the skyline from most of the *miradouros* in Lisbon. The devout, sad and ultimately mad Queen Maria I ordered its construction in 1779 to fulfil the vow she had made that she would build it should she give birth to a son and heir. (She did have a son, José, but was to outlive him.) Despite a profusion of multi-coloured marble and the soaring dome, the interior is as cold as Maria's tomb, a massive, black marble sarcophagus which is housed here. It's sometimes possible to climb to the base of the dome for the panoramic view.

The imposing façade of the Parliament building, which houses the national archives. It is often called São Bento after the old convent which used to occupy the same site (overleaf).

The *Jardim Guerra Junqueiro* opposite is invariably referred to as the **Jardim da Estrêla**, after the church. It's a local favourite, lush with tropical foliage. Old men play cards, small boys play football, children feed the ducks, geese and peacocks, and sometimes a band plays at the elegant bandstand, whose slim columns of wrought iron somehow manage to support an oversized roof.

FAR FROM HOME

Across the Estrêla garden, on the opposite side from the basilica, stands a tall iron gate in a high wall. A discreet sign says 'British Cemetery and Church of St George'. You press the bell and listen at the security speaker. There's no answer, and you push the bell again. Still no response, but be patient. Eventually the gate opens a little way and the resident guardian, a tiny, wizened old lady looks you over. If she decides your purposes are respectable, she lets you in. The gate clangs shut.

The British Cemetery is of more than British interest. Many German, American and Dutch Protestants are buried here, including Daniel Gildemeester, the Dutch consul and builder of most of the palace of Seteais at Sintra (see p.136). Admiral Horthy, the right-wing Regent of Hungary from 1920 until 1944, died at Estoril and was buried here, but with the fall of Communism, admirers moved his remains to his homeland in 1993. Another strange twist of history accounts for the memorial to Boer prisoners-of-war and internees, who died while held in Portugal during the South African War (1900-03).

Inside, the cemetery, the cedar, cypress, palm and pine trees form a forest canopy through which dappled sunlight plays on the gravestones. In nearly three centuries of use, the space has become crowded with crosses, urns, tall pyramids, ornamental railings and inscribed stones. If you're looking for a particular grave among the thousands, ask the gatekeeper quickly, before she vanishes. The establishment of the 'English Cemetery' as it was called (although there were many Scots, Welsh and Irish among the expatriate community) was a sensitive matter in the early 18th century. Portugal was a strongly Catholic country, the Jesuits were still a powerful force and it was not so much an English as a Protestant burial ground that was wanted. Even Protestant services had to be held in private houses or embassies, and permission for a church was only granted one century later. The Romanesque building you can see at the top end of the cemetery dates from 1885.

Look out for the grave of Henry Fielding, author of *Tom Jones* and father of the modern novel. You'll find it on the left of the main avenue in the second block, with an impressive plinth bearing a cataphalque, topped by an urn and stone flame. 'Died MDCCLIV. Age XLVII' reads the inscription, as well as giving a long Latin account of his qualities. In 1754, the year before the great earthquake, Fielding was suffering, by his own account, from 'a jaundice, a dropsy and an asthma'. He gave up hope of a cure at Bath and sailed to Lisbon for the warmer climate. No sooner had he arrived than he was denouncing it as 'the nastiest city in the world', not to mention the most expensive, with food likely to poison him. He was later to change his tune: 'My affairs will soon be in a fine Posture ... the Produce of the Country is preposterously cheap.' He felt better and news was sent to England of his recovery, but by the time it arrived, he had suffered a relapse and died near Belém on 8 October, aged 47. For some reason, his family did nothing about providing even a simple gravestone. That being so, the British community in Lisbon didn't see why they should pay for one. Even when the French consul had a memorial made at his own expense (inscribed in French), they turned it down without being shamed into action themselves. Finally, in 1830, a visiting chaplain collected the money for the present monument.

Major Museums

Gulbenkian Museum

Just north of the tip of Parque Eduardo VII, Lisbon's wonderful Gulbenkian Museum was created to house the thousands of works of art acquired by the Armenian billionaire and philanthropist Calouste Gulbenkian, who died in Lisbon in 1955 (see p.118). The marvels start with the building itself: it's the perfect size, not too many rooms, and has a feeling of space and a lovely garden setting. The quality of the exhibits is breathtaking. Gulbenkian specialized in certain fields – he knew what he liked and was willing to pay for it. Woe-betide anyone who wanted to bid against him!

The viewing starts chronologically with **Egyptian Art**, including ceramics and sculptures dating back to 2700 BC. These delicate and perfectly preserved pieces may change your whole view of ancient Egypt. There's nothing cold or heavy here.

A handsome statue of the Judge Bes is inscribed with hieroglyphs which date it from the reign of Pharaoh Psamtik I (7th century). The sleek bronze cats and kittens are infinitely appealing.

The small room devoted to **Greek and Roman Art** centres on a collection of rare gold coins from ancient Greece, which Gulbenkian especially loved. A 6th-century BC coin was minted by that noted gold enthusiast, Croesus, while a set of medallions may have been prizes at the Olympic

Games of 242 AD. Roman treasures include opalescent glass and jewellery.

A large section of the museum is devoted to **Middle Eastern and Islamic Art** – the rarest ancient fabrics, Persian carpets, Turkish ceramics, glassware and illuminated pages from the Koran. The picture windows here show the art of landscaping; the museum is surrounded by its own perfectly planned park, with sculptures, streams, ponds and cool green glades.

In the hall of **Oriental Art**, Chinese porcelain starts with the Yuan epoch (the time of Marco Polo) and goes on to some exquisite 17th- and 18th-century pieces, Chinese jade and rock crystal, plus Japanese prints and netsuke (carved toggles of wood or ivory, originally used to tie a medicine box or purse). As with everything in the museum, each exhibit represents the pinnacle of a particular style, miraculously unmarred over the centuries.

Gulbenkian's choice of **European Art** begins in the 11th century with illuminated parchment manuscripts. Tiny, exquisite ivory sculptures of religious scenes come from 14th-century France. There are also well-preserved tapestries from Flemish and Italian workshops of the 16th century.

Among the paintings by Dutch and Flemish artists of the same era, two Rembrandts have pride of place: a portrait of a helmeted warrior believed to be Pallas Athene or Alexander the Great (probably modelled by Rembrandt's son, Titus), and

Henry Moore sculptures are just some of the exhibits which overflow into the beautifully landscaped gardens at the Gulbenkian Museum, the creation of a great collector and philanthropist.

MR FIVE PERCENT

At the dawn of the Oil Age, a far-sighted Turkish-born Armenian put up money to help finance drilling in Mesopotamia (now Iraq), which was then part of the Turkish empire. Eventually he was to own 5 percent of the Iraq Petroleum Company.

Two world wars and the fuelling of millions of cars, aeroplanes and ships made Calouste Gulbenkian rich beyond imagination. He became an avid collector of antiquities and valuable art, beginning with Turkish and Persian carpets, Armenian and Arabic manuscripts and Greek and Roman coins. His passions spread to ancient Egyptian art, Chinese porcelain and Western painting, always looking for the most perfect examples in each of his chosen fields. He had become a British citizen, but in his later years preferred to live in Portugal. Here he established a philanthropic foundation based in Lisbon, to which he left most of his money and fabulous collections when he died in 1955. The Gulbenkian Museum is the result, along with many other cultural facilities in Portugal, including the Modern Art Centre, regional museums, educational institutes and orchestras.

Figure of an Old Man. The French collection shines in the area of furniture, tapestries and goldsmith's art from the 18th century, plus paintings by Boucher, Watteau and Fragonard. English art includes works by Gainsborough and Turner, and Romney's *Miss Constable.* Burne-Jones is one among several of the pre-Raphaelites represented – Gulbenkian was an admirer when their work was still out of fashion in the 1940s.

One room is dedicated to the 18th-century Venetian artist, Francesco Guardi, and the collection of his 19 *vedute* (views) and *capricci* (caprices) of Venice is considered the finest anywhere.

The French Impressionists are represented by Monet, Degas, Manet's charming *Boy with Cherries* and *Boy Blowing Bubbles,* and Renoir's *Madame Monet,* looking uncomfortable in a stiff blue dress on a white sofa.

The last room of the museum contains 169 items by Gulbenkian's friend, René Lalique (1860-1945), the versatile French artist whose style seems to sum up the Art Nouveau movement. Here are pendants, bracelets, necklaces and combs of assorted materials and unexpected motifs – serpents, crickets, beautiful women, lovers, butterflies and owls.

The museum is only one element of the Calouste Gulbenkian Foundation. Elsewhere on the premises are concert and exhibition halls, a library, bookstore and informal restaurant. The **modern art centre** in a separate building stages temporary exhibitions, mainly of current or recent Portuguese art.

Museu Nacional de Arte Antiga
(National Museum of Ancient Art)

'Ancient' Art is a misleading translation for a superb collection of western European art spanning the 15th to 19th centuries. Exhibits from former Portuguese colonial possessions and treasures imported from Japan and China during the Age of Discoveries include outstanding ceramics and glass, gold, silver and furniture. The museum is housed in a palace on a hillside just above the Lisbon docks, halfway between Praça do Comércio and Belém. If you get lost, ask for 'Janelas Verdes' (green shutters), the street it's on and also the name by which the palace and the museum are better known.

A major restoration of the building began in 1993. Until completed, many sections are likely to be closed, but arrange-

*E*very Portuguese museum has its quota of religious art. This polychrome medieval figure of the Virgin and Child is especially charming.

ments have been made for some 'star' items to be on show whenever the museum is open. Check with tourist information.

The first great name in Portuguese art, Nuno Gonçalves, painted *The Adoration of St Vincent* in the 15th century for Lisbon's convent of São Vicente de Fora. Six large panels show the patron saint of Lisbon receiving the homage of the Portuguese royal family and other dignitaries of the time. Many have been identified: a figure with a moustache in the left centre panel is taken to be Henry the Navigator, looking suitably devout. Dozens of other faces are shown in every range of distraction – boredom, amusement, ire – and a number of the assembled clergymen look ugly, evil or both. This is a masterpiece of group portraiture. The flowering of Portuguese painting in the 16th century, the movement known as the 'Primitives', is represented by the Lisbon School of brothers Gregório and Cristóvão Lopes and Cristóvão Figueiredo, as well as by many anonymous artists or those known only by titles such as 'The Master of Sardoal' or 'The Master of Setúbal'.

Outstanding early German Art includes Durer's *St Jerome*, Cranach's *Salome* with the bloody head of John the Baptist and, most extraordinary of all, *The Temptation of St Anthony* by Hieronymus Bosch. Painted around 1500, this tryptich is a typically fantastic piece of Bosch hallucination. Bizarre creatures – a crane rigged up like a helicopter, walking fish, animal-faced men – and the most hideous disasters are so grotesque that they evoke amusement now, but there's no evidence that the artist was anything but deadly serious.

On no account miss the collection of five Japanese 6-fold screens dating from around 1600. The subject is the arrival of the Portuguese in Japan, as seen through Japanese eyes, recorded in meticulous and hilarious detail. Almost all the foreigners are portrayed as villainous or arrogant and the locals, watching from their balconies, appear to be amused. Who wouldn't be, at the sight of these strangely garbed, long-nosed grandees with their fawning servants and black slaves, folding chairs and even, in one case, sunglasses?

There's much more to see in the rest of the museum: English, Flemish, French, Dutch, Italian and Spanish paintings, most of them meticulously restored; china and glassware from Europe and the Orient;

rare Portuguese ceramics, furniture and tapestries; and a bequest by Calouste Gulbenkian – a room of ancient sculpture, up to his admirable standards, including a Greek torso of marble from the 5th century BC and a statue of a lion from the palace of Emperor Tiberius at Capri.

Museu do Azulejo
(*Museum of Azulejos*)

The **Convento da Madre de Deus** (Convent of the Mother of God) makes a magnificent setting for a museum devoted to the art of painted tiles. It's some way from anywhere else you're likely to want to visit, but not hard to find and well worth the trip. Head north-east from the vast Santa Apolónia Station for just over 1km (0.8 mile), parallel to the waterfront but one street back from it. There, in a run-down area near a container terminal, look out for the convent's Manueline doorway, a survivor from the original building of 1509. A side door leads to the museum entrance and the interior of the **church**, which was rebuilt after the 1755 earthquake and gleams with gilded baroque woodcarving. Below a painted ceiling, two rows of enormous paintings of the life of St Francis hang on the side walls, the lower halves of which are covered by blue and white painted tiles from Holland, depicting scenes from rural life.

Apart from the deconsecrated church, the museum's exhibits fill the sacristy, a large and a small cloister and the rooms leading off them. The earliest tiles here were of Spanish-*mudéjar* manufacture, geometric Arabesque designs mainly in blue, green and white. Next came home-produced versions of the same type, followed by panels making up a larger, multi-coloured design such as a vase of flowers. The next fashion was for narrative panels. At first they were made in more than one colour, but by the early 18th century most were blue and white alone. Other colours returned later, but the fashion for blue and white has never gone away. Most panels were on religious themes, but not all: seven light-hearted ones show the rags-to-riches biography of an early-19th-century hatmaker. A few exhibits depart from the main theme. Look for the delightful Christmas crib (*presépio*) figures dating from the 18th century.

*T*he gilded and tiled interior of the church of the Convento da Madre de Deus. Originally built in the 16th century, it was destroyed by the 1755 earthquake, and then rebuilt. Today it houses some splendid art, and the convent is the appropriate setting for the Museu do Azulejo.

On the Tiles

Its roots may be in China, Persia, Arabia, the Netherlands and Spain, but the Portuguese have turned the art of the painted and glazed ceramic tile, the *azulejo*, into their own. Other nations restrict their use to bathrooms and kitchens, with perhaps a timid variation or two, but in Portugal tiles are used with unrivalled panache, inside palaces, churches and railway stations, on fountains and park benches and covering the outsides of houses to keep out the damp. Unique pictures are painted, sometimes on only four or six tiles, sometimes using hundreds to make up a vast panorama.

The Moors left many examples behind when they were expelled. That was especially true in Spain – where the Reconquest took so much longer to complete – where the technique was more advanced. There also were the artisans who knew how to make *azulejos*. The word itself comes from Arabic: *azzulayj* originally meant 'little stone' and may have been used first to describe the mosaics which the Arabs found in the former Roman empire. Then it came to mean the patterned ceramics used by the Persians to embellish their mosques, and which spread all over the Islamic world. It's tempting to assume some connection with *azul*, Portuguese for blue, since blue and white tiles are so common, but the word *azulejo* (pronounced Azoo-LEH-joo in Portugal) is much older than the fashion for blue, so the similarity is probably a coincidence.

Most of the Moors in Spain belonged to the Sunni branch of Islam, which forbade images of living things, so their tiles used geometric 'Arabesque' patterns, mostly of green, blue, yellow and white. Spanish *mudéjar* designs continued the tradition into the 16th century

A Nativity scene in polychrome azulejos is typical of the work of Portuguese artists in the first part of the 17th century.

and some found their way to Portugal: you can see examples in the Palácio Nacional at Sintra (see p.132) and in major museums (including those at Évora and Coimbra). Portuguese and immigrant Flemish artists started to produce tiles in Lisbon in the 16th century, but only with the Spanish occupation of 1580 to 1640 did the industry really get going. Blue and golden-yellow became the favoured colour combination, and pictures of vases of flowers, saints and religious scenes spread over anything from six to 48 tiles appeared at about this time. Exotic birds and other designs inspired by the discoveries used a growing palette of colours.

Towards the end of the 17th century the fashion suddenly changed. Multicoloured *azulejos* were out. and blue was in. A new period of prosperity had dawned, at least for the nobility and the merchant class. Palaces and mansions were built, and without exception their salons, corridors and gardens were adorned with ambitious scenes made up of vast numbers of *azulejos*. The factories worked night and day to meet the demand.

Why the love affair with blue? Blue and white Ming porcelain from China had begun to make its way by the Silk Route overland to Europe in the 16th century. Then Portuguese and, later, Dutch traders brought back greater quantities by the sea routes. The craze caught on and Ming began to fetch extraordinary prices. Dutch factories, notably at Delft, started to turn out their own blue and white china, at first imitating Ming but soon evolving original designs, including tiles. Many were imported into Portugal – you can see some at the Museu do Azulejo in Lisbon (along with the most magnificent collection of Portuguese tiles from every era; see p.120) and in their thousands at the Casa do Paço in Figueira da Foz (see p.177).

Blue and white's exclusive appeal lasted until the mid-18th century. The vast panoramas painted for baroque churches, monasteries and palaces made some artists famous, such as António de Oliveira Bernardes – his studio produced many scenes of Lisbon. His brother Policarpo created the celebrated scenes at Santa Marinha da Costa in Guimarães (now a Pousada). At the same time, exports to Madeira, the Azores, Brazil, Goa and even Macau transformed the appearance of every palace and most of the mansions and churches in the empire. Spain had virtually given up production and Portugal was left supreme.

The earthquake of 1755 may have been the trigger for a partial return to polychrome. All those identical buildings in the Baixa district of Lisbon required something to differentiate them, and a coating of colourful geometric-design tiles was applied to many. Besides, the colonists in Brazil, their buildings plagued with damp and decay, had discovered that tiles made a very effective weatherproof layer, and the idea was quickly taken up in Portugal too. Seaside towns such as Aveiro and the fishing village of Santa Luzia near Tavira still have rows of houses encased in tiles. Royalty also continued to favour *azulejo* scenes: the gardens at Queluz (see p.131) have some fine polychrome examples.

The taste for blue and white never went away. Some of the most colossal pictures ever created in any medium were produced around 1900 by Jorge Colaço for the Buçaco Palace (now the Palace Hotel, see p.176) and the São Bento Railway Station in Oporto (see p.189). In our own time, artists express themselves through the *azulejo* – what could be more durable? – and scarcely a new Portuguese house is built without its ration of the national art form.

The smaller cloister is surrounded by old geometric tiles. Notice the Manueline touch in the stonework, carved into a design of twisted cord fixed by buckles. On the upper level of the larger cloister, don't miss the **Great Lisbon Panorama**, an *azulejo* panel 36m (118ft) long recording every detail of Lisbon's riverside as it looked 25 years before the earthquake. In all, many thousands of *azulejos* are exhibited here, ranging from 15th-century polychrome designs to 20th-century art deco. Other displays explain how they are made, and you can buy some expensive reproductions of early designs as well as modern creations.

An excellent little restaurant opens every lunchtime (except Monday, when the museum is closed), in the original convent kitchen looking out onto a courtyard and garden. Naturally, it is lined with tiles, 18th-century originals illustrating all sorts of food. Judging by them, the monks ate pretty well.

Museu de Artes Decorativas
(Museum of Decorative Arts)

The Decorative Arts Museum is appropriately set in a 17th-century palace, next to Largo das Portas do Sol above Alfama. It is filled with the most choice furniture, ceramics, silver and carpets dating from 16th- to 19th-century Portugal and the Portuguese empire. Fine examples of woodwork are arrayed in rooms that often look lived in. Among the curiosities are a primitive version of a fold-up sofabed, children's rooms with miniature furniture, and an 18th-century picnic basket.

The museum, and an attached training school for cabinetmakers, bookbinders, engravers and other artisans, is run by the Ricardo Espírito Santo Silva Foundation, which was set up in 1953 by the donor of the collections, who was a member of a wealthy banking family. Students come from many countries to learn woodcarving and restoration techniques. The gold leaf used in gilding and bookbinding is made on the premises: two ounces (60g) of 23k gold yield 4,500 leaves measuring 8cm x 8cm, so thin that they disintegrate if touched by hand. They're sent all over Portugal and further afield: 40,000 leaves were used recently to re-gild the top of the fence and gates of Versailles in France. You may see conservation work going on in the museum, but if you have a special interest in visiting the workshops, ask at the tourist information office well in advance. The palace occupies a splendid vantage point just above the Miradouro de Santa Luzia, the lookout point from where you survey the roofs of Alfama.

Museu Militar
(Military Museum)

A big classical building with an elaborate portal, opposite the Santa Apolónia station, stands on the site of a foundry where 16th-century cannon were cast. Some of the weapons now on show date from much further back: crossbows, maces and lashes; 14th-century mortars; and even Vasco da Gama's two-handed sword, which is as tall as a man. The age of chivalry is represented by many suits of armour, custom-made for knights and their horses. A large, evidently nostalgic section specializes in World War I, including photos of Portuguese troops in the trenches of the Western front, faded uniforms, medals, bugles and helmets with bullet-holes as souvenirs. Room after room of dusty weaponry is likely to interest only the most dedicated enthusiasts. The patio of this building overflows with cannon and even a tank.

Palaces and Beaches Within Easy Reach of the Capital

The Portuguese 'Costas' around Lisbon offer a wealth of interest. North of the Tagus, the Costa do Estoril reaches west to Guincho. South of the Tagus, the shoreline of the so-called Costa Azul darts in and out of the Atlantic, swallowing the estuary of the broad Sado river. Colourful fishing villages are complemented by grand palaces inland at Sintra, whose mountainous beauty has been praised by travellers for centuries. Whether bathing at holiday spots along the Costa da Caparica, having a flutter in the casino at Estoril, or watching the bird life at the Serra da Arrábida nature reserve, you'll soon find enough to keep you occupied.

Costa do Estoril

The half-hour train ride from Cais do Sodré station in Lisbon to Estoril passes through dull-looking commuter suburbs which were once fishing and wine-growing villages. If you travel by car, the hectic traffic through Belém (see p.105) and along the coast is little inducement to stop. The route, which is known as the *Marginal*, is notoriously ac-

The 19th-century Palácio da Pena on a hilltop above Sintra is a multicoloured mock-medieval and Moorish fantasy. Rich in architecture, history, art and views, it formed the perfect romantic retreat for Queen Maria II.

cident-prone, so drivers can scarcely spare a glance for the sea view.

The Tagus estuary merges with the open sea at **Oeiras**, which is notable for the *quinta* or country estate of the 18th-century dictator, the Marquês de Pombal. His mansion, the Palácio de Pombal, more recently housed the Gulbenkian collections before they moved to the present museum (see p.116). Now it is the home of the National Agricultural Institute and not normally open to the public. If you have a specific interest in seeing the splendid gardens, enquire at the Tourist Office in Lisbon (see p.95) if they can make arrangements for you to visit.

The 16th-century **Fort of São Julião de Barra** on the next headland was built in the new Italian style as a massive gun platform to deter enemy ships from entering

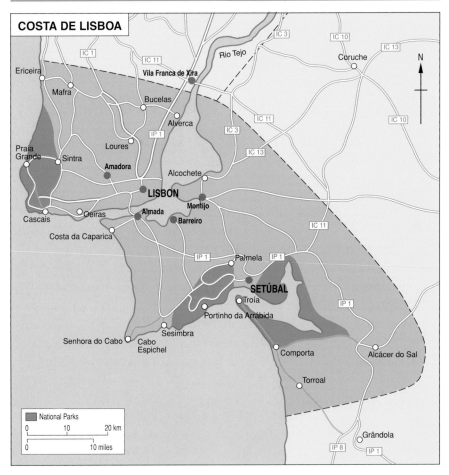

COSTA DE LISBOA

Ericeira
Mafra
Bucelas
Vila Franca de Xira
Rio Tejo
Coruche
IC 3
IC 10
IC 13
IC 1
IC 11
N
Alverca
IC 11
IC 10
Praia Grande
Loures
IP 1
IC 3
Sintra
Amadora
IC 13
Alcochete
LISBON
Oeiras
Almada
Montijo
Cascais
Barreiro
IC 11
Costa da Caparica
IP 1
Palmela
IP 1
SETÚBAL
Troía
IP 1
Portinho da Arrábida
Senhora do Cabo
Sesimbra
Cabo Espichel
Comporta
Alcácer do Sal
Torroal

National Parks

0   10   20 km

0   10 miles

Grândola
IP 8
IP 1

the Tagus. Later it became a grim prison: Pombal locked up Jesuit leaders here for 20 years, and this was also where the Miguelites tortured their Liberal enemies during the Civil War (see p.57). The round **Bugio Fort** you can see offshore covers the whole of a tiny islet. Started in 1586 it took a century of setbacks and restarts to complete this 'stone galleon'. Now the sea again threatens to undermine it and even the lighthouse is unmanned.

Carcavelos has long been known for its sweet, amber-coloured dessert wine (the English drank it even before they dis-covered Port), but development has swallowed up most of the vineyards now. The rural tradition clings on in the regular Thursday produce and craft market. Crowds from Lisbon come to the beach, even taking to the water in spite of notorious pollution, and the seafront is lined by restaurants and bars.

An alternative to the *Marginal*, the A5 *Auto-estrada* toll road, passes further inland, heading west from Lisbon's Praça Marquês de Pombal and through Monsanto Park (see p.112). There are exits just north of Oeiras, Carcavelos, Estoril and Cascais.

Estoril

Estoril first attracted visitors in the mid-18th century, when liver complaints were treated at the thermal baths. During the first half of the 20th century, many an exiled monarch found either this town or neighbouring Cascais an agreeable retreat from where they could dream of restoration. This was the home of the ex-kings of Romania, Bulgaria and Italy, as well as the claimants to the thrones of Spain, France and the Austro-Hungarian Empire. These days the residents are more likely to be retired and rich Portuguese, while visitors come largely for the golf and other sports facilities.

The railway station at Estoril is right next to the beach. On the other side of the tracks (and the busy Avenida Marginal) is a formal park with disciplined ranks of palm trees, shrubs, flower beds and ponds. You'll find the **Tourist Information Office** near the southwest corner of the park, just off the Marginal.

The park acts as the front lawn of the town's glitzy **casino**, which is owned by Macau tycoon, Stanley Ho. With its nightclub, restaurants, bars, cinema, exhibition halls, shops and gaming rooms, this is Estoril's one-stop after-dark amusement centre. Tour groups and excursions from Lisbon take in the combined dinner and show, a typical 'international spectacular' with cabaret turns, big production numbers and the obligatory scantily clad showgirls.

In spite of the modern decor, the casino – which employs about 200 croupiers – maintains an old-fashioned pace. Gambling – roulette, baccarat, blackjack, craps and a Portuguese game called French Bank – is suspended only two nights a year: on Good Friday and Christmas Eve. According to legend, one lucky gambler once broke the bank on Good Friday, prompting a superstitious management to declare it a holiday thenceforth. The 300 or so slot-machines are ready to relieve you of any

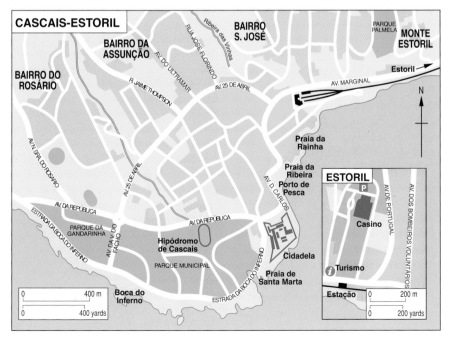

Crowds flock from Lisbon at weekends in summer to soak up the sun and throng the beach at Estoril, once the preserve of the retiring rich.

change you may have left. There's more evening diversion during July and August, when a **craft fair** sets up its stalls in the open air in the nearby streets. A summer music festival brings international artists and orchestras (see p.40).

In the quieter avenues off the park and up the hill, Victorian villas and sleek modern mansions sit in discreet solitude behind green curtains of palms, eucalyptus, pines and vines. Hotels tend towards the expensive and exclusive, unlike the beach, which can be packed with locals and Lisbon day-trippers. Unfortunately, the purity of the seawater is suspect this close to the mouth of the Tagus, although efforts to clean it up are said to be in hand.

Cascais

The railway continues along the shore for just another 2km (1.2 miles), running parallel to the Avenida Marginal, which cuts inland when the coast turns south. Were it not for the signs, you could hardly tell where Estoril ends and Cascais begins. There's a distinctly different atmosphere in Cascais though, for while Estoril is all resort, its neighbour lives a double life, in which fishermen coexist with the retiring rich and camera-toting tourists. Something is always going on at the fishermen's beach, **Praia da Ribeira**, even on holidays when the little blue, yellow and red boats are in port or dragged up on the sand. That's when groups of fishermen in Sunday suits gather to trade stories and local children turn the beach into a football field.

The workaday fishing scene attracts visitors to inspect the catch as it is unloaded from the boats into wooden trays, then rushed to the modern auction building. There the fish is sold by a reverse (Dutch)

Cascais became a popular summer escape from Lisbon in the 19th century, and then a place where those who could afford it retired to. Now it's a holiday resort as well as a working fishing port.

auction, in which the price starts high and decreases until somebody shouts a bid. You might not understand the auctioneer's chant, but you'll like the look of what he's selling – lobster, shrimp, hake, sardines and squid. Retail sales are in the hands of local fishwives who set up stalls outside the market. For the finished product, try any of the dozen or so restaurants within walking distance. The other beach, Praia da Rainha, is nominally for sunning and swimming, but it's cramped and the water is none too clean. Most visitors stick to their hotel pools.

The **main square** of Cascais is charming, with undulating designs in its mosaic pavement and a modern statue of King Pedro I, crowned tall and majestic. The Paços do Concelho (town hall) has stately windows with iron railings, separated by panels of *azulejos* depicting saints. The fire department occupies a place of honour between the town hall and a disused but attractive church. You'll find the **Tourist Information** not far away at Alameda Combatentes da Grande Guerra, No 25.

King Luis popularized Cascais in the 19th century when the royal family used the imposing 17th-century fort called the **Cidadela** (citadel) as a summer retreat. It was one of the few buildings to have survived the earthquake and tidal wave of 1755, and is now used for occasional official receptions and concerts. In a small chapel within the walls is kept the image of St Anthony, which is traditionally borne on the back of a white mule when Cascais celebrates a religious festival and procession.

On a hot day, the municipal park, Parque Marechal Carmona across the road from the Cidadela, is a cool relief. Beneath tall trees, swans preen beside ponds which are brimming with red and silver carp. The palace in this park is a museum – the **Museu dos Condes de Castro Guimarães**

– with archaeological relics, art works, old furniture, gold and silver. One prize exhibit is a 16th-century illuminated manuscript with a detailed picture of Lisbon harbour at the time of the great discoveries.

West of Cascais

The road west passes **Boca do Inferno** (Mouth of Hell), a geological curiosity where, in rough weather, the waves send up great spouts of spray, accompanied by ferocious sound effects. Nearby, an informal market has evolved selling all sorts of souvenirs, cheap clothing and the full gamut of plastic and trash. Just after the Farol da Guia lighthouse, a turning to the right leads into the **Marinha** country club, with golf, tennis and an equestrian centre.

The Costa do Estoril turns the corner at Cabo Raso and heads north to **Guincho** (or you can take the direct road across the headland), the first place on this coast where the water is likely to be clean. There's a choice of a sandy beach or rocks to fish from, but be careful, they face the open Atlantic. Often rough enough to suit expert surfers seeking the perfect wave, it has been the venue for international competitions. An old fort has been turned into a luxury hotel, and a number of good restaurants compete for your custom.

Just up the coast from Guincho you can see the windswept **Cabo da Roca**, the most westerly point of mainland Europe, marked by a lighthouse and souvenir shop. Neither is particularly attractive and the

*T*he plain pink exterior of the 18th-century palace of Queluz hardly prepares you for the elaborate flourishes that hide within.

views are not much different from those at many other points, but summer days still generate lines of traffic. If you want to visit this geographical extreme without the crowds, go early or late in the day. Beyond the cape, the long stretch of Praia Grande ('big beach'), Praia Pequena ('little beach') and Praia das Maçãs are too windy to attract large scale development. Further north, land has been designated a nature reserve and there's no coastal road at all until just before Ericeira (see p.139).

Queluz

Conveniently visited from Lisbon or anywhere on the Costa do Estoril, this pink rococo palace lies 14km (8 miles) west of the capital. Some organized excursions include Queluz, or you can drive here yourself. If you're coming from Lisbon, take the motorway from Campo Grande, or head through Monsanto Park and fork right (towards Sintra). You're scarcely out of Lisbon's mushrooming suburbs when you reach the sprawling palace. Alternatively, you can catch a commuter train from Rossio station to Queluz.

The **palace** was built for the Infante Pedro in the mid-18th century by Mateus Vicente de Oliveira and later extended by the French architect Jean-Baptiste Robillon, who also designed the superb gardens. It became the main official residence of the royal family in 1777 on the accession of Maria I, who had married Pedro, her uncle. However, the unfortunate queen suffered frequent fits of depression and eventually declined into madness. In 1799 the future King João VI took over as Prince Regent. He preferred other palaces, however, so by the time the French General Junot took Queluz as his headquarters in 1807 at the start of the Peninsular War (see p.55), the court had long since departed.

From the road, the palace seems relatively plain. Restraint is abandoned on the inside, however, where you'll find an endless succession of rooms swamped in

shabby splendour. The **throne room** is the most lavish of all, with walls and ceilings burdened with gilt and overpowering chandeliers. The Hall of Ambassadors has a floor like a huge chessboard, with many mirrors, and thrones at the far end. As you wander round, you will realise that Queluz is curiously laid out, with public rooms bordering living quarters almost incoherently.

The **gardens** go on and on with high clipped hedges in geometric array and bushes barbered into inventive shapes. Huge old magnolia trees and productive orange groves relieve some of the formality (don't pick the fruit!). Royal guests would have entered the garden via the pompous but original *Escadaria dos Leões* (Lions' Staircase). The fountains include some surprising statuary, such as sea monsters with faces like Pekinese dogs. During the early 19th century, dozens of live animals – not just dogs, but lions and wolves – were boarded at Queluz, which was then the site of the royal zoo. One rather original feature of the gardens is a controllable river, which is enclosed between walls covered in precious painted *azulejos*. This was created by diverting a stream to pass through the palace grounds, which was then dammed to raise the water level whenever royal residents wanted to take a boat ride.

If you time your visit right, you can stay for lunch in the royal kitchen. With giant old utensils, a huge fireplace and loads of atmosphere, the place is (logically) called **Cozinha Velha** – the old kitchen. It's a highly regarded restaurant run by the government *Pousada* group, which has plans to convert another historic building at Queluz into one of the chain's luxury hotels.

Most museums are closed on Monday, but Queluz takes Tuesday off – and any other day when visiting heads of state are in residence.

Sintra

'Lo! Cintra's glorious Eden intervenes, in variegated maze of mount and glen', wrote Lord Byron, while subjecting everything else about Portugal and the Portuguese to withering scorn. Artists and poets have enthused over Sintra for centuries. Lying west of Queluz and north of Cascais, a miniature mountain range catches the sea breezes, trapping moisture which nourishes the lush vegetation. Palaces, mansions and lovely gardens are half hidden on the forested hillsides. In days gone by, those who could afford to escape the summer heat of Lisbon retreated to this 'earthly paradise' (another often repeated accolade). Today, its fame attracts inevitable crowds and traffic, but even at a busy time a visit is worthwhile, although it's better to come early or late in the day. You can take in the two biggest palaces on an organized tour or easy day trip from Lisbon or Estoril, but ideally you should spend longer and preferably stay overnight to appreciate the atmosphere when the growling mass of tour buses has gone. As a bonus, the major monuments are floodlit at night.

Coming from Lisbon by road, you'll first reach the village of São Pedro de Sintra, which is known for its market (see p.137). The main town, Sintra-Vila, is another 4km (2·5 miles) west. Trains arrive at the station in the Estefânia district, just north of Sintra-Vila, and the **Tourist Information** is in the centre of Sintra-Vila, close to the Palácio Nacional. There are some wonderful walks, but the climbing and the distances between palaces and other attractions are better tackled on foot only by the fit and healthy.

Two massive conical chimneys render the **Palácio Nacional** an unmistakeable landmark, dominating this part of town. Note that on various maps and signs it's also

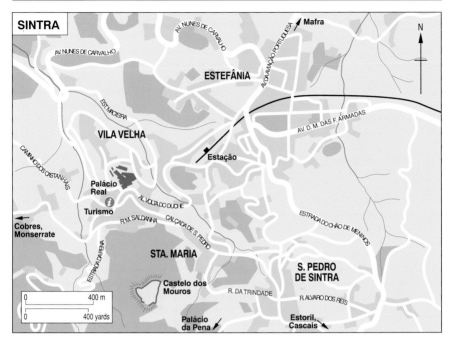

called the *Paço Real* (Royal Palace), *Paço da Sintra* and *Paço da Vila* (Town Palace). If you're driving, there's a large car park next to it. (The palace is closed on Wednesday.) The outside may look a little shabby, but the interior is full of treasures and is a fascinating medley of styles. The façade gives some clues, with its arabesque and Manueline windows, for this has been a summer home for Portuguese kings since the 14th century, and its architecture has become more and more mixed as wings were added over the centuries. Some of the oldest and most valuable *azulejos* in Portugal

A former royal residence, the rambling Palácio Nacional, with its twin conical chimneys, dominates the centre of Sintra-Vila.

A neo-Moorish fountain, where people fill plastic bottles with Sintra's fresh spring water.

are to be seen here, notably in the *Sala dos Árabes*, where the blue and green tiles date from the 15th century. The fountain here may have come from a Moorish palace which once stood on this site.

Every room of the Royal Palace has a story. For instance: in the 17th century the dull-witted Afonso VI was forced into abdicating for the good of the country, making way for his more effective brother, Pedro II. When a plot to restore Afonso to the throne was discovered, the former monarch was exiled to Sintra. For nine years, until he died in 1683, he was imprisoned in a simple room of the Royal Palace, where it's said that the worn floor is the result of his pacing up and down.

A spacious hall known as the *Sala das Pêgas* tells a more sprightly story, for this is where King João I (1385-1433) was caught in the act of kissing one of Queen Philippa's ladies-in-waiting. The king's response to wagging tongues was to say '*por bem*' (in a good cause) and to have the ceiling painted with 136 magpies – one for each lady-in-waiting – their mouths sealed with the same motto. Several other ceilings are worth craning your neck for, including that in the Manueline banqueting hall or *Sala dos Cisnes*, which is decorated with pictures of 27 swans in gold collars, each in a different position. The compartmented dome in the *Sala dos Brasões* features the crests of the noble families of the early 16th century, while other precious ceilings are decorated in the *mudéjar* style influenced by Moorish art.

In the kitchens you'll see inside those strange and enormous chimneys. Shaped like upside-down ice-cream cones, they were designed to draw up smoke when whole oxen were spit-roasted for a great royal feast.

Moorish Castle and Gothic Fantasy

The ruined **Castelo dos Mouros** (Moorish Castle) hugs a rocky ridge overlooking the town. It was probably built in the 8th or 9th century, soon after the Moors occupied Portugal, and Afonso Henriques and his crusaders took it in 1147. The crenellated ramparts are still impressive, but there's little left behind them to protect. A horseshoe-shaped Arab arch survives from the Moorish period, as well as parts of the chapel built after the Christian conquest, with Romanesque doorways and traces of wall paintings. The 10-minute walk from the road is well worth it for the views.

On the hilltop further up the same winding road, at over 450m (1500ft) above sea level, stands the **Palácio da Pena** (or Castelo da Pena), a rambling Romantic folly reached by way of a park so lush with flowering trees and vines it seems like a tropical rainforest. In 1511 King Manuel I ordered a monastery built on this site, but it was mostly destroyed in the earthquake of 1755. The present cocktail of Gothic, Renaissance, Manueline and Moorish architecture was designed as

*F*rom the ramparts of the Castelo dos Mouros, above Sintra, you can look across to the Palácio da Pena on the next hilltop.

a romantic retreat for Queen Maria II (1834-53) and her husband Ferdinand of Saxe-Coburg-Gotha. You enter across a mock drawbridge and through a tunnel. A diversion leads to a chapel and genuine Manueline cloister which survived the earthquake: the reredos is credited to the French sculptor Chanterenne, who worked on many of King Manuel's projects.

The interior is even more bizarre than the outside, with a succession of rooms decorated in painstaking pastiches of a dozen styles. The furniture is equally remarkable, and everything has been left just as it was when the royal family fled in 1910, following the deposition of Manuel II. On a clear day the view from the terraces sweeps all the way from the Atlantic to Lisbon. The heroic statue on a rocky crag was a piece of self-glorification by the architect of this fantasy castle, the German Baron Eschwege. (The palace is closed on Monday and public holidays.)

At the bottom of the steep driveway down from the Pena Palace, a road to the left (before you pass the Castelo dos Mouros) leads to the strange **Convento dos Capuchos**, once a hermits' retreat in the woods but long since abandoned. It comprises no more than a dozen grim little rock-cut chambers made more comfortable by a lining of cork (hence the nickname of the 'Cork Convent'). This would not only have kept the inmates warmer and drier, and reduced the noise level to assist contemplation, but it would have also cushioned the blows when their bald heads hit the low ceilings in the dark.

Seteais and Monserrate

A little way west of the centre of Sintra-Vila, the **Palácio de Seteais** (fancifully explained as 'seven sighs') is one of the most beautiful of the private palaces. Dating from the end of the 18th century, it was built for the Dutch consul in Lisbon, whose evident wealth came from his diamond business. It is now a luxury hotel, but even if you aren't staying, you are welcome to stroll in the main garden. The elegant central arch is said to have been added to mark a visit by João VI when he was Regent. You'll find that it leads to a terrace with a superb view down to the plain and up to the Castelo dos Mouros. If you use the hotel's bar or formal restaurant, you'll be able to take a look inside. The elegant public rooms are beautifully furnished with antiques.

Just over 2km (1.2 miles) further along the road, the **Quinta de Monserrate** was the home of a succession of wealthy Englishmen who liked to entertain in grand style. In the 1790s, the immensely rich and eccentric William Beckford lived here in a now vanished house, after fleeing from a homosexual scandal in England. The chief reason to visit now is the 30ha (75 acres) of subtropical gardens, rambling across the hillside. They were first laid out by English gardeners in the 1850s for Sir Francis Cook, a London textile merchant, and no expense was spared in importing exotic plants and even Etruscan tombs – which can still be seen. The Victorian-Moghul fantasy of a house, with its round towers, bulbous cupolas and elaborate decoration owing more to the Brighton Pavilion in England than any Indian original, was built for Cook at the same time. King Ferdinand was so impressed by the whole scheme that he awarded Cook the title of Viscount Monserrate. The estate became national property half a century ago, but lack of resources meant that large parts of the gardens were long left untended and the house is now empty and decaying. Monserrate today is a great, cool, shady forest park with magnificent trees and an

COUNTRY FAIR

On the second and fourth Sunday of the month, a huge market takes over the adjacent village of São Pedro do Sintra (allow time for even worse traffic than usual). In the engrossing open market, you can buy homemade bread, cheese and sausages, or a bottle of patent medicine sold by an old-fashioned, slick-talking hawker. There's an endless array of pottery, basketry, wood carvings, rustic furniture, religious statues and household goods. Antique collectors can have a fine time trying to tell the genuine from the fake, and anyone is welcome to rummage through a range of bric à brac, bygones and junk.

Here or in Sintra's pastry shops, ask for a packet of *queijadas*, miniature cheesecakes in paper-thin crusts. These local specialities may be the most delicate little cakes you'll come across anywhere in this sweet-toothed country.

extraordinary variety of species from all around the world.

Beyond Monserrate, the road descends to the hillside village of **Colares**, which is famous for its red wine. The original was so dark and tannic that it needed years in the bottle to mature, like the best Bordeaux, but it travelled well. Little is grown these days, but you may find the name on bottles of lighter red wines.

Mafra

The dimensions of the convent and palace of Mafra, 40km (25 miles) north west of Lisbon, are staggering. The frontage is often likened to Spain's Escorial but the similarity is only one of size, for Mafra is much less forbidding. In terms of length, though, it just has the edge, measuring in at over 220m (more than 700ft). According to one count, there are 7,000 windows and doors. The monumental project was conceived by King João V to mark the birth of an heir to the throne, as well as to proclaim his own religious fervour. Construction began in 1717, directed by a German architect with Italian experience named Ludwig (or Ludovice). As many as 50,000 artists, artisans and labourers *at a time* were engaged, finishing the work in an extraordinarily short 18 years. Money was no object: only the seemingly endless shipments of gold from Brazil could have made it possible. This is marble country, and on the trip from Lisbon you'll see marble quarries, mansions made entirely of marble, and even ordinary houses decorated – on walls, steps and patios – with mosaics of marble chips.

Marble is also used liberally in the **basilica** of the Mafra complex, where original effects are achieved by contrasting colours: white, black and shades of blue, red-brown and yellow. The statues are noteworthy, too, some being made of the almost luminous white Carrara marble from Italy.

Much of the convent building is in military hands and not open to the public, but a guided tour still takes you through an endless succession of chambers, corridors, staircases and galleries. The highlight is the great baroque **library**, with its vaulted ceiling, elaborate gilding and shelves housing over 30,000 books. It is much vaster than the library at Coimbra (see p.170), but dates from around the same time.

The convent **hospital** was designed so that patients in the 16 private sick-rooms could hear (and see) mass in the adjoining chapel without having to move from their beds. In the pharmacy, along with fine old apothecary jars, there is a gruesome display of some rather primitive medical tools.

With luck you may be in Mafra on the day of a carillon concert – usually heard

As many as 50,000 workers at a time laboured to build the colossal convent and palace of Mafra, sited close to vast marble quarries.

On the direct road back towards Sintra, you can see the remains of an important **Roman villa** site at the village of Odrinhas, with a large area of restored mosaic floor and part of a very early Christian church. The archaelogical museum at the site has an extensive collection of inscribed stones from the Roman and Visigoth eras.

in the late afternoon. Operated by an 18th-century Dutch machine the size of a house, the mellow tones of the carillon's 140 bells can be enjoyed for miles around. When the Flemish bell founders who cast them received João V's order, the story goes that they wrote back questioning whether he really wanted so many, in view of the enormous price they would have to charge. The king's response was to send twice the advance payment they had specified.

Ericeira

Another 10km (6 miles) further on from Mafra brings you to the coast and Ericeira, an attractive fishing town and resort which is a good place to have lunch. In 1910, King Manuel II and his family arrived here in less-than-leisurely style, having just received word at their apartments at Mafra of the Republican revolution in Lisbon. It was to Ericeira that they fled in order to board the royal yacht and sail into exile.

The town is expanding now, with apartments, villas and a few hotels on the outskirts. The old centre is charming, with unusually clean and narrow cobblestone streets, and whitewashed houses trimmed with blue and yellow. Life centres on the Praça da Republica with its open-air cafés, and along Rua Eduardo Burnay, which leads to the main beach. Restaurants overlooking the sea specialize in the fresh fish brought in by the local fleet.

South of Lisbon – the 'Costa Azul'

If you cross the Tagus by ferry or the Ponte 25 de Abril to see the statue of Christ the King, it's only another 10km (6 miles) to a fine stretch of beach, the Costa da Caparica. This is just one corner of a peninsula which is 30km (19 miles) wide and has varied scenery planted with olive and citrus orchards, with cows grazing among the trees. Further south, vineyards predominate – the Azeitão district produces a range of wines and the Setúbal region a well known muscatel.

The southern shore is sheltered by the mountain ridge of the Serra da Arrábida, which has been designated a national park. South from here is Sesimbra, a growing resort and an attractive old fishing town, from where a road runs west to the tip of the peninsula and bleak Cabo Espichel, an ancient sanctuary and pilgrimage centre. In the opposite direction from Sesimbra, at the eastern end of the peninsula is Setúbal, Portugal's third largest port and a city of great character, which looks southwards across the nature reserve of the Sado estuary (known for its bird life). Across the River Sado, the Tróia peninsula is a long finger of sand with superb beaches on the ocean side and a holiday resort at the northern end. Up river, the quaint old port of Alcácer do Sal is worth a special visit or a diversion.

Costa da Caparica

This is the nearest beach to Lisbon which can guarantee clean water, and it's becoming more and more popular with city people. Facing the open Atlantic, it can be windy and the sea may be too rough for anyone but seasoned surfers. The northern end of a huge arc of sand is lined by apartment buildings, gradually tailing off into a semi-legal shanty town as you go south. The road soon gives up, but a little railway with open carriages runs quite a way further to a series of numbered stops. The first few stops serve mainly family-oriented beaches, while some of the more distant sections are predominantly gay or nudist, or both.

Setúbal

The district capital is an easy 50km (31-mile) drive from Lisbon. The bus does it in one hour, or you can take the ferry across the Tagus and then the leisurely local train – a total of an hour and a half. Setúbal is not only a market town for the region, but also a major fishing port and a big shipbuilding and industrial centre, home to extensive docks and many processing plants. Don't miss the action in the fishermen's quarter at the western end of the waterfront when the brightly painted boats of all sizes return with the catch. This is a busy working city, but there are more parks, squares, statues and monuments than you would expect for its size, and narrow, inviting shopping streets twist through the old centre. If you have a car, look for a parking space in one of the paying areas along the central Avenida Luisa Todi.

It's pleasant to walk in the alleys around the Largo da Misericórdia, where the smell of roasting coffee may entice you to stop for a cup. The **Tourist Information** is close at hand in Rua da Corpo Santo, and also worth visiting is the regional tourism office nearby in Avenida Luisa Todi: it has a glass floor revealing the ancient Roman fish-salting tanks that were used as the foundations of an earlier building on the site!

Setúbal's greatest historical and artistic treasure, the **Igreja de Jesus**, comes as a surprise, half-hiding on the edge of the city centre and below the present street level. (Its newly-paved, sunken plaza with sloping sides has turned out to be a perfect arena for daredevil skateboarders.) The church was built shortly before 1500 by the French architect Boytac, who later created the magnificent Jerónimos monastery at Belém. Here in Setúbal he introduced some of the elements which were to become trademarks of the Manueline style. A dramatic main portal carved from reddish aggregrate (a 'natural concrete') leads to a simple vaulted interior made extraordinary by the use of stone pillars carved into twisted rope. The rope motif appears again on a smaller scale in the ribs of the apse, which is strikingly lined with 17th-century *azulejos*.

The adjoining monastery has now been converted into the town **museum**, with a wide-ranging collection including Roman and other archaeological relics, jewellery, coins, furniture and tiles. The stars of the show are the Portuguese 'Primitives', paintings of the 16th century, and some Flemish originals, which inspired the local artists. They've recently been cleaned and restored, so that the details and colours emerge with jewel-like brilliance – controversial but indisputably stunning. Fourteen of the panels displayed were painted in the Lisbon studio of Jorge Afonso in the 1520s to make up a great altar piece for the Igreja de Jesus. The largest, a powerful Crucifixion, was central in the top row; the Assumption, with its vivid golden-yellow background, was at the centre. The cloister was reconstructed after the 1755 earthquake, but excavation has revealed parts of the original patio. Not far away, facing the gracious little oval of Praça do Bocage, the **Igreja de São Julião** was rebuilt with two remarkable portals after the Manueline style had caught on.

If you've always dreamed of staying in a castle, now is your chance. The Fortress of São Filipe near Setúbal is one of the hotels operated by the Pousada chain.

The 16th-century **Fortress of São Filipe** above the town to the west dates from the Spanish occupation and the need to deter pirates (and the English). It's now a comfortable *Pousada*, a government owned hotel (see p.22), with a sweeping view. High on a ridge 6km (4 miles) north of Setúbal, just off the main road to Lisbon, the **Castle of Palmela** was once the headquarters of the knightly Order of Santiago and subsequently a monastery. Wrecked by the 1755 earthquake, it fell into ruin. Now it too has been restored and in 1979 opened as an even more luxurious *Pousada* with even more outstanding views. The monks' refectory houses the restaurant.

Serra da Arrábida

West of Setúbal a steep ridge 35km (22 miles) long and up to 500m (1650ft) high shelters the coast from the north winds and accounts for the Mediterranean vegetation. Almost the whole of the ridge has been designated a nature reserve, although the coast road has been disfigured by a cement factory. Once past the Fortress of São Filipe (see above), it soon starts to climb away from the sea, but look out on the left for a turn down to **Portinho da Arrábida**. Here you'll find a fine, spacious and sheltered beach, not usually too crowded, and excellent facilities for water sports, as well as a good restaurant.

Sesimbra

As well as being a growing resort, Sesimbra is still a working fishing town. In the morning the entire adult male population seems to be occupied on or near the beach, mending nets and taking the knots out of the tough plastic fishing lines. Next to a little fort built to protect the harbour, the beach is narrow but quite long, sheltered from the brunt of Atlantic waves and

141

*S*heltered from the north winds and Atlantic waves, Portinho da Arrábida, on the southern shore of the Arrábida peninsula, is a popular watersports centre *(above)*.

*T*he Moorish ramparts of the old citadel, rebuilt by Frankish crusaders, high above present-day Sesimbra. There's little inside to be defended nowadays *(below)*.

winds. Claims of 'a high iodine content' in the water can be taken with a pinch of salt: you're hardly likely to eat the seaweed or swallow enough seawater for it to make a difference. Holiday developments are now spreading over the hillsides, but they're reasonably unobtrusive.

The **castle walls**, silhouetted on the hilltop above Sesimbra, are the genuine article (though recently restored). In the Middle Ages the whole town was situated up there, protected against sea raiders by the ramparts and altitude. The Moors built the enclave, lost it to King Afonso Henriques in 1165, won it back again for a few years, then had to move out for good in 1200. Not much is left inside the walls, but it's still worth the 6km (4-mile) ride from present-day Sesimbra. A small but interesting archaeological museum has been set up in a room attached to the castle's 12th-century church, and the view down

to the curve of the coast and back to the Arrábida mountains is splendid. Three squat white **windmills** are survivors of a vastly greater number now vanished (although Portugal still has far more windmills left than Holland).

The dreary and windswept promontory southwest of Sesimbra ends at Cabo Espichel, a sailors' nightmare which attracts the most merciless Atlantic breakers. This is just the place for a lighthouse, but it's also the unlikely setting for the sanctuary of **Nossa Senhora do Cabo** (Our Lady of the Cape), where pilgrims have been coming since the Middle Ages. The two rows of arcaded buildings facing each other across the front of the 17th-century church were built to house the pilgrims, and an aqueduct was built to bring water. Sadly, the whole ensemble is now in a state of decay.

A different way back to Setúbal follows an inland route on the north side of the Serra da Arrábida. This is wine-growing country, and in Vila Nogueira de Azeitão you can tour the cellars of one of the best known producers, José Maria da Fonseca (and taste some of the wines). They still make the traditional dessert wine of the region, as well as dry reds and whites. On the outskirts of the town, the similarly-named but quite separate J.M. Fonseca Internacional also welcomes visitiors to its big modern winery.

The Tróia Peninsula

Just across the broad Sado river from Setúbal is a narrow sand spit, 18km (11 miles) long, with beaches stretching along the whole length of the seaward side. The **Torralta resort complex** has sprung up at the northern tip of the Tróia peninsula, with a golf course, tennis courts and holiday apartment blocks with pools. Discos and

The windswept Cabo Espichel was a popular place of pilgrimage for centuries.

supermarkets open in summer to cater to the holiday crowds. If you want more solitude, stroll south along the beach, or drive a short distance and walk through the dunes to the sea. Alternatively, go out of season, when the place becomes a ghost town.

On the sheltered shore facing the Sado estuary, extensive **Roman ruins** are almost certainly those of *Cetobriga*, a fishing and fish-preserving centre which tradition says was overwhelmed by the sea in the 5th century, perhaps by a tidal wave or maybe due to silting up. To reach the site, head south along the peninsula for 3.5km (2 miles) and take the sandy track to the left signposted 'Ruinas Romanas'. After another 3km (1.8 miles) you'll come to the shore, a little fishing settlement, and the entrance to the excavations. The main visible features are fish-salting tanks as large as 3m (10ft) square, port buildings, tombs and baths with traces of mosaic and marble lining. It seems certain that there is much more still to be uncovered. The name of Cetobriga, slightly modified, was eventually taken by

a new site, today's Setúbal.

From Setúbal to Tróia by land is a journey of over 100km (62 miles), but in summer you can be there in five minutes by fast passenger ferry. The car ferry runs every half hour in summer (and every hour for the rest of the year), taking 20 minutes, but it carries only about 30 vehicles, so at busy times drivers may face a long wait (especially for the return journey). If you have a car, you can make the best of this by returning the long way round, along the peninsula and east through Alcácer do Sal. The wetlands of the estuary (a nature reserve) are renowned amongst bird watchers and the whole area, with its mud flats, salt pans, still waters and silence, has an intriguing strangeness. Pine trees growing on the sand are tapped for their resin, and there's a scattering of cork trees and little isolated farms on the more fertile pockets.

Alcácer do Sal

Mercifully bypassed by the heavy traffic that thunders between Lisbon and the south, the quiet old town of Alcácer do Sal seems to have been forgotten by the 20th century. Picturesque houses, all white and tiled in red, spread along a rambling promenade on one side of the Sado, beneath the ramparts of a castle. Athough more than 40km (25 miles) from the sea, this was an ancient port, founded by the Phoenicians, important under the Romans and a Moorish stronghold. The name derives from the Arabic *Al Ksar*, meaning 'the walled city', while *do Sal* ('of salt') refers to the trade in salt, which is so essential for preserving fish. There are still salt pans on the Sado estuary, but the main activity around Alcácer is agricultural, growing rice and raising cattle.

The **Tourist Information** faces the river, and as in all the towns on the 'Costa Azul', it has particulary good literature. Next to Largo Pedro Nunes, in the lovely Espírito Santo church is the **museum**, where with the aid of some good displays you can get to grips with prehistory. There are also some striking Roman relics, including a stone carving showing a bullfighter on horseback. A climb to the **castle** is worthwhile for the views across the salt marshes and down to the town, where whole families of storks nest in the church towers. Like almost all castle churches in Portugal, the Romanesque 13th-century church is dedicated to Santa Maria.

(For the area south of Alcácer do Sal, see p.282.)

145

Architecture to Inspire, Resorts for Relaxation

Portugal's 'Silver Coast' stretches for over 250km (155 miles) from north of Lisbon to just south of Oporto. Sand and sea give way to many historic sights inland, including the abbeys of Alcobaça and Batalha, architectural masterpieces that are landmarks in Portugal's history. In addition, you'll find Óbidos, one of the prettiest medieval walled towns in the country, and Nazaré, a picturesque fishing village that has turned into a major resort. Fátima remains a magnet for Catholic pilgrims, while Tomar is home to one of the most extraordinary achievements of 16th-century Manueline design, the Chapter House of the Convento do Cristo.

Tour companies offer long day trips from Lisbon covering some of the greatest attractions in the southern part of the area. If you are travelling independently, you can see all these and more at greater leisure by staying overnight at Nazaré, Óbidos or Tomar. Further north, the old university city of Coimbra, the nation's capital before Lisbon, could serve as a base, or if you prefer the coast, the lively resort of

*T*he breezy Atlantic coast was perfect for harnessing windpower in bygone days. Most windmills have gone now, but Portugal still has more left than The Netherlands.

Figueira da Foz, where Wellington's expeditionary force landed in 1808.

Anyone following in the Duke's footsteps (see p.88) has plenty of ground to cover in the Costa da Prata. North of Mafra (see p.137), the town of **Torres Vedras** gave its name to Wellington's lines of defence running from the Atlantic to the River Tagus. This series of hilltop strongpoints was built on his orders to protect Lisbon, and was held by the British and Portuguese forces during the winter of 1810-11. The French battered against them, but were forced to retreat and eventually quit Portugal altogether. Dedicated students of military history can find traces of the Lines of Torres Vedras on the ridge above the town.

Vimeiro, nearer the coast, was the site of Wellington's second victory over the French at the start of the Peninsular War

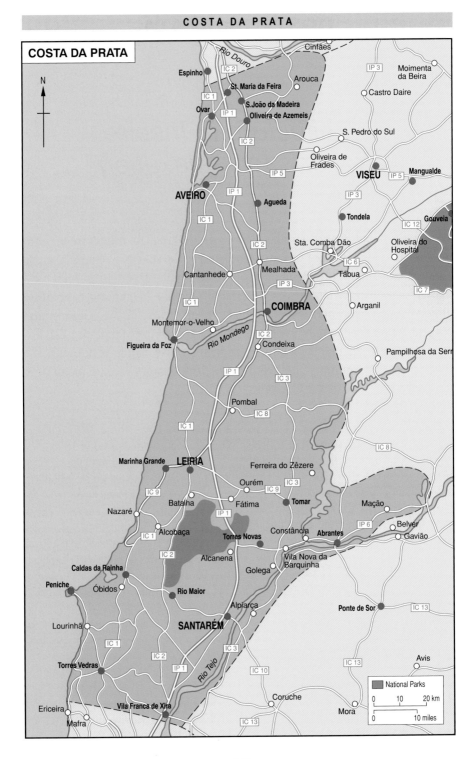

COSTA DA PRATA

N

Rio Douro

Cinfães

IP 3 Moimenta da Beira

Espinho

IC 2

Arouca

Castro Daire

St. Maria da Feira

IC 1

S.João da Madeira

Ovar IP 1

Oliveira de Azemeis

S. Pedro do Sul

IC 2

Oliveira de Frades

IP 5

VISEU IP 5 Mangualde

AVEIRO IP 1

IP 3

Agueda

IC 1

Tondela

IC 12 Gouveia

IC 2

Sta. Comba Dão

Oliveira do Hospital

IC 6

Cantanhede

Mealhada

Tábua

IP 3

IC 1

COIMBRA

Arganil

IC 7

Montemor-o-Velho

Rio Mondego

IC 2

Condeixa

Figueira da Foz

Pampilhosa da Serr

IP 1

IC 3

Pombal

IC 8

IC 1

IC 8

Marinha Grande LEIRIA

Ferreira do Zêzere

Ourém IC 3

IC 9

IC 9

Batalha Fátima

Tomar

Mação

Nazaré

IP 1

Constância

IP 6 Belver

IC 1

Alcobaça

Abrantes

Gavião

IC 2

Torres Novas

Alcanena

Vila Nova da Barquinha

Caldas da Rainha

Golega

Peniche Óbidos

Rio Maior

Alpiarça

Ponte de Sor IC 13

Lourinhã

SANTARÉM

IC 1

IC 3

Avis

IC 2

Rio Tejo

IC 13

IP 1

IC 10

Torres Vedras

National Parks

0   10   20 km

Ericeira

Vila Franca de Xira

Coruche

Mora

Mafra

IC 13

0   10 miles

148

in 1807. **Roliça**, further north and close to the main road near Óbidos, was the site of his first. Like most battlefields of the past, there's nothing more than a monument at either place to show what happened, so you'll need to carry a detailed history and maps if you want to fit the engagement to the lie of the land.

Peniche

On the coast north of Torres Vedras, the old port of **Peniche** was once an island, but an accumulation of sand gradually joined it to the mainland to form the present peninsula. The road into town passes through a defensive wall built across the neck of land, and more fortifications guard the seaward side. These were built by the Spanish during the 16th century, to hold off pirates or the English – much the same thing, in Spanish eyes – at the time of Sir Francis Drake. More recent history is recalled in the **fort**, which is now a museum telling the story of the political prisoners who were held here during the Salazar regime. Local handicrafts are also on display.

The **fishing harbour** is usually packed with colourful, storm-battered craft and is flanked by some excellent informal fish restaurants. It's worth collecting a town map at the nearby tourist office, where you can also arrange accommodation – just follow the signs to the **Turismo**. Peniche's huge sweep of sandy **beach** (facing north) is a local favourite.

In fine weather (and calm seas) you might take a trip to the island and bird sanctuary of **Berlenga**, which lies 12km (7 miles) offshore. A ferry runs from Peniche every day between June and September, and twice a day in July and August, taking about an hour to get there.

*S**creeching gulls escort every fishing boat in hope of some scraps. Like many other west coast ports, Peniche has a new, deep-water harbour for its fleet.*

The island was once the site of a monastery, but that was abandoned long ago since it was too easy a target for pirates. The impressive 17th-century **fort** of São João Baptista still stands, on an islet joined to the main island by a narrow causeway. Plans were announced a few years ago to convert it into a *Pousada*, but as yet the island remains home only to innumerable seabirds, who share it with a lighthouse and a few fisherfolk. Since it is a national bird sanctuary, you must stick to the marked paths when exploring. A bar and restaurant operate in summer, and boatmen run trips around the wonderfully convoluted coast with its caverns, cliffs, tunnels and weird rock formations.

Óbidos

Almost too perfect to be true, this jewel of a town is completely encircled by its high medieval walls. Equally hard to believe, it was once a *coastal* fortress until the sea inlet here silted up, leaving the quiet Óbidos lagoon cut off and the shoreline 10km (6 miles) away.

From the main car park, you can enter the town through the narrow southern gateway, which is partly lined with blue *azulejos*. Alternatively, head round the outside of the walls to a second way in at the north end, guarded by the 13th-century **castle**, with its high square and round towers. This is now a luxurious *Pousada*, but you can

still take a look and enjoy the view from the ramparts. Down at street level, Rua Direita runs from one gate to the other.

The narrow streets inside the town walls are enchanting, lined with whitewashed houses which have been decorated with improbable quantities of flowers. The place has probably never looked so neat and clean in all its history and is inevitably popular with visitors – come early or late in the day if you want to avoid the crowds.

It's a pleasure just to stroll about, climbing up to the battlements here and there and walking along the safer sections. Nearby, the parish church, **Igreja de Santa Maria**, faces the main square. Take a look inside at its 18th-century *azulejos*,

the strange blue ceiling, and the elaborately gilded tomb in the north wall. In the chapel to the right of the altar, the paintings of the life of St Catherine are by the Spanish-born Josefa d'Ayala, who came to live and work in Óbidos and who the Portuguese have adopted as their own (they usually call her Josefa de Óbidos). She died here in 1684, one of the first women to break the gender barrier and be recognized as a great artist. Also facing the square, the **Museum** in the 16th-century town hall was established by the Gulbenkian Foundation (see p.118). Occupying three levels (don't miss the basements), its varied collection is well set out and includes some very fine statuary. Exhibits on the Peninsular War incorporate weaponry from both sides and a clear topographical model of the Lines of Torres Vedras. Two maps (one printed in London in 1790, one in Portugal in 1808) are probably just like the ones used by Wellington to plan his strategy.

Óbidos was traditionally the wedding gift of the kings of Portugal to their queens. Leonor, the wife of João II, was so impressed by the sulphurous mineral waters 5km (3 miles) to the north that she had a hospital built at the site in 1486, thus creating the spa of **Caldas da Rainha** ('The Queen's Hot Springs'). During its heyday in the 18th and 19th centuries, it attracted fashionable people from all over Portugal, and a number of attractive

*T*he white-washed houses of Óbidos are trimmed with yellow and blue and stand secure behind a complete medieval wall. The town is almost too perfect to be true.

houses survive from that period. Rheumatism, arthritis and respiratory complaints are said to be cured here, and sufferers still come in notable numbers to immerse themselves in the baths.

If you're not ailing, then try to come on a Monday, market day, when stalls cover the Praça da Republica. The town has a reputation for its (gaudy) ceramics, including caricature figurines, and big green salad bowls shaped like cabbage leaves.

São Martinho do Porto

This little fishing town on a shell-shaped bay has turned more rapidly into a resort than anywhere else on this coast. The attractions are the sheltered sandy beach and water which warms up to temperatures noticeably higher than anywhere that faces the open sea. Development has been haphazard and often ugly, but the mainly local crowd generates a cheerful atmosphere in summer. The rest of the year the place can seem almost deserted.

Nazaré

Nazaré (meaning Nazareth in Portuguese) is the old fishing village that you may well have come across in pictures, but which is almost swamped by resort development now. The traditional wide, flat-bottomed boats which were once pulled ashore by oxen – and then tractors – have gone now, and most fishing activity is concentrated at the new port on the southern outskirts.

Despite the effects of tourism and industry, though, some of the old charm lingers on. Fishermen here really do wear black stocking-caps and plaid trousers and women still appear in black shawls and bright embroidered aprons. Only the cos-

The old fishing village of Nazaré has become a holiday centre, but its souvenir dolls still wear the traditional seven petticoats.

tumed dolls in the souvenir shops still wear seven petticoats, however (one for each day of the week – so it is said). In the old town behind the waterfront, many of the white-washed houses have turned into restaurants, their tables half-blocking the narrow streets.

Until the 19th century, most people actually lived up on top of the 110m (360ft) cliff at the northern end of the beach, in the area called **Sítio** – a good vantage point from where to watch for marauding pirates. These days, the cliff top is easily reached by a funicular, or by road, and Sítio, with its new clusters of holiday villas, suits those wanting to stay somewhere quieter than Nazaré. The restaurants offer just as good quality as those down below and prices can be more attractive. The views are superb, too, across green hilly countryside, closely packed tile roofs and miles of beach. The church of Nossa Senhora da Nazaré on Sítio's big square is notable for some fine Dutch tiles, rather than the expected Portuguese *azulejos*. In summer, row after row of tents cover half of Nazaré's beach.

Be warned, the coast here is open to the full force of the Atlantic and the sea can be too rough for safe swimming. If the town beach is too noisy for you, head for the wild open shore north of Sítio.

Alcobaça

Portugal's largest church is a majestic former Cistercian monastery (*Abadia Real de Santa Maria*), built to celebrate the 1147 victory of Afonso Henriques over the Moors at Santarém. The main structure was finished in the early 13th century, but an ill-suited baroque façade was added to the west front five hundred years later. Fortunately, the original west door and rose window were left uncovered.

*P*opular west coast beaches look like the tented camps of an invading army every summer. Some sort of shelter from the wind is often needed.

The interior has been rigorously cleared of almost all the accretions of the centuries; tiles and paintings, statuary and gilding, whether Gothic, Manueline, Renaissance or baroque, have all been removed in an effort to return to the imagined purity of the original. The unadorned limestone is immensely impressive, especially the soaring nave.

In the transept, standing about 30m (100ft) apart, are the **tombs of King Pedro I** and his beloved **Inês de Castro**, their effigies facing each other so that on the day of resurrection they will see each other as soon as they open their eyes. Each tomb is inscribed with the words *Até ao*

*T*he monastery of Alcobaça contains some of Portugal's most magnificent stone-carving, on royal tombs and around doors and windows.

fim do mundo ('Until the end of the world'). The bearded Pedro and the serene Inês are each tended by six sturdy stone angels and the tombs are decorated with some of Portugal's greatest medieval carving, depicting scriptural scenes. The incredibly delicate sculpture was slightly damaged in 1810 by French soldiers looking for treasure when they sacked Alcobaça after their setback at Buçaco (see p.57). In a side chapel, Pedro's ancestors Afonso II and Afonso III are buried in less elaborate sarcophagi.

Don't fail to visit the cloisters and other areas on the north side of the church (you'll need to buy a ticket). The **Cloister of Dom Dinis** dates from the 14th century, with the upper storey added 200 years later. The elegant **chapter house** is adorned with the figures of saints, and next to it is the monks' hall, stepped like a lecture theatre; a flight of stairs in between leads up to a **dormitory**, its superbly vaulted ceiling supported by 20 stone columns.

The 18th-century **kitchen** is on a huge scale, with monumental tiled fireplaces and sinks as big as baths. The sound of running water comes from a small stream which was channelled directly through the kitchen, to bring in water and carry away waste. Next door is the **refectory**, with a perfect little fountain for the monks to wash their hands under a vaulted canopy opposite the door.

At the west corner of the cloister, near the main door of the church, the **Sala dos Reis** (Hall of the Kings) has an incomplete collection of statues of the Kings of Portugal. The *azulejos* here show the life of St Bernard and the history of Alcobaça.

PEDRO AND INÊS

Passion, murder and revenge are the themes of many a story from Portuguese history, but one above all still has the power to move and shock, over six centuries later.

Inês de Castro, the daughter of a Spanish nobleman, came to Portugal in 1340 as lady-in-waiting to her cousin, Constanza of Castile, who had married Pedro, the heir to the throne. Pedro fell instantly and deeply in love with Inês. His father King Afonso IV had her banished, but when Constanza died in 1345, Pedro sent for her. They lived together openly for ten years and she bore him four children. A faction of the nobility at court suspected her of promoting Spanish interests by influencing Pedro, and persuaded Afonso that she should be removed. In 1355, three of them went to her house, Quinta das Lágrimas at Coimbra, and murdered her in cold blood. Whether the king ordered the killing or tacitly approved it is not certain. Pedro definitely thought so, and took up arms against his father, although he was subsequently persuaded to make an uneasy peace.

When he came to the throne himself two years later, Pedro swore to the Cortes that he had been secretly married to Inês the year before her death. According to the story as told by the national poet Camões, he had her body disinterred from its grave at Coimbra and taken to the Old Cathedral (see p.169). There it was seated on a throne and crowned, and all the nobles were forced to kneel and kiss her hand. Then she was buried at Alcobaça, where Pedro was to join her in 1367. Two of her murderers were subsequently hunted down and executed at Santarém (see p.165), the third escaped.

Batalha

Northeast of Alcobaça on the road to Fátima, the many-turreted **Mosteiro da Batalha** (Monastery of the Battle) was consecrated to Santa Maria da Vitória in gratitude for another great military success. King João I ordered the construction of this Gothic masterpiece to mark his victory over the Castilians at nearby Aljubarrota in 1385. The exterior is a vision of pinnacles and stone tracery almost as delicate as lace. The fine **west door** is decorated with over 100 statues of apostles and saints, and a central figure of Christ.

Inside, immediately to the right of the entrance, lies the **Capela do Fundador** (Founder's Chapel), which was added just after the church was completed. In the centre, beneath a magnificent star-shaped vaulted ceiling, stands the massive double tomb of João I and his queen, Philippa of Lancaster, their effigies lying side by side and hand in hand. Traces of colouring are still evident in the carved coats of arms, for this bare stone would once have been a riot of red, purple and gold. Niches in the south wall hold the tombs of four of their sons, including Henry the Navigator.

The **Claustro Real** (Royal Cloister), like the church, began as a straightforward Gothic work but as construction continued a couple of centuries later, the Manueline style was superimposed. Thus the columns and arches are decorated with the most unrestrained fantasies in filigree stonework. By contrast, the carefully clipped hedges in the centre of the cloister are regimented in geometric patterns.

Portugal's Unknown Soldiers are buried in the monastery's **Chapterhouse** and guarded by two riflemen. This vaulted chamber, nearly 20m (65ft) square, was an engineering wonder in its day (around 1400). Because of fears that the unsupported ceiling would fall, the architect is

*T*he Gothic monastery church of Batalha was built on the orders of João I to mark the victory of his army and their English allies over the Castilians in 1385 (opposite).

*T*he arches of the Claustro Real were later embellished with Manueline stonecarving in 'organic' designs and the Cross of the Order of Christ.

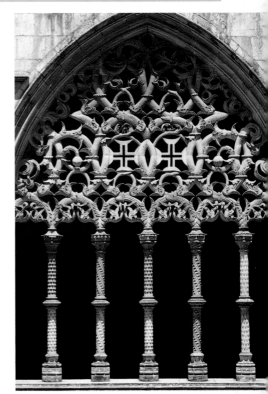

said to have employed only convicts under sentence of death to work on the project.

Be sure not to miss the last word of the Manueline architects, the **unfinished chapels** (*Capelas Imperfeitas*), which are attached to the eastern end of the church itself (access from outside only) and were intended as a royal mausoleum for Dom Duarte and his successors. Seven bays surround a central chamber, with the octagonal design completed by a breathtaking west door, carved into finely detailed tracery. Why was the project not finished? It seems that the fashion for this style of architecture vanished soon after the death of its patron, King Manuel, to be replaced by the geometric austerity of the Renaissance.

Just north of Batalha, **Leiria** is the chief town of the region and spreading fast. The old parts are worth exploring, particularly the imposing hilltop castle, visible from afar and often floodlit at night. This was first a Roman base, and then a Moorish stronghold for four centuries. Once through the gate in its outer wall, you'll see the chapel of Nossa Senhora da Penha, built around 1400 and roofless except for its lovely apse. Above it, the fortress-like royal palace is in better shape, from where a fine colonnaded balcony enjoys a giddy view. The summit is crowned by a massive 14th-century keep.

Fátima

Set in bleak hill country east of Batalha, about 135km (84 miles) north of Lisbon, this fast-growing town of smart apartment blocks and countless hotels was once just a poor village. Now it's one of the most important centres of pilgrimage in the Catholic world. Its 20th-century neoclassical **basilica** faces a square said to be twice as large as St Peter's in Rome.

A poor and humble mountain village became one of the Catholic world's centres of pilgrimage after visions were seen here in 1917. Mystery and secrets surround the events which caught the imagination of the faithful.

At a spot close by, on 13 May 1917, three young shepherds saw a dazzling vision of a 'lady all of light, more bright than the sun', sitting on the branch of an oak tree. According to one of them, 10-year-old Lucia dos Santos, who was apparently alone in hearing the lady's words, they were told to return on the 13th of every month until October, when she would reveal her identity and her message. The children spread word of what they had seen, and in spite of scepticism on the part of the church authorities, ever-increasing crowds gathered every month. Many claimed to have seen the lady, and identified her with the Virgin Mary. Finally, on 13 October, tens of thousands were present. This time a remarkable phenomenon was witnessed by them all: the sun blazed to a blinding intensity and coloured fireballs flashed to earth. Miraculous cures were claimed. According to Lucia, again the only one to hear the message, the Virgin identified herself as Our Lady of the Rosary and asked for a chapel to be built on the site. In addition, she revealed three 'secrets'. The first was a call for peace, pleading with sinners to repent, pray and make sacrifices. The second message predicted that if people did not heed the first, Russia would spread error throughout the world and persecute the church, and many

nations would collapse. (It is worth noting that the Tsar had already been overthrown in March 1917 and the Bolshevik revolution was only days away.) The 'Third Secret of Fátima' heard by Lucia was apparently so dire that the pope decided it should not be divulged, although there has been speculation that it referred to the end of the world. Each pope since that time has read it, and remained silent.

Two of the children, Lucia's young cousins Francisco and Jacinta, died soon after these events; Lucia herself became a Carmelite nun in Coimbra in 1949. She makes very few public appearances now, although she was seen at the 50th anniversary ceremonies at Fátima, attended by Pope Paul VI and an estimated 2 million faithful from around the world.

Today, pilgrimages are held on the 13th of each month from May to October. The most important observances, marked by midnight torchlight processions, occur on 13 May and 13 October. Around those dates, you'll need advance reservations for accommodation. Even on an ordinary weekday, though, you'll see crowds of pilgrims, some in wheelchairs, some kneeling in penitence. In spite of the nearby picnic grounds, parking lots and dozens of religious souvenir shops, most of the gaudiest side effects of a world-famous attraction have been avoided.

The **information office** is near the Chapel of the Apparitions, facing the huge sanctuary square, and can provide details of all events, including mass said in various languages at the Chapel and the Basilica. They also have a leaflet and map showing all the sites in the area.

Note: not all who come to Fátima have their minds on higher things. The local police issue a warning: if you're caught up in a crowd, watch out for pickpockets.

ious languages at the Chapel and the Basilica. They also have a leaflet and map showing all the sites in the area.

Note: not all who come to Fátima have their minds on higher things. The local police issue a warning: if you're caught up in a crowd, watch out for pickpockets.

Underworld

Fans of limestone **caves** can find a surfeit in the Serras de Aire, the uplands southwest of Fátima, where a whole network of grottoes (*Grutas* in Portuguese) was discovered by quarry workers between 1940 and 1964. The cave systems at Santo António, Alvados and Mira Daire are all about 12km (7 miles) from Fátima as the crow flies, rather more by the narrow country roads, but they are well signposted.

Being discovered in modern times meant they were not subject to much souvenir hunting, so the stalactites are in good condition. Mira Daire's caves are proba-

bly the most striking, and among the deepest in Europe, with a natural lake and artificial fountains 110m (360ft) below ground – an elevator takes visitors down. In all of the commercialized grottoes, the formations are given the usual treatment: fanciful names, multicoloured lighting and dramatic music.

Tomar

Tomar, a busy little town on the River Nabão, some 32km (20 miles) east of Fátima, would be worth a visit for its lovely old centre alone. That is completely overshadowed, however, by the mighty walls of the **Castelo dos Templários** (Templars' Castle) and **Convento do Cristo** (Convent of Christ) on the wooded slopes to the west. Together they form what is arguably the greatest assembly of medieval architecture in Portugal. You'll see them

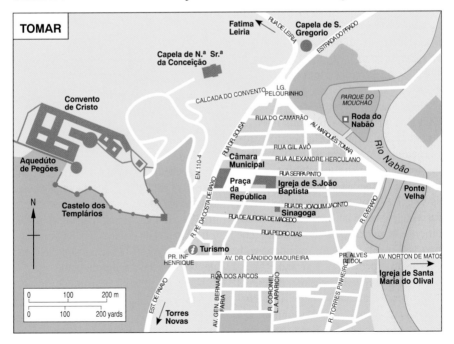

TOMAR AND THE TEMPLARS

The story of Tomar is intertwined with that of the Knights Templar (full name: The Poor Knights of Christ and of the Temple of Solomon), a military order formed in Jerusalem in 1119, after that city was captured in the First Crusade. Its first members, nine French knights, vowed to defend the holy places, protect pilgrims and fight the Moslems. Their courage, and the propaganda support of St Bernard who wrote their rulebook, led to the order growing rapidly, and it soon owned lands and castles right across Europe as well as in the Holy Land. In 1157, as a reward for fighting the Moors, the Portuguese Grand Master of the order, Gualdim Pais, was granted land at Tomar by King Afonso Henriques, on the understanding that he would build and defend a castle to help guard the newly-won territories. By 1190, their new fortress was strong enough to repel a Moorish counterattack.

Over the ensuing centuries, the order's increasing power (it was answerable only to the pope) led to conflicts and jealousies, until in 1307 King Philip IV of France seized its property and arrested its members. The Pope was somehow persuaded to disband the order in 1312, and King Dinis in Portugal was obliged to go through the motions of abolishing it in 1314. Far from persecuting its members, though, he gave refuge to many who had fled from other countries, and in 1320 he formed the 'new' Military Order of Christ, giving it the Templars' property and privileges. Its most famous member – and Grand Master from 1418 until his death in 1460 – was the Infante Henrique ('Henry the Navigator'). He used some of its revenues to finance the voyages of the Age of Discoveries and his caravels sailed under the order's banner of a red cross on a white background.

King João III (1521-57) reorganized Portugal's orders of knights into a monastic brotherhood, with himself at their head, and commissioned the great architect João de Castilho to create magnificent monastery buildings behind the castle at Tomar. Without its individual identity, however, the Order of Christ declined. French troops sacked and desecrated Tomar in the Peninsular War and the disbanding of monastic orders in 1834 was the final blow. (The novel *Foucault's Pendulum* by Umberto Eco, author of *The Name of the Rose*, includes a description of Tomar and the story of the suppression of the Templars.)

from a distance if you're coming from Lisbon, but on the road from Fátima they appear more suddenly as you round a bend above the town.

At the western end of the old town, by the **Turismo** and a statue of Prince Henry

The 16-sided, almost circular, Templars' Church at Tomar dates from the 12th century and follows a typical Templar design. It surrounds an octagon of tall columns enclosing the high altar.

walls, it dates from the first phase of building in the 12th century, although it was restored after lightning damage in the early 16th century. One addition at that time was the richly decorated, Gothic **south portal** of honey-coloured stone, with a central statue of the Virgin and Child. (The style is sometimes referred to as *plateresque*, because the carving looks like ornamental silver.) The church itself follows a favourite Templar pattern, with a central octagon of tall pillars around the high altar, a design inspired by the Holy Sepulchre at Jerusalem and other Byzantine models of the Near East. It is said that in the early years, the knights attended mass on horseback, standing in a circle around the altar. Due to conservation work, you may not be able to see all of the interior at close quarters.

On the east side, a passage lined with blue and yellow *azulejos* leads to the Gothic arches and double pillars of the **Claustro do Cemitério** (Cemetery Cloister, with 16th-century tombs), which was added in the time of Henry the Navigator. The nave and two-storey extension on the west side of the church was another of Manuel's additions. The lower level is a lovely **Chapter House**, with a shallow-vaulted ceiling and carved bosses. Above it is the **Upper Choir**.

The nave leads to the Renaissance two-storey **Great Cloister**, completed in 1587 under the Spanish usurpers (and sometimes labelled Claustro dos Filipes). This is a majestic if severe construction with square doors, round arches and circular windows, which could be straight out of an architectural textbook. Two elegant staircases descend to the lower level and a baroque fountain. If you go down, come up again to the smaller Claustro da Santa Bárbara and out into the open air.

T he Renaissance Great Cloister at Tomar was built in the 16th century. It obscures parts of the earlier Chapter House.

Take a deep breath and turn to face the **west front** of the Chapter House. Pinnacled buttresses, lacy incrustations, the circular upper window (a swirling design of bulging sails) and above all the decoration around the **central window** represent the ultimate in Manueline stone carving. Below the Cross of the Order of Christ, countless symbols of the sea celebrate the voyages of discovery: coral, seaweed, nets, anchors, chains, the artichokes eaten by sailors to combat scurvy, and especially rope – knotted, writhing and impossibly twisted. A figure of a bearded man supports a gnarled tree root at the base and lichens add a natural gilding. Several sculptures have been lost, but their absence is hardly noticed amid the profusion. The architect of this breathtaking *tour de force* was Diogo de Arruda, but the sculptors – surely more than one – are unknown. It dates from around 1515, by no means the end of the Manueline period, but nothing so exotic and alive was ever attempted again in the style.

On the winding road back to town, a left turn up past the walls of the Convent leads to a view of the arches of the **Aqueduct** (Aquedoto dos Pegões), which was built to bring water from the hills above. You can see where it reaches the Convent, but if you have your own transport or want to walk, take the rough but passable track signposted to Pegões. After 2.5km (1.5 miles), you'll come to a point where the arches of the aqueduct march dramatically across a valley. Where the land rises on one side, you can inspect the water channel at the top. A monument dated 1613 marks the completion of the work, dedicated by one Spanish interloper king to another – Philip II to Philip I, using their Portuguese numberings.

The Town Centre

The old town of Tomar lies directly below the castle, with the main square of **Praça da Republica** right next to the base of the hill. Narrow streets of little shops and attractive houses run down to the River Nabão. Parking can be a problem: you may have to leave your car at the edge of town (perhaps most safely at the Hotel dos Templários on the northern outskirts). Facing Praça da Republica, the Town Hall incorporates the surviving parts of King Manuel's palace, and the Church of **São João Baptista** (c.1510) has Manueline doors. Paintings by the 16th-century artist Gregório Lopes include a lurid decapitation of John the Baptist.

One block south of the square, at 73 Rua Dr Joaquim Jacinto, stands Portugal's best preserved medieval **synagogue**, which was in use until around 1500, when Jews were given the 'choice' of conversion or expulsion (see p.52). The plain rectangular building later served as a prison and storehouse, and is now a museum, with Hebrew tombstones and exhibits and gifts from all over Portugal and beyond. The building next door may have been a women's ritual bathhouse.

On the river near a medieval bridge, some fine 18th-century mill buildings include a preserved water wheel (not Moorish as implied, but certainly like the ones the Moors would have used). Over the river to the south, past the covered market, the 12th-century church of **Santa Maria do Olival** has been much rebuilt, but it contains several Templar tombs, including that of Grand Master Gualdim Pais who died in 1195.

Excursions from Tomar

In the rolling wooded country to the east, the River Zêzere has been dammed at **Castelo de Bode**, creating a beautiful artificial lake with an amazingly complicated shoreline. Its countless tranquil inlets and little islands attract a host of local sailors, windsurfers and anglers, especially on summer weekends. The Pousada de São Pedro has been installed in the house where the engineers who built the barrage used to live, and pleasure boats cruise on the lake and river.

The Zêzere joins the River Tagus at **Constância**, a pretty village spread over the slopes around both rivers. It's known in Portugal as the place where the national poet Camões was banished in 1547, for having the misfortune to write a love poem to the same lady-in-waiting in whom the king (João III) himself was interested. There's a plaque marking the ruins of the house where he is thought to have lived for three years, and a seated statue nearby, with quotations from his works. Every Sunday, market stalls line the river bank below.

Just 3km (2 miles) downstream, the picture book castle of **Almourol** stands on a little island in the Tagus. Built in the 12th century by the Templars under Grand Master Gualdim Pais, it stands where there was once a Roman and then a Moorish fortress, guarding the passage of the river and controlling movement along the valley. The tall keep and ramparts, eight slim round towers and main gate, make a splendid sight, one that has inspired romantic legends and tales of chivalry, star-crossed lovers and ghostly hauntings. A boat will ferry you the short distance to the castle from the north bank of the Tagus east of Tancos, near Vila Nova da Barquinha. (Take the N3 road, not the IP6, and look for the signs to Almourol. Coming from the east, it's just after the air base.)

Along the Tagus valley, 12km (7 miles) to the east of Constância, **Abrantes** has been a military base since Roman times. João I gathered his troops here before the Battle of Aljubarrota (see p.51), and it was occupied by both Junot and Masséna in the Peninsular War. Wellington also had his headquarters here before advancing to Talavera on his first foray into Spain. Head up through the narrow streets on the steep, south-facing slopes to the recently restored hilltop castle. Dating from around 1300, it was one of many built all over the country in the reign of the tireless King Dinis. The church of Santa Maria do Castelo now houses a museum collection of odds and ends as well as the medieval tombs of the counts of Abrantes.

M achines are making headway, but in rural Portugal farm animals still do a lot of the donkey work.

The 12th-century hilltop castle of Belver, built at a time when the valley of the River Tagus marked the boundary between Christian and Moorish territory.

Further east along the river, another romantic castle, **Belver** stands on its own conical hill where the Tagus valley narrows to a gorge. For historic reasons it's part of the region of the Alentejo, but is conveniently visited from Tomar or Abrantes. Its name is said to come from the words of a princess who had arrived in darkness and awoke the following morning to exclaim 'Que belo ver!', ('What a beautiful view!'). Climb the steps from the Largo do Pelhourinho in the middle of the village to the restored ramparts and you'll see what she meant: the castle commands vast distances in both directions. Inside the walls, the Chapel of São Brás has a Renaissance altar which arrived, according to tradition, in a mysterious boat to the sound of celestial music.

Santarém

Heading back to Lisbon from the north, you can pay a visit to this historic town, set on a hill overlooking the Tagus, 80km (50 miles) from the capital. The hill has probably been fortified since the earliest times, controlling traffic on the river, but the town takes its name from a 7th-century martyr, Santa Iria, a young nun who was accused of being unchaste and was murdered at Tomar. Her body was thrown into the Nabão only to be washed up downstream at a place then called Escalabis, where miraculous apparitions occurred, affirming her innocence.

Hearing the story, the Visigoth king of the time renamed the town Santa Iria. Under the Moors it became Santariya or Santarim, and was reckoned to be almost impregnable until it fell to a Christian army from Léon in 1093. The Moors soon retook it, but in 1147 Afonso Henriques and a band of knights captured the fortress by scaling the walls in a surprise night attack. The Abbey at Alcobaça (see p.153) was built in gratitude for the victory.

The outskirts are unpromising – Santarém has sprawled in recent years – and most of the interest is concentrated in the old town on the hill. You'll find the **Turismo**, which has excellent street plans and details of hotels and restaurants, in Rua Capelo Ivens at No.63. Not far away, the

165

central square, **Largo Sá da Bandeira**, is overlooked by the baroque **Seminário**, a 17th-century Jesuit church which now serves as the cathedral. The fine multi-windowed façade contrasts with a heavy and gloomy interior. In front of an earlier church on this site, King Pedro I watched while two of the murderers of his beloved Inês de Castro had their hearts torn out. From the square, the narrow Rua Serpa Pinto (it soon becomes pedestrian-only and takes another name, Rua de Såo Martinho) leads towards the majority of Santarém's notable sights. At Praça Visconde Serra do Pilar, you'll find the **Igreja de Marvila**, a church with a Manueline doorway; the interior is lined with early 17th-century tiles in *mudéjar*-style geometric patterns.

A short step to the east, the tall, Romanesque 13th-century São João de Alporão is now the **Archaeological Museum**, specializing in stone carvings, from Roman inscriptions to medieval masterpieces. Note the fine Gothic tomb of Duarte de Meneses, who was killed in 1464 in one of Portugal's periodic skirmishes in North Africa. The remains of his body are displayed nearby: one tooth. Opposite the museum, the Torre das Cabaças was originally part of the town's 15th-century fortifications.

One more church is worth finding, the **Igreja da Graça**, reached by turning a short distance down a side street between the museum and the Marvila church. Its Gothic west door echoes Batalha's (see p.155). Incredibly, the lovely rose window above was carved from one piece of stone. Inside, the tombstone of the accidental discoverer of Brazil, Pedro Alvares Cabral, is plain and unassuming (he may have actually been buried at his birthplace, Belmonte; see p.250). In contrast, the figures of Pedro de Meneses and his wife recline on a superb Gothic tomb. Pedro was luckier than his kinsman Duarte, successfully defending the enclave of Ceuta in Morocco (now a Spanish possession).

The extension of Rua de São Martinho, Avenida 5 de Outubro, leads to the superb miradouro (viewpoint) of **Portas do Sol**, part of the Moorish walls and 17th-century bastions which look out over a lovely garden towards the Tagus and its vast flood plain of the Ribatejo. Down near the river, a statue of Santa Iria was commissioned by Queen (and later Saint) Isabel in the 14th century. Tradition says that if the river reaches her feet, everywhere downstream will be flooded, including Lisbon. The water did come that high in 1979, but Lisbon escaped.

Santarém is the centre of a great farming region, and stages the National Agricultural Fair, generally the first week in June. It's also known for a splendid **food fair**, the Festival de Gastronomia, which takes place at the end of October and in early November. This culinary extravaganza showcases local fare from every region of Portugal, including specialities from the territory of Macau.

The Ribatejo area in which Santarém lies is the home of Portuguese bullfighting, and the bulls themselves are raised on the fertile lands that fill the view from the Portas do Sol. (Bullfights are held at the bullring and fairground on the south-western outskirts of town.) If you take a diversion across the Tagus, you'll see great herds of cattle grazing, and bird watchers should have a rewarding time in the wetlands.

The towns surrounding Santarém are at their liveliest at festa time or on market day, and there's little to distinguish one from another. If you're near Alpiarça on a Sunday or Thursday afternoon, with an hour to spare, you can visit the palatial **Casa dos Patudos**, which is now a museum. It was the home of the philanthropist and politician José Relvas (1858-1929), and still houses his extraordinary collection. Some of the ceramics are priceless and the azulejos are superb, including early *mudéjar* examples and large 18th-century panels depicting local life. Fine paintings by 19th- and 20th-century Portuguese artists, including Silva Porto, Carlos Reis, António Ramalho and many others, were bought or commissioned from the painters themselves. The authenticity of some of the other paintings, however, is more questionable, and you will be amazed or amused as the guides solemnly identify the alleged works of Rubens, Van Dyck, Boucher, Renoir and Leonardo da Vinci! A lovely Virgin Mary might just be the Memling they claim; a still life by Josefa de Óbidos is generally accepted as genuine (it's said that there used to be three here); and you might even be convinced by the Reynolds *Young Lady* – but as for the rest ...

Back across the Tagus and north of Santarém, **Golega** is a famous horse-breeding centre with a November fair, where bullfighters come to buy their steeds. Look out, too, for the parish church with its magnificent Manueline doorway and characteristic carved stone 'rope' around its tower and chancel.

Heading back towards Lisbon, it's hardly worth a diversion to see the industrial town of **Vila Franca de Xira**. The exception would be at festival time in July, the Fiesta do Colete Encarnados, and again in October, when bulls run through the streets. (Parking then is virtually impossible: from Lisbon, it makes sense to take the train.) The town's bridge over the Tagus was the nearest to the river mouth until the opening of the suspension bridge at Lisbon. It's still an important crossing and traffic can be heavy.

Coimbra

Celebrated in poetry and song and Portugal's capital city before Lisbon, Coimbra is known above all for its university, one of the world's oldest. The site is magnificent, a high hill overlooking the wide Mondego river. It was occupied by the Romans, Suevi, Alani, Visigoths and Moors, and taken by Christian forces in 872 only to be lost again in the Moorish resurgence of the 10th century. With the aid of the legendary El Cid, it was finally reconquered in 1064 and became part of the county of Portucale under the kings of Castile and Léon. When Afonso Henriques was declared king of an independent Portugal in 1139, Coimbra became his capital, and even after Lisbon inherited the title in about 1256, for years to come Portuguese kings preferred to make Coimbra their chief residence.

People remain passionate about the place. It's claimed to be the guardian of *Portugalidade* (untranslatable except as 'Portugueseness'); to speak the purest Portuguese; and to produce the greatest artists, poets and thinkers. (That the dictator Salazar was an economics professor here before taking over the country is rather an embarrassment.) Even the River Mondego is counted as superior: it rises and flows only in Portugal, whereas the Tagus and Douro start off in Spain!

Historic buildings crowd the slopes and crown the summit. There used to be even more until whole areas were razed during the Salazar era and replaced with the ugly 'University City' blocks, but enough riches remain to keep visitors busy for days. Mercifully, the perfect old university quadrangle was preserved. Other treasures include the Machado de Castro Museum and two cathedrals, especially the evocative *Sé Velha*.

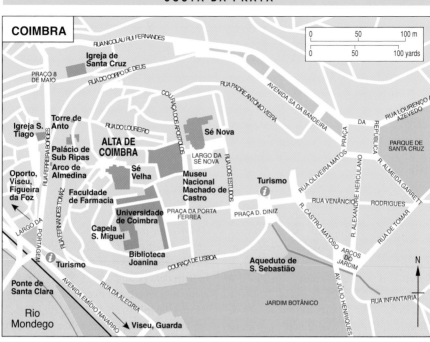

COIMBRA

RUA NICOLAU RUI FERNANDES

Igreja de Santa Cruz

PRAÇO 8 DE MAIO

RUA DO CORPO DE DEUS

RUA PADRE ANTÓNIO VIEIRA

AVENIDA SÁ DA BANDEIRA

RUA LOURENÇO A. AZEVEDO

DA

RUA DA REPÚBLICA

PARQUE DE SANTA CRUZ

Igreja S. Tiago

Torre de Anto

RUA DO LOUREIRO

COURAÇA DOS APÓSTOLOS

Sé Nova

PRAÇA

R. ALMEIDA GARRETT

ALTA DE COIMBRA

Palácio de Sub Ripas

Arco de Almedina

Sé Velha

LARGO DA SÉ NOVA

RUA DOS ESTUDOS

Museu Nacional Machado de Castro

Turismo

RUA OLIVEIRA MATOS

R. ALEXANDRE HERCULANO

RUA VENÂNCIO

RODRIGUES

Oporto, Viseu, Figueira da Foz

RUA FERREIRA BORGES

RUA FERNANDES TOMAZ

Faculdade de Farmacia

Universidade de Coimbra

PRAÇA DA PORTA FÉRREA

PRAÇA D. DINIZ

R. CASTRO MATOSO

ARCOS DO JARDIM

RUA DE TOMAR

LARGO DA PORTAGEM

Capela S. Miguel

Biblioteca Joanina

COURAÇA DE LISBOA

Aqueduto de S. Sebastião

AV. JÚLIO HENRIQUES

RUA INFANTARIA

Turismo

Ponte de Santa Clara

AVENIDA EMÍDIO NAVARRO

RUA DA ALEGRIA

Viseu, Guarda

JARDIM BOTÂNICO

N

Rio Mondego

0   50   100 m

0   50   100 yards

Weekday traffic can be a nightmare, but don't despair – sights are concentrated enough to explore on foot and it's best to leave your car in a supervised car park. There's one south of the Santa Clara Bridge, from where the walk to the city is longer, but by the best approach. Another is close to the north end of the bridge and the **Turismo**, where you can pick up a good street map. (Another tourist office is near the University, on Praça de Dom Dinis; see p.172.) Alternatively, if you don't

*F*ormer capital, guardian of Portuguese culture and tradition, the old university city of Coimbra clusters on the heights above the River Mondego.

want to walk to the top of town, you can take a chance on finding a space there, which is generally easier when the university is not in session. The drive up is not direct – one-way and pedestrian streets force you to make a long clockwise swing around the centre.

Walkers can make their way from the triangular Largo da Portagem by the Santa Clara Bridge and along the pedestrian shopping street Rua Ferreira Borges. Up to the right, the graceful **Arco de Almedina**, originally a Moorish arch but much rebuilt, leads by way of steep steps to the Upper Town. On the way, take a short diversion to the left along Rua de Sub Ripas to see a wonderful Manueline doorway in the Casa Sub Ripas. The tower next along the same road is the Torre de Anto, part of the medieval wall. Nicknamed after the 19th-century poet, António Nobre, who lived here, it's now a craft centre selling pottery and other products of the region.

The Upper Town and University

If you've walked up from the Almedina Arch, you'll soon come to the **Sé Velha** (**Old Cathedral**), begun in 1162 and built as much like a fortress as a church for those turbulent times. Several kings were crowned here, from Sancho I in 1185 to João I two centuries later, and some claim that it was the scene of the bizarre enthronement of the body of Inês de Castro (see p.155; other versions of the story place that event in Santa Cruz church at the bottom of the hill). The old cathedral has been much altered, but its fine Romanesque lines have survived, especially in the apses at the eastern end and the majestic rounded west door, repeated in the west window above it. Fine sculpture over the much later Renaissance north door show signs of fire damage. The impressive

*G*enerations of students have passed through the Porta Férrea, the 17th-century gateway which leads to the delightful main quadrangle of Coimbra University.

austerity of the interior focuses attention on superb Gothic carvings, the flamboyant 16th-century Gothic high altar, 16th-century Arabesque tiles in chapels on either side (many more tiles have been removed during restoration), and huge clamshell fonts. In the south aisle, steps lead up to the early 13th-century Gothic **cloister**, the oldest in Portugal.

From the eastern end of the old cathedral, beyond the 16th-century mansion which houses the university's Faculty of Pharmacy, steps up to the right lead to the **Praça da Porta Férrea**. The 'iron gate' of the name forms the main entrance to the old part of the university, which was built in 1634, and the figures in its niches

depict the founder, King Dinis, and King João III, who re-established it permanently in Coimbra. Through the gate, the **Old University quadrangle**, the Pátio das Escolas, is a thrilling sight, open on the south side with a view down to the River Mondego. A fine ensemble of mainly baroque buildings lines the other three sides, and another statue of João III tops a tall column. To the right as you enter the quadrangle, ceremonial staircases lead up to a colonnade, the *Via Latina*, where students line up for degree ceremonies. The central portico leads to the **Sala dos Capelos** (Graduates' Hall) with a gorgeously painted wooden ceiling from the mid-17th century. (Check at the desk here to see whether they are also selling tickets to the chapel and library).

In the corner of the quadrangle, the imposing clock tower dates from 1733. Its bell used to sound the nightly curfew for the students, who gave it the mocking name of *A Cabra*, the goat. Next comes the **Chapel** (Capela de São Miguel), with a fine Manueline doorway of 1517, gilded high altar and spectacular baroque organ painted in chinoiserie style. Small groups are admitted periodically to the celebrated *Bibilioteca Joanina*, the baroque **Library** next to the chapel. (You may have to join a crowd outside. If no one else has done so, press the bell to let the guides know you're there!) Built around 1720 in the reign of João V, its three halls with their upper galleries glow with rich carving of exotic woods and gilding. Its arches lead the eye to a portrait of the king, who had a taste for the extravagant: he also commissioned the building of Mafra with *its* famous library (see p.137). As for the venerable tomes, they're part of the décor: the really valuable (and useful) books are elsewhere.

Back in the world beyond the Porta Férrea, most of the work of the university goes on in stark modern blocks dating from the time of Salazar. Intended as a modern version of the old buildings, they've been generally castigated as a fascist caricature. In fact, there's a distinctly Stalinist look about them and their heavy sculptures, and they are grandiose but banal.

At the end of Praça da Porta Férrea, turn left along Rua de São João. At the next crossing, the **Museu Machado de Castro** is one of Portugal's best, named after an 18th-century sculptor. It's housed in buildings that are prize exhibits themselves: the former bishop's palace (begun in the 12th century) with Roman foundations, a Moorish tower and the church of

The gorgeously gilded baroque library of the university was paid for by João V out of his store of gold from Brazil. The benefactor himself is commemorated by a portrait at one end of building.

TATTERED GOWNS AND COLOURED RIBBONS

To many visitors, the university *is* Coimbra. Originally founded in 1290 – in Lisbon – by King Dinis, it is one of Europe's oldest universities. It was first moved to Coimbra in 1308, and was shuttled four more times between the two cities at the whim of various kings before finally settling in Coimbra in 1537. The mystery is why they didn't have one in each place, something which was not rectified until the 20th century.

In spite of a revolutionary reputation, the students preserve many old traditions, and you may see them in black *capas*, gowns torn into fringes at the hem, each tear supposedly representing a love affair. Ribbons in different colours attached to the gowns indicate the faculty: red for law, yellow for medicine, blue for arts, light blue and white for sciences and so on. Graduation in May is marked by a week-long festival and ceremonial burning of the ribbons (*Queima das Fitas*).

Like students all over the world, many live in bohemian style in old lodging houses which here are called *repúblicas*, 'republics' (similar to the American fraternities), with their own abstruse rules about admission and seniority. You might even come across a group gathered in a bar or out of doors on a fine evening, listening to one of their number singing the Coimbra *fado*. Quite different from Lisbon's version, it's usually sung by a man and not always as a lament; it can be political, satirical, and even funny.

São João de Almedina, which is probably on the site of the chief mosque but was rebuilt around 1700. The medieval sculpture collection near the entrance is a highlight, especially the little 12th-century knight on horseback, with his vizor lowered and armed to the teeth, and three painted figures of knights in chain mail. Go up and out on to the loggia, like a balcony high above the city, before continuing to the religious sculpture and early paintings, fine ceramics and vestments. There's really too much to take in, but don't miss the dramatic descent (the guides will show you) into a multi-level underworld, which is nothing less than the foundations of the Roman town of Aeminium. (One inscription dating from 305 AD actually uses that name for the city.) A grid pattern of passages between massive stone pillars is a storehouse of sculpture from the Roman and Visigothic periods.

Across the road from the museum, the **Sé Nova** (New Cathedral) was begun in 1598 by the Jesuits, but still wasn't complete when the Marquês de Pombal threw them out in 1759 for, among other offences, selling university degrees. Having been started in classical style, it was finished in baroque – you can see the change in the façade and the interior. It became the cathedral in 1772, when the choir stalls and Manueline font were brought from the old cathedral.

Botanical Gardens

If you walk straight ahead from the Porta Férrea between two of the monstrous modern blocks (the Faculties of Medicine and Science), you'll come to **Praça de Dom Dinis**, with a statue of that king. This was once the site of the medieval royal fortress, which was cleared away as part of a beautification scheme ordered by Pombal in 1772. Round to the right are the impressive arches of the 16th-century **aqueduct** and beyond them, the spacious 20ha (50 acre) Botanical Gardens, which were also part of Pombal's programme. Its terraces and paths are a popular place to walk and a lovers' rendezvous. There's still a rich collection of plants and trees, although some areas are untended.

The Lower Town

Down the long flight of steps from Praça de Dom Dinis, Rua Oliveira Matos leads to the busy **Praça da República**. Its cafés and bars are popular with the students and good for economical meals. The trees lining the square are the nightly sleeping quarters of tens of thousands of sparrows who make a deafening din at dusk. It's unwise to walk underneath.

The wide Avenida Sá da Bandeira sweeps downhill towards the centre of the lower town, the **Praça 8 de Maio**. The general level of the streets has obviously risen, because it's a few steps down to the entrance of the **Church of Santa Cruz**. A monastery stood on this site as early as 1131, and St Anthony of Padua is supposed to have studied here, but there's little trace of the early buildings. The present church was commissioned by King Manuel in the early 16th century, and his best architects, including Boytac and João de Castilho, worked on it, so some Manueline features are evident. The doorway has good sculptures by Chanterenne and João de Ruão (both French; the second name is the Portuguese rendering of Jean de Rouen!), but it's obscured by an odd, free-standing arch planted in front around 1800.

Portugal's first two kings, Afonso Henriques and Sancho I, were given new tombs in 1520, with effigies carved by Chanterenne. He also made the pulpit and was buried in the church. On the north side, the Manueline cloisters date from 1517. The Renaissance sacristy on the south side dates from 1624 and houses important paintings by Figueiredo and Grão Vasco (his *Pentecost*). More cloisters and a fountain behind the church have been turned into a public garden.

Rua Visconde da Luz runs from the front of Santa Cruz church and merges into the fashionable main pedestrian street, Rua Ferreira Borges (see p.000). Near the junction, down a street to the right, look for the original Romanesque traces of the Church of São Tiago, dating from about 1080. It faces Praça do Comércio, the focus of a maze of narrow alleys where you'll find some economical and entertaining bars and cafés.

If you have plenty of time and feel like a walk, head north from Praça da República to the left of the wooded Santa Cruz Park to the Mosteiro de Celas, another Manueline church, although the cloisters and other features are earlier. Further out in the same direction on its own hill, the church of Santo António das Olivais is dedicated to St Anthony of Padua, who was born in Lisbon (see p.000) but studied and taught in Coimbra before going to Italy. Azulejo panels from about 1730 show scenes from the saint's life.

South of the River

Across the Santa Clara Bridge from the city, the main road swings left along the south bank of the Mondego. Just beyond the junction, the next lane to the left leads to the church of **Santa Clara-a-Velha**, the chief relic of a convent begun in 1286 and consecrated under the patronage of Queen (Saint) Isabel in 1330. It was an unwise choice of location: the first of many floodings by the Mondego occurred the following year, and there were to be many more. Finally in the 17th century it was abandoned in favour of a site on higher ground nearby (Santa Clara-a-Nova). The tomb of Queen Isabel which had been here was moved as well, and most of the site was gradually buried beneath layers of mud. A few years ago, you would have seen only part of the walls and the lovely rose window at the west end of the church. Now 'restored', in effect completely rebuilt, it shows what modern Portuguese stonemasons can do.

About 800m (half a mile) to the east by the next road after the church, the *Fonte das Lágrimas* (Well of Tears) in **Quinta das Lágrimas** park is the traditional site of the murder of Inês de Castro in 1355. She was buried at Santa Clara-a-Velha but her body was later moved to Alcobaça (see p.000).

Next along the road south from the bridge, Portugal dos Pequenitos (meaning 'Portugal for the Very Young', although it attracts all ages) is an appealing garden with miniature versions of an eclectic selection of buildings, from typical cottages to famous monuments from all over the country, as well as giant African figures and other reminders of the former colonies.

A twisting cobblestone road climbs steeply (you can drive up if you wish) past the derelict São Francisco monastery to the colossal buildings of the Convent of **Santa Clara-a-Nova**. From the plaza in front there's a fine view across the river to Coimbra. The convent and church were built in the 17th century, to house the community of Poor Clare nuns driven out of the riverbank site (see above) by repeated flooding. The cloisters and much of the decoration were added in the 18th century. When Queen Isabel's remains were moved here, a new silver tomb was made, which can be seen near the gilded baroque high altar, with paintings showing the details of the actual transfer. (It is said that her body was 'undefiled'.) A statue depicts her showing the roses which miraculously took the place of bread and gold she was taking to the poor when her husband King Dinis complained of her extravagance and demanded to see what she was carrying. Her original 14th-century tomb is still preserved here as well, in the Lower Choir. The polychrome effigy shows the queen-saint robed as a pilgrim, and round the base of the tomb are more fine carved and painted figures of nuns and St Francis, and Christ with the Apostles. Look also for the touching little 14th-century tomb of one of Isabel's grand-daughters and the superb 18th-century organ with trumpets.

Conimbriga

Whether speeding along on the *Auto-estrada* or meandering by minor roads, it's worth turning off near the town of Condeixa-a-Nova just south of Coimbra to see the greatest Roman site so far excavated in Portugal. Late in the second century BC, after they had pacified most of the interior of their new province, the Romans took over this old Iron Age settlement. It's easy to see the attractions of the place, a plateau with the land falling away steeply on all sides except the east, where it was defended by strong walls. Under the Pax Romana, the threat of attack diminished and the town expanded beyond its old limits. It was an important staging post, roughly half way along the road from Lisbon to Braga, and later became the seat of a Christian bishopric. Judging by the quality of the art objects and the size of some of the houses, Conimbriga was a substantial and prosperous city.

As the Empire's power declined, increasing disorder and the threat of 'barbarian' invasions from the north forced the inhabitants to pull back inside a shorter and much stronger wall, built in the 4th century. The work was evidently urgent: you can see where it cut right through many houses which must have been levelled in the process. The new defences delayed but couldn't prevent the inevitable:

the city was sacked more than once by the Suevi in the 5th century. Under the Visigoths it was gradually abandoned in favour of a safer hilltop fortress, the Roman Aeminium 15km (9 miles) to the north. Oddly enough, the name was transferred too: Conimbriga evolved first into Conimbria and then Coimbra.

Following the signs from the main road, look out for the traces of the outer eastern wall and the remains of the aqueduct which supplied the city's water until the Suevi broke it down. At the gate, you'll need to decide whether to tour the excavations first, or the excellent **museum**, a modern building over to the left. In the hottest part of the day, you might choose the latter – it has a café too, and the light is better for viewing the ruins when the sun begins to go down. The museum's star exhibits include Roman jewellery, glass, coins, bronze statuettes and white marble sculpture (mainly fragments but often strikingly beautiful). There's a magnificent mosaic of the Minotaur in his labyrinth, a maze too intricate for the eye to follow and measuring fully 3m by 4m (roughly 10ft by 13ft). Just as interesting are the sections on daily life in Roman times, showing glass-making, carpentry, ironwork and agriculture.

Before heading for the site itself, buy one of the guide leaflets. The site is still difficult to follow, but without one, impossible. As you approach the ruins, you'll see the **4th-century wall** and gateway ahead of you. To the left are the foundations of several houses, shops, and part of a public bathhouse; and on the right under a protective roof, a palatial 3rd century villa. Labelled the **House of the Fountains**, its central pool and spouting bronze jets have been reconstructed by copying discovered fragments of the original. Great areas of mosaic floors include a superb illustration of a staghunt.

Just inside the city gate, the aqueduct ends near more shops, baths and a cistern. The rest of the scene is more confusing: you'll need the help of the site plan. The forum is straight ahead, and over the north wall nearby you can see the ruins of an amphitheatre. To the south are still more baths (close to the wall) with their complex brickwork heating ducts exposed. Although much has still to be excavated, Conimbriga is supreme among the remains of the Roman Empire in Portugal.

Luso and Buçaco (Bussaco)

In the hills northeast of Coimbra, the name of a gracious old spa town has become familiar to generations of visitors to Portugal. Few have ever been there, but they've drunk plenty of bottles of its mineral water, **Luso**. The place itself has a grand old hotel, a few *pensões*, a casino and, of course, a bath house where you can immerse yourself in pleasantly warm water (along with those seeking relief from rheumatism and other pains). Next door, the elegant Casa de Cha (tea house) is a 19th-century gem.

Steep roads climb out of Luso to the south-east and soon enter the **Buçaco National Forest**, a favourite weekend retreat for picnicers and walkers. It was first planted by Carmelite monks when they were granted the land in the 17th century, and some of the exotic trees they introduced still flourish, along with native Portuguese species which have since become rare elsewhere. The simple monastery built from local stone, timber and cork and decorated with pebbles was abandoned early in the 19th century. Then most of it was knocked down and the rest surrounded, dwarfed and almost buried by the extraordinary 'hunting lodge', actually a vast **summer palace** built for the royal family between 1887 and 1910. The style is fairy tale Gothic and neo-Manueline, with magnificent salons, furnishings, huge tile panels and terraces. Surrounding it all are some very fine formal gardens and then the green wall of the forest. For many years, the palace has been one of the grandest of grand hotels. Its restaurant is celebrated and the wine cellars are stocked with 180,000 bottles, most of them naturally the local Bairradas, including many superb old vintages.

You can visit the remnant of the convent, which played host to its most famous guest during the Peninsular War, when Wellington lodged in one of the monks' cells. A sign proclaims that he 'spent the night following the victory of Bussaco over the invading army of Masséna on the 27 September 1810 in this convent'.

Notice the cork-lined doors and beams, which are excellent for soundproofing and keeping in the warmth. Swords, bayonets, muskets, tools and, oddly, stuffed animals are displayed in some of the other cells, along with old prints of the campaign.

There's a more substantial Military Museum further up the wooded slopes. It gives the detailed history of the Battle of Buçaco, including maps, weapons, uniforms and other relics. An obelisk nearby honours the Portuguese-British army that gained the victory. No doubt Wellington's generalship was instrumental, but a prime cause of the French defeat seems to have been the over-confidence of Masséna, their commander. Considering the British troops to be 'useless' and the Portuguese mere 'canaille', he sent in his columns one after another against a strong defensive position. They suffered heavy losses and made no impression. Wellington retired in good order to his prepared 'Lines of Torres Vedras' (see p.243) while Masséna's army wasted time venting its frustration by sacking Coimbra.

Montemor-o-Velho

West of Coimbra, the new IP3 road stays north of the Mondego. You might be surprised to find that the low-lying land along the river is an important rice growing area. After about 30km (19 miles), a side road leads to the left and the romantic ruin of the fortress-palace of Montemor-o-Velho, high above the old town. The name comes from Monte Mayor, the Great Hill, and this site has been settled for thousands of years. It's worth the climb to walk around the 11th-century ramparts. The mainly 14th-century castle was a favourite with several kings. Its church of Santa Maria da Alcáçova, within the walls, was rebuilt in Manueline style – note the rows of twisted columns inside.

Figueira da Foz

This old fishing port where the River Mondego and the IP3 meet the sea is now the biggest and brightest holiday resort on the Costa da Prata. Its broad beach of golden sand, sheltered from the worst of the Atlantic's waves, first drew a crowd from nearby Coimbra, then from the rest of northern Portugal. With much improved roads from the border, it's now also popular with people from neighbouring areas of Spain. Hotels, apartments and restaurants are spreading along the seafront towards the village of Buarcos, but they're not too

Echoes of the Portuguese connection with Asia in the Iberian Peninsula: rice is cultivated in paddy fields on the flat lands of the lower Mondego valley near Montemór-o-Velho.

unsightly. If you need help with accommodation or would like an excellent street map, go to the **Turismo** on Avenida 25 de Abril, facing the beach at the town end.

Close by, **Forte da Santa Catarina** at the river mouth is typical of anti-pirate defences all along this coast. Started in the 16th century and strengthened over the next two hundred years, it now shelters the courts of the local tennis club from the prevailing sea breezes. There's a fine yacht harbour just up river; then comes the old town, with most of the growing industrial zone restricted to the opposite (south) bank.

The cultural spectrum ranges from a casino to the local museum, both located just inland from the yacht marina. Funded by the Gulbenkian Foundation – which is always a good indication of quality – the **Museu Dr Santos Rocha** is strong on archaeology and local crafts, industries and traditions. In the old town, the **Casa do Paço** is a fine mansion whose interior walls are covered by thousands of 18th-century Dutch Delft tiles, said to have been a cargo from Holland which ended up here by mistake. **Buarcos**, the old fishing village 3km (2 miles) away at the other end of the main beach, was a frequent pirate target (Dutch, English and North African), in spite of the strong ramparts which still line its seaward side. In the holiday season, it becomes a downmarket satellite of Figueira.

As for local entertainment, there is usually something to occupy your time. Different beaches offer a variety of sea conditions for different watersports; bullfights are staged regularly in summer; and bars and discos, as well as the casino, provide some nightlife. Figueira being a fishing port, there are naturally plenty of seafood restaurants – the local fish stews are famous. If you are looking for a

Three sorts of harvest are won from the sheltered waters near Aveiro: fish, seaweed, and here, salt.

From this point north, narrow at first and then expanding into wide channels and fully-fledged lakes, a maze of waterways protected by coastal dunes stretches for 60km (37 miles). At the half way point stands an ancient port which is sometimes fancifully labelled 'Portugal's Venice'.

change from the Algarve or just want to sample a really Portuguese flavoured resort, this is a pretty good bet, as well as making an excellent base for touring.

North of Buarcos, the landscape is flat, windswept and empty. The road runs about 10km (6 miles) inland, with only a couple of lanes leading to deserted beaches. Praia de Mira is an old fishing settlement between marshy lagoons and the sea, and retains a number of old stilt houses. Falling levels of water have gradually left more and more houses on dry land, except after a storm. You'll see signs that visitors are expected: a camp site and some summer-only bars, cafés and limited accommodation.

Aveiro

Any number of former ports in Portugal, from Caminha in the north to Faro in the Algarve, have slowly silted up. The accumulation of sand or mud has made them unusable and in some case even left them far inland. Aveiro's case is slightly different, however, for it was cut off literally *overnight* in 1575, when a great storm created a sandbar right across the mouth of the Vouga river. With its only outlet to the sea blocked, the river flooded the land all around, forming a huge lake, the *Ria*. Aveiro's trade and fishing industry, which had flourished on great hauls of cod from the Grand Banks off Newfoundland, was snuffed out. Only in 1808 was a channel cut through to the sea, draining some of the marshes, letting ships pass and heralding the return of a degree of prosperity.

At first, you may think you've come to the wrong place. There's a fair amount of industry nearby and the region's radically improved major roads seem intent on carrying you away from the town. (To reach the centre, take the exit marked 'Oeste' off the IP5.) When you do get near, it stands out: the oldest part covers the only little hill in an otherwise utterly flat landscape. The canals are few, but they complement the town beautifully and define its character. They're lined by some lovely houses, many faced with tiles and a surprising number in the Art Nouveau style which flowered in the early 20th century. The **Turismo** occupies one of a row of almost Dutch-looking houses facing a canal in Rua João Mendonça. It's a great source of maps and information on not only Aveiro, but the whole region stretching inland to the hills – labelled Rota da Luz ('Route of Light'). Ask here about excursions by boat on the Ria, too. You'll see various sorts of craft, ancient and modern, even some pedalos, moored along the canals. Just behind the Turismo, the **fish market** is liveliest in the morning. To try some of the good things sold there, visit any of the several informal restaurants close by.

Across the canal by way of Praça Humberto Delgado (more a broad bridge than a square) and up a short hill, you'll come to the **Misericórdia**, dating from the prosperous days of the 16th century. The inside has since been covered with blue and yellow *azulejos*. Continue along the same road and you'll come to a pleasant square called Praça Marquês de Pombal, which is faced by a Carmelite church with a richly gilded interior. Beyond the square, a left turn along Rua Santa Joana brings you to the former Convento de Jesus, now the **Aveiro Museum**. The chief attraction here, along with an impressive quantity of religious art, is the superb, mainly 18th-century chapel of Princesa Santa Joana. This daughter of King Afonso V decided to become a nun and lived here from 1475 until she died in 1489. No particular acts appear to justify her elevation to sainthood two centuries later, but it was celebrated by the making of a massive tomb. Constructed from carved and inlaid marble, and supported by winged angels and a phoenix, it's a work of great craft and little artistry. The church across the road is in fact Aveiro's cathedral, but lacks any specific interest.

Try to find time for a boat trip on the Ria, to see its bird life and three main activities: fishing, gathering seaweed for fertilizer, and managing the vast areas of salt pans. All have been threatened by pollution in recent times, but there's growing concern to clean up and protect the sensitive environment. A few high-prowed, brightly-painted *moliceiro* boats still work along the waterways, raking weed from the bottom and stacking it on deck. Washed clean of salt, it makes good fertilizer, putting humus into sandy soil. The Festa da Ria at the end of August features races and processions of all the varieties of traditional craft, which are specially decorated for the occasion.

There's no sign of them from town, but Aveiro has some fine **beaches**. Barra, next to the lighthouse which marks the channel from the sea to the Ria, is the nearest by road. North of the channel, São Jacinto is a lively little port and resort, backing on to an important nature reserve and bird sanctuary.

Oporto and the Green North West

This land of vineyards and forests was where Portugal began. It was taken back from the Moors early in the Christian reconquest, before Lisbon and long before the Algarve and most of Spain. 'Portucale', as the infant state was called, took its name from Portus and Cale, the settlements at the mouth of the River Douro; and Portus became the city of Porto (Oporto to most English speakers). The title of actual birthplace of independent Portugal is contested by two cities: the ecclesiastical capital, Braga, and nearby Guimarães, whose perfect medieval centre is guarded by the castle where Afonso Henriques was first acknowledged as king.

Other historic fortresses look over the River Minho where it marks the border with Spain. Just to the south, the valley of the Lima is one of the prettiest in the country and the region produces the famous *vinho verde*, 'green wine' (the name refers to its youth rather than its colour). Then, of course, there's Oporto, home of Port, the aristocrat among fortified wines. The Atlantic coast has some great beaches, largely a secret that the locals have kept to themselves, but which are now being promoted to take some of the pressure off the Algarve. Despite the label of Costa Verde (Green Coast), north-west Portugal is much more than a stretch of sand, and much more even than its historic cities. Inland, the mountains and lakes offer some of the finest scenery in the country, especially in the Peneda-Gerês National Park. The whole region still sees far fewer visitors than Lisbon and the south, but it's beginning to be discovered.

Depending on time, you can take a short trip on the River Douro to see Oporto from its best angle, or a week-long holiday on a luxury river cruiser.

Oporto (Porto)

It was inevitable that a thriving port should develop here (*O Porto* means simply 'the port'). The site is ideal: close to the sea but sheltered in the estuary of a great river which reaches far into the fertile interior.

The Douro narrows to a deep gorge at this point, and in days gone past the rocky heights of Penaventosa above the north bank were easily fortified and defended. Various civilizations have been based here – the Celts had a hilltop town where the cathedral and bishop's palace now stand – but such traces that remain of theirs and Roman and Visigoth occupations, are a matter for archaeologists: you can see virtually nothing of them above ground. The Moorish period, from the 8th to the 10th century, left its mark in a labyrinthine street pattern on the steep slope below the cathedral. Encouraged by the Spanish kings of Léon and Castile, crusaders then expelled the Moors and Oporto became the capital of the reconquered area.

Seeing the Sights

This can be a confusing city, with several distinct areas of interest. If you don't mind

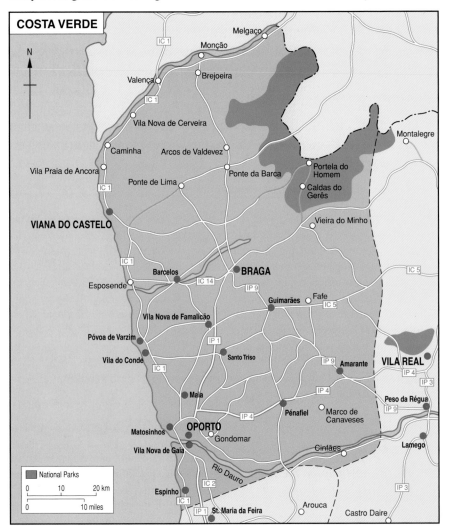

COSTA VERDE

N

Melgaço
Monção
IC 1
Valença
Brejoeira
IC 1
Vila Nova de Cerveira
Montalegre
Caminha
Arcos de Valdevez
Vila Praia de Ancora
Ponte da Barca
Portela do Homem
Ponte de Lima
Caldas do Gerês
IC 1
VIANA DO CASTELO
Vieira do Minho
IC 1
Barcelos
BRAGA
IC 5
Esposende
IC 14
IP 9
Guimarães
Fafe
IC 5
Vila Nova de Famalicão
IP 1
Póvoa de Varzim
Vila do Conde
Santo Triso
IP 9
Amarante
VILA REAL
IC 1
IP 4
IP 3
Maia
IP 4
Peso da Régua
Matosinhos
Pénafiel
Marco de Canaveses
IP 9
OPORTO
IP 4
Vila Nova de Gaia
Gondomar
Cinfães
Lamego
Rio Dauro
National Parks
0   10   20 km
0   10 miles
Espinho
IC 2
IC 1
IP 1
St. Maria da Feira
Arouca
Castro Daire
IP 3

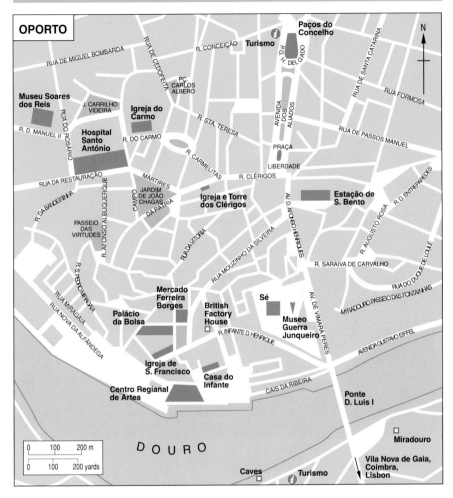

the steep hills, walking is the best way to get around, supplemented by taxis, buses or trams to go from one area to the next. The *Turismo* offices have a map showing the public transport routes as well as a detailed street plan, and local people are helpful: many speak English and even more, French. If you arrive by train or you're somewhere near the city centre, call in at the main **Turismo** opposite the City Hall at the northern end of the broad Avenida dos Aliados. There's another one not far away, on the south side of Praça de Dom João I.

One of the best introductions would be to see Oporto from the river. Better still, if you have a head for heights, try walking across the 1886 **Dom Luis I bridge**, 60m (almost 200ft) above the water, which was a great engineering feat for its time. It's the biggest free thrill in Oporto. The upper level of this double-decker iron structure soars from the Serra do Pilar (see p.192) on the south bank, straight to the top of the old city near the cathedral. Far beneath, the lower level links the quaysides of Oporto and Vila Nova de Gaia, where the Port

shippers have their lodges (see p.192). The tremendous panorama includes almost all of the city's landmarks.

Downstream you can see the Arrábida road bridge and the mouth of the Douro. Immediately below the bridge, parts of the old walls and crumbling houses cling to the steep slopes, while sheep graze in terraced gardens. Up river, ramshackle shanties are packed together like a third world slum on a site which has such a magnificent view that it's surprising it has not been snapped up as prime real estate. Beyond them, the **Maria Pia railway bridge** was designed by Eiffel in 1877, several years before his Paris tower.

The Old City

The **Cathedral (Sé)** was started by Count Henry of Burgundy (see p.49), but the solid granite building which you see now dates from the 13th century and later. João I and Philippa of Lancaster were married here in 1387, setting the seal on an Anglo-Portuguese alliance which had been established earlier. (Oporto later became the home of many English merchants trading in textiles, dried cod, fruit, cork and, of course, wine.)

Inside, the body of the cathedral is disappointingly narrow and cramped and has been cleared of most decorative features, with the exception of a famous and complex baroque **silver altarpiece**. When

T est your head for heights by walking across the Dom Luis I bridge, completed in 1886 and running high above the River Douro, to the heart of Oporto.

A t the highest point of the old city, Oporto Cathedral was the setting for the marriage of João I and Philippa of Lancaster in 1387.

French forces occupied the city in 1809, it was hidden from them behind a false wall. Don't miss the vaulted **cloisters** on the south side. Someone will come to open the door and take a small fee which also lets you climb to the Renaissance chapter-house, designed by the Italian architect Nasoni, who settled in Oporto in the 18th century. He also added the arcaded porch outside on the north side of the building. The nearby figure on horseback depicts a local hero, Vimara Peres, who won a battle against the Moors in 868.

Almost adjoining the Sé, the imposing **Bishop's Palace** is another Nasoni design. It now serves as local government offices and you can't go inside, but the road below it passes a small museum in the former house of the poet Junqueiro, with collections of furniture, china and silver. Just north of the cathedral, the stalls of an outdoor market (best on Saturday) cluster in the shelter of the rocky hilltop.

From the broad terrace in front of the cathedral's west door, near the tall *pelourinho*, you can look out over the **Barredo**, one of the oldest parts of the city, sloping down to the waterfront. It's a medieval jumble of tiled roofs punctuated here and there by the more modern materials of redevelopment projects. The narrow cobblestone alleys are so steep they turn into steps in places, and they're lined by decrepit houses tall enough to keep the street level in a state of permanent gloom. Stairs below the cathedral terrace lead to the Renaissance Jesuit church, **Igreja dos Grilos**, and on downhill into the picturesque squalor. It's best avoided at night and you should be careful of bag-snatchers at any time.

Ribeira - the Waterfront

Head down through the Barredo as directly as the maze allows, and you'll soon arrive at **Cais da Ribeira quayside** along the Douro. Few vessels tie up here now, for the riverboats lost trade to the railways and roads, and ocean-going ships can't get past the sandbars at the river mouth (they use seaports such as Matosinhos). You might spot an excursion boat or two, especially in summer, and larger cruise boats have recently begun to make week-long trips up the Douro (see p.198). A few market stalls set up along the quay and some of the little shops – tucked into remnants of the old city wall – cater for the sporadic tourist trade. The chief reason for people to come here, however, is to eat in one of the many restaurants that line the waterfront and adjoining streets and alleys. Mostly small and informal, these cover a broad price range and generally serve traditional Portuguese food – that means fish, naturally, but also

*T*he Ribeira quarter down by the River Douro is one place to look for some typical Portuguese restaurants. There is certain to be fresh fish on the menu, as well as the local speciality, tripe.

plenty of unusual meat dishes. Some switch rôles from workers' café at lunchtime to fashionable bistro in the evening.

The Cais da Ribeira runs from the Dom Luis I bridge westward to Praça da Ribeira, then the road diverts inland for a short way. Where it rejoins the quay, the **Centro Regional de Artes Tradicionais** (regional craft exhibition and shop) is worth a visit.

The Bolsa District

Leading uphill away from the river, Rua da Alfândega is home to the **Casa do Infante**, a fine four-storey mansion reputed to be the birthplace of Prince Henry the

---

TRIPE EATERS

Tripe is a local speciality: menus in back street dives and elegant restaurants alike list *Tripas à Moda do Porto* ('Tripe Oporto Style'), a filling stew which also includes bits of chicken, sausage, ham, beans, onions, herbs and spices. To the rest of Portugal, the Oporto people are known as *tripeiros*, tripe eaters, or in less polite graffiti scrawled by fans of rival football teams, just *tripas*. The label recalls a time when all the best cuts of meat were patriotically salted to supply Henry the Navigator's ships, while those at home had to survive on all the odds and ends left over.

Navigator in 1394. The event may well have taken place here, but the king's customs house which stood on the site has been rebuilt so thoroughly that it's unlikely that anything remains of the original. The present building houses the city archives, including a record of the birth (bemoaning the cost of the festivities). Only the entrance hall is open, with historic ship models and a few documents on show.

At its upper end, the street runs into the prince's eponymous square, **Praça do Infante Dom Henrique**. A right turn takes you along a street that's now also named in his honour: it used to be Rua Nova dos Ingleses. Appropriately, on the next corner (the junction with Rua de São João), you'll come to the **Feitoria Inglesa** (British Factory House), which is not a factory in the modern sense but an elegant four-storey mansion in unmistakeable Georgian style. Dating from the late 18th century, it was built for the association of British Port wine shippers as their headquarters, library and club.

Returning to the square, you're faced by the imposing classical façade of the 19th-century **Palácio do Bolsa** (Stock Exchange). Guided tours are offered (daily in summer, weekdays only the rest of the year), but if you're short of time there are better ways to spend 40 minutes. Costly materials – marble, mahogany and gold – were lavished on the interior, above all in the gilded *Salão Arabe* (Arabian Hall), an oval chamber imitating Moorish style at its most elaborate, which has been derided by some as a gaudy pastiche. Across the street, uphill from the Bolsa, the Port Wine Institute has its offices. As in Lisbon, the institute runs a bar where you can buy various ports by the glass, but not in this building. It's near the Palácio de Cristal (see p.190). Opposite, the old Ferreira Borges covered market, with its slim cast-iron columns, now serves as a spacious exhibition hall.

Where the Bolsa now stands was once the site of a convent attached to the **Igreja de São Francisco**. The church itself survives, right next to the Bolsa in the south-

*G*uides will proudly show you round the elaborately decorated 19th-century Palácio do Bolsa, Oporto's Stock Exchange.

west corner of the square. The style is solid-looking 14th-century Gothic – from the outside. Inside, it was transformed in the 18th century when almost every surface was encrusted with incredibly elaborate gilded carving: angels, birds, vines and bunches of grapes. A huge Tree of Jesse dominates the north wall; beneath it, the figure lying in a boat is *Nossa Senhora da Boa Viagem*, Our Lady of the Good Voyage. A combined ticket gains access to the church and its museum opposite, with some fine religious statuary.

A couple of streets away to the west, the **Museum of Ethnography and History** faces a small square called Largo de São João Novo. The palatial 18th-century mansion which houses it is currently undergoing a major renovation. When it reopens (check with the *Turismo*), you'll be able to see wide-ranging collections covering prehistory, the Roman period, ship models, folk art and costume, ceramics and glass.

The Centre and West

Oporto outgrew its medieval wall in the 18th century and has been expanding ever since. In all but a few places the wall has gone, but it's easy to follow the line it took: just watch for where the streets become broader and the houses bigger. For the best vantage point, head for the Igreja dos Clérigos, which was designed by Nasoni in the 1740s, although he added the **Torre dos Clérigos** bell tower later. Standing on high ground just north of the old city, it is still the most prominent landmark on the skyline and something of a symbol of Oporto. The small fee and the climb of more than 200 uneven steps are worth it for the spectacular views in every direction.

A couple of blocks to the east, the **Praça da Liberdade** makes the best claim to the title of city centre, alhough it con-

The imposing Praça da Liberdade in the centre of Oporto, where the city expanded beyond the line of the medieval walls.

sists of nothing more interesting than a collection of banks around the edge staring on to an equestrian statue of Dom Pedro IV. Leave the square by the south-east corner and you'll come to **São Bento railway station**. Even if you aren't planning a train journey, take a look inside the main entrance to see the huge panels of 20th-century *azulejos*. Some depict the history of transport, and a striking scene of the age of chivalry shows João I arriving for his marriage to Philippa of Lancaster.

Praça da Liberdade is open on the north side and continues uphill as the Avenida

189

dos Aliados, a broad boulevard with gardens down the middle. The baroque-revival City Hall stands at the top end, and one block to the east, **Praça de Dom João I** is the focus where Oporto's most elegant shopping streets meet.

West of the Torre dos Clérigos there has been a rash of redevelopment, but the 18th-century **Hospital de Santo António** is still an impressive sight. Enormous though it seems, it was never finished: the original plan was for a complete square. Behind the hospital in Rua de Dom Manuel II, the former Carrancas Palace (the French Marshal Soult's headquarters in 1809; see p.241) is normally the home of the **Soares dos Reis Museum**, named after a noted 19th-century sculptor. In 1993 it was decided that the building was in need of repair, and it was closed indefinitely. When the work is finished, Oporto's chief collection of fine art will again be on display, including works by Vasco Fernandes (O Grão Vasco), Gaspar Vaz and Josefa de Óbidos. The museum's other major strengths are in rare Chinese, Japanese and Portuguese ceramics, furniture, glass and silver.

Further along the same street, the leafy park called **Jardim do Palácio de Cristal** was the site of an 1865 glass and cast iron exhibition building. The dome which replaced it inherited the name, Palácio de Cristal, and stages conventions, fairs and sports events. Continue past the gardens and take Rua Entre Quintas to the left to Quinta da Macieirinha, a fine mansion which houses the **Museu Romântico**. After a look at its somewhat heavy 19th-century furniture and portraits, choose a glass of Port from an extensive list in the basement in the Port Wine Institute's **Solar do Vinho do Porto**.

If you've picked one of the big modern hotels to stay in, you'll probably find

yourself based some distance from the centre, very possibly on the long, straight **Avenida da Boavista**. Starting at Praça da Republica, it heads west to the Atlantic, punctuated only by the Rotunda da Boavista (or Praça de Mousinho de Albuquerque). Here, circled by heavy traffic, a tall monument to the Peninsular War is topped by a lion crushing a fallen eagle (symbolizing the British-Portuguese victory over the French). Not far away in Rua de Anibal Cunha, the Romanesque **Igreja de São Martinho da Cedofeita**

church dates from the 12th century, but has clearly been rebuilt more than once. If you're walking, the pedestrian shopping street Rua da Cedofeita is a useful route to the city centre.

Western Suburbs

Down river from the old waterfront area, the Ponte de Arrábida carries the *Auto-estrada* from Lisbon across the Douro, funnelling its traffic into Oporto's streets and often creating huge jams. Further west, in a quiet residential area south of Avenida da

T he Museu Nacional de Arte Moderna (Modern Art Museum), in the western residential suburbs, was set up by the Gulbenkian Foundation.

Boavista (about 3km/2 miles from the city centre), the **Museu Nacional de Arte Moderna** stands in its own beautiful gardens. Like the Centro de Arte Moderna in

Lisbon, this is a creation of the Gulbenkian Foundation, with frequently changing exhibitions of modern Portuguese artists.

Where the Douro meets the sea, Atlantic waves roll into the narrow river mouth, up past the long sand bar on the south side. On the north shore, **Foz do Douro** became Oporto's own seaside resort in the 19th century as well as a residential suburb. Several stretches of sand between the rocks were good for swimming and a string of seafront restaurants catered to the crowds carried here by the new electric tram service. One section of beach was adopted by the British community and labelled *Praia dos Ingleses*. Now, more than a century later, the sea is badly polluted by sewage and industrial effluents and the city authorities themselves warn people against swimming, or even going too close to the water when spray is in the air.

'Foz' and its restaurants are still popular, however, and the trams are still running. For a nostalgic tour you can take a Number 18 down Avenida da Boavista, reaching the sea at the 17th-century fort of **Castelo do Queijo**, a low, star-shaped cannon platform typical of the period. The line then follows the seaside promenade to the river mouth, guarded by another fort. North of Foz do Douro, the one-time fishing village of **Matosinhos** now has a big artificial harbour, making it Oporto's chief port and industrial zone, and adding to the pollution at Foz.

Vila Nova de Gaia

From any high point in Oporto, you'll notice the long, low buildings clustered on the south bank of the Douro, many with the names of Port shippers on their roofs in large white letters. These are the old *armazéns* (from the Arabic for warehouse) or **wine lodges**, mostly established in the 18th century, although some occupy even older buildings. They're used for the storage, blending and bottling of Port wine prior to export. Being north-facing, the site stays a little cooler, an advantage for keeping the wine (see p.193-196).

The **waterfront** of Vila Nova de Gaia (often called simply Gaia), is quickly reached from the Ribeira quayside in Oporto via the lower level of the Dom Luis I bridge. Alternatively, if you're starting from the city centre, take the upper level – unless you suffer from vertigo – and enjoy the view (see p.183). High above the south end of the bridge, the terrace in front of the former convent of **Nossa Senhora da Serra do Pilar** is another fine vantage point. This was Wellington's headquarters before he took Oporto from the French in 1809: he watched from these heights while his troops began the momentous crossing of the Douro (see p.241). The Renaissance church and its columned cloister are unusual, for they are both circular in plan, but they're not open on a regular basis and the adjoining convent buildings are occupied by the army. To reach the Gaia quayside, take the steep lane down to the right just after crossing the bridge.

Many of the shippers offer free tours of their premises with an explanation of the whole production process. At the end, you'll have a chance to taste one or two of the products, probably just their standard white and ruby ports – don't expect a prize vintage. There's quite a contrast between the tours you get at different lodges, ranging from smooth commercial operations with audio-visual programmes, multilingual guides and souvenir shops, to a personal briefing in a lodge where nothing seems to have changed for a century. The lodges situated further from the river tend to have fewer visitors.

Port

Many parts of Portugal have the right natural conditions for growing grapes, but the upper Douro valley where Port wine comes from is not one of them. Flowing out of Spain, the Douro cuts a deep gorge through a harsh landscape of bare granite and shale. The steep slopes are practically devoid of earth, and although there's plenty of sunshine, rainfall can be sparse and winters almost Arctic. In a paradox which New World growers have begun to appreciate, a harder life can make for finer wines.

Centuries of superhuman labour were needed to create walls and terraces and build up the soil to grow crops. The Romans probably planted the first vineyards, and by the 13th century the region's wines were beginning to travel. Rivers were the roads of those days, and the Douro gave easy access to Oporto and thence to the rest of Portugal. Then war and politics took a hand. All the best wine-growing areas of south-western France had once come under the English crown. By the 14th century they were lost and a seemingly endless war cut the English off from their favourite 'claret'. New sources had to be found. Even before the 1386 alliance between John of Gaunt and João I, English merchants were trading with Portugal. Thus they began to ship quantities of Douro and Minho wines from Oporto instead of French from Bordeaux.

The trade remained small scale until war with France broke out in 1678, and again in 1690. British merchants were already well established at Oporto, trading wool for dried fish, cotton and fruits, as well as wine. In the Methuen Treaty of 1703, Britain reduced the tax on Portuguese wine in exchange for lower tariffs on her woollen goods entering Portugal, and so the market received a further boost.

The barcos rabelos *which used to bring the Port wine down the River Douro from the vineyards to the shippers' lodges at Vila Nova de Gaia, only carry commercials now.*

With little control over production and storage, plus a voyage through the stormy Bay of Biscay, it's certain that a lot of the wine was more like vinegar by the time it reached England. No one knows who found that the addition of brandy stabilized it – the discovery may have been an accident. This 'fortification' had another advantage: when carried out during the fermentation, that process is quickly stopped, leaving a lot of the sugars unfermented and producing wines both sweet and strong. These suited English tastes and so Port became all the rage. More and more people could afford it, but the demand for ever greater sweetness and potency led to the use of all sorts of dubious additives. Wines were laced with various crude spirits, as well as elderberry juice to give a richer colour.

In 1727, the British Port shippers in Oporto formed an association, called a 'Factory', to improve their buying power with the growers and wine brokers. The rough stuff was damaging Port's reputation and the price they could get in Britain had begun to fall. They complained to the growers about the quality, but the dispute came to the ears of the energetic Marquês de Pombal, the king's minister and the effective dictator of Portugal at the time. His response was twofold. He fixed the boundaries of the region which was allowed to produce Port wine, and took measures to stop adulteration and counterfeiting. Less to the merchants' liking, in 1756 he formed a government monopoly to handle all sales to the shippers. Even so, they did well enough and by the end of the 18th century many familiar names had been established, including Croft, Sandeman, Warre, Taylor and Offley Forrester. Not all exports were in British hands: Dutch, German and Portuguese shippers were active too. French occupation of Oporto twice during the Peninsular War was a setback, but trade soon recovered. The shippers began to buy *quintas*, estates in the upper Douro so they could be close to the harvest and have a better idea of what they were buying. Some of the British even learned Portuguese.

Although new vineyards are blasted out of the hillsides with dynamite and levelled by bulldozers, picking is still done by hand, mostly by whole families of local villagers, who clamber over the terraces. The women and children do the picking, while the men ferry huge basketfuls on

THE BARON

Joseph James Forrester arrived in Oporto in 1831. He was one of a new breed of British merchant – one who learned fluent Portuguese and took the trouble to get to know the growers and labourers personally. He was on good terms with the local aristocracy, and was created a baron (*Barão*) himself. As a talented artist, he painted fine watercolours of the region, and he was the first to map the upper Douro accurately. He campaigned against putting additives in the wines, such as elderberry juice to enrich the colour. More controversially, he was in principle opposed to fortification, claiming that the upper Douro's wines at their best could stand on their own without it, and bear comparison with the best of Bordeaux and Burgundy. Tragically, he was drowned in 1861 when his boat capsized in the rapids on his beloved Douro near Quinta de Vargellas. His body was never found: it was said his money belt was full of gold for paying growers and it pulled him to the bottom of the river. Today he is widely honoured in the business (and the firm of Offley Forrester is still active), while the Pousada at Alijó carries his name, Barão de Forrester.

their backs to the waiting trailers. Traditionally, the grapes are then trodden in stone tanks called *lagares* by teams of men working 8-hour shifts. It's hard labour – imagine doing underwater exercises for that long – but the whole community gathers round and turns the treading into a continuous party. Bare feet apply just the right pressure – enough to release colour from the grape skins, but not to break the pips and produce bitter flavours. Some growers still stick to the old way, swearing that it makes better Port, but modern mechanical crushers have inevitably taken over most of the work.

Fermentation starts right away, during the crushing, triggered by the natural yeasts on the grapes. When the grapes have been trodden, they're left to ferment in the *lagares*. If they're crushed mechanically, the fermentation takes place in closed vats, and the pressure of the carbon dioxide gas generated is used to pump the juice around and mix up the must (the mass of juice and grape debris). That does the job of human feet in extracting the colour and tannin from the skins. Fermentation goes on for two or three days at a temperature of about 28°C (83°F) until the must reaches around 6% alcohol, about half the sugars having been converted. Then the juice is run off into a big wooden cask called a *tonel*. This is the point when the half-made wine is fortified by adding one part of grape alcohol (like colourless brandy) to every four parts of wine. The alcohol content of the mixture jumps to around 20%, enough to stop the yeasts from working and halt the fermentation.

The new Port rests in its casks at the quintas until spring, when most of it is moved to the shippers' lodges in Vila Nova de Gaia, on the south bank of the Douro opposite Oporto. Until the 19th century when the railway took a share, it was all floated down the river, riding

---

TRADITION VERSUS TECHNOLOGY

Australian and American winegrowers dedicated to controlling every factor to 4 decimal places are inclined to throw up their hands in horror. To them, Port is made under conditions that make a mockery of modern oenological science. In an era where wine labels round the world proudly trumpet 'Cabernet Sauvignon' or 'Chardonnay', many Douro growers don't even know what sorts of vines they've got. Port comes from as many as eighty different varieties, some of them nameless.

Methods of preventing oxidation may appear primitive, but they seem to be effective. Fermentation is left to yeasts that occur by accident, but nature often knows best, and they work perfectly well at the lower concentrations of alcohol reached before fortification stops it anyway. Temperature regulation – considered essential elsewhere – is still a new idea. Yet these wines can live for 30 years or more in their old wooden casks before bottling; and the finest vintage Ports may spend over 50 years in a bottle, finally to emerge as some of the most sublime and complex wines in the world.

---

treacherous rapids on flat-bottomed boats called *barcos rabelos* – you can still see a few moored at Pêso da Régua and Vila Nova de Gaia. The casks were usually not full when they started, so that they would float if the boat capsized. It's said this gave the boatmen a chance to tap off a portion to drink: if the cask had been full, they would have been tempted to top it up with river water. It may have been a relief to the shippers when, by 1960, new dams on the Douro stopped the remaining boat traffic. Nowadays almost all the wine goes by road tanker.

In the cool, dark lodges of Vila Nova de Gaia, the wines rest in their casks. (The traditional Port cask, known as a

Port lies for years in oak barrels in the cool dark warehouses of Vila Nova de Gaia, on the south bank of the Douro.

'pipe', holds 115 imperial gallons, or about 523 litres. The production of a *quinta* and the size of a shipper's business are still measured in pipes.)

The shippers already have a shrewd idea if the year has been a good one. They know from experience which growers are likely to have made the best Port, and frequent tastings tell them how every wine is developing. About 18 months after harvest, the process of blending begins. Perhaps three years in every decade, a consensus starts to emerge that the Port of a certain year is particularly fine. The shippers 'declare a vintage', proclaiming their intention to bottle their blend of the best wines of that year as vintage Port, putting all their prestige behind its marketing.

Needing to be laid down for at least 10 years and handled only with great delicacy, it's almost more like an investment than a drink. Britain has always been the main market – in the past every country

house and town mansion had a cellarful (some still do) but the US is catching up fast.

Vintage Port is the flagship of the business, although it only represents perhaps 2% of the volume. All the rest, from rough-and-ready young ruby to subtle old tawny, constitutes a fascinating range of wines, spread right across the price range. If you've never tried a cool white Port as an aperitif (a French favourite) or a rich late-bottled vintage, your visit to Portugal could be something of a revelation.

Although a couple of the largest (Sandeman and Real Vinicola) are open on Saturday and even on Sunday mornings, it's best to go during working hours, and not too close to lunchtime. Then you'll have a chance to see something happening, even if it's only a modern bottling line. The traditional Port-carrying *rabelo* sailing boats tied up at the quayside are just for show now, but in summer you can take a trip up and down the river on one of the tour boats.

South of the Douro, a flat coastal plain suffers from messy development. The main roads stay inland, and the couple of minor beach resorts aren't worth a diversion – if for no other reason than simply because the seawater this close to Oporto is suspect. The situation is different at **Espinho**, 20km (12 miles) south, where the current keeps it clean. Here, a brash, down-market holiday centre has grown up around an old fishing village, with a hotel and casino complex standing oddly in the middle of wasteland at the northern end. Appropriately for a plain town, the grid-pattern streets have numbers, not names. There's plenty of space on the beach, even when the mainly local summer crowds are here. At the south end, colourful high-prowed fishing boats are hauled ashore by tractors and some of the catch is sold on the spot. For more solitude, explore the beaches and dunes that extend for the next 40km (25 miles) south towards Aveiro (see p.178)

The Lower Douro

Your first sight of the 'River of Gold' may be as it emerges from a gorge to flow past Oporto and the Port shippers' lodges of Gaia on the the last lap to the sea. If you have an ambition to travel the length of its valley, you can. A road sticks close to the north bank for most of the way, occasionally switching to the south side or climbing away from the river when the valley walls become too steep – for a road that is, since there's always a rough track, sometimes hacked out of the rock. After the *rabelo* boats had delivered their precious cargo, they had to make their way upstream. When the wind was from the west, they could sail; when it wasn't, the men had to fix a rope and walk these towpaths, pulling the boats behind them.

Unless you have unlimited time, it's better to skip the less interesting lower reaches, which is exactly what the Douro

CRUISING THE DOURO

Where once the *rabelos* laden with barrels of Port drifted downstream or ran the rapids, a riverboat like a floating hotel now carries 80 passengers on week-long cruises in comfort and ease. From Oporto it travels upstream to Entre-os-Rios, where the Tâmega River meets the Douro, and then on towards the Port-growing region. Several locks have to be negotiated on the way, including one of the highest in Europe. Thanks to the locks, the boats are able to climb the barrages which have smoothed out the rapids. The river cuts though narrow gorges, then meanders lazily through broader plains and past villages which it used to flood on a regular basis before it was tamed.

At Peso da Régua, the Port vineyards begin, the 'hanging gardens of Portugal' notched like rough staircases into the steep, slaty slopes. The cruise makes leisurely progress, stopping at Pinhão, Pocinho and Barca de Alva at the Spanish frontier, which marks the end of the navigable reaches of the Douro. There are side trips at each port of call: to a vineyard, or a *quinta* for dinner, or sightseeing tours to castles. Travel companies offer various other options before and after the cruise, including trips to Santiago de Compostela in Spain.

Line trains do, only joining the river about 60km (37 miles) inland (see p.78 for details of the small railways of this region). They then run along the north bank through the *vinho verde* (and not Port) villages and vineyards.

The main road east from Oporto doesn't follow the Douro at all: a side road cuts south-east to join the river at Mesão Frio. Finally, at Peso da Régua, the Port wine region of the Upper Douro begins (see p.230 for further information).

The North Coast

Between Oporto and the Spanish border you'll find historic towns full of character, fishing ports, fast-growing holiday resorts and stretches of shore you can have all to yourself. The weather isn't as reliable as it is further south, nor is the sea as warm, but with countless opportunities for excursions inland and a big choice of places to stay – including rooms in private houses and *quintas* – you have one of the most rewarding parts of Portugal.

Vila do Conde

This fishing and boat building town grew up where the River Ave meets the sea, 26km (16 miles) north of Oporto. The first settlement was probably on the hill where the massive 18th-century **Convent of Santa Clara** stands, dominating the medieval quarter. It's now a boys' reform centre, but at weekends you may be able to see inside the Gothic church. Begun in the 14th century and rebuilt in the 16th, it's notable for the finely carved tombs of the founder Afonso Sanches (an illegitimate son of King Dinis) and his wife. The fountain in the cloister used to be fed by an **aqueduct** 5km (3 miles) long, built in

the 18th century. You can still see part of it here and other sections inland to the north, including some of the original 999 arches. The builders thought that the number 1000 would have smacked of perfection, and only God is perfect.

Even if the Santa Clara church is closed, it's worth going up the hill for the view over the river and boatyards, where a few rugged wooden fishing vessels are still constructed. Below the hill in the old town, the 16th-century **Igreja Matriz** (parish church) has a superb Gothic door. Manueline features are evident, as they are in the rope-like carving of the *pelourinho*, and many houses in the quiet streets have windows and doorways in the same style.

Vila do Conde went into a long decline when the river silted up in the late 18th century. Two things have given it a new lease of life: an artificial harbour for the fishing fleet and an influx of summer visitors attracted to the long clean beach. The town has expanded north along the coast, where you'll find several bars and restaurants but few places to stay. The old town has *pensões* and an *estalagem*; and the **Turismo** at Rua 25 de Abril can help to find rooms. They're all likely to be full in the last week of July and the first week in August, when Portugal's biggest craft fair takes over every available space, each province with its own pavilion and demonstrations. Vila do Conde itself has been known for its bobbin lace since the 17th century – ask at the *Turismo* if you want to visit a lace-making cooperative.

If Vila do Conde hasn't sprouted hotels and apartment blocks, it may be because neighbouring Póvoa de Varzim already has so many. The old town centres are 5km (3 miles) apart, and as one spread north, the other expanded to the south.

Now they've joined up, but there's a world of difference between them.

Póvoa de Varzim

Dedicated to the holiday business, this resort has all the hotels, bars, discos and restaurants you would expect. A wall of white high-rise buildings looks out over a broad avenue to a vast stretch of sandy beach, half covered in summer by row after row of striped beach tents. Leisure craft pack the marina and showgirls strut the stage of the pink and white **Casino**.

Look closely, however, for this modernity is only one street deep. This is an age-old settlement, one of the few sheltered bays in the region, and was probably first inhabited by fisherfolk migrating down the coasts of western Europe (and not by the local Celts). Their descendants still bring in the fish and mend their nets right opposite the casino. Deeply religious, they take statuettes of Our Lady and their patron saints to sea and parade life-size images through the streets to the seashore at Easter and during summer festivals. On Assumption Day, 15 August, the figure of *Nossa Senhora da Assuncão* is taken to the harbour to bless the fishing boats.

A squat 18th-century **fort** guards the harbour and traditional life goes on in the quiet streets of the old town around **Praça da Almada**. Before exploring, collect a street map from the **Turismo**, just behind the Casino at 160 Avenida Mousinho de Albuquerque. You'll see the strangest contrast between ancient and modern at **A-Ver-o-Mar**, adjoining the northern outskirts of Póvoa. The roads deteriorate to mud and dust, and at first sight the foreshore appears to be dotted with thatched huts, like an African kraal. Close up, you'll see that they're stacks of drying seaweed, to be sold to farmers as a soil improver and to industry as a source of alginates (to keep ice-cream soft and toothpaste squeezable, amongst other uses). Next to the ramshackle shanties of the seaweed gatherers and their lines of washing, hopeful builders are putting up new apartment blocks.

In a maze of lanes just inland from Póvoa, factories at Beiriz and Terroso produce colourful carpets and blankets. The same villages are known for their silversmiths, whose jewellery and ornaments are sold in Póvoa's shops. In a store behind the Casino you can actually see them at work.

Rates, 14km (9 miles) east of Póvoa, has one of the best 12th-century Romanesque churches in the country, built soon after the reconquest. (To find it, follow the IC5 road and look for signs to Rates to the north.) The interior, triple-apsed eastern end and worn west door with its carved capitals are all very fine. A statue outside honours Tomé de Sousa, the first governor of Brazil who was born in the village.

Stretches of sandy coast continue as you go north, but large-scale development peters out. In many places the sea can only be reached by lanes through little farms, and you might find yourself sharing remoter beaches with only the seaweed gatherers. **Ofir**, on a sand spit between the sea and the River Cávado, has a few big hotels, holiday houses and campsites shaded by pine trees. There's a wide range of sports facilities, both land and water based – the sheltered estuary suits waterskiers and small boats. Across the river, the little town of **Esposende** is more concerned with light industry and fishing, and only a couple of resort hotels face the beach. At Mar (San Bartolomeu do Mar), a narrow road gives access to a vast and unexploited length of shoreline. If you're prepared to walk a bit, you can be alone even in high summer.

Viana do Castelo

Port, holiday resort and historic city – the capital of the Alto Minho region is all these and more. The fast-growing outskirts may look unpromising, with smoking factories and highways often choked with traffic, but the old centre is delightful, full of architectural gems, friendly and informal, with the attractions of a bustling harbour, famous festivals and folk music, good food and wine. The beach is across the estuary of the River Lima, and can be reached by a short ferry trip or a 4km (2.5-mile) drive. With unusual foresight, the coastline south of the river has been designated a protected area, saving it from a rash of high-rise building. Apart from camping, most accommodation is in the lively little city itself and not in a tourist ghetto.

Almost every town on the Atlantic coast of Portugal evolved on an estuary, giving boats a place to shelter, and Viana is no exception. It was at the forefront of progress during the era of the great voyages of discovery, and for centuries the fishing fleet has ranged as far as Newfoundland in pursuit of cod. In the 16th century, English merchants based here were exporting Minho wines, though the trade later moved to Oporto. Today, gracious buildings, public and private, are evidence of the prosperity of that time.

One such building, the 1468 Hospital Velho in Praça da Erva, now houses the **Turismo**, where you can pick up a recommended booklet and numbered map with descriptions of dozens of marked sights. From the railway station (where there's also hope of parking a car), it's just off the broad Avenida dos Combatentes da Grande Guerra which leads to the harbour. If you take the more attractive **Rua Candido dos Reis**, you'll first come upon the lovely **Palácio dos Condes de Carreira** (now the

Town Hall) and then the admirable main square – in fact a triangle – the **Praça da República**. The battlemented **Old Town Hall** (*Antigos Paços do Concelho*), with open arcades at street level, dates from the early 1500s and the tall, elegant fountain in the centre carries the date 1554. Most unusual is the 1598 **Misericórdia Hospice**, whose three-storey façade has balconies supported by granite caryatids.

The modest Cathedral, which in the past has been downgraded to parish church, has a fine 15th-century Gothic door with figures of the apostles. The interior was ravaged by fire in 1809, and the eventual repairs saw the addition of the present trompe l'oeil decoration. Continue along Rua Sacadura Cabral and Rua da Aurora do Lima to reach the river, where there is a cluster of restaurants in the narrow streets to the right.

West along the waterfront, you'll come to the Fort (Castelo de Santiago da Barra), begun on the orders of Philip II of Spain when he gained power in Portugal in 1580. The dusty space beside it comes alive with market stalls on Friday. Signs nearby to Praia do Norte just north of the harbour shouldn't be taken too literally. The 'North Beach' they refer to is tiny and rocky, though popular with anglers. Viana's main **beach** is Praia Cabedelo, south of the Lima estuary. You can catch a ferry from the quay, near Largo 5 de Outubro, or drive over the two-deck Ponte de Viana, the iron bridge designed by Eiffel and opened in 1878 – now a notorious bottleneck, partially relieved by the new highway bridge further east.

Viana's religious and folk festivals are renowned throughout Portugal and beyond. In early August, the Festa de Santa Cristina is marked by a procession and parade in vivid traditional dress, the women loaded with gold ornaments. On the weekend near-

One of the most attractive town centres in Portugal, that of Viana do Castelo, is also the setting for some of the most colourful processions and festivals.

est to 20 August, the Festa da Senhora da Agonía (Our Lady of Sorrows) is anything but sorrowful, with a religious procession on Friday and a great parade of floats from all the nearby villages on Saturday, including gigantones (stilt-men with huge papier maché heads). In the streets and squares there's eating, drinking and dancing unlimited. Like most Portuguese festivals, it climaxes in a storm of fireworks.

On the northern edge of Viana do Castelo, the wooded **Monte de Santa Luzia** dominates the scene: a funicular and a zig-zag road climb to the most ob-

vious landmark, a heavy-looking basilica finished in 1926. There's a fine view from the terrace, and and an even better one from the hotel (part of the *Pousada* chain) higher up. The road to reach it was cut right across an ancient citânia, or fortified **hilltop town** from the Celt-Iberian period. In places, you can see where it sliced through prehistoric houses. Now there's a more respectful attitude to the past: walkways being constructed above the site will give a bird's eye view.

Little Afife, 10km (6 miles) north of Viana, has yet to exploit its beautiful sands, but **Vila Praia de Ancora**, a further 5km (3 miles) on, is a popular resort. The tiny harbour, protected by a fort, is still used by fishing boats – notice the lights to guide them through its narrow entrance. Some of the catch appears within hours on menus at the local restaurants. The town has expanded south along the beach, but it is still on a pleasantly human scale.

The Valley of the Minho

Ever since Afonso Henriques asserted its independence, Portugal's short northern border has been marked by the last 110km (68 miles) of the broad River Minho on its meandering progress to the Atlantic. Not surprisingly, kings of León and Castile and later of a united Spain often threatened to invade (and sometimes did). As a result, every town along the river was heavily fortified and garrisoned right up to modern times. These days, the invading Spanish army consists of shoppers looking for bargains. The most spectacular fortress serves as the backdrop for market stalls, while another has been beautifully converted into a *Pousada*.

A 17th-century fort, chapel and convent, sadly vandalized, cover most of the island of **Ínsua**, which can be seen in the estuary from the rather scruffy beach at Moledo. The main road turns upstream, past the walls of the old port of **Caminha**, which has only been used by shallow craft since the river silted up. Around the main square, Largo Silva Torres, impressive Renaissance buildings tell of the town's former importance. The battlemented 16th-century clock tower, topped by an ironwork belfry, stands on a much older base. Through the arch beneath it, in Rua Ricardo Joaquim da Sousa, the **Turismo** is housed in one of many elegant mansions. Continue past the lovely little Largo Calouste Gulbenkian to the **Igreja Matriz**, the parish church, which is almost surrounded by thick 17th-century ramparts. Dating from the 15th and 16th centuries, it's distinguished by two fine doorways and other stone carving, including some Manueline trademarks, plus a gorgeous interior with *azulejos* and a complex wood-panelled ceiling in *mudéjar* style.

Vila Nova de Cerveira

Up river and 12km (7 miles) from Caminha, one of the prettiest towns in the Minho is hidden behind its old walls. Although a few Spanish day-trippers arrive by car ferry across the river, the majority cross by the bridges at Valença, its neighbour upstream.

In the heart of the old town, the central square called the Terreiro is faced by the massive gateway and steep, angled entrance ramp of the 13th-century **Castle**, built on the orders of Afonso III. Although married to the daughter of his northern neighbour, the king of Castile and Léon, Afonso evidently felt safer with the insurance of good defences. Inside the castle, old buildings have been adapted and new ones constructed to create the luxury Pousada de Dom Dinis. Its modern two-storey restaurant, with an upper level mostly of glass, fits in rather well and gives a good view of the river and Goyán on the Spanish side, as does a walk on the castle walls. The little town is something of an arts and crafts centre, with galleries and shops selling pictures, metalwork, blankets, stone carvings and pottery.

Valença do Minho

The north's most spectacular fortress stands on a low hill near the river, with massive double walls and a deep rock-cut ditch completely surrounding a compact medieval town. The immensely thick outer ramparts were built in the 17th and 18th centuries and withstood more than one Spanish siege. Their sharply angled zig-zag pattern is often called Vaubanesque, after the French engineer Vauban who developed the style (see p.263).

A big car park is located by the main gate, the monumental **Porta da Coroada**, where you pass through a tunnel in the outer wall. The space between the walls is taken up by shops and market stalls and it's often a seething mass of Spanish bargain hunters loading up with clothes, toys, shoes, drinks and whatever represents a saving at the time. More prices are marked in pesetas than escudos! Through the inner wall, many old houses have been turned into shops and the narrow streets can be jammed with cars that have found their way in. Some parts are still quite unspoiled, and if you can wait until evening, calm returns.

At any time, you can escape the crowd by walking along some sections of the walls, but watch out for slippery slopes with no guard rail. If your budget will run to it, the modern but well designed Pousada de São Teotónio stands above the ramparts, looking over the river towards the Spanish town of Túy. There's a choice of other accommodation and places to eat both inside and outside the walls.

The modern frontier town has far outgrown the walls. Expansion was first boosted by the building of an iron bridge over the Minho, an Eiffel design, 330m (1,100ft) long, completed in 1885. By the 1980s an average of over 20,000 people a day were using it. Now a new road bridge has relieved the border congestion, but added even more to the total traffic: you'll see more Spanish-registered cars than local.

Monção, 18km (11 miles) of winding road up the river from Valença, is another border fortress with a history of sieges, although its walls are far from complete now. With only a ferry connecting it to Spain and no bridge, it gets far fewer visitors, and has consequently retained a more original ambience, notably in the attractive old centre. The Romanesque parish church, built in the 13th century but much altered in the 18th, contains the tomb of Deu-la-Deu Martins, who got the better of a besieging Castilian army in 1368. She baked bread with the last of the defenders' supplies and threw it over the walls, calling out that there was plenty more where that came from. Believing her, the besiegers gave up and went home. (It's a popular tale which you may come across in several other Portuguese towns!) Restaurants specialize in river fish and the region produces some of the best *vinho verde* wines, notably those from the Palácio de Brejoeira estate. You'll pass the imposing palace itself on the road south towards Ponte da Barca (see p.204).

During their war with Castile in 1386, King João I and his English ally, John of Gaunt, Duke of Lancaster, negotiated the king's marriage to Lancaster's daughter, Philippa, in the unprepossessing little vil-lage of Ponte de Mouro, 7km (4 miles) to the east. Another 16km (10 miles) away, built around a fort on a hill overlooking the Minho, **Melgaço** is the Portugal's most northerly town, the last before the border. It's well off the usual tour routes, and not much happens apart from the rural market on Friday morning. You might come this way if you're heading for the Serra da Peneda, the northern half of the Peneda-Gerês National Park (see p.220).

The Valley of the Lima

Rising in Spain and flowing through the Peneda-Gerês National Park and down to the sea at Viana do Castelo, the River Lima cuts through some of Portugal's greenest and prettiest scenery. The area is

*R*oman legionaries thought the Lima was the mythical Lethe and believed that crossing it would make them lose their memories. You can just forget about the traffic.

not overrun with visitors, apart from at Ponte de Lima in high summer. The local tourism authorities are particularly energetic, publishing maps of suggested walks and efficiently arranging accommodation. This area has led the way with schemes such as TURIHAB (see p.23) offering rooms in private homes, including luxurious country estates.

You could tour the valley in either direction, or both, travelling up one side, for instance, and then down the other. Each side of the river has its own attractions, and so do all the seasons. Spring and summer see a spate of religious and flower festivals in the towns and villages, while the corn and grape harvest is celebrated in riotous September fairs. Autumn colours are superb, and winter is the time for eating the famous lamprey from the river.

Ponte da Barca

The little town of Ponte de Barca is expanding fast in the suburbs, but in the midst of it all, you'll find a charming old quarter next to a bridge of ten arches, built in the 16th century in place of a bridge of boats (which probably gave the town its name). The colourful Tuesday market fills the spaces along the Lima with stalls and brings in a crowd from the surrounding villages. You can hire a boat to go on the river, and the water is usually clean enough for swimming.

Just 6km (4 miles) to the west, the village of **Bravães** on the N203 south of the river boasts the finest **Romanesque church** in Portugal. Wonderfully preserved 12th-century stone carvings surround the west and south doors: saints, fantastic animals, birds and mythical figures and capitals of stunning complexity. Inside, Renaissance wall paintings of the Virgin and Child and the Martyrdom of St

*P*retty Ponte de Barca is a good centre for exploring the attractive valley of the River Lima.

Sebastian were found when later paintwork was removed in the 1940s.

North of Ponte da Barca, the N101 climbs to a rocky pass before dropping into the valley of the Minho at Monção (see p.203). If you head east, you'll soon reach an entrance to the northern part of the Peneda-Gerês National Park (see p.220). If you want to follow the Lima downstream, the road on the north side of the river winds past picturesque villages and steep terraced hillsides. A number of beautiful quintas in the area have rooms available; check first with the Turismo in Ponte da Barca or Ponte de Lima.

Ponte de Lima

The impressive **bridge** that gave Ponte de Lima its name was built by the Romans, and the long, graceful 14th-century reconstruction you see now incorporates a lot of their work, notably in the arches that span dry land on the right (north-west) bank. On the left bank, the bridge leads straight into the old town. Only pedestrians can use the narrow roadway these days (other traffic crosses by the new bridge downstream), and the tree-shaded embankment is perfect for continuing the stroll. Wide stretches of sand along the river serve as a beach, a public laundry and a site for the market, a great tented camp set up every second Monday.

With some of its walls and towers still standing and many fine granite or whitewashed houses, there's hardly a jarring note in the lovely old town centre. The tower near the bridge houses the local library: its proudest possession is the original town charter granted in 1125 by Dona Teresa, mother of Afonso Henriques, Portugal's first king. Some mansions and palaces date from the 15th or 16th centuries, including the **Paço do Marquês de Ponte de Lima**, with its superb Manueline windows. The **Turismo** in Praça da Republica has street plans and detailed suggestions for local walks, ranging from 7km to 15km (4 to 9 miles). The countryside certainly makes it worth lingering; everywhere you'll hear birds singing and church bells ringing in the distance, see the family cow being led on a

*T*he riverside town of Ponte de Lima is a good base for local walks. It is famous for its September harvest festival, as well as for its bridge built on Roman foundations.

rope, and pass little fields hemmed in by high vines and growing an amazing variety of produce.

The festivals of São Jorge, São João and especially Corpus Christi are all held in early summer, with lots of processions and masses of flowers. The Feiras Novas ('New Fairs', dating from the 12th century) in mid-September combine a harvest celebration, pageant, fireworks and general bacchanalia.

The Southern Minho, Cradle of the Nation

One hour's drive from Oporto – and even closer to each other – lie two historic cities which formed the nucleus that was to grow into Portugal. Guimarães was probably the birthplace of its first king, while Braga was the Romans' regional headquarters and later the country's ecclesiastical capital, a title which it retains to this day. Both places have expanded almost explosively in recent years and the area is one of the most dynamic and densely populated in the country. It is also packed with great sights and treasures, including the Celt-Iberian stronghold of Citânia de Briteiros and the oft-illustrated monumental staircase of Bom Jesus. The craft centre of Barcelos, lying nearest the coast, is not technically in the southern Minho and not the most important centre, but you may want to adjust your route and timing to be there for its famous market day.

Barcelos

This picturesque old town west of Braga would be worth a visit any day of the week, but every Thursday from dawn to mid-afternoon it's the site of the biggest **market** in Portugal. The **Campo da Feira** (or Campo da República), a vast open space about 300m (330 yds) across, becomes a sea of covered stalls. Fast-talking itinerant traders, farmers and smallholders and wizened old ladies sell everything imaginable. The ubiquitous cheap clothing, jewellery, plastic goods and cassette tapes are all there, and plenty of local food and livestock. The big attraction to visitors is the concentration of crafts: wood carving, lace, linen, baskets and especially pottery, from functional kitchenware to purely ornamental pieces, including gaudily painted primitive figures which are probably a distant echo of pagan times. You can find some appealing and funny designs, but they're made in such quantities that originality is rare, and generally found only at a high price in art galleries. Traffic can be a problem at both ends of the day – Barcelos has been provided with new bypasses to reduce the disruption for those *not* going to the fair – and it can be impossible to park anywhere near the centre.

MIRACULOUS BIRD

All over Portugal you'll find brightly painted cockerels made of pottery or wood, for sale in every market and souvenir shop. The crowing cock is practically a national symbol, but its home is Barcelos. As the story goes – and there are many variations – a pilgrim passing through the town was unjustly accused of theft and sentenced to death. He was allowed one last request, and asked to see the judge who had condemned him. Finding that gentleman just sitting down to dine off a roast, he pointed to the cooked cockerel and said: 'May that cock crow if I am innocent!' Some maintain that the bird rose instantly from the plate and did so, but according to another version it didn't move until the judge had sent the man off to the gallows. The judge hurried to the execution chamber to find the man already hanged, but the noose had not tightened enough to kill him and he was saved.

There's much more than the market to see in Barcelos. The first settlement grew up next to a bridge over the Cávado river, and the old part of the town extends from the restored 15th-century **bridge** to the Campo da Feira. In the south-west corner of the Campo, the domed octagonal church of **Nossa Senhor Bom Jesus da Cruz** set a fashion. Built soon after 1700, its shape was copied and its white stucco walls with granite outlines and details became a Portuguese trademark for a century. In the Campo's north-west corner, the **Terço Church** of the same period has a superbly carved and gilded pulpit, standing out from a wall entirely covered with blue *azulejos*.

Leaving the Campo, past the octagonal church you'll see the solid **Torre Nova** (or Torre de Menagem), formerly a strongpoint in the 15th century town wall. Now it houses the **Turismo** and a **craft shop**, which is stocked with a selection of pottery and souvenirs. Oxen with decorated yokes pulling cartloads of musicians

The Tuesday market at Barcelos is celebrated as the biggest in the country, with the greatest selection of craft work.

are a miniature version of the real thing seen in many Minho parades.

Keep right for the pedestrian-only Rua António Barroso, the main artery of the old town, which is faced by 15th- and 16th-century houses and an unusual little classical theatre, still in use. A left turn leads to the Igreja Matriz, the parish church, where you'll find a statue of Nun' Alvares Pereira, commander at the Battle of Aljubarrota, and his son oppposite the Romanesque west door and rose window. The ruin to the south of the church was once the fortified Palace of the Counts of Barcelos, guarding the bridge over the Cávado. Damaged in the 1755 earthquake, it

The ruins of the Palace of the Counts of Barcelos has been imaginatively turned into an outdoor museum for the display of stone antiquities.

then stood empty before collapsing some years later. Now, as the **Museum of Archaeology**, the shell has been imaginatively used to display stone capitals, columns, crosses and sarcophagi. One cross, the 14th-century Cruzeiro do Senhor do Galo, depicts the last-minute rescue of the condemned man in the story of the crowing cock.

Braga

Not so long ago, the business of Braga was exclusively religion. The old city was concentrated around its cathedral, huge archbishop's palace and numerous other churches, but now, industrial and commercial expansion has ringed it with broad boulevards and sprawling suburbs. Nothing suggests that this was once the im-

Gracious old houses, small shops and cafés line the streets in the centre of Braga, Portugal's ecclesiastical capital for a thousand years.

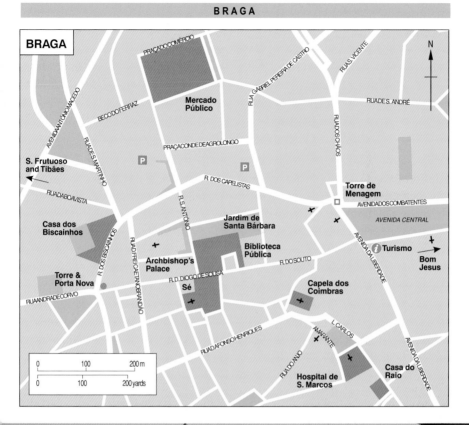

BRAGA

PRAÇA DO COMÉRCIO

RUA DE S. VICENTE

RUA DE S. ANDRÉ

RUA GABRIEL PEREIRA DE CASTRO

AVENIDA ANTÓNIO MACEDO

BECO DO FERRAZ

RUA DE S. MARTINHO

Mercado Público

PRAÇA CONDE DE AGROLONGO

RUA DOS CHÃOS

S. Frutuoso and Tibães

RUA DA BOAVISTA

R. DOS CAPELISTAS

Torre de Menagem

AVENIDA DOS COMBATENTES

R. S. ANTÓNIO

AVENIDA CENTRAL

Casa dos Biscainhos

R. DOS BISCAINHOS

Jardim de Santa Bárbara

ⓘ **Turismo**

Bom Jesus

R. DE FREI CAETANO BRANDÃO

Archbishop's Palace

Biblioteca Pública

R. DO SOUTO

AVENIDA DA LIBERDADE

Torre & Porta Nova

R. D. DIOGO DE SOUSA

Sé

RUA ANDRADE CORVO

Capela dos Coimbras

L. CARLOS

RUA AFONSO HENRIQUES

AMARANTE

AVENIDA DA LIBERDADE

RUA DO ANJO

Hospital de S. Marcos

Casa do Raio

| 0 | 100 | 200 m |
| 0 | 100 | 200 yards |

VENANCIO

PAGO

portant Roman town of Bracara Augusta, which stood on the slope south of the cathedral. Today it has been largely built over, although there is one area of excavations, but this is closed to non-specialists. Nothing survives from the time of the invading Suevi, either, who made this their capital in the 5th century, or indeed the Visigoths, who followed and established a bishopric. Moors and Christians then fought over the region for more than 300 years, and Braga had been largely destroyed and abandoned by the time the Moors were finally expelled.

Reconstruction began, and the cathedral was started before 1100. The Archbishop of Braga supported Afonso Henriques in the creation of an independent Portugal, although he and his successors continued to claim the spiritual leadership of Spain as well. As lords of Braga, their power rivalled that of the king for 600 years. In the 1790s their control of non-church matters was reduced, and the sacking of Braga by French forces in the Peninsular War came as a further setback. Even when most of its property was confiscated by the state in 1834 and 1910, the church remained a potent influence, usually backing right-wing and reactionary movements such as the military coup of 1926 which led to the Salazar dictatorship.

The days when priests and nuns outnumbered the rest of the population are long past. This is a dynamic, modern, secular city, but the archbishop is still the leader of Catholic Church in Portugal, which incorporates the vast majority of the population. Braga's religious ceremonies at Easter, Christmas and other holy days are the most devout and lavish of anywhere in the country.

The old and modern cities collide at the top (north) end of the broad **Avenida da Liberdade**, where it runs into **Praça da República**. Call in at the **Turismo** on the corner, in a beautiful Art Deco building, where you can pick up a good street map marked with the major sights. If you're driving, look for a parking place one block north and west in Praça Conde de Agrolongo.

The historic centre is concentrated to the west of the arcaded Praca da República. Just off the square, the **Torre de Menagem** of 1378 is all that's left of a fortress which was once part of the medieval city walls. Leaving it on your right, continue along the charming pedestrian street, **Rua do Souto**. On the right, it opens into Largo de Paço (Palace Square), surrounded on three sides by the elegant arcades and walls of the old **Archbishop's Palace**. Its 14th-century nucleus was augmented regularly, and the parts you see here date from the 18th century. A fire in 1866 did enormous damage, but now restored, the vast building houses the public library and various university departments. The north side of the palace is more fortress-like, contrasting with a beautiful formal garden.

Almost opposite the palace, across Rua do Souto, the *Sé*, or **Cathedral**, is a most unusual and confusing building in a broad mixture of styles, from 11th- and 12th-century Romanesque origins through Gothic, Renaissance and baroque additions. A courtyard flanked by important chapels (see p.211) and a small, classical 18th-century cloister lead to the north door of the cathedral itself. (Long-term restoration projects mean you may have to pick your way through a building site.) The dark interior is notable for some fine tombs, including that of Afonso, brother of Henry the Navigator, at the south-west corner. He died in childhood in 1400. Superb stone carving around the west door and the south door

The Museum of Religious Art in the cathedral at Braga has a wealth of exhibits, but most unlabelled, like this medieval crucifixion.

survives from the 12th century. You'll get a good view of the exterior from this quarter: the ornamented roofline and belfries were added in the 16th century.

Many more of the cathedral's highlights are hidden, and generally seen only at the end of a half-hour tour for which there's a small fee. This begins with the **Museum of Religious Art**, a succession of rooms stuffed with undoubted treasures of a thousand years: gold, silver, jewelled chalices and crosses, statues and vestments. Annoyingly, they're all unlabelled and unexplained and the custodians who show visitors around are unlikely to enlighten you. The Upper Choir gallery over the west end of the cathedral has some striking 15th-century stalls and two stunning, carved and gilded 18th-century organs.

The chapels near the north courtyard are usually kept to last. The **Capela dos Reis** contains the tombs of Count Henry of Burgundy and his wife Teresa, parents of Afonso Henriques, the first king of Portugal, as well as the dessicated body and effigy of Archbishop Lourenço, the fighting prelate who was wounded at the Battle of Aljubarrota. If the count's effigy is a true likeness, he must have been very short, although, strangely, his son is said to have been a giant. The **Capela de São Geraldo**, with the tomb of the first archbishop of Braga, is lined with 18th-century azulejos painted with scenes from his life. The last word – and the last stop on typical tours – goes to the 14th-century **Capela da Glória**, built by Archbishop Gonçalo Pereira for his own finely carved tomb. The walls are covered by mudéjar frescoes, an amazing catalogue of arabesque design.

Continuing along Rua do Souto, which changes its name here to Rua Diogo de Sousa, you'll come to **Largo do Porto Nova**, which was originally just outside the medieval walls. The contrast in the cityscape looking one way or the other is still striking. Turn right along Rua dos Biscainhos to reach the 17th-century mansion of **Casa dos Biscainhos**, which is so impressive it outshines the exhibits in the museum of decorative arts which it houses. Statuary, azulejos, plasterwork and carved wood make this a truly masterful architectural creation.

Other handsome buildings face two neighbouring squares east of the cathedral. In **Largo São João de Souto** the church of the same name is partly covered with blue azulejos, while the adjoining **Capela de Nossa Senhora da Conceição** has some fine 16th-century sculptures. Next to it, the **Casa dos Coimbras** was a Manueline house of 1525: the characteristic windows are preserved in the restored building, which is now a finely-housed electrical shop. The next square, Largo Carlos Amarante, is named after the architect of the 18th-century **Hospital de São Marcos** on the south side. It was he who topped the façade with waving figures of the Apostles. Just beyond it, the elaborate baroque **Palácio do Raio** (1754) is faced with unusually deep blue azulejos, but the effect is spoiled by vivid purple-blue paint. From here, Rua do Raio leads quickly back to Avenida da Liberdade, downhill from the Turismo.

Near Braga

Appropriately for an ecclesiastical capital, excursions from the city include more churches and religious sanctuaries. If this sounds like an overdose, don't worry. They're all completely different – from each other as well as from anything in Braga itself. Other attractions date from the pre-Christian era, and the countryside and views are reason enough in themselves to go exploring.

The little **Chapel of São Frutuoso** is a rare relic of the Visigoth era. Almost overtaken by the expanding suburbs, it lies 3km (2 miles) northwest of Braga and just off to the right of the road to Ponte de Lima. Built in the 7th century, then abandoned when the Moors occupied the area, it was restored in the 11th century, although the original cross shape was reduced to the central dome and one arm, ending in an elegant apse and decorated with alternating pointed and rounded arches. It's usually closed and the priest no longer lives very near.

Continuing on the road towards Ponte de Lima (N201) for about 1km to Dume, a sign to the left points to the monastery (Mosteiro) of São Martinho at **Tibães**. The enormous 17th-century church and attached decrepit monastery buildings are 4km (2.5 miles) away along a narrow lane. Once the home of the biggest Benedictine community in Portugal, it's now almost deserted, although the government has plans to develop it for leisure purposes. Meanwhile, the caretakers may let you in to see the wreck of the formal gardens and the

derelict cloisters. The church is still used and sometimes open: the gorgeous gilded altar and other 18th-century woodcarving is worth the diversion.

Bom Jesus

Bom Jesus has been illustrated as often as any site in Portugal, with the possible exception of the 'Palace' on the *Mateus Rosé* bottle (which is in the same baroque style of granite and white stucco). People come to Braga just to see the magnificent, monumental **double staircase** which

climbs to the Bom Jesus sanctuary high on a hill about 5km (3 miles) east of the city. You can walk up (some pilgrims are said to do it on their knees), but it's a lot eas-

One of the great sights of Portugal, the elaborate 18th-century double staircase up to the Bom Jesus sanctuary church, is easily reached on the outskirts of Braga.

drive up the nearby road. A more original way is to take the water-powered funicular, installed in 1882 and recently renovated. A spring nearby provides the water, which runs into a tank in the upper car so that it descends, pulling the lower car to the top. Hotels, restaurants, sports facilities, picnics and walks through the woods make the trip popular.

The staircase was the brainchild of a diminutive dynamo, Archbishop Rodrigo de Moura Teles (who is said to have been very short), and work started in 1723. Even critics of the Catholic church have conceded that if it was going to spend vast sums on 'useless' works, there was a lot to be said for employing artists and artisans to build something beautiful.

Each landing has side chapels, an elaborate fountain and granite statues. At the uppermost level, they depict the New Testament villains Caiaphas, Annas, Herod and Pontius Pilate. Further down, the fountains show the Five Senses: touch, taste, smell, hearing and sight. Even higher up the hill from the 18th-century Bom Jesus church, and also accessible by road, the modern Monte Sameiro sanctuary church marks an important pilgrimage site, but offers little of interest apart from the view.

Citânia de Briteiros

The pre-Roman inhabitants of Portugal liked to live on hilltops: they were more easily defended, and heathier too, as rain and natural drainage carried away the detritus and breezes cleared some of the the smells and insects. Around 700 BC the Celts began to take over Neolithic sites and founded many new ones, traces of which are found all over northern Portugal. Smaller settlements are known as *castros*, larger ones are called *citânias*, although the line between them is blurred.

The most spectacular of them all is Citânia de Briteiros, which lies between Braga and Guimarães, on a back road which also passes the Bom Jesus sanctuary. Coming from Braga, continue for a further 14km (9 miles) past Sobreposta to find the citânia on your right. From Guimarães, turn right off the busy main road at Caldas das Taipas and follow the signs.

Probably first settled around 300 BC, the site sprawls across the summit and southeastern slopes of a steep hill, 336m (1,100ft) high. At first it looks chaotic, scarcely more than the foundations of walls and houses, mostly circular in plan. Follow the numbered map which you can get from the caretaker and you'll begin to discern details: paths (too narrow to call streets), small squares, larger buildings and water conduits. Make your way to the flat hilltop for the best view of the triple defensive walls, up to 2m (7ft) thick. On the southern edge of the plateau, two re-built stone houses with conical thatched roofs were the work of the local archaeologist Martins Sarmento (1833-99). He excavated here from 1875 until 1884, and in the ruthless fashion of the time, removed the most exciting discoveries. The saddest loss was of many intriguingly carved stone lintels and doorways, which can now be seen along with many other artefacts in the Martins Sarmento Museum in Guimarães (see p.218).

The most remarkable feature left at the citânia was discovered later, at the south end of the fenced area (and also visible from the road, just below the entrance gate). This so-called **funerary monument** has caused much controversy. Some experts think it may be a bath house, since it has a water tank and what looks like a furnace as well as a miniature atrium. Also still in position is a fine curved portal with a 'ship's propellor' motif (a favourite symbol of the Celt-Iberians). If this was a bath house, it was tiny by Roman standards.

When the Romans first penetrated this part of Portugal in the 2nd century BC, they either failed or didn't attempt to take over all the Celtic strongholds. Life in Citânia de Briteiros seems to have continued without much change until about 20 BC, when it was one of the last settlements to be subdued. The later architecture shows signs of Roman influence, and it is assumed that the inhabitants were increasingly Romanized up until the 4th century AD, when the site appears to have been abandoned.

Martins Sarmento also dug the **Castro de Sabroso**, not far to the south-west but reached by a different road. If you like your historic sites unfenced, overgrown, lonely and unmarked, try this one. From Caldas das Taipas, take the road signposted to Falperra. After 2.8km (1.7 miles) turn right (before reaching Sande). Near the top of the hill the road deteriorates into a rough track to a quarry. The castro covers the hilltop to the right. The wall is still substantial, several house foundations can be seen and the view is superb, but here again, any notable objects have been removed. The best are in the museum at Guimarães.

Guimarães

The people of Guimarães are in no doubt as to the importance of their city. A sign in the city centre asserts: *Aqui Nasceu Portugal*, 'Here Portugal was born'. When Henry of Burgundy was granted the county of Portucale by Alfonso of León and Castile, he set up his court at Guimarães, where his son, Afonso Henriques, was probably born around 1110. Henry died roughly two years later, and as early as 1127, documents began to refer to the young Afonso as King of Portugal. He defeated a challenge from his mother, Teresa, and her Spanish allies at São Mamede, 15km (9 miles) to the south,

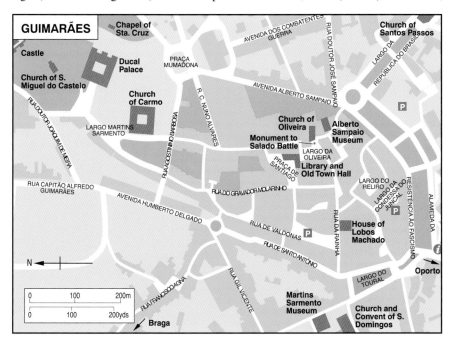

in 1128, and ruled from Guimarães until 1139. Proclaimed King Afonso I in that year, he then moved the capital to Coimbra, nearer to the lands which had been newly reconquered from the Moors.

Guimarães retained some of its importance as a royal counterweight to the power of the archbishops of Braga, and was later part of the vast holdings of the Dukes of Bragança. It has grown rapidly in recent years and is now a centre for clothing and shoe manufacturing, with great tracts of new housing. It's not difficult to find the heart of the city, and there's plenty to see, with most of it concentrated into a small area, where it's a pleasure to walk. There are also two superb museums which shouldn't be missed.

The Historic Centre

The castle on a low hill to the north is a landmark by which to orientate yourself. From there, the pendant-shaped old city, still with some of its old walls, runs down to a curved garden boulevard at the southern end (the Alameda da Resistência ão Fascismo). The **Turismo** at its south-west corner has excellent numbered and illustrated street maps.

Logic and chronology suggest starting at the top of the *Sagrada Colina* ('Holy Hill'), the site of the **Castle**. Standing on a rocky outcrop above the grass-covered slopes, the great square keep and seven towers with their spiky battlements have become a national symbol seen on banknotes and stamps. Count Henry's castle was started at the end of the 11th century, but is built on earlier foundations, and due to many additions and restoration it's hard to tell what survives from when. Unfortunately, it isn't open to visitors.

The stalls of a lively open air market fill the area to the north-east every Friday.

Henry's son, Afonso Henriques, is said to have been born in the castle and baptized in the font still standing in the little Romanesque **Chapel of São Miguel** (usually locked), which must have been brand new at the time.

The massive **Ducal Palace** just down the hill from the castle and chapel is an inaccurate 20th-century reconstruction. As such, it has been castigated as a pastiche and a fraud. The fact that the rebuilding was the work of the Salazar régime only made the critics more virulent. Like it or not, it's worth closer inspection. The original fortress-palace was built in the 1420s for Afonso, soon to be the first Duke of Bragança, but following the execution of the third duke, it was abandoned and gradually turned into a vast ruin, used as a source of stone for other buildings. In the 1930s it was rebuilt to serve as a grandiose northern residence for the head of state and other important visitors. Radical changes were made in the process, including cutting off the flight of steps which once climbed from the courtyard to the upper level chapel. Although they may look weird, the spindly brick chimneys are claimed to be authentic.

If you have plenty of time in Guimarães, take the 45-minute tour of the interior. The great ceremonial halls may feel like a stage set, but they're furnished with a fine collection of antiques: 15th-century weapons; 16th- and 17th-century furniture, including chests made in Portuguese India; Chinese porcelain; and portraits, carpets and tapestries (those showing Portuguese battles in North Africa are copies of 15th-century originals).

Rua de Santa Maria leads down into the lovely old town, first passing the long façade of the 17th-century **Convent of Santa Clara**, formerly one of the richest foundations in Guimarães. It's now the

Town Hall, with the archives housed in the chapel, the marvellous gilt carving of which is now in the Museu Alberto Sampaio (see below). The street passes under an arch (part of the elegant Arch House), before an opening to the right leads to the triangular plaza of **Largo de Santiago**. At the far end stands the 14th-century **Old Town Hall**, with open arcades at ground level supporting the council chamber and its battlemented roof. Here you come to the focal point of **Largo da Oliveira**.

On the east side of the square, the Colegiada de **Nossa Senhora da Oliveira** (Collegiate Church of Our Lady of the Olive Tree) was rebuilt by João I in gratitude for his victory at Aljubarrota in 1385. Striking features from that time are the Gothic west door and blind window above. The north tower in Manueline style (see the rope-like decoration) dates from around 1520, while a stone canopy of Gothic arches standing near the church commemorates victory over the Moors at Salado in 1340. It's said that this is also the spot where the Visigoth leader Wamba stuck his olive-wood staff into the ground in 672, vowing that he

T he spindly brick chimneys of the Ducal Palace are said to be copies of the originals.

would accept the position of king to which he had just been elected when it put forth leaves, and not before. The obliging staff then sprouted immediately.

On the north side of the square, several handsome town houses of the 15th to 17th centuries have been converted into the guest rooms and restaurant of the Pousada de Santa Maria da Oliveira. Rua da Rainha, running out of the south-west corner of the square, leads to a tangle of little streets and interconnecting squares, lined by stately mansions, quaint toytown houses and ramshackle tenements.

The Alberto Sampaio Museum

The *Museu Alberto Sampaio* is housed in parts of the old convent of Nossa Senhora da Oliveira. The curators have been selective, only showing a fraction of the collection, and the printed information is excellent. You have to take a guided tour, probably in Portuguese, but leaflets (some in English) in each main room make it quite easy to follow. The 13th-century **cloister** – worth seeing in its own right – is a fine setting for precious *azulejos* and stone carvings, including Visigothic capitals, while the lovely 14th-century *Santa Maria a Formosa* ('the Beautiful') is the star among outstanding polychrome Gothic sculptures. A separate room shows off the gilded wood carving saved from the Santa Clara convent.

Upstairs in the **Aljubarrota room** are two national treasures, one being the tattered and blackened tunic which was worn by João I at the actual battle. The other is a silver-gilt tryptich of the Nativity, which is thought to be the work of Guimarães silversmiths, made for this church in thanksgiving for the victory at Aljubarrota. More superb silver, ceramics and paintings by the 16th-century master António Vaz are amongst the other highlights of the museum. On the stairs down, don't miss the fresco of John the Baptist.

Emerging from the museum and the old town, you'll see at the end of an avenue and garden the tall twin towers of the **Igreja dos Santos Passos**. They were added in the 19th century to the elegant, bow-fronted baroque church designed by Andre Soares. To the left, another garden boulevard curves around the line of the former city wall, past the tourist office and into tree-lined **Largo do Toural**. This is the focus of modern Guimarães, thronged with people and frequently choked by traffic. For an instant contrast, return to the 16th-century by cutting back into the old town to **Largo da Condesa de Juncal**.

The Martins Sarmento Museum

Just off Largo do Toural along Rua Paio Galvão, the **Museu Martins Sarmento** bears the name of the 19th-century excavator of Citânia de Briteiros (see p.214), although the collection doesn't concentrate solely on archaeology. The displays are not always logically organized, and labels are laconic, but the staff will produce detailed catalogues if you show an interest.

The museum occupies the former convent of São Domingos, and the larger objects fill the 14th-century **cloister**. On the obligatory tour, the guides hurry past undistinguished paintings and colonial bric-à-brac to reach the main attractions, notably the **Celt-Iberian finds** from the citânias. Not all are on a grand scale: note the fine

*T*he atmospheric Largo de Santiago, in the centre of the old walled city of Guimarães, is one of several attractive squares.

bronze tools and votive objects such as animal sculptures and a carriage pulled by men and oxen. The eye is drawn to the decorated stone doorways, some with a rope motif foreshadowing Manueline designs. Even more impressive are the **Pedras Formosas**, curvilinear portals which may have been the entrances to burial chambers. Two Lusitanian warriors with round shields have lost their heads; originally they would have been 3m (10ft) high. Biggest of all is the **Colossus of Pedralva**, a seated granite figure with a snake-like phallus. This is also the most puzzling exhibit, for it could be Celtic, or older, or it may even have been made much more recently.

Penha

Halfway up a hill, 7km (4 miles) southeast of Guimarães, the Monastery of **Santa Marinha da Costa** commands an almost aerial view of the city. The site seems to have been a religious centre from Roman times (there are traces of a temple), and probably earlier. A monastery was founded by Queen Mafaida, wife of Afonso Henriques, in 1154, but the massive buildings you see today date from the 18th century.

Now they form one of the biggest and most impressive hotels of the *Pousada* chain. Some guest rooms are in former monks' cells, but don't assume that they're spartan or even small; on the contrary, they're luxurious and quite spacious. The public rooms, meanwhile, are on a scale to impress a Roman emperor, and the grand ceremonial staircase is a tour de force in 18th-century *azulejos*. Earlier features discovered during reconstruction have been cleverly left exposed. Even if you aren't staying, look into the cathedral-sized restaurant.

Further up the hill, a leisure complex and the modern sanctuary of Nossa Senhora da Penha attract picnic parties and pilgrims. Plans are well in hand to build a cable car to the top.

Amarante

Amarante is somewhere to savour. On the way to Vila Real and the north-east, or the Upper Douro, and easily reached from Guimarães or Oporto, the town and its setting on the Tâmega River are equally lovely. The old part clings to a steep slope west of a handsome, high 18th-century bridge, only wide enough for one-way traffic, while newer areas spread around a modern bridge and over the nearby hills.

Occupying a prime position next to the river and the older bridge, the **Church of São Gonçalo** and its convent stand on the site of a Roman temple.

The church you see now was started in 1540 but interrupted when Philip II of Spain seized the throne of Portugal (as Filipe I). It was completed in 1620 while the Spanish were still in power, and the five-arched upper gallery of the façade features the statues of Kings João III, Sebastião, Henrique, and Filipe I. It comes as a surprise that the Portuguese didn't remove the interloper. The extensive convent buildings now house the Turismo and the town museum, with a collection of the Cubist paintings of Amadeo de Sousa Cardoso and work by other local artists.

Amarante seems to have been associated with a fertility cult, for there are echoes of it in some of today's customs. At the feast of São Gonçalo on the first Saturday in June, the young and unmarried give each other cakes shaped like phallic symbols. São Gonçalo's 13th-century **tomb**, much older than the church itself, stands to the left of the rich baroque high altar in a little chapel lined with blue and yellow *azulejos*. Over the centuries Gonçalo has become the patron saint of spinsters still seeking a husband, and the face and extremities of his multi-coloured effigy have been eroded by the touch of countless hopeful hands.

Up a steep slope facing the church, the round 18th-century Church of São Domingos has unusual doors, reminiscent in style of the 18th-century English furniture designed by Thomas Sheraton. The tiny interior holds some superb statuary, a stepped altar and Calvary scene.

If you're heading east to Vila Real (see p.232), the rustic Pousada de São Gonçalo makes a convenient stop. Just off the new IP4 road 24km (15 miles) from Amarante, its superb views and notable cuisine offer good value.

Peneda-Gerês National Park

In a great arc next to the border with Spain, the mountains, forests, waterfalls and remote villages of the 72,000ha (180,000 acres) of **Peneda-Gerês National Park** offer something for everyone. This is wonderful walking and camping country and a paradise for botanists and bird-spotters. Roads are few, but you can enjoy some spectacular scenery. Dozens of Roman milestones – a greater concentration than you'll see anywhere else – mark the old military highway from Braga into Spain. Several rivers cut deep valleys through the mountain ranges and some have been dammed; the artificial lakes have become arenas for watersports.

You can't cover both the northern (Serra da Peneda) and southern (Serra do Gerês) sections of the park by road without leaving the boundaries and re-entering at another point. Some routes involve crossing into Spain, so note that hire (rental) cars cannot normally be taken across the frontier. If you have your own vehicle, certain documents are required or advised (see p.14).

Gerês and the Southern Park

Easily and quickly reached from Braga, this is by far the most popular part of the park, and there can be a lot of summer and weekend traffic. At **Cova**, three lakes meet, attracting anglers, sailors and windsurfers. A *Pousada* near **Caniçada** makes a luxurious base, but there's a range of other accommodation too. North of Cova, the road begins to climb and after 7km (4 miles) reaches the old spa of **Caldas do Gerês**, just called Gerês on some signs. A line of formerly grand old hotels in faded pastels faces the one main street. Next comes the spa building, followed at the top of town by the **Turismo** and, just above it, the **National Park office**, which sells the best map of the area (available in English), marked with all roads, most footpaths and a host of prehistoric, Roman and later sites. The staff will advise on walks and the current condition of tracks, including their suitability for different types of vehicle. Dozens of different forays are possible: here we suggest a few examples.

Roman Footsteps

North of Caldas do Gerês, the road zigzags ever higher towards what looks like an impassable wall of granite mountain. It's only 11km (7 miles) to the Spanish border at **Portela do Homem**, named after the river crossing just below it, and even if you don't intend to enter Spain, do go as far as the frontier to see a group of eight **Roman milestones**, up to 2.5m (8ft) high. This point was 'Mile XXXIV', the top of the pass on a road built in 80 AD, between *Bracara* (now Braga) and *Asturica Augusta* (Astorga). To trace its route on the Portuguese side, turn back from the border to the river, whose cold crystal waters must have been a welcome relief to the marching legionaries with their heavy equipment. (A footpath along it makes an attractive walk.)

Just over one kilometre (half a mile) beyond the bridge, an unsurfaced track cuts back to the right and down to the river. There it joins the Roman road again, through the woods past a remarkable cluster of 15 milestones. Many inscriptions are still clear, giving the name of the road, the distance from *Bracara* and, in some cases, the name of the emperor at the time the stone was erected. After another Roman mile (about 1.5km), you'll see no fewer than 18 columns, of differing heights and in varying states of repair.

The track follows the shore of a lake before taking leave of the Romans and turning south to **Campo do Gerês**. Just beyond it at a fork in the road, yet another Roman milestone has been set up with a crucifix on top. The left hand path winds its way back through forest to Caldas do Gerês, and is passable by car except after snow or heavy rain. Walkers taking this route can divert to visit traces of a Celt-Iberian citânia (signposted).

The Road East

A twisting but driveable track leading south-east from Caldas do Gerês carries a lot of weekend traffic for the first 3km (2 miles) to a *miradouro* (viewpoint) looking out over the lakes to the south. After that, it's much less busy along the terraced slopes, where little farms take advantage of the southern aspect to grow fruit, vines and corn. **Ermida** sees a fair number of visitors but further east you'll see even fewer cars, apart from the August arrival of *émigrés* back from France for a holiday.

Further east, you'll come to one of the remotest parts of Portugal, and north of **Outeiro** the land rises to a plateau of wild moorland, rocky outcrops and occasional patches of cultivation. Despite the harsh conditions, this seems to have been a centre of Neolithic settlement, and a number of dolmens and other standing stones remain. **Tourem**, overlooking a reservoir shared with Spain, is a dead end, with limited accommodation. East of Outeiro, a rough road follows the valley of the Cávado to Montalegre.

The Serra da Peneda

Head east from Ponte da Barca (see p.204) or Arcos de Valdevez and you'll soon be in the northern arm of the National Park. A narrow, winding road leads first to the little village of **Soajo**, famous for its *espigueros* (or *canastros*) – grain stores for keeping the heads of corn (maize). In other parts of Portugal they're made of wood, but here these tall, narrow structures are built to last, out of stone. Twenty of them, a century or two old, stand on stone 'mushroom' pillars, set around a stone threshing floor. You'll see more of them at **Lindoso**, which is overlooked by its restored castle, a 13th-century keep with 17th-century outer ramparts.

A rough but passable road north through the park starts west of Soajo. The stone-built villages along the way can look even more deserted than usual in rural Portugal. That's because when the cattle, sheep and goats are taken up to higher pastures in summer, many of the people go with them, living in straw and stone shelters. At **Lamas de Mouro**, one road leads through wild country strewn with giant boulders, down to the valley of the Minho at Melgaço (see p.203). If you have time, head east first, to the remote village of **Castro Laboreiro**, almost 1,000m (3,300ft) up. It's well known for its own variety of fierce sheep dog, bred not only to herd the sheep but to fight off the wolves which still roam these mountains.

Off The Beaten Track in the Rugged North East

The north east sees fewer visitors than the rest of the country, but offers everything from the high mountain ranges of the Serra da Estrêla national park to the Port wine vineyards of the upper Douro. Past invaders found this region hard to conquer: it is cut off from Lisbon and guarded by fortresses in the east and the cities of Bragança and Chaves in the north. The Celtic hero Viriatus held out against the Romans here, and this was once a refuge for Jews expelled from Spain. Still remote and unspoiled, but also accessible by new highways, this is one of Europe's last truly untrampled escapes.

Viseu

Set among pinewoods and rolling hills at the gateway to the Dão wine region, this ancient town claims to have been a stronghold of the Celtic hero Viriatus in his campaign against the Romans (there's no firm evidence for the local belief that his last battle and assassination took place here in about 139 BC). What is more certain is that the famous painter Vasco Fernandes (c.1475-1541), usually called *O*

*T*he valley of the Zêzere cuts through the Serra da Estrêla National Park, which offers Portugal's highest mountain range and finest walking country.

Grão Vasco ('The Great Vasco'), was born in the area. Some of his best works, created for Viseu's cathedral, are on display in the museum which bears his name. The granite hill crowned by the cathedral was a Celtic *castro* and then a Roman settlement. It's now the centre of the old city, where most of the town's sights are concentrated. In recent years Viseu has expanded rapidly along broad, tree-lined avenues, spreading out below the hill.

If you're driving, you'll arrive at **Praça da Republica** (also called Rossio), the heart of the lower town, with a statue of Henry the Navigator – one of his titles was Duke of Viseu. The helpful **Turismo** can provide a good street map – you'll find the office just to the south in Avenida Calouste Gulbenkian, opposite a public park. On a busy day it can be worth parking in Rossio

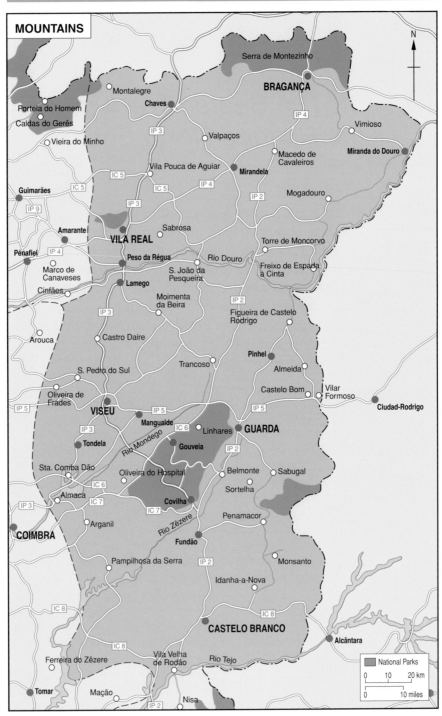

MOUNTAINS

N

Serra de Montezinho

BRAGANÇA

Montalegre

Chaves

IP 4

Portela do Homem

Caldas do Gerês

Vimioso

IP 3

Valpaços

Vieira do Minho

Macedo de
Cavaleiros

Miranda do Douro

Vila Pouca de Aguiar

IC 5

Mirandela

IP 4

IC 5

Guimarães

IC 5

Mogadouro

IP 9

IP 3

IP 2

Sabrosa

Amarante

VILA REAL

Torre de Moncorvo

Penafiel

IP 4

Peso da Régua

Rio Douro

Freixo de Espada
à Cinta

Marco de
Canaveses

S. João da
Pesqueira

Lamego

Cinfães

Moimenta
da Beira

IP 2

Figueira de Castelo
Rodrigo

IP 3

Castro Daire

Arouca

Pinhel

Trancoso

Almeida

S. Pedro do Sul

Castelo Bom

Vilar
Formoso

Oliveira de
Frades

Ciudad-Rodrigo

IP 5

VISEU

IP 5

IP 5

Mangualde

IC 6

Linhares

GUARDA

IP 3

Rio Mondego

Gouveia

IP 2

Tondela

Sta. Comba Dão

Oliveira do Hospital

Belmonte

Sabugal

IC 6

Sortelha

Almaca

IC 7

Covilhã

IP 3

IC 7

COIMBRA

Arganil

Rio Zêzere

Penamacor

Fundão

Pampilhosa da Serra

IP 2

Monsanto

Idanha-a-Nova

IC 8

IC 8

CASTELO BRANCO

IC 8

Alcântara

Ferreira do Zêzere

Vila Velha
de Ródão

Rio Tejo

National Parks

0   10   20 km

Tomar

Mação

0   10 miles

Nisa

IP 2

224

and walking. Otherwise, you may be able to negotiate the narrow streets up to the Adro, or **Praça da Sé** (Cathedral Square) and leave your car there. Small boys will probably offer to guard it for you.

The most eye-catching building on the square is not, in fact, the cathedral, but the 18th-century **Igreja da Misericórdia**. Typical of Portuguese baroque, its best feature is the highly decorative white stucco façade framed in granite. The church is frequently locked, but the interior is not particularly striking. The **Sé** (cathedral) on the other hand presents a quite dull 17th-century west front to the square, but is full of notable features inside. The stone vaulting is carved like knotted ropes, a trademark of Manueline design, celebrating the great voyages of discovery of the time (about 1500), while the gilded retable (main altarpiece) is a replacement for the one that held the 14 paintings to be seen now in the neighbouring Grão Vasco Museum. The interior must have been sumptuously decorated in the past. Notice how the stone walls were scratched to hold plaster and no doubt *azulejos*, some of which are still in place. Don't miss the double-decker **cloisters**, with the Renaissance lower level formed of massive columns and arches. Blue *azulejo* panels here date from as early as the 17th century.

Museu Grão Vasco and the Old Town

A visit to this museum should persuade you that, contrary to what you may have come to expect, Portugal did, in fact, manage to produce more inspired works than the heavy, derivative pictures which adorn so many of its walls. Here, dull religious art is forgotten in the superb works by Grão Vasco. The museum adjoins the north side of the cathedral, taking up three floors of what was once the bishop's palace.

On the upper level, you'll find the Vasco paintings, including a fine *St Peter* and a *Crucifixion*, and those of his younger contemporary, Gaspar Vaz, all cleaned to reveal something of their original colours. The famous 14 scenes from the Life of Christ which came from the cathedral were once all attributed to 'O Grão Vasco'. Now, it's agreed that some entire paintings and parts of others are by less talented followers. The best are complex and dramatic, with fine portraiture and vivid colour combinations. Details of dress and daily life (of the Portugal of Vasco's time, not the Holy Land of Christ's) are remarkably realistic, and some of the background landscapes are brilliant miniatures. Notice the *Adoration of the Magi*, with King Balthazar in the guise of a feather-bedecked Brazilian Indian chief (Brazil having been discovered a mere 20 years earlier), and the climactic *Arrest in the Garden, Crucifixion, Resurrection, Ascension* and *Pentecost*. On the lower floors, look for work of Portuguese landscape painters and Impressionists, and varied religious sculptures and reliquaries, some with windows to display the treasure they once held. (The museum is closed on Mondays.)

It's worth wandering the maze of alleys and steps that make up the **old town**. Just south of Cathedral Square, Rua Dom Duarte leads to the busy Rua Direita; both are lined with patrician houses from the 15th to 18th centuries, as well as craft stores and pastry shops selling the local sugary specialities. For a choice of regional products, try the covered **market**, almost back at Rossio. The Dão wines are some of Portugal's best known, and the local cheeses are celebrated.

There's much more to see in Viseu if you have the time. The **Carmo** and **São Francisco** churches have good *azulejos*, and the **Museu Almeida Moreira** displays an art and furniture collection in a fine, Moorish-style house at the north end of Rossio. (The house and contents were left to the city by Almeida Moreira, the first curator of the Museu Grão Vasco.)

On the northern outskirts of Viseu, near the main road north, a statue of Viriatus ('Viriato' in Portuguese) stands near the still-visible outlines of the camp which the Romans set up after they had arranged his assassination. The name, Cava de Viriato, is purely imaginative; there is no evidence for it.

Around Viseu

A worthwhile excursion to the east takes you across the River Dão, which gives its name to some reliable Portuguese wines, especially the smooth, velvety reds. The vineyards are spread along the valleys of the Dão and the Mondego to the south, and it's possible to stay at some of the

quintas and manor houses in the area: check with the *Turismo* office in Viseu. High on a ridge between the two rivers, **Mangualde** is notable for some handsome mansions and the fine, late 17th-century Palácio dos Condes de Anadia (not normally open to visitors, but you can see the exterior). West of Viseu, the little hill resort of **Caramulo**, a slightly faded spa, surprisingly boasts an **art museum**, the Fundação Abel Lacerda, with paintings ranging from the Viseu school (including a Grão Vasco *John the Baptist*) to Picasso

and Dali. The adjoining **Car Museum** has vintage vehicles, from an 1899 Peugeot to classics by Rolls Royce, Bugatti and some of the personal limousines of the dictator Salazar, who was born at Vimieiro on the Dão, not far to the south.

Viseu is now linked to the coast (at Aveiro, see p.178) by the smooth IP5 road which sweeps through some beautiful hill country on the way. If you have plenty of time, the old route winding along the wooded valley of the Vouga river is even more picturesque. Sadly, trains no longer run on this section of the Vouga Line, which followed the same route. At the eastern end of the valley, **Termas de São Pedro do Sul** has been a spa since early times – the round-arched bridge stands on Roman foundations. The town still attracts local weekenders, who stay in the handful of old-fashioned hotels and take boats on the river.

Castro Daire, in rugged country 35km (22 miles) north of Viseu, stands on a hilltop towering over the deep valley of the River Paiva. The site has been occupied since Neolithic times: dolmens and standing stones are found in the area. The attractive town square is lined by some fine old houses, and there's some great scenery along the winding road to the west, where the river cuts a gorge through the mountains of the Serra de Montemuro.

Lamego

Lamego sits in a fertile valley ringed by rugged hills south of the Douro. This is another ancient site, taken in turn by Celts, Romans, barbarian invaders and Moors, before the Christian reconquest came in the 11th century. Agriculture was, and still is, the foundation of its prosperity, and Lamego is known for its sweet and sparkling wines, which are popular all over Portugal. You can visit the producers – ask at the **Turismo** just off Largo de Camões, the main square, when you call in to collect a good town map. The ancient walled citadel is just to the north, with the Rua do Castelinho its main artery, old gates at either end and the remains of the 13th-century **castle** looking down over jumbled stone houses.

The **Sé** (Cathedral) on the south side of Largo de Camões has a fine square tower from the 12th century. Otherwise it dates from the early 16th century, including the beautiful cloisters. At that time, artists of the Viseu school (including Grão Vasco) painted 20 pictures for the altarpiece. Sadly, only five of them are known to exist today. You can see them in the excellent **Museu de Lamego**, installed in the old bishop's palace facing the square. Two, the *Annunciation* and *Visitation*, seem to be in a different league from the rest, more direct, realistic and with superbly executed portraits and background scenes. The *Creation of the Animals* is charming – notice the unicorn.

Elsewhere in the museum, the huge and magnificent Brussels tapestries are the best in Portugal, while the gilded 18th-century chapel of St John the Evangelist, saved from the vanished Convent of Chagas, is a jewel. Wooden statues of St Peter, St Paul and the Virgin and Child from the 13th century are outstanding. Even more intriguing are the 14th-century statues of a heavily pregnant Virgin Mary, *Nossa Senhora de O* (they seem to have been characteristic of this region).

Staircase and Shrine

Tales of miraculous cures turned Lamego into a place of pilgrimage and led to the building of the tiled baroque church of **Nossa Senhora dos Remédios** on a hill to the southwest of town. Finished in 1771, it stands at the head of an elaborate flight of granite stairs, inspired by those at Bom Jesus (see p.213) and completed over the next century and a half. How many steps? Certainly more than 600, but everyone comes up with a different number, having been distracted by the statues and shrines, fountains, *azulejos* and chapels that line the pilgrims' progress. Some make the climb on their knees; others drive up a winding road through parkland to the top. (Take the turning just above the point where the road from Castro Daire intersects the steps.) The view alone is worth the climb, and there's a hotel and restaurant in case the effort has given you an appetite.

The weeks before and after 8 September each year bring the biggest influx of visitors (all accommodation will long since have been booked). Religious processions are only a small part of the celebrations. Extras include a rock music festival and traditional fair, and the approach to the steps is lined with market stalls.

*F*ountains and statuary, azulejos *and shrines embellish the ceremonial staircase of Nossa Senhora dos Remédios.*

A sedan chair kept your feet out of the mud, but it must have rocked and rolled like a small boat in a storm. *(Museu de Lamego)*

The elaborate double staircase of the pilgrimage church of Nossa Senhora dos Remédios at Lamego followed the pattern of Bom Jesus, near Braga. It's a long climb, up more than 600 granite stairs. You can rest at the top in the shade of chestnut trees and admire the view. The less energetic can drive up.

The Port Vineyards

From Lamego the road north twists and turns for 13km (8 miles) to **Régua** (full name Peso da Régua), a river port on the Douro. This used to be where the Port wine from the vineyards began its boat trip downstream to Oporto. Then the railway was built along the upper Douro valley, and the wine went by train, most of it from further up the line at Pinhão, although you'll see a long brown loading shed at Régua station, too. These days, it's transported even less romantically by road.

However, the headquarters of the wine-growers is here at the **Casa do Douro**, and through them or the small **Turismo** opposite the railway station, you may be able to arrange a tour of a local cellar or visit a vineyard. You'll get an insight into the business if you can stay in one of the manor houses or *quintas* on the wine growing estates which offer rooms. Again, ask at the *Turismo* about accommodation, but don't expect to find a room in a *quinta* during *vindima*, harvest time (end of September, beginning of October). Even though

the Port doesn't ride the railway any more, you can (see p.78 and p.193, Port).

Upriver about 22km (14 miles) from Régua, **Pinhão** is at the heart of prime Port country. This is where the soil and climatic conditions are reckoned to be at their best, rugged though the land might seem to an untutored eye. Everywhere you look, the steep slopes along the Douro and up the side valleys have been carved into terraces through centuries of toil. Most of the vinyeards are quite small, and there are as many as 30,000 growers in the demarcated Port region, although not all produce Port; many unfortified wines are made as well. Undoubtedly, however, the business is changing, with the big shippers increasingly becoming major growers. New vineyards are being blasted out of the hillsides with dynamite and scraped into shape by bulldozers. Wider terraces allow machines to do some of the cultivation.

At harvest time, the vineyards are a frenzy of activity. Women and children do most of the picking while the men clamber up and down the slopes, as sure-footed as mountain goats, carrying huge 60kg (132lb) baskets of grapes on their backs. Fortified by generous amounts of wine provided by the growers, family groups of a dozen can pick as much as 6 tonnes of grapes in a day, while their songs echo round the valleys.

Trás-os-Montes

The remote region 'beyond the mountains' with its harsh winters and baking hot summers has always been the poorest part of Portugal. The first settlers were enticed here by gifts of land from the early kings, and they were later joined by refugees fleeing from religious or political persecution, but the area was never more than sparsely populated. A string of fortresses was built along the Spanish frontier to defend it – the soldiers sent to man them looked on the posting as a punishment. Towns and villages are far apart and had to be self-sufficient. The upland moors, scattered with giant granite boulders, are home to flocks of hardy sheep, and here and there a sheltered valley allows the planting of fields and orchards and, in the south, grapes and oranges on the sunnier slopes. Trout from the clean mountain rivers are a local speciality, and the hams and smoked sausage are famous throughout Portugal. Now new roads are making travel much easier. The best time for a visit is either spring, when the almond trees are in blossom, or early autumn, while the days are still warm.

HOME AND AWAY

Emigration has been a fact of life in rural Portugal for centuries, but in the 1960s and 70s it became a flood, especially from the deprived north-east. This time the destinations were the more prosperous countries of Western Europe, in particular France, and today there is scarcely a family in the region without relatives in Paris, where the Portuguese community numbers around half a million. In summer you'll see more French-registered cars than local, but it's not an influx of tourists, just the *emigrés* returning for their holidays, showing off their BMWs and taking over all available accommodation.

Many of them eventually come home for good, after long spells in France, Germany, and even America. Their elaborate, modern houses stand incongruously alongside traditional stone huts, which the previous generation shares with the family livestock. Some of the returnees have injected a new dynamism, setting up businesses and campaigning for state investment and EU aid.

Vila Real

As the administrative centre of Trás-os-Montes, Vila Real is one of the region's least typical towns, with its industrial development, mushrooming suburbs and traffic snarls. The old walled town, built where the rivers Corgo and Cabril meet, has long since been outgrown, but is still worth exploration; some sections of wall survive, and there's a giddy view down into the gorge which traditionally made this such an easily defendable site. The strangely anonymous **Turismo** is in part

of an old mansion at the upper end of the broad central avenue (Avenida Carvalho Araújo No. 94) and has a good local map.

Vila Real's two major sights are, in fact, some way out of town, and the road to them is easy to miss. Head east on the small road towards Sabrosa (you may see signs to Mateus). About 3km (2 miles) from Vila Real on the right but out of view lies one of the most frequently pictured sights in all of Portugal, the country house shown on every bottle of *Mateus Rosé*. Officially called the **Solar de Mateus**, the house represents the zenith of the local version of baroque, with its white stucco and extravagantly carved stonework. The large entrance fee is almost justified by the formal gardens, lake and

A less familar view of the Solar de Mateus and its manicured hedges than the one seen on certain wine bottles. The mansion is a fine example of Portuguese baroque.

views. The house has been spruced up recently, and inside there are period pictures, furnishings and assorted exhibits, including letters from 19th-century statesmen.

Another 5km (3 miles) in the direction of Sabrosa, just after the little village of Constantim, look out for an obscure national monument sign where a minor road forks to the left. Between the two roads, **Panóias** looks at first glance to be no more than a scattering of massive boulders. These are worth a closer look, for this was an important pre-Roman – and later a Roman – sacred site, perhaps selected because the rocks resemble great animals. It's believed to have been dedicated to the god Serapis and used for sacrifices. You'll probably have the place to yourself, unless the guardian decides to show you round. Steps and little cisterns, rectangular or round, have been cut into the rocks, which in places have also been shaped as the foundations of buildings, now vanished (though it would appear that some large stones have been re-used in nearby houses).

Steep steps lead up the highest rock, away from the entrance, where five tombs over 2m (7ft) long have been carved out, recessed to take covering slabs. The grooves cut into the boulders are presumed to have channelled blood from the sacrifices. Grim thoughts aside, it's quite an evocative place, overgrown with mosses and lichens, home to an unusual number of birds, and with fine views over pinewoods and vineyards. The nearby village with its church bells hanging in the open looks as if it hasn't changed in centuries.

East of Vila Real

Perched over a pretty valley full of terraced vineyards, **Sabrosa** is one claimant to being the birthplace of Magellan (Magalhães in Portuguese), whose ship com-

pleted the first circumnavigation of the globe in 1522 (although he himself was killed in the Philippines). They don't make much of the connection here, only a bookshop bears his name.

Up on the plateau, **Alijó** produces a respectable red wine and some handsome old houses in the town centre are evidence of past prosperity. The Pousada Barão de Forrester, situated near the main square, is named after the Scotsman who campaigned to improve the quality of Douro wines, mapped the region, was created a baron and eventually drowned in a boating accident in the river in 1861 (see p.194).

The attractive little town of **Murça** is known for a pre-Roman statue of a powerful looking wild boar, carved lifesize out of one piece of granite. This Porca de Murça, on his plinth in the town square, is the most famous example of several such figures found in the area. The usual guess is that they were Celtic fertility symbols, although some scholars have suggested they are even older.

Mirandela has expanded rapidly, as improved roads have made it much more accessible. Next to a curvaceous new bridge over the Tua, an old stone bridge with 20 arches of varying shapes and sizes is now for pedestrians only. It dates from about 1500, but stands on piers built by the Romans.

Climbing the narrow cobbled streets to the top of the old town, you'll come to a square dominated by the 17th-century town hall, with its elegant loggia. It was once a palace of the Távora family, who were all-powerful in the area until they were accused of being involved in a plot to assassinate the king, Dom José, in 1758. The dictatorial Marquês de Pombal (see p.54) ordered the execution of leading members of the family and the seizure of their property.

Chaves

Occupying a strategic position on the border with Spain, Chaves was once a Roman spa known as *Aquae Flaviae*, and its hot springs are still channeled into baths in which those with rheumatism, hypertension and liver disorders immerse themselves. The **bridge** the Romans built across the Tâmega in 104 AD still stands, carrying more traffic than ever. Tamed since then, the river now passes through only nine of the bridge's twenty arches: many of the others have been blocked off, but you can inspect both them and two well-preserved Roman **milestones** standing on the central piers. *Chaves* means 'keys', and the town was certainly one of the keys to northern Portugal (suffering several Spanish occupations or sieges), but the name probably came from successive corruptions of the Roman version.

Uphill from the bridge, Rua Direita leads to Praça da República, its stone *pelourinho* carved in typically twisted Manueline style. The adjoining Praça do Camões is supervised by a statue of the long-lived Afonso, first Duke of Bragança (1371-1461). Surrounding buildings include the **parish church** with a Romanesque door, the Misericórdia church, town hall and a regional **museum**, with many Roman artefacts, coins and inscribed stones, as well as exhibits on the traditional life of the area. Behind it rears the tower of the 14th-century **castle**, its terrace and gardens scattered with Roman stonework and commanding a great view of the town.

You'll find the **Turismo** at the top of the long, triangular Terreiro de Cavalaria; it has occasional craft displays and offers useful maps and literature. Just a block away to the east, Forte de São Francisco is one of a pair of 17th-century fortresses on this side of town.

At **Outeiro Machado**, about 6km (4 miles) west of Chaves, a great boulder is almost completely covered by the best display of prehistoric rock carvings in Portugal. To reach it, take Rua do Teniente Valadim south-west at the opposite end of the triangle of streets from the Turismo. Follow signs to **Arte Rupestre**: after 4km (2.5 miles) of minor road, they point to the right along a dusty or muddy track, depending on the season, but usually passable. Another 1.5km (1 mile) brings you into open country and a sight of the rock, which is about 50m (160ft) long.

Lying low and not very prominent, it looks unremarkable at first, but close up you will begin to make out the shapes carved on the upper surface. Lichen and erosion haven't improved the clarity, but hatchets, paddles, ladders and gridirons can be made out. Without other evidence, there's no technique for dating them exactly: they could be Celtic, perhaps from around 500 BC, or earlier.

The road from Chaves east to Bragança soon starts to climb and twist through rugged country. A rough track to the north leads up the powerful but abandoned hilltop castle of Monforte, on the site of a Roman fort which in turn stood on an earlier castro. Most of what you see, including the great square keep, dates from around 1300, when King Dinis reinforced Portugal's defences against Castile.

Bragança

There's no mistaking the frontier atmosphere of Bragança. This remote fortress town looks north and east to the Spanish border, across wild country which was deliberately kept unpopulated for one thousand years. Only recently has much attention been paid to the roads, the theory having been that inaccessibility would

*S*tern guardian of the north-east frontier: the castle and citadel of Bragança.

deter invaders. It didn't always work: Moorish armies took Bragança several times; the forces of Léon and Castile also passed through, and their Spanish successors seized it more than once. Students of English history have known the name, in their own spelling, since Catherine of Braganza married Charles II in 1662, handing Bombay to the British as part of her dowry. She never lived here, however, for the ducal family (who had become the royal family with the restoration in 1640) found it too bleak and isolated and preferred their palace at Vila Viçosa (see p.264).

New roads and EU membership have brought an increase of Spanish traffic, notably since Oporto is now the most convenient port for quite a large region of Spain. In Bragança, suburbs have sprung up and a one-way traffic system of board-game ingenuity has been introduced. One wrong turn and you're sent to the edge of the city and deposited in a dusty building site. Even the locals can't fathom it, so if you have a car, don't try to use it to explore the centre. The excellent **Turismo** is in a new building, a couple of blocks north, on the road towards Zamora in Spain.

Citadel and Castle

You can drive up to the **citadel**, right through the eastern gateway in the well preserved walls. Inside, the castle with its own wall stands over the northern ramparts. The magnificent **keep** is now a **military museum**, which is worth a visit even if you are not interested in military matters. Notice the stonemasons' marks on the lower courses of the keep before taking a giddy climb to the top of the ramparts. Now glassed over, the beautifully restored keep is crammed full with exhibits on every floor: prehistoric and Roman weapons; medieval armour and superb early firearms; Peninsular War sabres and muskets; and trophies from Angola and Mozambique – relics of Portugal's colonial past. The top floor covers World War I, with evocative dioramas of trench positions on the Western Front.

The smaller **Princess Tower**, according to legend, held various noble ladies who had been locked up by their fathers or husbands to keep admirers at bay. Next to it, two commonly found features in Portuguese towns are combined: a *pelourinho* (see p.41) has been spiked into the back of a prehistoric granite figure of a wild boar. The former is topped with unusually grotesque figures and the boar, like some other examples, has a hollow in its head.

Across the street there's a picturesque huddle of old houses, some surviving from the medieval town. Many are in a poor state and unfortunately threatened with clearance in a programme intended to 'sanitize' the citadel.

The middle of the citadel is dominated by the white tower of the 18th-century **Igreja de Santa Maria**, with a fine barrel-vaulted, painted ceiling, and an elaborate gilded altar. Next to the church is a greater rarity, the five-sided, 12th-century town meeting house known as the **Domus Municipalis**. It's a gem of genuine Romanesque architecture, recently restored to the original design of open arches around the upper floor. These had been blocked up at some time in the past, presumably because the town elders didn't care for cold winter draughts. If you wait for a while, someone will come with a key to open the council chamber, the lower level of which was a water cistern.

The Lower Town

Cars have to leave by the same gate they came in by, but walkers can stroll down through the western gate. Just beyond it, a right turn leads to the main street (here called Rua São Francisco) and the charming little church of **São Bento**, with its painted *trompe l'oeil* ceiling and traces of wall painting. In the same street to the west, the church of **São Vicente** had to be rebuilt in the 17th and 19th centuries, on a Romanesque base. This was where Pedro I claimed to have married Inês de Castro (see p.155). A little further along and across the street, **Museu do Abade de Baçal** is named after the local abbot who collected most of the museum's exhibits, including Celtic carvings (more wild boars) and Roman inscriptions, coins, books, paintings, church vestments, and regional costumes.

The street runs past a typical 18th-century Misericordia and ends at the rather plain Cathedral, which is adjoined by the local market and riverside gardens. On a hill across the river to the south, the Pousada de São Bartolomeu has a great view of the citadel and town.

North and west of Bragança, the land rises through grassland and oak forests cut by sheltered river valleys to the Montesinho mountain range along the Spanish border. The area has been declared a Natural Park, giving some guarantee against development. In its isolated villages, a way of life survived for centuries in which land was held in common and work was allocated by an elected committee. Elaborate ceremonials to ward off the evil eye and assure fertility certainly have pre-Christian origins. Electricity, television, roads and cars seem bound to change all this.

Here and elsewhere around the northeast, look out for strange U-shaped buildings with sloping roofs. They're pigeon houses, where the birds are reared for their droppings (a fertilizer), and for the pot.

Following the Border

For those in a hurry, a direct road links Bragança with Guarda (see p.249), but if you can afford a day to meander, take the much more interesting route which sticks close to the border with Spain. You'll see more livestock than people in the villages on the way, for the traditional granite houses are gradually being abandoned. **Outeiro** has a strange old church with double Romanesque doors, and a hilltop ruin of a castle, reached by a good path.

Miranda do Douro

On the heights above the gorge of the Douro facing Spain, this remote outpost has marked the frontier ever since Afonso Henriques carved out his new kingdom of Portugal in the 12th century. When relations were good, it flourished from trade, but in war it was seized more than once and often attacked by Spanish forces. During one siege, in 1762, the castle was largely destroyed when the gunpowder store blew up,

When walking in towns, look up to see details such as this little statue of saintly Queen Isabel above a church door in Bragança.

killing most of the defenders. Soon afterwards, the local bishop moved to Bragança and Miranda's cathedral was downgraded. The little city dwindled in importance, although Wellington came here in 1813 (he was hoisted across the river in a basket, suspended beneath a rope bridge).

Now prosperity has returned. Traffic from Spain arrives across the top of an impressive dam built to generate hydroelectric power. At weekends, thousands of people cross from Spain for the shopping, and whole streets of stores have opened, full of shoes, ceramics, umbrellas and port. Goods are carried away in whatever will hold them – baskets, suitcases and bin-liners.

Wellington in Portugal

Napoleon's declaration of war on Portugal on 20 October 1807 may have seemed a minor matter to him, but it started a train of events that would lead to his downfall eight years later.

Portugal had been an irritant to him for years, refusing to give up her neutrality and her extensive trade with Britain. With Spain his ally, albeit a reluctant one, he expected the all-conquering French army to make short work of the smaller nation. Her ships could be seized and added to his fleet, and her ports closed to the British. He ordered General Junot to invade. Portugal invoked the old alliance made with England in the 14th century and often reaffirmed since, and called for aid. When Junot's small and exhausted column entered Lisbon on 29 November 1807, they found that the Portuguese royal family, most government ministers and many other leaders had sailed for Brazil in British and Portuguese ships, taking with them all the gold and treasure they could carry.

Wary of getting involved in a land war on the the continent, Britain had been looking for other ways to get at Napoleon and his Spanish allies. A force had already been assembled with the idea of invading Spanish colonies in South America. Selected to lead it was the youngest lieutenant-general in the British army, Sir Arthur Wellesley, who had already made a name for himself campaigning in India. As Viscount and then Duke of Wellington, he was to make a greater one.

Following the invasion of Portugal, the French emperor took another fateful step: he seized King Ferdinand of Spain, forced him to abdicate and replaced him with his – Napoleon's – own brother, Joseph Bonaparte. Spain exploded in rebellion. Spanish and Portuguese deputations arrived in London to urge Britain to join them in attacking the French occupiers. The destination of Wellesley's expedition was suddenly changed from South America to Portugal.

The First Campaign

Wellesley went on ahead, putting in at Oporto on 24 July 1808, where he arranged to link up with Portuguese troops at Leiria. At sea again the next day, he joined the invasion fleet. The landing began on 1 August, at Figueira da Foz, chosen because its fort had been captured from the French by a number of brave students from Coimbra University. Getting 9,000 men ashore in small boats in raging surf was a slow and dangerous business, and a number were drowned. Joined by 6,000 Portuguese at Leiria, the army marched south towards Lisbon, passing through Batalha on 14 August. By coincidence

Sir Arthur Wellesley, later Duke of Wellington, architect of victory in the Peninsular War and Napoleon's Nemesis.

this was the anniversary of King João I's victory of 1385 which the Abbey of Batalha commemorated. It was a favourable omen, for João had been helped by English archers, and in the abbey his effigy is shown hand in hand with his English queen, Philippa.

On that same day they reached Alcobaça, another victory memorial, and on the 16th Wellesley was standing on top of the castle at Óbidos, looking south at the small French force sent out to shadow him. Next day, near the village of Roliça, he attacked, to gain the advantage of numbers before enemy reinforcements arrived. The French, anxious to avoid being surrounded, retreated. Wellesley had won the day, but he unfortunately had too few cavalry for pursuit to be possible.

Vimeiro

News came of ships carrying 4,000 more British soldiers and Wellesley moved south to Vimeiro to cover their landing. Unfortunately, as well as this welcome addition to his strength, London had sent the ageing and cautious General Sir Harry Burrard to take over command. Having decided against an advance on Lisbon, Burrard returned to his ship to sleep, leaving Wellesley in charge on shore for a few hours more.

Now fortune took a hand. Word came after midnight on 21 August that Junot himself was approaching from the south with the main French force. At 9am they were in sight, but due east of the British and Portuguese who had to be hurriedly redeployed to face the threat. Coolly, Wellesley placed his men in strong defensive positions on the Vimeiro ridges and hilltops, many of them just behind the skyline and out of sight of the attackers. To counter the Napoleonic practice of sending *tirailleurs* (skirmishers) ahead of the main force to cause confusion, he posted skirmishers of his own at the bottom of the hills to interfere with the French advance. When Junot ordered his columns to assault the heights, they were thrown back again and again until finally they broke and ran.

Meanwhile Burrard had appeared on the scene. He at least had the sense to allow Wellesley to complete the day's work, but then refused again to order an advance on Lisbon. Next day, yet another and still more senior general arrived to take over, the third commander in 24 hours. This one, Sir Hew Dalrymple, not only disregarded Wellesley's plans to exploit the British successes, but completely ignored the man who had won two battles in five days.

French Go Home

The wily Junot chose this moment to send a party under a flag of truce to propose a French withdrawal from Portugal. Sir Hew agreed, and an armistice was signed. Even Wellesley put his name to it, feeling it his duty to show loyalty to the new commander, although he had taken no part in the negotiation. On 31 August the agreement was ratified by Junot in Lisbon and Dalrymple in Torres Vedras. The British then moved their headquarters to the more agreeable surroundings of Sintra and the treaty became known as the Convention of Cintra (British writers always spelled it with a C). When its terms were made public, there was an explosion of fury in Britain and Portugal. Not only were the French being let off the hook, they were to be transported home in British ships and allowed to carry away all 'their' property, including a great deal of loot from Portuguese churches and palaces.

The British general whom Wellesley most admired, Sir John Moore, had by this time reached Portugal, and the two met at Queluz, which had been Junot's headquarters. Wellesley told Moore he believed there were only two generals

Sir John Moore, who died from wounds at Corunna. His death brought Wellington back to Portugal.

who inspired confidence among the troops, namely the two present at that meeting. One of them would have to lead the liberation of Spain and, said Wellesley, 'You are the man'. The next day he sailed for England.

Setback

Back in London, Wellesley was widely condemned for the notorious Convention of Cintra, but he rode out the storm and eventually most of the blame for the easy terms was attached to Dalrymple and Burrard. Meanwhile, Napoleon in person led a fiercer and more effective onslaught in Spain. Madrid was taken, and most of the uprisings across the country were put down. Sir John Moore conducted a skilful retreat: many survivors from his small army were successfully evacuated from Corunna (La

Coruña), but he died there on 16 January 1809. Napoleon handed over command in Spain to Soult, who immediately launched a second invasion of Portugal. By the end of March he had taken Oporto, and again the Portuguese had to call for help. Wellesley told the British government that 20,000 men would be needed merely to hold Portugal. A new expedition was ordered, and he was the obvious choice to command it.

Beginning Again

On 22 April 1809, Wellesley was back in Lisbon, to a welcome of dancing in the streets. Within two days he had formulated a plan: to march north immediately, liberate Oporto, cross into Spain and link up with the Spanish resistance to advance on Madrid.

He sent the army ahead to Coimbra and joined them there on 2 May. Pausing for a week of reorganization, he divided the Portuguese among British brigades to speed up their training and gave every brigade a company of riflemen in order to build on their success at Vimeiro.

The Passage of the Douro

On 12 May the force reached Vila Nova de Gaia, home of the Port shippers' lodges on the south bank of the Douro opposite Oporto, just as Soult's engineers blew up the bridge across the river. His men had already seized or destroyed every boat – or so he thought – but as Wellesley watched from the clifftop convent of Serra do Pilar, a local barber reported that four wine barges lay undamaged, unguarded and hidden under overhanging cliffs on the north bank. He had also found a single rowing boat on the south side. In broad daylight, a party of volunteers rowed across the 200m (220 yards) of open water and brought back the barges, all without being seen by the French.

Wellesley didn't hesitate. 'Well, let the men cross,' was his laconic command.

Thirty at a time, the soldiers were carried over. The first to land occupied a seminary building and prepared to defend it, covered by British guns on the other bank. After an hour, 600 had made the crossing, few enough against Soult's 23,000. The French launched attacks on the seminary but were driven back. All this time, Soult was sleeping, after a night's preparation which had now proved incomplete. Rudely awakened, he refused at first to believe that the enemy was in the city, but it was already too late to save the day. The people of Oporto enthusiastically joined in ferrying the rest of the army across the Douro, and the French were in full flight. Soult and his staff had no choice but to follow, leaving a fine meal on his table. At 4pm, Wellesley sat down to enjoy it himself. Celebrations went on all night, fuelled by a flood of wine given away by the ecstatic British Port shippers.

Next day the pursuit began, to Braga and north-east through the mountains, following a trail of burning villages and abandoned equipment. In spite of appalling weather, Soult and his tattered survivors were able to make their escape, leaving their stragglers to the vengeance of the Portuguese. At Montalegre on 18 May, Wellesley gave up the chase. Portugal was once again clear of the French.

The crossing of the River Douro and capture of Oporto from the French led to their expulsion from northern Portugal in 1809.

Foray into Spain

The army regrouped at Abrantes on the Tagus in June, and on 4 July began to cross into Spain. Wellesley conferred with the veteran Spanish Marshal Cuesta on how best to move against the two French armies now between them and Madrid. The British commander was for taking them on one at a time, but Cuesta found reasons for delay and as a result, the French were able to combine their forces. On 27 July close to the walled town of Talavera on the Tagus, they attacked. As at Vimeiro, Wellesley had occupied a good defensive position. Outnumbered two to one, he faced a succession of crises, but after two days' fighting it was the French who were forced to retreat. When news of the victory reached London, the king made Sir Arthur Wellesley a Viscount. He couldn't keep the same name (his elder brother had a prior claim), and there wasn't time to consult the new lord, so his younger brother William had to decide for him. He chose the title of Viscount Wellington, apparently because of the similarity. When he heard, Arthur declared it 'exactly right'.

Talavera had been costly: Wellington had lost a quarter of his men. Now reports came of new French armies, led by some of Napoleon's best marshals, present and future: Kellerman, Mortier, Ney. The Emperor himself threatened to take the field, but when trouble with Russia took precedence, he put Masséna in command. There was no choice for Wellington but to withdraw into Portugal.

Winning Defence

In September 1809, Wellington paid a private visit to Lisbon and then spent some weeks riding all over the hilly country to the north of the capital which he had seen the previous year. With remarkable foresight, he ordered the covert preparation of a chain of fortified positions between the Tagus and the sea – the 'Lines of Torres Vedras'. A year later, they would be needed.

The first half of 1810 was used by the French in building up their forces in Spain and trying to suppress resistance there. The British government wanted to pull out of Portugal, but Wellington persuaded them to reinforce him, although not in the numbers he asked for. In August, Masséna crossed the border and started to attack the great star-shaped fortress town of Almeida. A shell ignited the main magazine, killing most of the defenders and forcing the rest to surrender. Wellington pulled his army back, moving his headquarters from Celorico to Gouveia. Masséna advanced to Viseu.

Now the British commander saw a chance to fight one more battle on advantageous ground before withdrawing to his defences in front of Lisbon, which had so far been kept secret from the French. The 50,000 British and Portuguese occupied the towering north-south Buçaco ridge, 15km (9 miles) long and largely bare, not wooded as it is today. Masséna had 66,000 men, most of them veterans who had never known defeat. As Wellington had calculated, the French commander could not and would not ignore the challenge, and at dawn on 27 September he began the attack. Used to easy victories and almost as contemptuous of the British as of the Portuguese, he was fatally over-confident, launching his columns one after another at the ridge, which seemed to be thinly defended. Wellington had as usual positioned more men and guns out of sight behind it. When the day was over, Masséna had made little impression and had lost 4,600 men, four times as many as the British and Portuguese combined.

The Buçaco ridge was no place to linger, victory or no victory. Still

Retreat from Coimbra.

outnumbered, Wellington's forces quickly slipped away to the south. Passing through Coimbra, the French were not far behind, but Masséna's army stayed to loot the city, and the monastery of Alcobaça in its turn. Meanwhile, Wellington supervised the occupation of his Lines of Torres Vedras. By 10 October, he was ready. Five lines, 152 forts and many lesser positions in a band up to 37km (23 miles) long and 10km (6 miles) deep, guarded every road and pass leading to Lisbon. A few days later, Masséna's vanguard began to discover the sort of force that they were up against. Unwilling to risk another Buçaco, the 'old fox' lay down for a month to await reinforcements. In an inspired piece of confidence-boosting, Wellington ordered a grand ball to be held in Lisbon.

With many of his men sick, his generals quarrelling and communications severed by vengeful Portuguese irregulars, Masséna retreated to winter quarters of his own near Santarém. For three months only minor skirmishes disturbed the growing boredom.

Pursuit

Suddenly, the fox was off and running. On 5 March 1811, covered by a thick mist, Masséna's army was in retreat. Increasingly disorganized, they were in constant danger of being cut off. Herded by Wellington and harried by Portuguese guerrillas, they made for Spain. Everything that was not essential was abandoned, and Portuguese peasants were tortured and killed in their hundreds to make them reveal hidden food. By 3 April, Masséna was across the border, having lost nearly half of his army in the campaign. On 10 April, Wellington issued a proclamation:

'The Portuguese are informed that the cruel enemy ... have been obliged to evacuate ... The inhabitants of the country are therefore at liberty to return to their homes.'

It was not yet over. A French garrison was besieged in Almeida and on 2 May Masséna marched a revived army to its relief. Outnumbered, Wellington waited in a strong position on the heights above Fuentes de Onoro. True to form, Masséna ordered a head-on attack. He almost succeeded, but in the end had to give up the attempt, although he declared a victory (on the grounds that through the mistakes of some British officers, the defenders of Almeida managed to escape).

Spain Again

Masséna was dismissed and replaced by Marmont, Napoleon's youngest marshal. Wellington laid siege to the Spanish border fortress of Badajoz, the twin of Elvas in Portugal, but had to give up for lack of effective artillery. In addition, up to half his men were laid low by disease and stronger French forces were approaching. He continued to blockade Ciudad Rodrigo, the second key Spanish stronghold further north, and in January 1812 besieged and took it. A grateful government in London elevated him from Viscount to Earl Wellington, while the free Spanish Cortés made him Duke of Ciudad Rodrigo. In March he tried again to take Badajoz and after almost a month of heavy losses it was successfully stormed, although for once his troops went out of control in drunken scenes of pillage and rape.

With the two 'keys' to Spain in his hands, he advanced for the first time deep into the interior with a British, Portuguese and Spanish force of 46,000. Marmont's equally strong army marched to meet them. They clashed at Salamanca on 22 July, and the French were decisively defeated. On 12 August the victorious allies entered Madrid to a tumultuous welcome ('King' Joseph Bonaparte having fled). It was during this stay that Goya painted his best portrait of Wellington (others which he produced were not from 'the life').

Now for the first time things began to go seriously wrong for Wellington. An assault on Burgos failed, valued officers were either killed or captured, and new French armies again outnumbered him. In October he cut his losses and pulled back once more across the border into Portugal.

Farewell to Portugal

The army moved into bleak winter quarters near Vilar Formoso. Wellington set up his headquarters in the little village of Freinada – the fine stone house still stands. With spring came a new confidence: fresh supplies, more artillery and troops, and news of yet more French disasters following Napoleon's retreat from Moscow. By May, Wellington was ready for what he intended would be the last campaign. He took a third of the army back to Salamanca and then rode to meet the rest, who had marched south through the wilderness of Trás-os-Montes. On 29 May 1813 he crossed the gorge cut by the Douro at Miranda do Douro, swaying above the white water rapids in a wicker basket hauled by ropes and pulleys. The next day he joined the main force to lead them over the border and into Spain.

'Farewell Portugal!' he cried, turning his horse and waving his hat in an uncharacteristically theatrical gesture. 'I shall never see you again.' Wellington had already shown himself a master of manoeuvre and strategic defence. Now began a victorious advance through Spain and France to Paris and, after the '100 days' of Napoleon's last throw, to Waterloo.

The spacious 16th-century **former cathedral** is richly decorated: notice the fine choir stalls, like a gilded arcade framing paintings. The odd little statue, painted and clothed, called *Menino Jesus da Cartolinha* (Little Jesus in a Top Hat) has a story behind it. In battle with the Spaniards in 1711, a small boy armed with a sword appeared to lead the Portuguese at a moment of crisis and revived their spirits. The day was saved, but afterwards, the boy could not be found. The victors declared that it must have been Jesus who had inspired them. None of that, however, explains the figure's top hat.

Behind the church, the ruins of the bishop's palace have been turned into an attractive garden. Back along the main street, the **Museu de Terra da Miranda** occupies a fine 17th-century house in Praça João III. The collections cover local archaeology from every era as well as the folk traditions of the region. Miranda is renowned for its *pauliteiros* (stick dancers), who perform stylized sword-fights, and its varied traditional dress.

The much-improved road south-west to Mogadouro passes through farmland and orchards and a succession of villages from where half the population has emigrated abroad. At Lagoaça, a short diversion east gives some fine views of the Douro gorge. The main road heads west, but continue south through a wild and rocky landscape to **Freixo do Espada-à-Cinta** ('Ash Tree of the Belted Sword'). The name may commemorate an occasion when King Dinis strapped his weapon to an ash tree, or it could just be a corruption of an older name. An ancient ash tree lends credence to the first story, next to a tall seven-sided tower surviving from Dinis's 13th-century fortifications. A statue honours Jorge

*N*ot much is left of the walls of the fortress of Freixa do Espada-à-Cinta, but King Dinis' seven-sided tower still dominates the little town.

Alvares, born in Freixo, who charted the sea route to Japan in the 16th century. The Igreja Matriz, the impressive parish church, was rebuilt around 1520 in Manueline style. From the same time, 16 paintings of the Life of Christ are attributed to Grão Vasco, including the *Flight into Egypt*, *Last Supper*, *Betrayal* and *Crucifixion*. In the valley and on the terraced hillsides, almond orchards blaze with white and pale pink blossom in February and March. Sheltered spots are warm enough for orange groves and vineyards: this is the eastern limit of the Port wine region, although its output goes to make table wines rather than Port itself.

At Barca de Alva the frontier turns south and the wide and placid Douro flows west through Port wine country to the sea. Sizeable boats could come this far upstream, and a ferry (probably the *barca* in the name)

The medieval walled town of Castelo Rodrigo covers the slopes of a hill, while the ruins of a mighty castle crown the heights.

used to carry traffic across the river. Then the railway from Oporto was built and took all the business. Now things have changed again, with barrages and locks, one of them the highest in Europe, making it possible for cruise vessels to get through. Week-long holidays take in the sights along the way in some luxury (see p.198). The railway no longer crosses into Spain or even reaches Barca de Alva, but stops at Pocinho.

The walled town of Castelo Rodrigo, built in the reign of King Dinis as a bulwark against Castile, was frequently involved in wars and sieges, and wrecked more than once by the Portuguese themselves, for backing the wrong side. Long deserted, the once-romantic hilltop ruins are in currently being reconstructed as a 'tourist attraction', but are worth a diversion for the view. At nearby Figueira de Castelo Rodrigo, the parish church has a gilded baroque interior and a strange arch assembled from S-shaped blocks of granite.

Almeida

Like Elvas to the south (and many other similar towns), this fortress town was built in the low, star-shaped pattern first developed in the 16th and 17th centuries, its bastions and deep tunnels designed to withstand the new power of artillery. Almeida was the key to northern Portugal and in 1810, the French under Napoleon's Marshal Masséna attacked. By ill chance, a trail of gunpowder from a leaking keg was ignited by an incoming shell, setting off the ammunition store in the church. In a huge explosion, heard by Wellington and his army some miles away, the church and half the castle simply vanished, killing hundreds of the defenders and forcing the remainder to surrender. Besieged in their turn the following year as Masséna retreated, the French blew up some of what was left and made their escape, largely thanks to incompetent British officers ignoring Wellington's orders.

Given this history, it's a surprise that so much remains to be seen at Almeida, including gateways surmounted by coats of arms; tunnels; ramparts; a parade ground, and the vast *Casamatas* (Barracks), whose chambers and dormitories could house 5,000 men. There's now a Pousada inside the walls, with 21 rooms and a restaurant serving the local dishes and wines.

Vilar Formoso stands where the main road and rail connections from central Portugal cross the border. On the Spanish side, Fuentes de Onoro was the site of one of Wellington's greatest victories, though its impact was dulled by the fiasco at Almeida (see above). Paradoxically, a new road from Guarda has brought more traffic but by-passes Vilar Formoso. That and the reduction of customs checks within the EU have made it rather a backwater except on Saturday, when bargain hunters from Spain pack the shops and markets. Otherwise, most people speed past without giving it a second glance.

Followers of Wellington's campaigns will want to take the minor road south from the town centre, past an old steam locomotive on a pedestal, looking for a sign to the right to **Freinada**, 5km (3 miles) off the road. Apart from the TV sets and the cars of the returned emigrés, the village can't have changed much since the winter of 1812-13, when it was Wellington's headquarters. On a handsome stone building in the main square opposite the church, the inscription reads: 'Quartel-General de Lord Wellington, Marquês de Torres Vedras, Comandante-Chefe do Exército Luso-Britânico. Novembro 1812 – Maio 1813'

By following the border, you'll miss **Pinhel**, between Barca de Alva and Guarda, which is actually worth a diversion if you have the time. The hilltop town itself has an attractive central square, gardens, fine old houses and decaying walls. Keep climbing to reach the remains of the castle, with two towers (one with a fine Manueline window) and some archways. On the road to Guarda, it's easy to imagine you're seeing neolithic monuments everywhere, in this land of granite outcrops and walls that alternate large and smaller stones. Look out for a fine dolmen near Martianes, on the east side of

*P*inhel is another of the frontier castles built on the orders of Dom Dinis to defend his kingdom against Castile.

the road, 1.6km (1 mile) north of the turning to Pêra do Maço. Five great upright stones form a small enclosure, and three of them support a massive slab, forming a Stone Age burial chamber.

Guarda

Guarda's name signals its rôle – to hold back the Moors after it was taken from them by King Sancho I during the 12th century. Later, it was an important link in the chain of strongholds against Spain. Lying at an altitude of 1,040m (3,410ft) on the north-eastern edge of the Serra da Estrêla mountain range, this is the highest city in Portugal, cool and fresh in summer and swept by icy winds and frequent snow

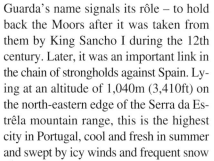

*M*odern statue of King Sancho I in Guarda, tireless crusader against the Moors. He took the upland city from them in the 12th century.

in winter. The grim, grey granite **Cathedral** looks suitably like a fortress, apart from the flying buttresses and carved gargoyles. More relief is provided by Manueline features added around 1510, notably the twisted columns of the main door and interior, which is bold and spacious. It looks out over a handsome arcaded square, the Largo de Camões, where you'll find the **Turismo**. The statue commemorates Sancho I.

An alley at the south-east corner of the square passes under **Torre dos Ferreiros**, one of the gateways in the city walls. To the left, you're faced by the typical baroque façade of the Misericórdia, with white stucco framed in stone. A few steps to the right of the church, the old bishop's palace has been rebuilt as a local **museum**, with exhibits relating to archaeology and folk customs, and the natural and military history of the region.

Serra da Estrêla Natural Park

South-west of Guarda, Portugal's highest mountains offer some of the best scenery, unusual towns, walks and climbs, and snow in winter. There's even some organized skiing. You could use Guarda as a base, but there's a better choice of accommodation closer to the heart of the park at Manteigas or Covilhâ (see below). If you're driving, the endless hairpin bends in the roads can seem tortuous, but the surface is well maintained and soon cleared after snowfalls. Here, we follow one of several possible circuits with diversions and suggested walks.

Belmonte, just off the main road south from Guarda, is dominated by its rebuilt castle. It was the birthplace of Pedro Alvares Cabral, the man who is credited with discovering Brazil: he bumped into it by accident on his way to the Cape of Good Hope in 1500. Various items can be seen here commemorating his voyage: the **castle** has a model of his ship; a statue of the Virgin Mary which he took with him is kept in the parish church; and the old church of São Tiago near the castle has a Cabral family chapel. The oldest houses and narrow alleys below the castle are the old Jewish quarter, whose inhabitants became 'New Christians' under duress in the early 1500s (see p.52). In Roman times, Belmonte was a garrison town, and Centum Cellas, the three-storey stone ruin just to the north may have been the *praetorium* (military headquarters).

The decorative Misericórdia church in Guarda in typical 17th-century Portuguese style of white stucco and granite outlines.

Covilhâ, spread across the terraced eastern slopes of the Serra da Estrêla, is turning into something of a centre for visits to the park. The Turismo in the main square can supply leaflets and maps, find accommodation and provide guides to accompany serious walkers and climbers. The statue in the square depicts the 15th-century explorer Pero de Covilhâ, who travelled by land to India, Arabia and Ethiopia, where he remained having been appointed a provincial ruler.

With all the sheep you'll see in the area, it's not surprising that the town has a long established wool industry, said to have been modernized with the help of English weavers in the 17th century. Among the products are the blankets which still keep the local shepherds warm. Further up the hill on the slopes above Penhas da Saúde, 1,500m (4,920ft) high, ski tows and lifts serve Portugal's only organized ski resort (although when it snows local families flock to the mountains on Sunday to slide down the slopes on sleds, trays or even plastic sacks). Most of the year, it's a great centre for hikes to waterfalls in the hills. The highest peak in the country, the Torre (1,993m/6,540ft), is 2km (1.2 miles) south from the top of the pass on the road up from Penhas. A tall statue of Our Lady of the Shepherds is carved into a niche in the mountainside.

North of Penhas da Saúde, a road follows the valley of the Zêzere – as pretty as its name – to the spa village of **Caldas de Manteigas** and on to the town of Manteigas (meaning 'butters', for which it's known, as well as cheeses). The countryside around offers superb walks and views.

The winding road west of town passes the Pousada de São Lourenço, another great base for exploring the area, before descending to **Gouveia**, where the infor-

In northern Portugal, outcrops of granite boulders can look like crouching animals, or the Stone Age monuments which some of them are.

mation centre for the whole Serra da Estrêla park has maps of the footpaths and leaflets on flora and fauna. The office is in an old mansion at No. 8, Avenida Bombeiros Volontarios.

On the old road back towards Guarda, **Linhares** is an ancient village which was once a Roman town – the ruined castle on a crag has Roman stonework in its lower walls. Typical of the Serra, there are more sheep and donkeys here than people. The parish church has three remarkable paintings which the locals claim to be by Grão Vasco, and many experts are

251

inclined to agree. The villagers are prepared to resist any attempt to remove the pictures for 'authentication' or conservation, in case they don't come back. Head along the path due west towards Figueiró da Serra and you will find you're walking along a Roman road, complete with its original paving of heavy stones.

Southern Slopes

The region known as the Beira Baixa (Lower Beira) is gentler country than the mountain ranges to the north and west. Woodlands and orchards alternate with farmland, punctuated here and there by a hill or rocky outcrop, standing out like islands. Any high place was invariably the site of an ancient settlement. You'll see fortifications everywhere, for there was never a time without some sort of threat, usually from Spain.

Sabugal was long disputed between Spain and Portugal, which explains the imposing walls of the castle at the south-west end of the town. Its five-sided tower and crenellations like long sharp teeth are being restored, and the ramparts made safe for walking. About 12km (7 miles) west on a rocky spur, the magnificent walled town of **Sortilha** was a stronghold of the Moors until they were driven out in the 12th century. Stones marked with Arabic patterns and script can still be seen in the walls of some of the houses inside the ring of fortifications, and the parish church has an intricate *mudéjar* ceiling. The inhabitants are aware of the potential of their picturesque home to attract visitors: antique shops have opened, several of the old houses have comfortable rooms available, and there's a choice of good rustic restaurants.

Penamacor, high on a hill next to the main road south is far less well preserved. For a view of the town and surrounding countryside, climb up its steep streets to the crumbling castle keep which lies among tumbled ruins.

Monsanto

This very ancient and unique place is a quintessentially Portuguese village. You'll see it from far off, on a rocky pinnacle towering above the plain, and reach it by well signposted country lanes. (From Penamacor head first for Medelim.) The road up climbs ever more steeply into a landscape of great granite boulders. The village begins, with houses beside, below and practically *inside* the huge rocks. The streets narrow until you can't drive any further, and parking can be a problem. You're still a 15-minute walk from the top, and almost any path will do, provided it heads generally uphill.

The **castle** at the top augments the natural defences with stonework the Incas wouldn't have been ashamed of, and the views to the south are breathtaking. The Romanesque **church**, probably from the 13th century, is roofless but otherwise almost perfect, and there are rock-cut tombs nearby. Back in the village, tourism has arrived, with postcards on sale at Stone Age houses, and one of the latest additions to the Pousada chain.

Down the hill again, back to Medelim and 6km (4 miles) south, you'll come to the sleepy village of **Idanha-a-Velha**, once the important Roman town of *Civitas Igaeditanorum*. Settlements like this that did *not* make use of defensive hilltops were a sign of the Romans' confidence that Lusitania had at last been pacified. Even the circling walls were probably added later, as the empire declined. You can see a fine double-arched **gateway** through them, next to the present-day road, straddling a paved Roman street grooved by cartwheels.

After the barbarian invasions, the Visigoths ruled, and one of their later elective kings, Wamba, is said to have been born here. The lower courses of stonework of the defensive **Templars' Tower** are Roman, probably the base of a temple, while nearby, the remarkable early Christian **basilica** was built by the Visigoths, perhaps also on Roman foundations. You'll find it near the tower, surrounded by the organized chaos of an archaeological dig. The roof has been repaired, and the nave and two aisles are lined with local discoveries, including fine pieces of statuary. The guardian is normally on duty during museum hours, or he will come to open up if you show an interest. Notice how a

mihrab facing Mecca was made in the eastern wall when the church became a mosque under the Moors. Ask to see the extraordinary cruciform **baptismal font**, which is lined with marble and has recesses for the priest and sponsors to sit while water was poured over the candidate.

Castelo Branco

The chief city of Beira Baixa is pleasant and busy, with broad avenues, parks and gardens. As a frontier fortress, it was wrecked and rebuilt too often for much of the medieval town to survive, apart from a few streets leading uphill towards the ruined castle, on the highest point. The main sights lie along or near the central avenue, Alameda da Liberdade, where you'll also find the **Turismo**.

Don't miss a stroll in **O Jardim do Antigo Paço Episcopal**, the gardens of the former bishop's palace. Laid out in formal baroque style in the 18th century, they're an intricate series of terraces with fountains and fishponds, sculptured hedges and a hundred or more statues: the apostles, the signs of the zodiac, Faith, Hope, Charity, and the kings of Portugal. The palace will house the **local museum** when the current reconstruction is complete.

The church of **São Miguel** enjoyed cathedral status until the bishops moved away in 1881. It has a fine, solid Renaissance interior with an impressive barrel-vaulted roof.

*T*he 18th-century gardens of the old bishop's palace in Castelo Branco feature statues of all Portugal's kings up to that time. The Spanish interlopers are shown as smaller than the rest.

Border Castles, Roman Cities and Rolling Plains

The Alentejo takes up most of southern Portugal. Much of this 'land beyond the Tagus' (*Alentejo*) is a vast plain dotted with cork trees and swept by hot, dry winds in summer. Coming from the north or east, as hills topped by eagle's-nest castles give way to tracts of prairie-like wheatlands, local drivers on the way to the Algarve view the Alentejo as something of an endurance test. There is much to see though, from the mighty fortress at Elvas to the marble town of Estremoz. Here, also, you'll find Évora, one of Portugal's most historic cities, still an architectural jewel surrounded by olive groves and vineyards.

Castelo de Vide and Marvão

Starting in the hilly north-eastern corner of the Alentejo, if you're coming from the north the route through the mountains will bring you to the Tejo gorge at **Ródão**, with superb views into the valley. Continue via **Nisa** (a dull sprawl with a huge and dusty market place) towards the Spanish border and you'll soon be in a region of wooded hills, close to **Castelo de Vide**. The town's

All over Portugal, but especially in the Alentejo, cork trees characterise the landscape. Actually a form of beech, they provide most of the world's cork.

waters were known by the Romans, who could never discover a spring without diverting it into a bath-house. The idea was taken up by the Moors, who were here for 500 years until around 1200. The old part of the town grew up in their time and retains the look of a North African casbah. For the next seven centuries, the habit of taking baths for the sake of cleanliness declined, but it was replaced by the belief that the waters could cure everything from skin diseases to gout, and Castelo de Vide became a health resort and summer retreat. Like all the spas in Portugal, its fountains are a magnet for day-trippers from the cities, armed with bottles in which to take some of the elixir home.

Once through the apartment buildings of the suburbs and into the old walled town, head first for the lovely main square,

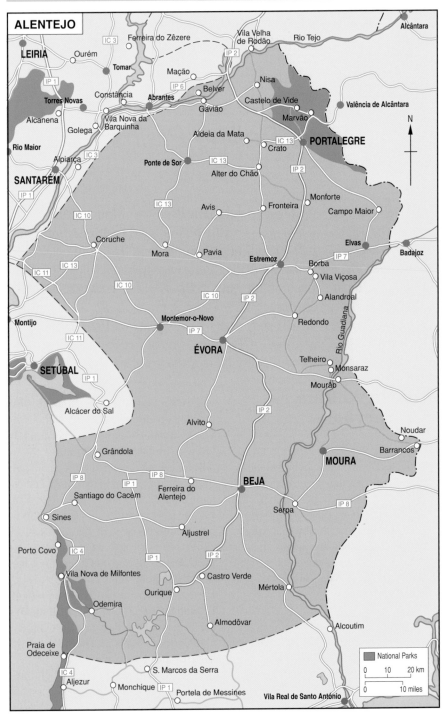

ALENTEJO

LEIRIA
Ourém
IC 3   Ferreira do Zêzere
Vila Velha de Rodão
Rio Tejo
Alcântara
IP 2
Tomar
Mação
Nisa
IP 1
Constância
Belver
IP 6
Torres Novas
Abrantes
Castelo de Vide
Valência de Alcântara
Gavião
Alcanena
Vila Nova da Barquinha
Marvão
N
Golega
Aldeia da Mata
PORTALEGRE
Rio Maior
IC 13
Crato
Alpiarça
IC 3
Ponte de Sor
IC 13
SANTARÉM
Alter do Chão
IP 2
IP 1
IC 13
Avís
Monforte
Fronteira
IC 10
Campo Maior
Coruche
Elvas
IP 7
Mora
Pavia
Estremoz
Borba
Badajoz
IC 11
IC 13
Vila Viçosa
IC 10
IC 10
Alandroal
Montijo
IP 2
Montemor-o-Novo
Redondo
IC 11
IP 7
ÉVORA
SETÚBAL
Telheiro
IP 1
Monsaraz
Mourão
Alcácer do Sal
IP 2
Alvito
Noudar
Grândola
Barrancos
IP 8
IP 8
MOURA
IP 1
Ferreira do Alentejo
BEJA
Santiago do Cacém
Serpa
IP 8
Sines
Aljustrel
Porto Covo
IC 4
IP 1
IP 2
Vila Nova de Milfontes
Castro Verde
Ourique
Mértola
Odemira
Almodôvar
Alcoutim
Praia de Odeceixe
IC 4
S. Marcos da Serra
National Parks
Aljezur
0   10   20 km
Monchique
IP 1
Portela de Messines
0   10 miles
Vila Real de Santo António

Rio Guadiana

WHICH WAY SOUTH?

If you're making for the Algarve, there's a choice of routes, each with its own rewards. People in a hurry coming from Lisbon usually take the new IP1 down the middle of the Alentejo, but in so doing sacrifice interest for speed. The west coast has a handful of lovely little sheltered coves and beaches, long popular with locals but only just being discovered by foreign visitors, and further east, most roads lead through Évora, just as they did in Roman times. The IP2 takes you to Beja – well worth a stop – and eventually joins up with the IP1. A more attractive but slower option takes in Serpa and Mértola, the latter unique in Portugal for its church, which has scarcely changed since it was a mosque 750 years ago. The best plan is to take one way south, and a different route on the return journey.

To see the Alentejo at its best, come in spring, when it is transformed into an emerald carpet sprinkled with wild flowers. Even as early as February, birds are already nesting and the fields are full of young lambs and calves. By March and April the days can be hot and the sky a cloudless blue. The roads are empty, few visitors are about, finding accommodation poses no problem, and you'll be all the more welcome.

Praça Dom Pedro V. The **Turismo** near the big plain church of Santa Maria will provide you with a useful street plan and key to the sights, as well as a good map of the surrounding area.

The narrow, cobbled Rua da Fonte climbs steeply from the town fountain towards the castle, but first you'll pass through part of the old *Judiaria* or **Jewish quarter**. Notice the stone doorways, many still with their ogival Gothic arches. Some come in pairs, one large, one small, which was the traditional Jewish style. Near the top where two of the alleys cross, the for-

mer **synagogue** dates from as early as the 13th century. The simple building comprises just two plain rooms with three storage silos under the floor, and a few relics on display. At the top of the hill stands the **citadel**, updated by the addition of star-shaped bastions in the 17th century. Inside the ramparts, the **castle** itself is empty but impressive, but there's also a charming and unusually well kept medieval village. The little church of **Nossa Senhora de Alegria** is beautifully tiled inside and out. Here and on the way down (almost all the lanes and steps lead back to the main square) you'll see flowers everywhere, in gardens, pots and window boxes.

The **Serra de São Mamede**, the uplands surrounding Castelo de Vide, have been declared a 'Natural Park' to give some protection to the profusion of wildlife and monuments. There's a great view of the town from the chapel on top of **Monte da Senhora da Penha**, 3km (2 miles) to the south-west. Several prehistoric dolmens and *menhirs* (tall standing stones) are not far away, at Fonte das Mulheres, Carvalhal and Santo António das Areias, further east.

Only 12km (7 miles) to the east, **Marvão** is like an eagle's eyrie, dominating the surrounding country from the top of precipitous cliffs. From afar, the sight is dramatic: unlike Castelo de Vide, the view is uninterrupted by modern development. At first, the fortifications look impregnable, but in fact a fairly gentle road leads up to the main gate. Inside, it's usually so quiet that you would be forgiven for wondering if the place has been asleep for the last couple of centuries. Little white houses with brown wooden doors line the narrow alleys and flights of steps, but there's scarcely an inhabitant to be seen.

This superb defensive site has been occupied since the Stone Age, and the region

around is peppered with remains from every era. In Marvão itself, however, any older traces are concealed beneath buildings which date from no earlier than the Christian reconquest of the 12th century. By 1300, the walls had been extended to take in the whole of the long narrow hilltop, and extra bastions were then added in the 17th century during frontier wars with Spain. Peaceful times brought a decline in importance, which was further accelerated in the 1960s by an exodus of the town's younger population, bound for the big cities or emigrating to France. The place might have been abandoned altogether if it hadn't been 'discovered' by a group of Lisbon artists, who use some of the houses as second homes. Other buildings have been turned into holiday accommodation, including the Pousada de Santa Maria, a *pensão* and a number of rooms to let. Ask at the **Turismo** (on the south side, near the centre of town) for details and a town plan.

The narrow end of the hilltop was cut off by multiple walls to defend the **castle**, which looks as if it has evolved naturally out of the rock. The walls have been well consolidated and a climb to the end is rewarded by stunning views. The old church of Santa Maria has been turned into the **Municipal Museum**, keeping its lovely wooden altar and *azulejos*. Collections of Stone Age arrowheads and axes, Roman glass and jewellery from excavations in the valley below, religious statuary, lace and traditional costume are well displayed.

There always seems to be a profusion of flowers in the clear mountain air of the Serra de São Mamede Natural Park. Wild flowers thrive in this remote area.

The village of Marvão was left almost deserted when most of the locals emigrated. Now artists, weekenders and foreign visitors are rediscovering it.

Portalegre

The busy chief town of the northern Alentejo has mercifully been granted a bypass to relieve some of its traffic problems. The walled upper town is still impressive, crowned by a great twin-towered **cathedral** in white stucco and heavy stone. Gracious 18th-century mansions all around tell

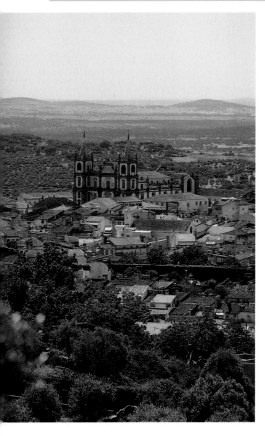

The busy capital of the northern Alentejo, Portalegre, grew up on a hill at the foot of the Serra de São Mamede. The walled upper town has good views out over the plains.

gregate. Just uphill to the south, in a former convent shared by the local Rover car showroom and an agricultural cooperative, an unmarked door and flight of stairs leads to a **tapestry workshop**. In spite of the lack of publicity, they're quite happy to take you on a quick tour through the great hall, where twenty women weave bright designs copied from modern paintings on two rows of looms. The large tapestries are generally commissioned for corporate head offices and foyers of luxury hotels. The guide doesn't even try to sell to visitors.

of past prosperity; across the cathedral square, one of them houses the local **museum**, with fairly typical collections of antiques and especially textiles – Portalegre used to have thriving silk and carpet factories. The bustling lower town centres on Largo Lourinha (or Rossio), where the **Turismo** is and where buses and taxis con-

St Anthony of Padua, who was actually born in Lisbon, is one of Portugal's chief saints. The museum in Portalegre has a collection of folk art recording the events of his life.

Crato, 16km (10 miles) to the west, was once the headquarters of the Knights Hospitallers (or Knights of the Order of St John of Malta). Its castle, one of the most powerful in this part of Portugal, held out so long against a Spanish invasion led by John of Austria in 1662 that when it finally fell he vengefully had it blown up. The ruins, above the church to the east of the modern town, are overgrown with flowering shrubs and are now used as an extension of the adjoining farm. You may be able to get inside and investigate if you can find someone with a key. Massive vaulted chambers give an idea of the power of the old fortress, which is now such a tranquil rural scene. The town's textile factory is similarly abandoned, with a storks' nest topping its tall chimney.

In a landscape strewn with boulders like huge animals, it's quite easy to imagine you're seeing the work of Stone Age people everywhere. For the genuine article, head west of Crato on the road towards Aldeia de Mata for 7.2km (4.5 miles) and off to the left, about a ten-minute walk away, you'll see a beautifully preserved dolmen, complete with capstone.

Almost adjoining Crato to the north, the little white cottages of **Flôr da Rosa** are spread around a wide village green. On a totally different scale, the vastly imposing 14th-century **convent** and fortress-like church were empty shells until quite recently. Now an ambitious scheme is well under way to convert them into a *Pousada*. The convent's founder and fighting cleric, Álvaro Gonçalves Pereira, is entombed in the church, and his son, Nuno Álvares Pereira (João I's constable), is depicted in a statue on the green. There are plans to restore the convent's gardens, laid out in a Maltese Cross to mark the connection with the knights at nearby Crato.

Horse Country

South of Crato, **Alter do Chão** is the most appealing little town in the area, with an impressive restored castle and fine baroque mansions. Call in at the **Turismo** – right opposite the castle in the town centre – for local information. **Alter Pedroso** ('rocky') is a much older hilltop village 5km (3 miles) to the east, where life appears to have stood still for centuries. Its ruined castle, on the site of a pre-historic *castro*, was another victim of John of Austria's spite (see opposite). On the way there, look out for another dolmen on the left of the road after 3km (2miles).

Anyone with an interest in horses shoud try not to miss the *Coudelaria de Alter Real*, the **royal stud farm** founded in the 18th century by João V. Just follow the signs to Coudelaria out of Alter do Chão for 2km (1.2 miles) to the north-west to reach the gate. Scores of superb horses graze the green pastures beneath the olive trees, and if you're there in spring, you should also see plenty of foals. Seasons come early here, and the first births can be expected at the end of January.

You're welcome to pay a visit to the palatial buildings and if you time your arrival for about midday, the horses will be filing in for lunch. Two pure strains are bred here, the iron grey Lusitanian and the chestnut Alter do Chão, both still prized for police, ceremonial, bull fighting and riding school use. A little museum of equipment is housed in a former stable (note the marble drinking troughs and other fittings). There's a collection of royal and other coaches, too; one coach is still in occasional use, for errands to the nearby town. Should you be in the area at the end of April, ask about the date of the annual horse auctions, the event of the year at the Coudelaria.

Empire Builders

Although Alter do Chão was a Roman foundation, it was razed on the orders of the Emperor Hadrian having supported a rebellion. For the most solid evidence of Roman presence in the area, take the road towards Ponte de Sor. About 12km (7 miles) from Alter do Chão, soon after a side road off to Avis, cross the River Seda near Vila Formosa by what is perhaps the best preserved **Roman bridge** in the entire empire. Take the side track down to the river for a close look. Not one stone in its six massive arches has been moved since it was built over 1800 years ago as part of the highway from Lisbon to Mérida. The 5m (16ft) roadway is paved with stone blocks as it would have been then. No weight restrictions apply, so 50-tonne juggernauts can rumble across without giving it a thought.

Cut across country to the south east (towards Monforte), until you reach a sign to **Torre de Palma** after about 24km (15 miles). (If you are coming *from* Monforte, take the old road that passes under the new IP2, which bypasses the town.) You'll cross another fine, solid bridge on Roman foundations, and 5km (3miles) from town reach the sign to Torre de Palma. Not far along the lane there are some impressive farm buildings, including the fortified tower that gives the place its name. Keep left to find the extensive excavations of a large Roman settlement: a villa now protected by a vast plastic roof, baths, more modest housing for the estate workers, an early Christian church and cemetery. A few damaged mosaics have been left in place, but the best have been removed to Lisbon, and are at present in storage awaiting the completion of renovations to the museum of archaeology at Belém. To see what you're missing, ask the guardian of the excavations to show you pictures.

The Alentejo is littered with such sites. Apparently unprotected by any defensive walls, they show how peaceful it was at the empire's zenith, and the destruction that befell when Roman power declined.

Monforte itself has some picturesque little streets leading up to an old walled citadel and a *capela dos ossos* with a wall of skulls – one of several in the region (see below).

A route linking the sights of the area makes a great day's excursion from Estremoz (see p.265), and you might add **Avis**, a quiet hilltop town which gave its name to the dynasty that ruled Portugal between 1385 and 1580. **Sousel**, lying just north of Estremoz, has one of the country's newest *Pousadas*.

Border Fortresses

Set amid cork plantations just a few kilometres from the Spanish border, **Campo Maior** was one of the chain of frontier castles created or strengthened by the tireless builder Dom Dinis to defend his kingdom. Again and again it withstood Spanish sieges, particularly after the restoration of Portuguese independence in 1640. Its greatest disaster was not the result of an attack; the powder magazine in the main tower blew up when it was struck by lightning in 1732, the explosion levelling most of the town and killing hundreds of people. The castle was rebuilt more or less as you see it now, without a keep, and a handful of defenders were able to hold off the whole French army for 13 days during the Peninsular War.

Like Monforte, the town has a *capela dos ossos*, but if you only want to see *one* of these, wait until you get to Évora.

There's a happier atmosphere at the famous local festival in the early part of September, when the cobbled streets and squares are almost roofed over with paper chains and flowers in a blaze of colour. Campo Maior's fortifications are impressive by most normal standards, but pale into insignificance beside those of neighbouring Elvas, only 18km (11 miles) to the south.

Elvas

No sooner have travellers from Spain crossed the border than they're faced by one of the greatest fortresses in Europe. The sight must have been daunting to past invaders. The circle of walls was strengthened after the Christian re-conquest in 1229, not just to hold off a Moorish counterattack but to thwart the ambitions of Castile, and later Spain. Elvas fell quickly to Philip II of Spain in 1580 when he claimed the throne of Portugal, but following the revolt of 1640 and the restoration of Portuguese independence, it was successful in holding out against vastly superior Spanish forces. In the late 17th century the whole town was encased by massive 'Vaubanesque' **bastions** and outworks, their pointed forms creating a characteristic star-shaped outline.

Huge as they are, the defences at Elvas are not the first sight that greets you if you're coming from Lisbon. On the west of Elvas, the view is dominated by the extraordinary **Amoreira Aqueduct**, whose arches – up to five tiers and 31m (102ft) high – march 1.1km (1,200 yds) across the valley (the whole aqueduct is over 7km/4 miles long). Started in 1498, it was not completed until 1622 – a year which far predates the aqueduct in Lisbon (see p.113), as people here will point out. Based on Roman

MASTER OF DEFENCE

Although Sébastien le Prestre de Vauban (1633-1707) has lent his name to the system of military architecture referred to as Vaubanesque, he didn't actually invent it. The ideas had been around ever since powerful cannon had made their appearance in siege warfare in Italy during the 16th century, battering the typical high, medieval fortress walls to rubble. By Vauban's time, two needs had become evident: to devise defences that could stand up to bombardment, and to find ways to use the new firepower against the besiegers. Walls became lower, very thick and sloping, and were angled to deflect incoming cannonballs. Sharply pointed bastions stood out from the walls, their shapes calculated to allow the defenders' cannon and muskets interlocking fields of fire, and deep moats, second and third lines of defence and outworks kept the attackers at a distance.

It was Vauban who published the most influential treatise on the subject. He made his mark as a young officer in a corps specializing in sieges and fortification and was appointed personal advisor to King Louis XIV in his twenties. At the age of 43 he became a field marshal, and was later created a marquis. In the course of his career he directed hundreds of sieges all over Europe, sometimes on the side of the defence, sometimes planning the attack.

models, for all its monumental size it carries only a tiny water channel, and the job could have been done equally satisfactorily by an ordinary pipe. Although the builders of the time could easily have made a sufficiently leakproof pipe, they didn't actually understand enough about hydraulics to see that it would work.

The main road carries thunderous international traffic south of the walls, but you can drive all the way round the outside – a trip well worth making. There's an entrance, the **Olivença Gate**, in the middle of the south side, just after the *Pousada*. (If you are driving and have problems parking, there is usually space near the castle.) If you head straight along Rua de Olivença, you'll come to **Praça da Republica**, which has mosaic paving in a striking box design. The **Turismo** here will give you an excellent street plan. The church of **Nossa Senhora da Assunção** (the former cathedral) at the other end of the square was rebuilt in the 16th century. It's notable for a light and airy interior, unusual grey ceiling paintings and some fine blue and yellow *azulejos*. Up the hill behind it, in Largo do Dr Santa Clara, the strange, studded 16th-century *pelourinho* has been reconstructed from fragments. Facing the square, **Nossa Senhora da Consolação** preserves the eight-sided plan of an ancient Templar church (see p.161). If it's open, seize the chance to see the domed interior, which is almost completely covered in 17th-century *azulejos*.

At the upper exit from the square, a tall **arch** topped by an elegant loggia was almost certainly part of the Moorish town walls before the defended area was enlarged. Beyond it, some of the narrow streets of the old town still have a typically Moorish look and at the top of the slope, the **castle** was originally built at the same time. It's now dwarfed by the later fortifications but the views from the tower are superb, especially over the town and northwards to the 18th-century **Graça Fort**, one of two outlying strongpoints. **Santa Luzia Fort** to the south-east is the other.

If time allows, stroll clockwise around the ramparts from the castle to São Vicente Gate, looking north-east across the bastions facing Spain. Then take your choice: either continue round the walls or cut back through the town centre.

Borba

Bypassed by the road from Elvas to Estremoz and Lisbon, this town is even whiter than most places in the Alentejo. Anything that isn't made of the local white marble is painted white. Borba is also known throughout Portugal for its wines, agreeable dry reds and whites. The central square is attractive, but it wouldn't be worth a diversion if you were not heading for Vila Viçosa, only 5km (3 miles) to the south-east. The road between the two is lined by marble quarries, piles of earth spoil, stacks of marble and loading cranes.

Vila Viçosa

It's easy to see why the dukes of Bragança chose to live here. Not long after the title was created for the illegitimate son of João I in the 15th century, the ducal court packed up and left the bleak north-east frontier for these gentler lands.

The lower town is laid out like a park with tree-lined avenues and squares. A vast empty space called Terreiro do Paço (Palace Square) is faced on one side by the austere classical front of the **Ducal Palace**, built during the 16th century. Along with outbuildings, gardens and 20 sq km (8 sq miles) of enclosed hunting grounds, it forms the centre of an enormous country estate. The family seems to have had a passion for the chase: the palace is full of antlers and other gloomy trophies. The 8th Duke only reluctantly accepted the crown as King João IV after the 1640 expulsion of the Spanish: he would have preferred to stay in Vila Viçosa and hunt. In 1861 Pedro V was carried home to the palace from a hunting expedition dying of typhoid. The sad associations continued:

Carlos I and Crown Prince Luis Filipe spent their last night here before going to Lisbon where, on 1 February 1908, they were assassinated (see p.58).

Inside, the palace is like a time capsule, preserved from that moment. You have to wait for a guided tour, which lasts about an hour, is quite expensive, and will probably be in Portuguese only. There's a succession of dark and formal halls, with heavy furniture, tapestries and portraits – including one of Catherine of Bragança (see p.53). Displays of silver, Limoges and Sèvres porcelain, and priceless early books amassed by the exiled Manuel II serve as a prelude to a visit to the private apartments of Carlos I and Queen Marie-Amélie, which in their detailed intimacy exert a powerful fascination. The royal clothes are still hanging in the wardrobes and family photographs stand on the dressing tables. Dom Carlos was an accomplished artist – a considerable improvement on the talents of many royals and statesmen – and many of his paintings hang on the walls.

The kitchens gleam with hundreds of copper pots and pans, some of which are big enough to make soup for an army. You'll be shown out into the French-style formal garden, with the choice of a separate visit to the **Collection of Coaches**, including the one in which Carlos and his son were shot in 1908. The usual exit is to the road north of Palace Square, through the remarkable **Porto dos Nós** (Gate of Knots), which is carved in stone in typical Manueline style.

The quaint little **upper town** inside its walls seems almost deserted: the castle, which has been thoroughly restored, is worth a visit mainly for the views of the Bragança palace and estate, and for a glimpse of local life.

Estremoz

The white towers of the citadel at Estremoz stand up from the plain like a distant ship, but the place has long since spread beyond the confines of its walls. Through a chaos of marble quarries and traffic, you'll come to the sprawling lower town, all dazzling marble (or whitewash) and red roofs. The enormous main square, Praça Marquês de Pombal or Rossio, is the focus of activity. Traders sell local pottery: earthenware water coolers, cooking pots, colourful plates and the painted figurines called *bonecos de Estremoz*. (Fine examples are on display in the local museum in the citadel, see below.) The Saturday market fills the square with stalls offering still more pottery, as well as all the produce of the Alentejo – fresh and dried fruits, vegetables, cured hams and superb cheeses made from ewes' or goats' milk. The small **Turismo** is in an offshoot of the square at the south end.

Pass through the beautifully preserved medieval walls into the upper town and you are in a different world where chickens scratch around in the narrow cobbled streets. It's more like a village, until you reach the great battlemented tower called the **Torre de Menagem**. Next to it, the imposing white **Palace** was rebuilt in the 18th century and again in recent times when it was converted into the Pousada Rainha Santa Isabel, one of the most beautiful and luxurious in the chain. Even if you are not staying or dining, ask inside if you can see the restaurant, a long hall under soaring arches. It was once a stable! Don't miss a climb to the top of the tower, starting at the *Pousada* door. The views of the town and countryside are magnificent: notice the typical, 17th-century zig-zagging ramparts which were added outside the citadel walls.

The *Pousada* takes its name from the saintly Queen Isabel, wife of King Dinis the fortress-builder, who was esteemed in Portugal for her charity towards the poor (see p.174). Her statue stands in the upper town square, commemorating her death here in 1336. She was still travelling widely and involved in good works in her 70's when she fell ill. You can see the room where she spent her last days in the arcaded house – part of an old palace – which stands across the square from the *Pousada*. It's now a chapel in her memory, with panels of *azulejos* showing scenes from her life.

Also facing the square in another fine old building, the charming **Municipal Museum** has fine collections of local crafts, including *bonecos de Estremoz* and a well displayed archaeological section.

Some of the pottery on sale in Estremoz will have come from **Redondo**, which lies half-an-hour's drive to the south through hilly country covered with eucalyptus forest. On the way, the isolated 14th-century **Convento de São Paulo** has been turned into a palatial luxury hotel by the owning family. In common with *pousadas* and many other places to stay, prices are practically halved from November to March.

Évora-Monte

Nearer to Estremoz than Évora and just off the road between the two, look out for a castle keep high on an isolated hilltop. As you approach, it looks more and more like a clay replica, but underneath the regrettable coating of new cement lies a genuine 16th-century tower with a four-leaf clover plan and Manueline 'knotted rope' stonework. Climb up through the three floors, each supported by four massive pillars, to the roof: the view makes you feel as if you're flying with the swallows that con-

gregate in thousands on the tower. Take a stroll in the old village too: the church of Santa Maria has a fine gilded altar and 16th-century wall paintings. In 1834, the War of Two Brothers (see p.57) was ended in a house in Rua Direita with the signing of the Convention of Évora-Monte.

Évora, Queen City of the Alentejo

There's so much to see in and around this lovely old regional capital that you could spend several days here. A full range of accommodation for overnight and longer stays is available, although it would be wise to make reservations in summer and at spring weekends. A short visit is worthwhile just to see the highlights, and day excursions from Lisbon and the Algarve are organized by a number of tour companies.

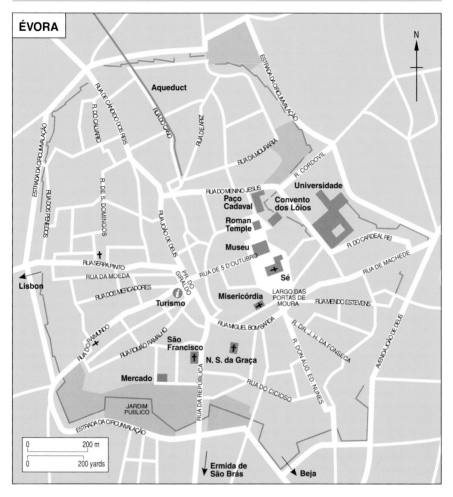

Some of Portugal's best megalithic sites show that this area was important in early times. The hilltop was the site of Celtic Ebora, which was taken by the Romans in

*T*he cathedral of Évora, built like a fortress in the turbulent 12th century. Its tranquil Gothic cloisters were added later. The treasury houses a fine collection of religious art.

the 2nd century BC. Relics of their time include the best preserved Roman temple in the country. Typically, few traces are left of the Visigoths who followed, but the Moorish presence for over four centuries gave the old town its present look – a maze of steep narrow streets and white-washed houses, still inside the line of the Roman walls. The freelance Christian warrior, Giraldo Sem-Pavor ('the Fear-less'), took Évora from the Moors in 1166 and presented it to Afonso Henriques. Many later Portuguese kings favoured

267

Évora and it expanded rapidly. A new wall was built enclosing a much greater area and this is the one that you can see today, reinforced in the 17th century by the same angular bastions as other fortresses in the region.

The city was neglected after the Spanish seizure of the throne in 1580. Even the restoration didn't bring Évora back into favour, with Portuguese kings preferring Lisbon and the palaces in its vicinity. Matters were made worse in the 18th century when the dictatorial Marquês de Pombal closed Évora's university. The population declined from an estimated 70,000 to only 5,000 and even today has only risen to around 50,000. Paradoxically, the town's beautiful state of preservation (especially the 16th-century buildings of its zenith) is partly due to centuries of neglect when there was little development.

Looting and slaughter by the invading French in 1808 was another setback for the town, after which it remained a backwater. It returned to centre stage when young officers of the military garrison played a central role in the plotting that led to the 1974 revolution. Afterwards, they revealed that to avoid eavesdroppers, they had often met in the open air at the Roman Temple.

The best way to get around is on foot: the main sights are close together. If you are driving, confusing streets and parking problems make it sensible to find a safe place for your car and leave it. Try the top of the old town, near the Roman temple and *Pousada*, or nearby, opposite the police station. (If you later find yourself at the bottom of the hill and too hot and tired to walk back up, take a taxi.) Call in at the **Turismo** in Praça do Giraldo to collect maps and leaflets. They have a particularly informative leaflet on Stone Age monuments in the area.

The Upper Town

The 2nd-century **Roman Temple** (sometimes called the Temple of Diana although there is no evidence of such a dedication) is the best preserved in Portugal, with 14 of its fluted granite columns still intact. They were probably saved because the spaces between were walled in for centuries: the building served for a long time as a butchery. The Corinthian capitals are carved from marble, but so covered in lichen it's hard to tell. Most of the base of the temple remains, although severely worn: to stop it crumbling further, you are requested not to

climb on it. Stroll over to the gardens to the west for a view over the city and down to the 16th-century **Porta Nova Aqueduct**. Facing the east side of the temple, the **Convento dos Lóios**, dating from the late 15th century, has been turned into high grade accommodation in the form of the Pousada dos Lóios. The vaulted Gothic cloisters (with a Renaissance upper level) are now part of the hotel, and are notable for the wonderful **Chapterhouse doorway**: beneath the complex ogee curves of the apex of the door, twin horseshoe arches in Moorish style stand on slim, twisting marble columns (a Manueline feature). The monastery church of St John the Baptist next door is private property, with restricted opening times. A beautifully light interior is the setting for fine 18th-century *azulejos* and the tombs of the Melo family, the

*S*tanding at the highest point in the old city of Évora is the best-preserved Roman temple in Portugal. It is a good place to start a walking tour.

convent's founders. A little further along the street, the twin towers of the family's palace, also called the **Cadaval Palace**, were adapted from the medieval fortifications, and, the entire site stands on Roman and Moorish foundations.

The **Museum of Évora** is housed in the former archbishops' palace facing the south side of the Roman temple. In and around its central courtyard, fine sculpture shows how the local marble has inspired artists from Roman times up to the present day. Look out for part of a classical frieze, the extraordinary head of Silenus (dating from 1st or 2nd century AD) and, among later work, Renaissance tombs and figures, Manueline doorways and fine *azulejos*. Upstairs, the mostly religious pictures include Flemish works by artists who came to Portugal in the 15th and 16th centuries. One of them, Frei Carlos, painted the portrait of Catherine of Bragança as a girl. There's a lovely *Holy Family at Supper* painted around 1660 by Josefa de Óbidos (here called by her Spanish name of Ayala).

The Cathedral

On the slope below the museum, the granite *Sé* (Cathedral) is one of Portugal's finest churches. Started soon after the reconquest, the powerful Romanesque structure was largely complete by the mid-13th century. Between oddly asymmetrical towers, the main door is flanked by marble columns which are topped by superb figures of the Apostles, also in marble. Inside, the mortar layers in the walls have been highlighted in white, giving a strange striped effect. The deep chapel behind the main altar was entirely lined with multi-coloured marble in the 18th century. Don't miss the **Gothic cloister** on the south side, below the level of the cathedral itself. Arabesque patterns in the stonework,

especially in the circular openings in the arcade, show Moorish influences. Perhaps *mudéjar* craftsmen (Moors converted to Christianity) worked on the building. The marble effigy of the founding bishop, Pedro, shows him with angels attending his rest. Nearby, there's a fine coloured statue of the Madonna and Child.

Entered through the south tower, the cathedral's **Treasury** is far more remarkable than the average collection of religious relics. A 13th-century ivory figure of the Virgin Mary opens up into a tryptich, entirely filled with tiny carved scenes from her life. Rotating slowly on a turntable, a jewelled reliquary was designed to hold a fragment of the True Cross.

More Évora Sights

Évora is ideal for walking tours: there's something to be seen round every corner. Behind the cathedral at the eastern end, alleyways lead to the **Paço Basto**, adapted from a Moorish palace which incorporated parts of the Roman wall. The gracious **Old University** buildings beyond it date from the 16th century: take a look through the gates at the baroque, two-storey arcaded courtyard. The reopening of the university in 1979 has given the city a lively student presence.

Rua do Conde de Serra da Tourega leads south past gracious, whitewashed houses to the elegant square, **Largo das Portas de Moura**. This was where the road to Moura emerged through twin towers in the wall – still visible in restored form – and under a Roman arch which was knocked down in the 1550s. It was replaced by the **Renaissance fountain**, with a marble globe on a curved column. Near the gate towers, Rua da Misericórdia leads to Igreja da Misericórdia, with 18th-century *azulejo* panels of scenes from the life of Christ. Continue past the church of **Nossa Senhora da Graça**, built in classical style at the pinnacle of imperial expansion. Carved granite 'flaming balls' probably represent the globe but also serve as an inadvertent reminder that the Inquisition was most active here at the time, burning a number of heretics.

Further on at Praça 1 de Maio is the **Igreja de São Francisco**. This Gothic barn of a church, topped by little conical pinnacles, was finished around 1500. The great portal leads to a door with the beginnings of a Manueline look. Inside, you see the same striped effect as in the Sé. The main 'attraction' is the macabre side chapel, **Capela dos Ossos**, lined entirely with hundreds of skulls, thousands of bones and a whole hanging skeleton, exhumed from cemeteries in the 16th century. This display of bones seems to have been a fashion in southern Portugal at the time, perhaps to encourage repentance before it was too late. Over the chapel entrance, a wry inscription: *Nós, ossos que aqui estamos, Pelos vossos esperamos* ('We bones here are waiting for your bones') scans neatly in Portuguese.

Out in the fresh air and across the square stands the city's covered **market**, jammed with local produce and pottery. Along the outer walls close by, both sides of the 17th-century bastions have been turned into pleasant botanic gardens. At the entrance, the partly restored **Palácio de Dom Manuel** shows some of the Manueline features – including curved windows – named after him and added during his reign. Looking south over the city wall near here, you'll see the curious **Ermida de São Brás**, all pinnacles, pillars and battlements. The style, which preceded Manueline in these parts, is called Gothic-Mudéjar.

Head back from Praça 1 de Maio to **Praça do Giraldo**, the city's focal point – once the Roman forum. Harmonious

In the heart of Évora, the Praça do Giraldo, named after the freelance leader who expelled the Moors in 1166, was once the site of the Roman forum.

four-storey, 17th-century buildings line the long cobblestoned square, arcaded along the eastern side, and in summer, café tables with sunshades take up the central area. The old Moorish quarter (*Mouraria*) was inside the old city wall nearby, and you can see traces of the *Judiaria* (Jewish quarter) in the narrow streets to the northwest of the square.

Excursions from Évora

All over Portugal in museums, country houses and many hotels you'll see carpets and wall-hangings from **Arraiolos**. Set on a hill north-west of Évora, this is an attractive town of white houses with doors and windows framed in blue. Look out for the House of the Arches and the baroque Fountain of the Muleteers. Shops along the main street sell everything from little souvenirs to huge carpets, and some of them will invite you to their *fábricas*, the workshops behind or above the stores. The carpets are sometimes wrongly described as 'tapestry', but they're made by cross-stitch embroidery and are not woven. You'll see teams of women bent over giant sheets of canvas, their needles flying with amazing speed as they build up the patterns of flowers and geometric designs or fill in areas of background. Even at the speed they work, it takes weeks to make one of the bigger rugs, so you can understand the reason for the high prices charged. Modern *arraiolos* (the town's name has long been a generic term) are quite coarse affairs compared to the work of the past.

The industry may have begun in Moorish times, but the present tradition probably had its origins when fine woven Persian carpets and rugs were brought back from India in the 16th century. Although they became the height of fashion, they were far too expensive for all but the very rich. These local versions imitated the eastern designs using home-produced wool and traditional dyes.

The region is rich in **Stone Age monuments**. If you want to track down some of the harder-to-find sites, the Évora tourist office has helpful booklets with maps. One of the most important, west of Évora and south of the main road to Montemor-o-Novo, is the great stone circle of **Almendres**, which is actually an irregular oval and not quite complete. In the lanes to the south, 3km (2 miles) west of the hamlet of **São Brissos**, a dolmen has been almost encased by a tiny Christian chapel, Nossa Senhora do Livra Mento Anta. (A similar example can be seen at Pavia, to the north of Arraiolos.)

Monsaraz

Situated away to the east near the Spanish border, Monsaraz may look remote on a map, but the roads are fine and fairly quiet, even by Alentejo standards. Monsaraz is a picturesque village inside the walls of a fortress, and the whole area is sprinkled with enough sights to make it a great day's excursion from Évora, Estremoz or wherever else you might be based in the region. An even better plan is to stay overnight – there's an attractive inn just outside the walls and a notable restaurant in the village itself. At weekends, the place is becoming increasingly popular with the Portuguese themselves, and reservations are necessary.

The tops of bastions added outside the old walls in the 17th century serve as convenient car parks. Inside the walls, you can stroll along the perfect little Rua Direita, lined with 16th- and 17th-century houses, many with Gothic doorways. Drop in at the **Turismo** for some local information, including how to find the Stone Age monuments in the region. In the 16th-century **Igreja Matriz** the most notable sight is a 13th-century tomb, wonderfully carved from two pieces of solid marble. The top part depicts a crusading warrior, Gomes Martins, sword in hand, his feet on a lion, now headless.

The **castle** at the end of the street was once a Templar stronghold (see p.161) and then belonged to their successors, the Order of Christ. Today the inner compound serves as a bullring. Climb the walls for an incredible panoramic view of fields and scattered olive and cork trees, where nothing seems to stir and the silence is broken only by birdsong.

Around Monsaraz

The area around Monsaraz has some impressive megalithic monuments, presumably the focus of ancient fertility rites. South from town towards the Guadiana river, opposite a big farm called **Xerez**, an unusual square of standing stones, 22m (72ft) across, surrounds a smooth granite *menhir* 3.5m (11.5ft) high. A taller stone, 5.5m (18ft) high and with indecipherable carved markings covering its lower surface, stands to the left of the side road to **Outeiro** from Telheiro, just north of Monsaraz. The **Turismo** in Monsaraz can provide you with a map showing how to find other sites.

If you still haven't overdosed on castles by this time, there are more to choose from. Across the Guadiana, **Mourão** gets few visitors to its fortress, which is still guarded by cannon dated 1701, but there is nothing inside. Unusually, the parish church is built into the 14th-century walls, incorporating one of the towers. A French engineer called De Langres, a follower of Vauban (see p.263), added a new outer line of typical 17th-century bastions during the wars with Spain, but then changed sides and sold his designs to the enemy. The Portuguese got their revenge when he was shot by one of their marksmen while advising the Spanish at a siege of Vila Viçosa. Strangely, his additions are now in worse shape than the older walls.

If Mourão's castle is empty, at least it has a living town. **Noudar**, by contrast, is entirely deserted, as is most of the country around. This most remote of all the border castles, reached by a rough but passable road from Barrancos, stands high on a ridge above the Murtega River on the very border of Spain. The region only came to Portugal as part of the dowry of a Castilian princess, Brites, when she married Afonso III, and Castile and, later, Spain both tried to get it back. The castle suffered in every war from then on, and the village has been abandoned since 1893. There's been some recent excavation and minor reconstruction, but take care when walking round – the exposed holes of the dungeons are just waiting for new occupants.

West of Monsaraz, on the way to Reguengos, stop in at the village of **São Pedro de Corval** to see the potters at work, turning out plates, jars and candlesticks. Depending on the time of your visit, you may see the kilns being loaded or emptied, or the cheerful designs being painted.

South from Évora

The improved highway IP2 to Beja (see p.275) bypasses **Portel** with its fine hilltop castle. It likewise skirts round the little agricultural town of **Vidigueira**, where Vasco da Gama's remains were taken in 1539 after they were brought back from India. He had died there 15 years earlier, soon after arriving on his third voyage to take over as governor of the Portuguese possessions. Although born in Sines, he had been made Conde (Count) of Vidigueira by King Manuel for his services, including his voyages to India in 1498 and 1502. His statue stands in the square, and the chapel where he was buried is in gardens on the edge of town. In 1898, the remains were moved again, to the church of the Jerónimos monastery in Belém (see p.106).

In olive groves 5km (3 miles) to the west, beyond the village of Vila de Frades on the road to Alvito, a substantial two-storey ruin called **São Cucufate** seems to have been part of a Roman settlement. Sometimes described as a villa, it was probably more like a farmhouse, with a barn below for animals and living quarters above. Although so many such buildings were destroyed, this was saved by being converted into part of a convent. The frescoes inside date from around 1600. Excavations are in progress to reveal more of the Roman remains.

An alternative route to Beja, slightly slower but more picturesque than the IP2. goes through **Viana do Alentejo**. The curious castle which dominates the town started out as a conventional creation of King Dinis in 1313. When it was selected as the venue for a royal wedding in 1482, all sorts of decorative battlements and pinnacles were added. Less appealing are the recent cement reinforcements, including coatings to the big conical tops of the towers. Take a walk round the top of the restored walls, and then have a look inside to see the church, which was transformed for the same wedding and later given a Manueline portal.

Across rolling wooded hills to the south, the quiet little town of **Alvito** has

CORK TALK

All over the country you'll see the blackened bare trunks of the cork trees, and curved sheets of their bark piled by the roadside or on the back of a truck. Portugal produces 80% of the world's cork, and most of that comes from the Alentejo. The hardy cork oak – actually an evergreen member of the beech family – can put up with poor soils and low rainfall, so it is suited to the marginal land on which wheat cannot be grown. Growers have to take a long term view (something which the Alentejo's big landowners were able to do), because trees need to be 25 years old before the bark can be stripped for commercial use. Then it takes another nine years or so before a second crop is ready. It's this regeneration that makes the cork oak special, since most trees die if the bark is removed.

Once harvested and dried, the rough outer crust is removed. Wine bottle corks are then punched out by machines which can manage as many as 15,000 an hour, before they are bleached, washed and graded for porosity. Those with the fewest pores give the most reliable seal.

The Greeks and Romans preserved their wine in jars by floating a thin layer of olive oil on top. In the Middle Ages the preferred method was to stuff an oily rag in the neck of a bottle. Corks caught on in the 16th century and have been a part of the magic of wine ever since. Even so, there's a threat to Portugal's cork industry. Plastic is cheaper and its use is increasing for low priced wines. Worse news is that poor quality corks have to take the blame for 'corked' wines – the rogue bottles that smell like blocked drains. Scientists trace the problem to compounds sometimes produced in the bleaching process, but the cork exporters are fighting back with tighter quality control and campaigns promoting the image of the natural product. Tradition is on their side. Pulling off a plastic cap just isn't the same.

a castle which is even more of an oddity than Viana's. No higher than the surrounding country, it doesn't seem designed for serious defence at all, with its twin horseshoe, mock-Moorish windows outlined in fancy brickwork. Built by the local barons at the same time as Viana was remodelled, it fell into disuse in the 19th century and was occupied by gypsies. Even recently, rooms around the courtyard were adapted to serve as shops while other parts crumbled. The House of Bragança charitable foundation stepped in to rescue the castle, and a new use was found. Conversion to a luxury *Pousada* was completed in 1993, with the interior beautifully restored. You may be put off by the smooth cement rendering of the outside, but it's not so unlike the decaying stucco it replaced. Elsewhere in Portugal, the same technique has regrettably been applied to stonework, for example at Évora-Monte and Sagres (see p.311).

Beja

Beja, in the middle of the vast grain belt of the lower Alentejo, was one of the chief cities of Roman Lusitania, with the distinction of having been founded by Julius Caesar. He called it *Pax Julia*, 'the peace of Julius', after signing a treaty with the defeated local chiefs, and the present name comes from the way the Moors said it (Arabic turns the P sound into a B). Roads fan out from Beja now as they did then, to Lisbon, Évora and Seville, and there's choice of routes to the eastern, central and western Algarve. It can make a convenient stop, and there's plenty to see, but there's also a surprising shortage of accommodation.

The hill on which the city stands is crowned by the tall keep of the castle – a landmark which competes for attention with an even more massive grain silo as you approach across the great plains. Climb the hill following signs to the

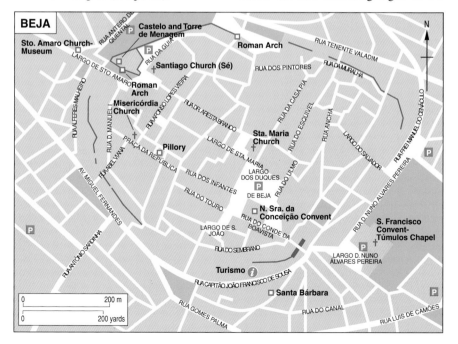

centre: the **Turismo** in the pedestrian Rua João Francisco de Sousa at No 25 has some of the best maps and literature you could hope for. The curve of this street, incidentally, follows the line of the vanished city wall (other sections survive). Beja is an ideal walking city, and it hardly matters where you start.

The Regional (or 'Queen Leonor') Museum is a must, even for those resistant to museums. The collections are interesting enough, but the building that houses them, the **Convento de Nossa Senhora da Conceição**, is utterly extraordinary. It was founded in 1459 by the 1st Duke and Duchess of Beja, the parents of Queen

Leonor (who married João II), and of the future King Manuel I. Enjoying royal patronage from the beginning, it became immensely rich. The baroque church is a vision of gilded carving, with a marble tomb of the founder and, on the right, an intricately inlaid alter, also of marble – rose, golden-yellow, black, white and grey.

*T*he building and its contents are equally remarkable: the Convento de Nossa Senhora da Conceição at Beja houses a museum of art and of the archaeology of the region. A detail of the cloister (above).

The adjoining cloister and chapterhouse are the real treasures, for the walls and vaults are covered by Spanish *mudéjar* tiles from the 15th and 16th centuries, stark, geometric blue and green tiles from Seville from the same era, and stunning early Portuguese *azulejos*. The 16-18th century religious paintings in the furthest rooms are mostly unremarkable, apart from a superb portrait of St Vincent.

In the 'Coat of Arms' room, the grille made of pierced terra cotta tiles in Arabesque designs dates from the 15th century. It is said to have been through this screen that a nun, Mariana Alcoforado, first saw the French nobleman who became her lover in the 1660s. Her supposed letters reproaching him for deserting her became romantic classics when they were published in book form in 1669, as *Five Love Letters of a Portuguese Nun*. You'll see an English translation on sale in Portugal today. Upstairs, the archaeology of the region is well covered, notably the finds from Stone Age to Roman times. (Keep your ticket: it covers another fine museum, Santo Amaro; see below.)

Rua do Conde de Boavista along the side of the museum leads downhill to Largo Nuno Álvares Pereira. On the opposite side of this square, with a public garden behind, the Convento de São Francisco was long derelict but is now being converted to a *Pousada* (due to open in 1995). Leaving from the front of the museum, Rua dos Infantes (with a choice of restaurants) leads to the long **Praça da Rebública**, with a Manueline pelourinho. The tall arcaded porch at the other end was formerly a covered market but now fronts the Misericórdia church. Behind it and to the right, you'll come to the castle, adjoining a section of city wall. The archway of a Roman gate has been reconstructed in front (there's another downhill to the east). The landmark **Torre de Menagem**, like the similar tower at Estremoz (see p.265), was built in the reign of King Dinis, but its excellent state of repair dates from a 1940 restoration. Inside, climb the spiral staircase to the three floors, each with one vaulted chamber. The view from the top seems limitless, and it's said that in pre-pollution days you could see the sea, over 100km (62 miles) away.

Below the castle and just outside the line of the old city wall, the **Church of Santo Amaro** stands on 7th-century Visigothic foundations and possibly those of a Roman temple too. Now it is a museum, beautifully displaying stone carvings from those times and the Moorish era. The Visigoth columns, pilasters and capitals are a revelation: because so little of their architecture survives, it's often assumed they just took over Roman buildings and created little themselves. This exhibition, unique in Portugal and only paralleled by one at Mérida in Spain, refutes that idea. It was the interminable wars of the Reconquest and, of course, earthquakes which destroyed a rich Visigothic and Moorish heritage.

If you want to visit one of the Alentejo's biggest Roman excavations, take the road towards Aljustrel from the Beja bypass. At 3.6km (2.2 miles), turn right along the rough track signposted to **Pisões**. Dusty when dry, muddy when wet, it's passable except to low-slung cars after heavy rain. After 4km (2.5 miles) you'll reach the extensive site, with the foundations of a villa, elaborate baths, mosaics, and the outlines of many smaller shops and dwellings.

Serpa

Across the Gaudiana river, 30km (18 miles) east of Beja, this is another hilltop town of white houses, and the focus of the local agricultural region. Whereas Beja has expanded and gives an impression of prosperity and activity, Serpa is a sleepy backwater, despite being famous throughout Portugal for its creamy, round, sheeps' milk cheeses. If you want to stay overnight, the Pousada de São Gens, with an excellent Alentejo restaurant, is 2km (1.2 miles) south of town, on the summit of a hill.

The Guadiana River near Beja. Further south it marks the border with Spain.

Serpa itself is ideal for strolling round – collect a street map from the **Turismo** in Largo Dom Jorge do Melo, right in the middle of the old walled town. The adjoining Praça da República is lined by fine mansions. In the opposite direction, steps lead up to the castle, which was wrecked by Spanish invaders in 1707. Parts of it seem precariously balanced, but they've been that way since that time. Also beginning at the *Turismo* but heading west along Rua das Portas de Beja, you'll come to Serpa's most prominent feature, a tall **aqueduct** along the line of the old wall, fed by a well and a chain of small buckets at one end and supplying a palace at the other. It's an elaborate affair to produce a trickle, and is still capable of working.

Mértola

South of Serpa the road climbs into a region of wooded hills and valleys, all apparently deserted. Suddenly, round a bend in the road, you're faced with the sight of a white town on a ridge, dominated by an old castle. Mértola enjoys a superb defensive position, on the sharp point where the River Oeiras joins the Guadiana, with walls across the third side of the narrow triangle.

European Union regional money has generated a lot of expansion recently, and funded imaginative cultural projects. Even before they were finished, Mértola awarded itself the label *Vila Museu*, 'Museum Town'. If that sounds a bit serious, it's misleading. This is one of the most delightful and fascinating places in the whole of Portugal.

The **Turismo** in the central Largo Vasco da Gama has detailed, numbered street maps, which are essential if you're to find the wealth of intriguing sites. Cars do penetrate the steep and narrow alleys

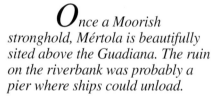

*O*nce a Moorish stronghold, Mértola is beautifully sited above the Guadiana. The ruin on the riverbank was probably a pier where ships could unload.

of the oldest part, but the only reason to try driving here yourself would be if you are renting a room in one of the houses. If that's the case (and an overnight stop is highly recommended), fold back the side mirrors and be ready for a test of reversing skills. Otherwise, walk.

The **castle**, which was the headquarters of the Knights of the Order of Santiago until they moved to Palmela (see p.141), gives a fine overview from its restored walls – see how many storks' nests you can spot. The cistern could be re-used today and the 13th-century vaulted tower, when open, is impressive. Just outside the

walls, excavations are unearthing Moorish and Roman foundations.

Close by the castle entrance, the white, pinnacled **Igreja Matriz** – parish church – is alone enough to make Mértola unique in Portugal. Inside, twelve columns divide a single hall into five aisles one way, four the other. Unmistakeably, this is the unaltered plan of a mosque. To confirm it, look behind the altar. A mihrab, or Arabesque arch over a niche on the southeast wall, indicates the direction of Mecca. An arched doorway in the same wall also survives from the Moorish building. Everywhere else in the country, mosques were destroyed in the battles of the Reconquest, or drastically changed during conversion to churches. In this enchanting

building, only the roof appears to have been rebuilt, supported by Gothic arches.

Near the tip of the town, an old house is scheduled to become an Islamic museum, bringing together inscribed stonework and other finds formerly scattered around various locations. Across the street, the Museu de Arte Sacra combines religious relics – statuary, silver and vestments – with ceramics and an active jewellery workshop, where you can watch young women silversmiths at work. Back towards the centre, pay a visit to the handsome Camara Municipal (Town Hall): its Roman foundations have been ingeniously converted into the **Museu Romano**, a fine collection of glass, coins, jewellery and sculpture superbly displayed and cleverly lit.

*M*értola's former mosque, re-roofed with Gothic arches but otherwise little changed when it was turned into a church in the 13th-century.

Mértola was the highest point up river that ships could reach, 80km (50 miles) from the sea. Below the town centre you'll notice the quay, which is used for launching canoes now. There, or by the steps from the clock tower, take a walk down to the water's edge for a striking view of the town from below. A little way downstream, the remains of a strange construction may be Roman in origin, or built by the Moors out of Roman brick. It's tempting to see this as the relic of a bridge, but it was probably a fortified jetty linked by causeway to the town wall, allowing supplies to be brought in even when the place was under attack.

Up in the new town, one more museum shouldn't be missed. A brand new building opposite the fire station covers the foundations of an early Christian basilica, probably dating from about 300 AD. Called the **Museu Paleocristão**, it uses imaginative display techniques to recreate the church and show off sculpture and other relics.

The eastern approach to the Algarve continues through almost empty country. A turn off to the east leads down to the frontier on the Guadiana, and the old Moorish port and stronghold of **Alcoutim**, opposite the Spanish town of Sanlúcar. (Only small boats cross to the other side, and not regularly.) You're already in the Algarve at this point, and you can continue along the river through orange groves and smallholdings, or return to the main road. Either way, you'll soon reach Castro Marim (see p.297).

The West Coast Route

From Alcácer do Sal (see p.145), traffic on the main road south may be heavy as far as Sines. After that it's usually only busy at summer weekends. Every significant town is bypassed but several are worth a short diversion. That is certainly true of **Santiago do Caçem**, which spreads down the slopes below its castle, now just a double line of walls, partly Moorish and partly built by the knights of Santiago. The town's name similarly combines the two influences: Kassem is said to have been one of its Arab rulers. As usual, the hilltop ramparts give a great view, but here they also enclose a cemetery. If you haven't visited one in Portugal, you may find it quite strange, with its tall family vaults and pictures of the departed.

Down in the town, facing the small public garden in the Praça do Município, a former prison used during the Salazar era is now the **museum**. A cell has been preserved, and other rooms furnished in the way they might be in typical houses of the region. The chief items of interest are the finds excavated at nearby Roman *Miróbriga*. To find the place itself, follow Rua de Lisboa from Largo 25 de Abril, the modern centre of town, and turn right after 600m (660yds) by a restored windmill. You'll find the site of **Miróbriga** on a low hill to the left after about 1km (0.5 mile). Spread out over a large area, it was clearly a substantial settlement. Facing the forum, part of a temple to Jupiter crowning the highest point has been tentatively reconstructed. Nearer the entrance, an old chapel houses an informative exhibition about Roman Lusitania, and a paved Roman street leads quite steeply down to the baths, with a well preserved heating system and foundations. Presumably as law and order fell apart in the failing empire, the town was moved to the steeper and more easily defended hill where Santiago's castle now stands.

Given that Portugal needed a petroleum industry, somewhere had to be found for it. There could have been many worse choices than **Sines**, where Atlantic winds and tides quickly sweep away pollution. Industrial development has been restricted to a quite small area, although its towers and smoke plume are visible from far away along the coast. You'll probably be grateful for the bypass – in fact there's no need to go any nearer than Santiago do Cacém – but if you have the time, it's quite an education to take a closer look. The old town, parts of the castle and governor's palace where Vasco da Gama is said to have been born are still there, beyond a maze of highways and pipelines. A road sweeps right around the town: one six-lane elevated section even covers part of the beach.

Attractive beaches both north and south of Sines are popular with the locals, especially at summer weekends, but protection from the Atlantic rollers and winds is a rarity. At a few points on this coast, where a river estuary creates some shelter, you'll find a handful of fishing settlements. A narrow road south of Sines leads to the enchanting little village and tiny harbour of **Porto Covo**. You might swim off the rocks when it's calm, but just 2km (1.2 miles) to the south there's a fine beach where the force of the ocean waves is broken by an offshore island, Ilha do Pessegueiro. Reached by a rough track along the coast, or a longer way round by road, the beach is quite undeveloped apart from a restaurant. The 17th-century fort on the shore is in excellent shape – notice the deep, rock-cut moat – but another on the island is a ruin. They were both built to resist the attacks of pirates, who frequently raided this coast, carrying off anyone they could catch.

Further south, **Vila Nova de Milfontes**, on the estuary of the River Mira, was another target of the pirates: the ivy-covered castle which stands above the pretty harbour was built in response. Now it's a select guesthouse. The town is one of the Alentejo's most popular resorts, and the little beaches can be crowded in summer with both Portuguese

---

BARBARY PIRATES

For centuries, Algerian and Moroccan raiders were the terror of the seas, preying on shipping and coastal settlements. Important captives were sometimes released in return for a ransom, but the rest faced a life of slavery. Portugal was not the only hunting ground: the whole of southern Europe was constantly threatened. Coastal towns were either given massive fortifications – which can still be seen at practically every Portuguese port and river-mouth – or else abandoned and rebuilt inland, giving fishermen a long walk to their work. As defences improved, the pirates found softer targets as far away as France, and in the early 17th century even descended out of the blue on villages in south-west England and Ireland. The scourge gradually declined as the British, French, United States and other navies took command of the seas, and by the beginning of the 19th century it had almost vanished. When France occupied Algeria in the 1830s, partly on the pretext of suppressing piracy, it became no more than an evil folk memory.

---

and foreign visitors, who now build holiday homes here.

A few more tiny resorts to the south are no more than dots in an empty landscape. The coastal route reaches the Algarve at Odeceixe (where a mainly German contingent removes its clothes) and then continues to Aljezur (see p.313).

The most scenic approach, if you don't mind tortuous twists and turns, goes through Odemira and Santa Clara-a-Velha, where a *Pousada* set amid forests and lakes makes a convenient staging post. The road then climbs through wild country dotted with mimosa trees covered with golden flowers in springtime. The top of a mountain ridge marks the border of the Algarve, before the road winds down to Monchique (see p.306).

ALGARVE

Sunshine and Sport on the Southern Strip

The southernmost province of Portugal is a great holiday playground. Sea temperatures may be a little cooler than the Mediterranean, but there's even more sunshine than you'll find at many resorts, with some 3,000 hours per year. Vast stretches of golden sand alternate with tiny coves backed by cliffs of coloured sandstone. There are, of course, crowds, but what better way to escape than by boating to your own peaceful hideaway on an offshore sandbar? Every sort of watersport is offered, and tennis and golf are played for most of the year. The Algarve is truly a place for relaxation.

It comes as no surprise to most people that even though the Algarve forms only a tiny fraction of Portugal, it gets more visitors each year than the rest of the country's regions combined. Mass tourism has undeniably changed the face of this coast – where once there were isolated fishing villages, there are now sprawling hoiliday complexes – but many areas were spared development and have since become protected. The eastern, central and western

Relax on the beach or immerse yourself in the clear waters. The coloured sandstone sculpted by the elements and the little sandy coves could hardly be anywhere but the Algarve.

Algarve all have their own distinctive scenery and character, and once you get up into the hills, it's entirely different again. Don't believe the clichés about the Algarve being just another tasteless holiday resort; there is much here that is typically Portuguese, especially if you come outside the summer months.

Faro

All that many visitors see of the Algarve's capital is the airport when they arrive and depart. This is a pity, for although Faro is not an obvious holiday destination in itself, it's a cheerful place with a fair amount of character, some interesting sights, and good restaurants and nightlife. The expansion and prosperity of the last

ALGARVE

N

Rio Guadiana

Vila Real de Santo António
Monte Gordo
Castro Marim
Manta Rota
IP 1
Tavira
Olhão
Alcoutim
S. Brás de Alportel
FARO
Mértola
Vale do Lobo
Quinta do Lago
Loulé
Almodôvar
Vilamoura
Quarteira
Castro Verde
Balaia
IP 2
Pademe
Portela de Messines
Albufeira
Serra do Caldeirão
Ourique
Algoz
IC 4
Rio Mira
Algar Seco
IP 1
Carvoeiro
IP 1
S. Marcos da Serra
Armação de Pêra
Silves
IP 1
Monchique
Portimão
Serra de Monchique
Lagos
Odemira
Ponta da Piedade
Rio Mira
Luz
IC 4
Aljezur
Salema
IC 4
IC 4
Praia de Odeceixe
Vila Nova de Milfontes
Sagres
Vila do Bispo
Cabo de S. Vicente

National Parks

20 km
10
0
10 miles
0

286

ALGARVE ALL YEAR ROUND

Every season has its attractions. In January and February there's a sea of white and pink almond blossom: the trees were supposedly introduced by a Moorish king to console a captured princess who was pining for the snows of her northern home. In February, the birds are already nesting, while golfers pour south in their thousands from cold northern Europe. March to June can be ideal, though the sea won't have warmed up – choose a hotel with a heated pool. July and August are the busiest months and if you're in the mood for a particularly sociable holiday, this is the time to come. In September and October things have calmed down, but the sea is still warm. Even November and December compensate for short and possibly grey days with extra-low prices and empty car parks.

20 years may have come mainly from tourism, but this is far from being a completely 'touristy' town.

It was probably the Moors who chose the town's present site early in the 8th century. At that time it faced the open sea (the offshore sandbars and mudflats have built up since). As late as 1596 during the Spanish occupation, an English fleet under the Earl of Essex could sail right up to the walls of Faro to sack and burn it. (The earl established his cultural credentials by stealing the books from the bishop's famous library first, and presenting them to the Bodleian Library in Oxford.) The 1755 earthquake (and others) compounded the destruction, so few earlier buildings survive today.

The town is spread around the inner harbour. Only yachts and small craft can use it, by wending their way through a maze of channels, lowering their masts and creeping in under the railway tracks.

Boats take visitors through the Ria Formosa nature reserve (see p.289) and are available for sport fishing out in the Atlantic – ask at the **Turismo**, which faces the south side of the harbour.

The Walled Town

Armed with a street map from the *Turismo*, walk through **Arco da Vila**, a castle gate rebuilt in the 18th century. The quiet cobblestone streets beyond converge on the **Sé (cathedral)**, which was originally built on the site of a mosque. Over the centuries earthquakes took their toll and only the tower over the main door survives from the 13th-century Gothic building. The hand-

A REGION APART

The Algarve was occupied for 500 years by the Moors – the Moslem Arabs and Berbers who invaded from North Africa early in the 8th century – who found the climate perfect for their orange trees and olive groves. The Moorish influence remains to this day in agriculture, music and the layout of the old towns and villages, and many place names – Albufeira, Aljezur, Armação – still give away their Moorish origins. Even the region's own name comes from the Arabic *Al Gharb*, 'The West' (strictly speaking, we ought to say just 'Algarve' and not 'The Algarve', since *al* means 'the').

The Christian Reconquest was not completed here until the mid-13th century and even after that, the region retained a certain degree of autonomy, isolated by mountains from the rest of the country. Until the end of the monarchy in 1910, the kingdom was known as 'Portugal and the Algarve', and the ports along the coast were the logical starting point for expeditions to Africa, whether invasions of Morocco or the great voyages of exploration sent out by Henry the Navigator from his headquarters at Sagres, the south-westernmost point of Europe.

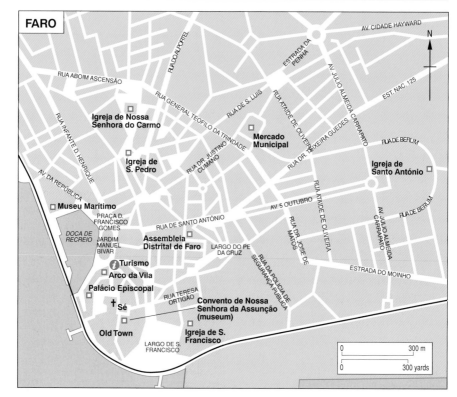

FARO

RUA ABOIM ASCENSÃO

RUA INFANTE D. HENRIQUE

AV. DA REPÚBLICA

RUA DO ALPORTE!

RUA GENERAL TEOFILO DA TRINDADE

RUA DE S. LUÍS

ESTRADA DA PENHA

AV. CIDADE HAYWARD

N

AV. JULIO ALMEIDA CARRAPATO

EST. NAC. 125

RUA ATAIDE DE OLIVEIRA

RUA DR. TEIXEIRA GUEDES

RUA DE BERLIM

Igreja de Nossa Senhora do Carmo

Igreja de S. Pedro

RUA DR. JUSTINO CUMANO

Mercado Municipal

Igreja de Santo António

RUA DE BERLIM

Museu Marítimo

PRAÇA D. FRANCISCO GOMES

DOCA DE RECREIO

JARDIM MANUEL BIVAR

RUA DE SANTO ANTÓNIO

AV. 5 OUTUBRO

RUA ATAIDE DE OLIVEIRA

AV. JULIO ALMEIDA CARRAPATO

Assembleia Distrital de Faro

LARGO DO PE DA CRUZ

RUA DR. JOSE DE MATOS

i **Turismo**
Arco da Vila

Palácio Episcopal

RUA TERESA ORTIGÃO

RUA DA POLICIA DE SEGURANÇA PUBLICA

ESTRADA DO MOINHO

✝ **Sé**

Old Town

Convento de Nossa Senhora da Assunção (museum)

Igreja de S. Francisco

LARGO DE S. FRANCISCO

| 0 | 300 m |
| 0 | 300 yards |

some 18th-century Bishop's Palace stands opposite, behind the orange trees which line the spacious Largo da Sé (cathedral square). On the other side of the cathedral, the 16th-century Convento de Nossa Senhora da Assunção faces a smaller square, Praça Afonso III. It ceased to be a convent in the 1830s, but then it swapped water for wine and became a cork factory. Now restored, it houses the **Museu Arqueológico e Lapidar** in the lovely two-storey cloister and surrounding rooms. The labelling is limited, but the exhibits here are certainly worth seeing. Some of the best finds from nearby Roman *Ossonoba* (see p.291) are here, including marble busts and mosaics. A magnificent mosaic floor measuring 9m (30ft) by 3m (10ft) shows the head of Neptune, but sadly the lower half of his face was destroyed by the bulldozer which unearthed it. The museum also features Portuguese ceramics, *azulejos* and paintings.

Outside the Walls

Back beside the harbour, the shaded seats set out in the **Jardim Manuel Bivar** are a favourite meeting place. A small **Maritime Museum** in the port office displays ship models and historic equipment, and as in most Algarve towns, the area of shops and restaurants along Rua de Santo António and the adjoining streets is partly pedestrianized. At the top end, facing Praça da Liberdade, the **Ethnographic Museum** (*Museu Etnográfico Regional*) makes a good job of illustrating the crafts, dress and ways of life of the Algarve in the setting of rooms furnished in traditional style. On the broad Largo do Carmo, the impressive baroque **Igreja do Carmo** is notable for a *Capela dos Ossos*, a chapel entirely lined with human skulls and bones. Dating from 1816, it's much newer than the chapels at Évora (see p.271) and elsewhere in the Alentejo, and the bones look distinctly fresher. Backing

The fishermen of Faro just 'carry on fishing'; the growth of tourism provides them with a bigger market than ever for the catch.

PARQUE NATURAL DA RIA FORMOSA

The great arc of barrier islands, dunes, mudflats and sheltered water between Faro's old shore line and the open sea has only existed for the last few centuries. Ocean currents carried sand from beaches further west and dropped it in long bars off the coast, with the result that silt washed down by rivers couldn't drain away and began to fill the lagoon. Tidal mudflats formed and grew into islands; plants established themselves and the new land was stabilized. Wetlands like this are increasingly rare, since all over Europe they have been drained for farming and building. This one has been under threat from many quarters, notably local industry, building work along the beaches, and the airport. Now it is officially a nature reserve.

The designated park stretches for 55km (34 miles) from Praia de Anç2o, next to the luxury resort of Quinta do Lago west of Faro, to Cacela Velha east of Tavira. Protection makes economic sense – its waterways are an important breeding ground for fish and shellfish, and the growth of 'eco-tourism' has made it a magnet for visitors outside the summer. Bird-watchers can spot dozens of migrant and resident species: flamingos, storks, egrets and herons, as well as the aptly named stilts, with the longest legs of any bird in proportion to their size, and the endangered purple gallinule. Sheltered waters along the Ria Formosa are also ideal for learning to windsurf.

A riot of gilded decoration embellishes the baroque Carmo church in Faro, but most people head for the adjoining, skull-encrusted Capela dos Ossos.

on to the same square, the 16th-century **Igreja de São Pedro**, rebuilt after the great earthquake, contains a finely carved, multicoloured Last Supper. You'll find some of Faro's nightlife in the narrow alleys between the Largo do Carmo and the harbour, where bars and loud discos keep going until 4am on summer nights. (Bear it in mind if you are thinking about accommodation in town!)

On the western edge of Faro, the former church of Santo António do Alto is now a museum of religious relics, of St Anthony in particular. Its tower offers one of the few good views over the city and south to the sea, 6km (4 miles) away across the Ria Formosa.

Faro's Beaches

In spite of first impressions, Faro does actually offer a number of beaches. On the seaward side of the outermost islands there's an almost endless stretch of gently shelving sand. In summer, ferries leave from the jetty near Largo da Sé for the **Praia de Faro** on Ilha do Ançao (not quite an island in fact: it's joined to land at the western end). You can also get to it by road past the airport and over a single-lane causeway. Only a short section of the beach has a road along it, lined with holiday houses and huts, a few restaurants and very limited accommodation. Near the south-east end of the road the waves are

often perfect for surfing. The parts of the beach which the road doesn't reach are less crowded and largely undeveloped. As part of the Ria Formosa nature reserve, they should stay that way.

Inland from Faro

On the main road north, 7km (4 miles) from Faro a turn to the right is signposted to Estoi. Before you reach the village itself you'll come to **Milreu**, the ruins of a **Roman villa** dating from the 2nd to 6th centuries AD. It was part of the town of Ossonoba, which was either destroyed or abandoned around the time of the Moorish invasion. The guardian can provide you with a numbered plan so you can trace the outline of the villa and the usual baths, with parts of the underfloor heating system. All the rooms were decorated with mosaics: some are on view, some have been taken to museums, and others have been covered up to protect them. One small bath, the size of a jacuzzi, is lined with fine mosaics of fish, designed to look their best when the bath was full of water. The most prominent feature at the site is the tall brick ruin across the Roman street (still paved in places) from the villa. Thought to have been a temple to water gods, more fish mosaics, beautifully preserved, embellish the walls. It was adapted – probably by the Visigoths – as a Christian church, which may account for its preservation, while nothing of the rest of Roman Ossonoba remains above ground level.

In the village of **Estoi**, just along the road, a gateway next to the church leads up a long a path to the 18th-century **Palácio dos Condes de Carvalhal**. The baroque house, small as palaces go, is closed for major renovations. As the local authority which owns it is short of money,

The palace of the counts of Estoi is currently being restored, but you can still walk in the grounds.

they have made little progress and plans to turn it into a museum are stalled. Parts of the grounds are open, including a ceremonial staircase decorated with sections of mosaic from Milreu and elaborate balustrades. They're worth the walk.

Further up the hill, **São Brás de Alportel** is a sleepy sort of place except on Saturday, market day. A few villas with pools cater for those who prefer the hills to the coast. The little Turismo in the main square has few suggestions to offer apart from the charming Algarvian Costume Museum (Museu Etnográfico do Trajo Algárvio), in a big old house close by. It's well set out, and displays are changed reg-

ularly to feature different regions. The Pousada de São Brás is 2km (1.2 miles) to the north, prominently sited on its own hilltop with stunning views.

Loulé

West of São Brás de Alportel through orchards of orange, fig and olive trees, you might expect the next town to be much the same. Instead, Loulé is big and prosperous, with wide modern streets – one a full scale boulevard – as well as an unchanged old town. The famous **Saturday market** seems to take up almost every open space, and the regular daily market in a fine pseudo-Moorish hall is one of the best in the Algarve. The fresh produce is superb, and it can be a good place to buy souvenirs, too. Local people credit Loulé with lower prices than the coastal towns where tourism has pushed them up. The Carnival here in February is the biggest and brightest in the region, with parades, lurid fancy dress, dancing in the streets and – by

Portugal's restrained standards – unbuttoned revelry and drinking.

The long, narrow market building opens off **Praça da Republica**, which is more like a section of avenue than a square. It used to run just outside the town walls, and at the lower end a left turn leads straight into the old quarter. The **Turismo** is immediately on the right, together with a small local museum in the shadow of a section of **castle ramparts**. Originally Moorish but rebuilt in the 13th century, the ramparts have been restored again and you can walk along a short section to enjoy the view. If you hear the sound of hammering while you're up there, it is the copper-beaters in their workshops off the streets below. Down on ground level again, you can watch them, and the town's potters, saddlers, carpenters and lace-makers. Buying direct from them may not save you much money, but there's added appeal to a memento if you know who made it.

Carry on through the narrow alleys to the south and you'll soon reach the 13th-century Gothic parish church, almost certainly on the site of a mosque. This is the south-west corner of the Moorish wall, with little houses nestling against its remnants. Through the archway south of the church, head left along Rua Duarte Pacheco. Just off it, to the left on Avenida Marçal Pacheco, the Misericórdia church has a fine Manueline portal and a lovely little whitewashed interior. Facing the following street to the left, a superb Gothic arch is all that

remains of the Convento da Graça, which was destroyed in the great earthquake. Now, it leads only to someone's back yard.

The villages around Loulé are noted for their latticework chimneys, made of clay and painted shining white. They're now copied en masse, cast in concrete and put on practically every new villa in the region, whether necessary or not. You'll find some of the best originals in **Salir**, up a new road to the north of Loulé. The lower part around the parish church is pretty enough, but climb to the hilltop just above, where the original tiny village grew up inside, around and on top of a Moorish castle, no doubt using its stones as building material. Only the base of four massive turrets and some foundations are left. Easily reached to the west of Salir, Alte is more famous and almost as picturesque (see p.303).

*M*oulded chimneys are an Algarve tradition which has been continued even on houses with no fireplace. The Barcelos cockerel is a northern import.

East from Faro

Offshore islands and mudflats like those which shield Faro from the open sea continue almost all the way to the Spanish border. This is the *Sotavento* or leeward coast, quite different from the western Algarve's coloured rocks and cliffs. Its resorts are smaller and lower-key, but each of the three main towns is distinctive: Olhão as a dedicated fishing port; Tavira for its unusual elegance; and Vila Real de Santo António for its rigid 18th-century chessboard layout. You could drive from Faro and be over the border into Spain in half an hour by the new IP2 *Via do Infante*, but it's more rewarding if you can take the time to explore.

Intensive agriculture is taking over some of the coastal plain, following in the steps of southern Spain in growing early crops for northern markets. Other development near Faro is messy, even by the standards of the area, and there's no temptation to linger. The first sight of **Olhão** might be discouraging too. The outskirts are exceptionally ugly, but remember that this is a real working port with a major fishing industry. Give the old town a chance: it's unusual in having mostly flat-topped houses instead of the Algarve's standard, sloping red-tile roofs. The **bell tower** of the baroque parish church in the centre is the only high point from which to get a view, and a forest of ironmongery designed to pick up distant TV stations rather spoils the early 20th-century 'cubist' look which artists once enthused about. Morning is the best time to see the action at the **fish market** in two big buildings on the waterfront – the auction bidding is electronic these days. Gardens nearby are quite pleasant, with park benches panelled with *azulejos* showing traditional fishing scenes.

From the jetty at the east end of the market, ferries leave for the **beaches** on the bar-

Colourful fishing boats of traditional design set out from every harbour and cove along the Algarve coast.

Tavira boasts more fine houses than any other Algarve town

rier islands. Connections are much more frequent in summer, and at busy times traffic can be chaotic and parking inadequate. Security has occasionally been a problem, so don't leave anything in your car.

Of the two islands, **Armona** to the east is 20 minutes away. **Culatra** to the south takes 30 minutes, but the first stop is at a seedy fishing settlement so it's worth taking an extra 15 minutes on the boat to reach Farol at Culatra's western tip. Both islands are dotted with holiday chalets and ramshackle huts, but the further you walk, the greater the privacy (each has its nudist area). The water on the landward side is naturally warmer and calmer, but a lot of the shore is unpleasantly muddy.

Back on the mainland, Fuseta is a sheltered fishing village with brightly painted boats bobbing at anchor. In the background, salt-pan workers rake a harvest of crystals into white pyramids. As you head east, look out for the Manueline doorway in the church at Luz de Tavira.

Tavira

The only truly elegant town in the Algarve has somehow avoided the excesses that have disfigured so many others. Presumably the local authorities and population can take the credit. Despite its patrician appearance, this is a hard-working town and fishing port. Since the River Gilão

MOMENT OF GLORY

Olhão claims to have been the first town in Portugal to rise against the French when they occupied the country in 1808. Following their example, the rest of the Algarve clubbed together and threw out the invaders. A 17m (56ft) fishing boat crewed by men from Olhão sailed to Rio de Janeiro to carry the good news to the exiled Regent, Dom João (later King João VI). No doubt he was pleased: he honoured the town with the title of *Vila Nobre de Olhão da Restauração* (Noble Town of the Restoration), but declined to return to Portugal for many years. As for the fishermen, they sailed home again. It was nothing extraordinary for them. The men of Olhão had been fishing for cod every year on the Grand Banks off Newfoundland since the 16th century, and would continue until late in the 20th century, when stocks almost vanished through over-fishing.

silted up, only small craft have been able to reach Tavira itself, but bigger boats can use the dock at the river mouth and reach the sea by a dredged channel.

A site this good was surely settled from earliest times, but the only solid relic is the old seven-arched **bridge** across the Gilão, which was rebuilt in the 17th century on Roman foundations. One of the piers gave way in 1989, so a temporary metal bridge now carries the traffic, with the original reserved for pedestrians only. Its spacious square bays are a favourite meeting place, each one having the capacity to seat 30 people. Just off Praça da Republica, near the southern end of the bridge, the town hall's medieval-style arcades have been rebuilt. You'll find the **Turismo** under the arches, next to a sculpted head which is said to depict Dom Paio Peres Correia, the knight who led the attack that expelled the Moors in 1242.

Directly across Rua da Liberdade, the main shopping street running up from the river, look for the **Misericórdia**, a 16th-century Renaissance church up steps at the end of a short side street. Notice the strange carving round the door, including some figures which are apparently playing guitars (or lutes). Uphill on the same side, all that remains of the 13th-century castle is part of the wall, which is worth climbing for a view over the town and the lovely public garden below in the castle grounds.

The church of **Santa Maria do Castelo** took over the site of a mosque. Inside, through a simple Gothic doorway, the tombs of Paio Peres Correia and the Sete Caçadores, seven knights killed by the Moors during a truce, lie in the chancel. After damage in the 1755 earthquake, the solid reconstruction was clearly meant to survive another. Tavira has many more churches, 16 in total, but most are locked.

The Turismo leaflet tells you about some, and may be able to guide you to the key-holders who can let you in.

Handsome mansions from the 17th and 18th centuries face the river on both sides. Near the temporary metal bridge, there's a busy produce market. The road along the river and past the market building leads to a jetty at Quatro Águas, where a ferry leaves for the offshore Ilha de Tavira in summer. The north side of the island is mainly muddy, and the best beaches at the eastern end can be crowded on summer weekends.

Two very different villages face the island across the lagoon. The traditional houses of Santa Luzia are mostly tiled all over as a measure against the damp. In contrast, **Pedras d'el Rei**, 4km (2.5 miles) west of Tavira, was built before the 1974 revolution as a Club Med village. The holiday company installed the miniature railway that runs in summer across the mud flats of the Ilha de Tavira to the beach at Barril. With the revolution, Club Med left and never returned, but the chalets and the railway still function. You have to cross a rickety pontoon footbridge to reach the island and open-sided train.

Tavira to the Spanish Border

At Conceição, by a church with a fine Gothic doorway, a side turning leads to **Cabanas**, a collection of villas next to a 17th century fort. At low tide, you can join the clam diggers and walk across to the beach on the offshore island. A rare piece of high ground is crowned by an old village and fort at **Cacela Velha**, where the only concession to tourism is to welcome diners at its shellfish restaurant. Here, the Ria Formosa nature reserve which begins west of Faro (see p.289) comes to an end. At **Manta Rota**, only sand dunes separate the holiday village from the open sea.

Praia Verde lives up to its name with plantations of pine trees. The authorities have actually forced the removal of some unlicenced buildings to try and preserve the open space before **Monte Gordo**, the last and biggest resort in the eastern Algarve. Its monster apartments, hotels and casino form only a narrow strip along the broad shelving beach. An ugly shanty town spreads out behind, and at the eastern end, a pine forest makes a sheltered all-year-round site for tents and caravans.

On the banks of the Guadiana River facing Spain, **Vila Real de Santo António** is a curiosity. Designed by the Marquês de Pombal as a model town, it replaced an earlier town which had been inundated by the sea. The perfectly rectangular street pattern echoes Pombal's plan for Lisbon's Baixa district (see p.93). Centred on a tall obelisk, the main square named after him is paved in a dramatic sun-ray mosaic of black and white. Astonishingly, the whole central area was built in only five months in 1774, using dressed stone brought from Lisbon at immense expense (in spite of plentiful local supplies of which the dictator was apparently unaware). On the eastern side of Praça Marquês de Pombal, the Manuel Cabanas Museum commemorates the artist whose works, especially woodcuts, were the foundation for its collections of art and ethnography. The classical parish church stands on the north side, and orange trees and 18th-century mansions complete an elegant ensemble.

Although it's likened to a chequerboard, driving in the middle of Vila Real is a more complicated game. Dead end, one-way and excavated streets make it better to park by the river and walk. The **Turismo** is on the riverside Avenida da República near the terminal for the car and passenger ferry to Ayamonte in Spain. Cruises on the river

*T*he central square of Vila Real de Santo António is paved with a dramatic radial pattern in mosaic and named after the man who planned it, the Marquês de Pombal.

also leave from the jetty here. Like most border towns in Portugal, Vila Real is a magnet to Spanish shoppers – many prices are given in pesetas as well as escudos.

The road north leads to Mértola (see p.279) or to Spain by way of an elegant new bridge over the Guadiana, but first passes **Castro Marim** – no more than a couple of streets fringing two ruined hilltop fortresses. In Neolithic and Phoenician times it was an island, and every power since then has fortified the site. The castle was built after Afonso III completed the Reconquest, but its square keep, round turrets and curved walls were probably

Castro Marim, where this church is, facing Spain, used to be an island in the surrounding marshes.

Moorish additions. It was the first headquarters of the Order of Christ in 1319 before they moved to Tomar (see p.161).

Fortaleza de São Sebastião on the hill nearer the river is just the surviving part of the extra defences added in the 17th century. The whole of the surrounding saltmarsh, Sapal de Castro Marim, has been designated a Marshland Reserve: it is home to kingfishers, snipe, marsh eagles, several species of heron and divers. The information office in the castle can tell you about accommodation and walks through the reserve.

West from Faro

The coastal terrain changes quite suddenly west of Faro, from flat landscapes fringed by long open beaches to rugged rocks and coves. The *Barlavento* ('windward') coast has the beaches featured in a million postcards, with cliffs of red and yellow sandstone forming a backdrop. An apparently random selection of fishing villages seems to have been buried by development, while others appear at first glance to be untouched. Both impressions are misleading. In the middle of almost every package tour magnet, you'll find an old quarter where traditional life still goes on. Even here, though, half the houses may have been bought by outsiders. Most of the Algarve's golf clubs are on this stretch of coast, some of them attached to luxury holiday estates with their own sports compexes.

Say 'EN125' to Algarve regulars and you'll evoke a grimace, shiver or horror story. This notoriously inadequate road running from end to end of the coast frustrated locals and visitors for years. Now the fine new '*Via do Infante*' of *Auto-estrada* standard offers a fast alternative for much of the way, taking pressure off the 125 which still has to be used for short journeys.

Some 14km (9 miles) west of Faro, immediately before the road to Almancil, look for a sign to **São Lourenço**, a simple white church on a small hill overlooking

the road. The interior, including the vaulted ceiling, is competely covered with blue and white azulejos dating from 1730. **Almancil** itself is a shabby but friendly little town with grocery shops, video rental stores and restaurants, mainly serving British expatriates and visitors from the nearby resorts and villa developments.

Two such resorts are reached by a narrow road out of Almancil. **Quinta do Lago**, a vast, sculpted, pine-wooded world of its own, has the feel of an American-style exclusive country club, with a luxury hotel, golf courses, tennis, horse-riding and watersports. The estate takes in part of the Ria Formosa reserve, with a sheltered lake, dunes and beach. **Vale do Lobo**, another self-contained environment with golf and a big tennis centre, is longer-established and slightly more compact, and centres on the Dona Filipa hotel and little beach facing the open sea. At both places, facilities are open to all, but residents benefit from discounts and the chance to reserve in advance. If you aren't staying, you won't get on the golf courses at popular times.

Quarteira and Vilamoura

Also reached from Almancil, or from further west, most of **Quarteira** is a concrete forest of soulless apartment blocks. In the shaded canyons between them, you'll find 'English breakfast all day', fish and chips, bars and discos. The long beach with breakwaters isn't one of the most attractive in the area, but believe it or not, there is a real old town at the western end. Make your way through the narrow streets to the **fish market** next to the sea, where an auction is held every morning. Several good, informal fish restaurants right next to it attract plenty of local people, so you can be sure of fair prices. On Wednesday, crowds jam the area for the general weekly market.

By contrast, at neighbouring **Vilamoura**, the only sign of an old town is the excavated Roman site (see below). The vast holiday complex started from scratch about 25 years ago and keeps on spreading. There's a casino with a floor show and no fewer than three golf courses (inspirationally called Vilamoura I, II and III). At the heart of it all, the **marina** is a big artificial harbour, bristling with the masts of hundreds of yachts and cruisers. Hemmed in by bars and restaurants, shops and apartments in a mish-mash of resort architecture, it's attractive in its way.

Cerro da Vila, a Roman, Visigoth and Moorish site, stands on the only piece of naturally raised ground in the area, just

Elegant living, Algarve style, at Vilamoura.

north of the marina. It's a limited site, with some mosaics, walls and foundations of a villa insensitively consolidated with a lot of cement. Small finds such as clay lamps, tools, fishhooks and coins are on display.

West of Vilamoura a busy, narrow coast road leads through orange groves and mostly haphazard development. The low-rise Sheraton Algarve at Pine Cliffs is an exception, set in one of few retained patches of pine trees, which shade the villas and 9-hole golf course. The coast here features strange formations of coloured sandstone: you have to pick your way down quite steep paths to some of the beaches. The pretty cove at **Olhos de Agua** is a forest of umbrellas in summer, when the holiday crowd share it with the brightly-painted boats of the fishing fleet. Praia da Oura, a smallish stretch of sand, is backed by scrubland and apartment complexes, hotels and villas.

Albufeira

All you'll see at first is the package tour resort which years of unstoppable growth have produced. More and more streets were added and lined with apartments, discos and English pubs. A whole satellite town, Montechoro, was built on the hill to the east. The traffic pattern is almost incomprehensible, but it's worth finding the old fishing town which first attracted holidaymakers here. Don't try to drive into its maze of narrow streets: all you'll be able to do is drive out again.

The name of Albufeira is Arabic in origin, from *Al Buhera* ('Castle by the sea'), and the cluster of little houses on the hillside has a Moorish look. In truth, nothing is that ancient. The castle was rebuilt to hold off pirates and the English and then destroyed in the 1755 earthquake, while a fire during the 19th-century War of Two Brothers (see p.57) razed most of the old centre. It still retains a surprising charm, though, and the beaches are still beautiful with their famous rock formations sticking out of the sand. The **Turismo** is at the seaward end of Rua 5 de Outubro.

Some of the best restaurants are next to the fishermen's beach, Praia dos Barcos, where the small boats of the fishing fleet are hauled up the sand by tractor. If the town beaches are too crowded, try São Rafael, Coelho and Castelo to the west. Vale de Parra has a choice of coves and the broad Praia Grande, with a golf course behind.

Inland from Albufeira

Whenever you need a break from beach life and bars, there's always a complete contrast close at hand. **Paderne**, 13km (8 miles) northeast of Albufeira, is a quiet village surrounded by orange groves. To find a perfect spot for a picnic, follow signs to nearby Fonte and continue for 2km (1.2 miles) along the rough track, passing under a new road bridge. On top of a low hill you'll come to the ruin of a **Moorish castle**, set above a river bend and guarding the valley. There's little sign of later stonework in the walls, but a Gothic church was built inside after the Christian Reconquest. Down in the valley you'll see an old bridge on Roman foundations, ten minutes' walk away by an overgrown path.

The fast new IP1 whisks Lisbon-bound traffic up and over the mountains, bypassing all the villages on the way. At **São Bartolomeu de Messines**, the church has been rebuilt so often you can spot half a dozen styles. Notice the heavy twisted pillars, naive polychrome statuary on main and side altars, and a superb marble pulpit. To the

Cafés spill out into the streets of Albufeira, a perfect town for walking – and a nightmare to drive in even where it's permitted.

West of Albufeira

Various attractions are positioned to take advantage of the tourist traffic on the EN125. At **Gaia**, a Florida-style marine show features leaping dolphins and performing sealions. Further west near Alcantarilha there's a water park with slides (and another near Lagoa). **Porches** is known for its pottery. The roadside shops are piled with souvenir pieces in off-putting quantities – they can look much better when you get them away from the mass. If you visit one of the potteries (look for the signs to *Olaria* and *Olaria Pequena*), you may find something more original made by one of the foreign or local artists who have settled here.

east, **Alte** has made the most of its label of 'most picturesque Algarve village'. Set on a hillside, it has a notable parish church with a Manueline doorway and 18th-century *azulejos*, but most people head for the stream and mill at Fonte Grande to picnic in the shade or to eat at the restaurants. In summer, tour groups come to 'folklore' dinners at nearby Pequena Fonte.

The inland village of **Pêra** seems unaffected by modern times and leaves the tourism business to its coastal neighbour, **Armação de Pêra**, where huge apartment blocks face one of the longest beaches in the Algarve. The fishing village to the west is dwarfed but not overwhelmed. Two lovely

The potters of Porches turn out huge quantities of colourful earthenware, including bold and original designs.

A bay near Armação de Pêra, the essence of the Algarve, whose lovely beaches entice visitors back year after year.

coves are hemmed in by cliffs and separated by a headland crowned by the little white church of **Nossa Senhora da Rocha**.

Lagoa (the 'lagoon' has dried up long since) is the Algarve's wine capital, where the *vinho da casa* which is served in most of the region's restaurants has been bottled. South along the coast, the pretty cove at **Carvoeiro** is far too small for all the building that's going on. Once a simple fishing village clustered around a square, it's now hemmed in by villas which are spreading far over the hills. At **Algar Seco** to the east, cliff walks lead to strange rock formations carved out by the waves and winds. Gaps in the cliffs have created small but beautiful beaches at Carvalho, Benagil and Praia da Marinha, which is famous for a natural double arch.

Silves

In Moorish times, Silves was capital of the Algarve, known as *Chelb*, a magnificent city of palaces and gardens which put Lisbon in the shade, a centre of culture, and a flourishing port where sailing ships unloaded treasures from the east. It's all hard to believe when you see the sleepy town of today, lying far from the sea on a muddy stream which flows sluggishly by, for Silves is now literally a backwater. The rust-red sandstone walls that protected its citadel still stand, but inside there's only a garden, water cisterns and excavations.

The Arab empire was in decline when Sancho I of Portugal recruited a group of northern Crusaders to add to his army for an assault on the Algarve. The siege of Silves in 1189 echoed that of Lisbon 42 years before. The citizens held out for three months before starvation forced surrender and the Crusaders moved in. Sancho wanted an orderly handover, but the city was sacked and many of its people slaughtered. The Moors recaptured Silves two years later and retained it until finally forced to evacuate the Algarve in 1249.

The silting up of the Arade River gradually choked off trade, and when the bishopric of the Algarve was moved to Faro in 1577, the population of Silves was recorded as only 140. The 1755 earthquake reduced the almost deserted place to ruins.

Silves makes a pleasant excursion, but offers very little accommodation. If you want to stay, the **Turismo** in Rua 25 de Abril can help, and provides a good street map. Take in the views on a walk around the restored **castle ramparts**. Just below the gate, the **Sé** (Cathedral) stands on the site of an earlier mosque, from which the columns on either side of the Gothic doorway may have been salvaged. The high vaulted interior is impressive. The little Misericórdia church opposite isn't usually open, but note a Manueline side door, one of many in the Algarve.

Next to Praça do Município with its open air cafés, the high tower and archway called **Torreão das Portas da Cidade** was once a barbican in the city wall. Just up the hill in Rua da Porta de Loulé, don't miss the **Museu de Arqueológia**. Local enthusiasts formed the collections and gave them to the town, and now they have been imaginatively displayed in a new building, built over the centrepiece of an old Arab well. Other highlights are a stone relief carving from 700 BC, Roman bronzes, Moorish and Portuguese ceramics and coins.

The pedestrianized **old bridge** over the Arade is signposted as Roman, but no more than the foundations are original. On the third Monday of each month, the open space along the river is covered by a huge market; on other days it's a much smaller affair. On the left of the road towards São Bartolomeu de Messines, look out for the **Cross of Portugal**, a 16th-century stone carving under a canopy. One side depicts the Crucifixion, the other shows Christ being taken down from the Cross. About 10km (6 miles) away up a side turning, the **Barragem do Arade** (the dam on the Arade river) forms a big reservoir. It has a reputation as a beauty spot, but when water levels are low – and they usually are – it is secondary to more attractive excursions inland.

Portimão

This is a working port and town where tourism happily coexists with everyday life. Industry and the holiday business are both growing, confirming that many visitors like to be part of a 'real' community. Portimão's reputation as the Algarve's best shopping town compensates for the lack of monuments or other specific attractions.

First a Phoenician and then a Roman settlement, the town lies on the estuary of the Arade, downstream from Silves, whose trade it took over as the river silted up. Portimão is the self-proclaimed 'sardine capital of the world', equipped with a cannery and a new dock and fish market across the river. Some excursion boats include a visit there as part of the trip. The old Sardine Dock has been mainly turned over to leisure use, but its informal quayside restaurants still serve up the fresh grilled product. You'll find a vast range of eating places in the town, and competition keeps the prices down – the few hotels here don't even bother to run restaurants. Most holiday accommodation is in the seaside suburb, Praia da Rocha.

An impressive new bridge over the Arade and a bypass have eased notorious traffic problems, but once in the town don't try to drive: the one-way system is designed to prevent you from getting where you want to go. This is a place for walking, even if many street names seem to be missing. Collect a map from the **Turismo**, which is at the top end of Largo 1 de Dezembro, a square just inland from the riverside gardens. A series of roughly parallel streets off Rua Direita (west from the square) contains most of interest; the pedestrianized Rua Vasco da Gama (continuing as Rua do Comércio) forms the major axis.

Ferragudo across the river is a lot scruffier, but its restaurants are making a name for themselves. The riverside **Fortaleza de Ferragudo** (not open to visitors) was built to deter pirates. Its twin, the clifftop **Fortaleza da Santa Catarina** stands on the Portimão side where the river meets the sea. Except in winter, the sheltered courtyard is used as a café by day and a restaurant in the evening, but you can always walk in and climb on the walls for the view of **Praia da Rocha**, a vast stretch of sand studded with rocky outcrops – islets when the tide is in. When the fashion for immersing yourself in the sea reached Portugal around 1900, grand hotels appeared on the cliffs and well-off families built holiday homes. A few British visitors discovered the town too, and in the 1930s it became an intellectuals' retreat. You can still see some of this former elegance along the seafront. The space behind is filling up fast with towering apartment blocks. **Praia do Vau**, to the west, is on a much smaller scale with an attractive little beach.

Amid the new development, take the trouble to find the old fishing village of **Alvor**, which was probably the Portus Hannibalis founded by the Carthaginians. In 1189, the Crusaders landed here and massacred the Moorish population before besieging Silves (see p.304). The **parish church** has a fine west door, like a Manueline version of Romanesque, shaped by multiple rounded arches with strange heraldic decorations. The style is continued in the south door and the arches over the chancel. Traces of colour suggest that the whole interior was once painted. Outside, a long sand bar protects the lagoon where Alvor's fishing fleet moors, and auctions take place at any time of day under a shelter near the water. The beach on the seaward side is a dazzling strip of white sand.

Two of the best golf courses, Portimão's small airport and the Quinta da Rocha nature reserve (noted for its variety of wading birds) share the flat land west and north of Alvor. The **Alto** golf course is one of the Algarve's newest, and the last to be designed by the late Sir Henry Cotton. He was also responsible for one of the first courses, that at the **Penina** hotel and resort which opened in 1966.

Inland to Monchique

An outing to the mountains is a favourite diversion with tour groups, and **Caldas de Monchique** is one of the popular destinations. If you're travelling independently, go early or late in the day to miss the crowds. There's nothing much to do except enjoy the cooler air, and stroll up to the spring where the locals fill plastic bottles and cans with fresh water. This has been a spa since Roman times, and enjoyed a resurgence in popularity in the 19th century, which accounts for the elegant but faded buildings around the shady square. Now most of the water is piped into the big bottling plant downhill from the village.

Just north of Caldas, **Monchique** is much larger, and an agriculture and forestry centre for the mountain region. Woodcarving is still a flourishing craft, basketry is another. Try to come on the second Friday of the month for market day. The **Igreja Matriz** (parish church) has a famous Manueline doorway with five radiating pinnacles joined by twisting stone 'rope'. A steep walk takes you up to the empty shell of the 17th-century **Convent of Nossa Senhora do Desterro**, from where the views are fine. Also here, you'll find the biggest magnolia tree in Portugal – an especially impressive sight during the spring, when it's covered in blossom.

More views can be enjoyed from **Fóia**, a peak 8km (5 miles) to the west and at 902m (2,962ft) the highest point in the Algarve. It's cool up here even in summer and the souvenir stalls do a brisk trade in hand-knitted woollens. A road goes up Fóia, but **Picota**, another high point, is a vigorous 4km (2.5 mile) walk to the south-east.

From Monchique the old road to Lisbon continues to climb through eucalyptus forest – these Australian natives flourish in Portugal and have the great merit of being able to survive a fire and regenerate rapidly afterwards. At the top of the ridge, a landscape of open grassland dotted with cork trees takes over and you're out of the Algarve (see p.283).

Returning from Monchique to the coast you don't have to take the same route, for a new mountain road leads west to Marmelete and on to Aljezur (see p.313).

Lagos

Perhaps better than anywhere else on the Algarve coast, Lagos ('LAH-goosh') has preserved a happy balance of local life and tourism. It's a market town and fishing port, prosperous and attractive, with expanding light industries on the northern outskirts, and wonderful beaches some distance away to the north-east and south.

The Moorish walls were strengthened after the Christians took the town in 1241 and whole, restored sections survive today. The 1415 expedition which captured Ceuta in Morocco left from here. Henry the Navigator, who took part, lived in the governor's palace at Lagos when he was not at Sagres (see p.311), and some of the

*O*nly fishing boats and pleasure craft use the town quay at Lagos today, from where great sailing ships once set out on voyages of exploration and conquest.

*T*he interior of the little church of Santo António in Lagos is completely covered with baroque carving, gilding and azulejos. The painted ceiling was added following the reconstruction of the roof after the 1755 earthquake.

ships used in his voyages of discovery were built in the yards here. A seated statue of the man himself can be seen gazing out to sea from **Praça do Infante**, which is next to the waterfront Avenida dos Descrobrimentos. The squat **Forte da Ponta da Bandeira** guarding the small harbour is typical of 17th-century anti-pirate defences. Its real drawbridge now leads to a small museum. Ferries run in summer from the harbour to the beach of Meia Praia (see p.310).

The first slaves brought from Africa in the 15th century were sold under the arcades of the handsome, classical **Custom House** facing Praça da Republica. A discreet sign says Mercado de Escravos, but assertions in the tourist literature that this was 'Europe's first slave market' can be discounted. Have they forgotten the Romans?

The young King Sebastião is said to have addressed his troops from the windows of the Renaissance church of **Santa Maria**, on the opposite side of Praça da República, be-

fore the ill-fated 1578 expedition to Morocco (see below). A short step out of the square along Rua de São Gonçalo, the little church of **Santo António** is a jewel box crammed with gorgeously gilded baroque carving and blue *azulejos*. The story goes that the statue of St Anthony in the church used to receive an army officer's pay. A tomb in the floor is that of 'Coronel Hugo Beaty' (Colonel Hugh Beatty), an Irishman who commanded the Lagos regiment. He seems to have been unusual, if the inscription claiming he was a Catholic convert is true, for most of the many Irish who served in continental armies were born Catholics. The **municipal museum** next to the church houses religious and folk art, a few pictures and archaeological finds. It's currently due for major restoration and so could be closed for some time.

Rua da Silva Lopes leads into the restaurant-lined Rua 25 de Abril – the tables fill most of the street when the weather's fine. Look down the narrow alleys leading off it for art galleries and craft and antique shops, but don't expect any bargains. Further on, the **Turismo** is in Rua Marquês de Pombal.

The focus of this part of the old town is **Praça Gil Eanes**, where all eyes are drawn to an extraordinary statue of Dom Sebastião. If the sculptor, José Cutileiro, wanted to make him look ridiculous, and fatally naive, he succeeded. The king cuts an undeniably memorable figure, in his 'kitchen foil' astronaut suit, with his pink childish face peeping out from beneath a helmet like a bouffant wig. He's certainly the centre of attention, and backpackers and bikers seem to have adopted his statue as a rendezvous.

The daily fish and produce **market** is along Rua das Portas de Portugal at the waterfront, but the really big market takes place here on the first Saturday of each month.

BATTLE OF THE THREE KINGS

Not content with expelling the Moslem Moors, the most zealous of the Portuguese periodically took the fight to the enemy by attacking Morocco. As often as not, such invasions ended in disaster, none greater than that led by the young King Sebastião, 'the Regretted'. He succeeded to the throne when only a child, and even when he came of age never stopped dreaming of Crusading glory. A dispute between the Sultan of Morocco and a deposed rival seemed to offer him the chance. Allying himself with the deposed al-Mutawakkil, Sebastião landed at Tangier in 1578 with 20,000 men, but the Portuguese were outnumbered and had to retreat along the coast. While crossing a river in flood, they were attacked by the forces of Sultan Abd al-Malik. Thousands were drowned or captured, and both Sebastião and al-Mutawakkil were washed away, while Abd al-Malik – who had been ill even before the battle – died the next day.

Half the noble families of Portugal were in mourning, or bankrupted by the ransoms demanded for those taken prisoner. Sebastião's death without an heir, quickly followed by that of his elderly great uncle Henrique in 1580, brought catastrophe in the form of 60 years' rule by Spanish usurpers.

Lagos Beaches

A long arc of sand called **Meia Praia**, across the river to the north-east from Lagos, is reached by ferry in summer or the road bridge at any time. You can only get to the eastern end of the beach by walking, so it's often quite empty. The well-established Palmares golf course occupies a good position overlooking the bay.

South of Lagos, the **Ponta da Piedade** peninsula features a stunning array of strange multi-coloured rock formations: arches, caves and pinnacles. Take a boat trip for the best views – some leave from steps at the tip of the peninsula, below the lighthouse. The beaches here are picturesque coves. **Praia de Dona Ana** is one of the most beautiful, and most photographed, but **Praia Camilo** is usually less crowded.

Luz, 8km (5 miles) west of Lagos, is still a working fishing village, with a broad beach and partly sheltered bay which are excellent for watersports. There's a growing number of villa developments in the town, and the old fort has been turned into a restaurant.

The Western Tip

You'll notice a sudden change of scene as soon as you're clear of the outskirts of Lagos: rolling countryside that seems almost empty of people, fewer trees, and no more big resorts. A fast new highway from Lagos to Sagres has replaced the narrow old track and made the area much more accessible, but it still has an 'end of the road' feel that appeals to the eccentric and adventurous. Battered old minibuses and camper vans congregate, and hippies preserved in a 1960s timewarp feel at home.

On the coast west of Lagos, **Burgau** is already established as a fledgling resort. The little harbour and beach are hemmed in by houses, and fishing boats are pulled up on a slipway which doubles as the one-way road through the village. There's a small sports centre some way inland and new building work is likely to fill the space between.

A pretty valley winds down to the sea at **Salema**, which is further along the development route than Burgau. The fishing village has lost some of its charm, with an apartment hotel built right in the centre and a scattering of holiday homes around. Here and all over the Algarve, both Portuguese and foreign outsiders have been buying up some of the old cottages. The locals patiently watch, and somehow traditional life goes on, side-by-side with the ebb and flow of the tourist season. Continuing west, the little town of **Vila do Bispo** is bypassed by the main road. Take a diversion to see its charming main square and church with 18th-century azulejos and ceiling frescoes.

Sagres

Even before the arrival of the new road, the village at the south-western extremity of Europe had been growing in anticipation. Half the houses are new, and many of them offer rooms, so there's no shortage of accommodation. Hotels, including the Pousada do Infante, have a fine view of the historic promontory and fortress and the south-facing Mareta beach. Others look over the sheltered harbour, tucked into a bay on the eastern side, off which the Martinhal islets are a favourite with scuba divers. The water is always cold, and you'd need a particularly calm day to swim at Mareta, but the eastern beaches enjoy more protection. The clifftop walks near Sagres are spectacular – take binoculars to spot nesting birds and ships rounding the cape, and try to be there for the superb sunsets.

Ponta de Sagres is the fortress peninsula near the village. There would have been earlier fortifications, but this one dates from the 18th century. If it looks to have been built still more recently – yesterday in fact – that's the unfortunate effect of a smooth layer of cement applied in a controversial 1991 'restoration'. Beyond the immensely thick rampart (you can drive through the tunnel), a chapel and small house were rebuilt after the earthquake. Climb above the fortress gate for a view of the 'wind rose', the points of the

compass marked in stone lines on the ground. There is no agreement about its age. Romantics like to think it dates from the time of Henry the Navigator himself; others suggest it was laid out when rebuilding work was begun in the 1790s. After restoration in modern times, it's again in poor condition. A stone sundial in the wall above is also of unknown date, while a building once labelled as Henry's house and then used as a youth hostel has been demolished. Its obtrusively modern replacement may become a 'Visitor Centre'.

Meanwhile, imagination can take flight. There's the raging sea below and an empty horizon, and on calmer days the remarkable sight of local men fishing from the 40m (130ft) cliffs with rod and line. Apparently fearless, standing at the very edge of the

---

IN SEARCH OF THE NAVIGATOR

Everyone agrees that a connection exists between Sagres, 'the sacred promontory', and *Infante Dom Henrique*, Henry the Navigator. Dissension begins when it comes to deciding just what that connection was. With a better, safer port available at Lagos, where he spent a lot of time, it seems unlikely that Sagres served as anything but a temporary base for the Infante's ships.

Legend insists that his school of navigation was here. Unfortunately, the two sites which compete for the distinction – Ponta de Sagres and Cabo de São Vicente – were sacked and burned by Sir Francis Drake during his operations to 'singe the King of Spain's beard' (while Spain ruled Portugal) more than a century afterwards. The earthquake of 1755 effectively completed the destruction. Henry's library and papers have been lost, and restorations, including misconceived 20th-century efforts, have probably wrecked any chance of finding the answers by archaeological methods.

precipice ('one or two fall off every year', they say), they're after sargo (sea bream) and other varieties that fetch a high price. When a big one bites, they don't risk hauling it straight up and losing it on the way. Instead they drop a keep-net on a rope down the fishing line and over the catch, flip it upright and pull the prize to the top.

The usually windswept road around the cliffs to the northwest passes a smaller fortress, the 17th-century **Fortaleza do Beliche**, perched high above a raging sea. Except in winter, a restaurant run by the Pousada do Infante operates inside the walls. There are also four guest rooms.

Cabo de São Vicente (Cape St Vincent) is another possible site for Henry's think tank. It was probably a Phoenician and then a Roman shrine – such headlands had great significance for them – and to ancient mariners it was *o fim do mundo*, 'the end of the world'. Geography dictated that the British and Spanish navies would frequently clash in battles off the cape, and Admiral Jervis was made Earl St Vincent after he and Nelson defeated a much larger Spanish fleet here in 1797.

The lighthouse from 1846 isn't usually open to visitors, but the views from the terrace below are dramatic enough. The convent, which was sacked by Drake, tumbled in 1755 and abandoned in 1834, was consecrated to St Vincent, whose remains may have been kept here before the Moorish invasion.

*T*he south-western tip of Europe, Cape St Vincent near Sagres, the last sight of their homeland for Portuguese sailors as they set out on voyages of discovery.

On the Algarve's west coast the Atlantic is colder and rougher. Just a few lanes and tracks cross the wild moorland scenery to a handful of beautiful sandy bays. Resort development is minimal, and out of summer you'll have this coast to yourself. The one big planned development, the **Vale de Telha** holiday complex south-west of Aljezur, has had its problems. Of hundreds of villas projected, only a few have been built, along with a hotel and sports facilities. There are some excellent but unsheltered beaches here, but sadly the tree cover, young plantations included, has been lost in fires. The place looks as if it is suffering from nuclear fall-out.

Aljezur itself is an attractive little town of white houses and red roofs. Its hilltop castle has been a ruin since the 1755 earthquake, but the view is worth the climb. Further north, Odeceixe is the last village in the Algarve. Its beach offers some shelter and with a few other remote bays in the area it's become a centre of German 'alternative society' in July and August.

SAINTLY ODYSSEY

Cabo São Vicente, or Cape St Vincent, is named after a 4th-century Spanish priest who was martyred by the Roman governor of Valencia. When the Moors invaded Iberia, the saint's body was taken as far west as possible, to the Algarve's 'Sacred Promontory'. Eventually this was also overrun by the Moors and the holy relics disappeared.

After the Reconquest, Afonso Henriques, first King of Portugal, sent out a search party to find the remains. Legend has it that the explorers were guided on their journey by a pair of ravens, which then accompanied the ship carrying the relics back to Lisbon.

Today, the seal of the city of Lison commemorates the legend with a sailing ship and ravens fore and aft.

When You Want to be Up and Doing

The days can be as full as you like: watersports in summer at the beach; golf and tennis all year round on the Algarve coast; and hiking and bird-watching in the national parks and nature reserves. Wherever you are, there's likely to be a festival or market going on not far away. For the evenings, the resorts are well supplied with diversions, and many of the bars and clubs offer live entertainment. In Lisbon the place for night owls is the Bairro Alto, home to the elusive, utterly Portuguese *fado*.

Shopping

A rich legacy of traditional crafts makes Portugal a happy hunting ground for those in search of handmade goods. Embroidery and lace, copper and brass, pottery and painted ceramic tiles, leather work and basketry fill the *artesanatos* (craft shops) *en masse*. At the other end of the scale, it's possible to find unique pieces, made by craft potters or woodworkers, but priced as the works of art they effectively are. If you can't find particular specialist shops,

At festival time streets can be roofed with streamers or scattered with flower petals. Wherever you are, there'll be some sort of celebration not far away.

ask at the local *Turismo*: they will usually have the information.

Many possible purchases are large, heavy or fragile – or all three – and the bigger stores and *artesanatos* will pack and ship goods for you. Major credit and charge cards are widely accepted in shops in cities and main towns, but less so in small towns and not at all in markets. Except when negotiating the purchase of an important antique, or a piece of bric-à-brac in a flea market, the days of haggling about prices are over.

The small shopkeeper is still very much alive in Portugal. Even Lisbon's various quarters are like overgrown villages with mostly local family-run shops. The Chiado was the elegant exception, but its two department stores were razed by a fire in 1988 and rebuilding proceeds slowly. The landmark Amoreiras Centre in Lisbon's north-western suburbs offers 350 shops and other services under its multi-coloured towers. It's a magnet for local shoppers, but visitors may find it less interesting to wander than the old streets.

Hours

Most shops open Monday to Friday 9am to 1pm and 3 to 7pm, and on Saturday from 9am to 1pm. The new shopping complexes usually operate from 10am to midnight or even later, often on Sunday as well. Some city centre shops may also stay open at lunchtime. Town and country markets usually get going by 8.30am and run through to mid-afternoon.

Antiques

Even experts in their own countries may be on unfamiliar ground here, because of the very 'Portugueseness' of what's available. Old ceramic plates and *azulejos*, religious sculptures and paintings, and local styles in silver and furniture are hard to assess, and the line between precious relics and junk is ill-defined. Lisbon has hundreds of antique shops where you can gain some experience if you have the time. The biggest concentration is along Rua Dom

---

TAX REFUNDS

If you live outside the European Union, you can recover the VAT (sales tax) on larger purchases (roughly over 12,000 escudos). Shops displaying the 'Tax Free for Tourists' sign will give you a special cheque. At your departure airport, show the goods and receipt and have the cheque stamped by customs and you will receive the refund in cash. If leaving by land through Spain, have the cheque stamped by customs at the point where you finally leave the EU. Where there is no Tax Free desk, you can get a refund by mail.

Pedro V and from Bairro Alto down to the waterfront at Cais do Sodré.

Pottery

Different parts of the country have their own distinctive styles and colours, possibly preserving Moorish, Roman and even older patterns. The range is vast, from fine porcelain to unglazed red, black or gaudily coloured earthenware. The Barcelos cockerel (see p.206) can now be found all over Portugal, but little groups of clay musicians, sometime animals playing instruments and riding on a cart, are still a Barcelos speciality. Estremoz and the nearby towns make glazed and unglazed cooking pots and

The skill of Portugal's copper-beaters is a legacy from the time of the Moorish occupation.

polychrome figurines known as *bonecos*. Some of the most elegant porcelain comes from the Vista Alegre factory near Aveiro.

Hand-painted ceramic tiles, **azulejos**, have adorned Portuguese walls for centuries, and they're still made in great quantities for use in modern houses. Antique tiles are collectors' items: some early or intricate examples are priceless. Reproductions of historic designs are sold at the Museu do Azulejo in Lisbon (see p.120) and you can visit modern factories at Belém and near Sintra. Every city has showrooms where you can buy a single blue and white tile square or a batch to assemble into a picture when you get home. Some places will paint and fire tiles to order if you want to create your own unique design.

Some More Ideas

Look for **baskets** in the markets as you travel round the country: they're likely to be cheaper than in the craft shops because people will be buying them for everyday use. Each region has its own ways of weaving willow, reeds or straw into baskets for the farm or home. They're strong, useful and can be beautiful. As souvenirs they have the advantages of light weight and strength. Less easily transported are handmade **wickerwork** chairs and tables. Carved wooden **yokes**, whch are still used for harnessing oxen, can make striking headboards or chair-backs. Nicely carved scale models serve as hat-racks.

The craftsmen of Loulé (see p.292) continue a tradition at least as old as the Moorish occupation, hammering out **copper and brass** cooking utensils, including the local *cataplana* (see p.28), pots, pans and coffee sets. Charming toy-sized versions solve packing problems.

Portugal is the world's leading **cork** producer, and not only to make stoppers

T he basketweaver's craft has scarcely changed for thousands of years. You can find useful and beautiful examples in all shapes and sizes.

for millions of wine bottles. You'll find insulating ice-buckets, and decorative uses too, including picture frames and intricate cork sculptures.

Thousands of women on the island of Madeira produce **embroidery** that is known worldwide. The linen or organdy tablecloths are admirable but expensive. Hand embroidery also comes from the Azores and some mainland villages and towns, notably Viana do Castelo. The celebrated traditional dress of Viana and other towns and regions is expensive, but you can find miniature versions on **dolls**.

Hand-embroidered cross-stitch **rugs** have been made for three hundred years at Arraiolos, an Alentejo village. The antique examples you can see in museums are intricate copies of Oriental designs. Today's versions are more bright and cheerful and much coarser, but still expensive. You can also have them made to order – at an even higher price.

Gold and silver are priced at the prevailing world rate, but the amount added for workmanship is often less here than elsewhere in western Europe or North America. The art of **filigree jewellery** may have been introduced by the Moors in the 8th century. It is used in gold or silver brooches in the form of flowers and butterflies, or a Portuguese caravel in full sail.

You will often see women sitting in their doorways, knitting pullovers in complex designs, rugged fishermen's sweaters or baby clothes. **Knitwear** in general is reasonably priced. In the Alentejo, they wear long woollen **cloaks** in winter, usually brown, with fur collars. Miniature models are made for children. Among everyday **clothes**, you don't find the bargains of the past, but Portugal is still a fairly low-cost producer of casual and sports wear.

Lace is made at a cooperative in Vila do Conde on the north coast and by a few individuals. Among the **leather goods** you might find a belt, purse or pair of shoes, but it may have been made in the Far East: imports are increasingly taking over.

If you find **wines** you particulary like, they will no doubt be cheaper here than at home, but only worth carrying in quantity if you have your own vehicle. A bottle or two of **Port** might be a good memento, perhaps the white aperitif version or a late bottled vintage, which would travel well. **Madeira** wine from the sunny Atlantic island was designed to travel in the first place, and even to be improved by it.

A few traditional lace makers can still be seen juggling their bobbins.

Sports

Watersports

The Algarve has warmer and usually calmer water for **swimming** than the more exposed west coast, but you should always be aware of the possibility of dangerous undertows. Except at popular beaches in summer, there won't be any lifeguards or

*T*he designers of the
Algarve resorts seem to be aiming
at the same sort of fantasy garden
created by the Moors a thousand
years ago.

*U*p and away. Just a few
minutes of basic instruction and
practically anybody can go
parascending.

flags. Where flags are flown, a red one is a warning to stay on shore, a yellow one urges great caution. Atlantic currents and tides generally guarantee clean water, but exceptions are the Estoril coast as far west as Cascais, the mouth of the Douro near Oporto and other short stretches affected by sewage and industrial outflows.

Windsurfing is the number one watersport and boards can be rented at most larger resorts. The open sea is often too rough for any but the experts, but the calm water sheltered by the Algarve's sandbars suits beginners.

Scuba diving is a fast growing activity, especially along the western Algarve coast: equipment and instruction are available at Alvor, Lagos, Luz and Sagres. Beaches which are protected from the open ocean may have small **sailing** boats, rowboats and pedalos for rent by the hour, while experienced sailors in search of more seaworthy craft can ask at the local yacht marina or sailing club.

Fishing is a national passion (see p.77), and all along the coast you'll see anglers casting from the beaches and perched on rocks, cliff edges or piers. For deep-sea fishing – generally for swordfish, but occasionally shark, tuna or marlin – you can rent a boat with a knowledgeable captain at Setúbal, Sesimbra, and at Faro and other Algarve ports. A permit is required for fishing in the rivers and lakes; tourist information offices can give advice.

Golf

The Algarve's courses, 18 at last count, and a handful near Lisbon and up the west coast, are remarkably varied. Wooded or open, amid sand dunes or rolling hills, many of them were created by world-renowned designers (see p.80). More British, German and Scandinavian golfers head for Portugal in winter and especially early spring than to any other golfing destination. When some flights land at Faro, you'll see as many golf bags as suitcases on the baggage belt. Some of the best courses are attached to hotels and green fees are waived or reduced for their guests, who also have priority in reserving start times. Several travel operators offer golf packages.

Tennis

Many hotels have their own courts, some floodlit. Some country houses which take paying guests under the TURIHAB or similar schemes (see p.23) also have courts. Some of the Algarve's big tennis centres offer individual lessons, or a week

or two of total immersion when the professionals will take your game apart – you'll just have to hope they put it back together before you go home.

Horse Riding

You can go horse riding, with or without an instructor, at the Lisbon Country Club, Marinha Club at Cascais, or at one of the many riding stables and schools around the country. Some of the larger country estates also keep horses for their guests to ride. There is no organized horse-racing in Portugal at present – the gambling which provides the financial support for it in other countries is illegal here (though that may soon change with the introduction of new legislation).

Fishing is a Portuguese obsession. You'll find the local anglers in action at every vantage point, like these rocks at Guincho.

Spectator Sports

Football (soccer) is the one activity which can stir up the usually restrained Portuguese to a frenzy of partisanship, whether for the national team or their local favourites. Bitter rivals, Benfica and Sporting from Lisbon and FC Porto, are the three big clubs guaranteed to pack the stadiums. On evenings when a match is

The nature reserve surrounding the Algarve resort of Quinta do Lago is ideal for a gentle outing.

being played, fans fill the bars around the country for a riotous few hours to watch it on TV. The season runs from September to May.

The world championship **Formula One** Grand Prix motor race takes place at Estoril's autodrome in late September.

Bullfights

The bullfight in Portugal is different from the Spanish version, since the bull isn't killed (at least not in view of the audience – most are despatched shortly afterwards). Only those bulls which have proved themselves unusually brave and agile survive to be used as breeding stock.

Stone carvings show that bullfighting was known to the Romans, but the present Portuguese form dates from the 17th century when it was the standard way for young aristocrats to show off horsemanship and courage.

At a typical *tourada,* eight bulls weighing in at half a tonne each enter the arena in turn. Some are fought *à antiga portuguesa* – the old Portuguese way – by a *cavaleiro* in 18th-century costume on a

Soccer has the status of a national religion. One of the top teams, Benfica, plays at the Stadium of Light in the suburbs of Lisbon.

magnificent high-stepping horse. During each chase the *cavaleiro* stabs a ribboned dart into the bull's shoulder. When the quota of darts (*farpas*) has been inserted, the horseman salutes the crowd with his three-cornered hat and leaves the field. In the second act of each fight, eight brave young men (*forcados*) leap over the barrier into the ring to face the bull on foot. In their traditional tasselled caps, they line up behind the head man, who taunts the bull into charging and then jumps over its horns, grabs it round the neck and holds on for dear life. The bull's horns are padded, but can still cause serious injury. The rest of the *forcados* then try to wrestle the bull to the ground with their bare hands.

Other bulls may be taken on one at a time by a *toureiro,* on foot and unaided, who dominates the bull with his cape. Again, when he leaves the ring, eight unarmed *forcados* take over. When they succeed in subduing the bull, they stand aside to let him get up before bowing out. Cows or oxen are then sent in to escort the mystified bull out of the ring.

The centre of Portuguese bullfighting is the cattle breeding region of the Ribatejo, northeast of Lisbon, where fights are held regularly in every town, notably Santarém and Vila Franca de Xira (where the bulls sometimes run through the streets first; see p.167). Lisbon's Campo Pequeno, Cascais and many other towns stage bullfights, often in conjunction with a *festa.* Bullfights are not an Algarve tradition, but some are organized there for the tourist industry.

The season runs from Easter Sunday to October. Seats in the shade (*sombra*) are more expensive than those in the sun (*sol*), and there are night performances as well. For a more comfortable performance, rent a pillow from the usher. Children under six are not allowed in.

Entertainment

Opera, ballet, **concerts** and recitals are concentrated in Lisbon, where the main season is during the winter. The Gulbenkian Foundation has its own symphony orchestra and ballet company and funds performances all over the country. In summer your best chance of getting to a concert, classical or jazz, is at one of the music festivals, which attract soloists and ensembles from many countries (see p.39). Rock concerts are mainly confined to Lisbon, apart from some visiting groups at the big Algarve resorts in summer. If you catch a live band in a club or show, the chances are that it will be African, from the old colonies of Cape Verde or Guinea-Bissau, with an Afro-Latin sound. In pop music there's a lot of interchange with Brazil.

Theatre is mainly confined to the big cities and is naturally in Portuguese, but **movies** are usually shown in the original language with Portuguese subtitles. In Lisbon, *Diário de Notícias* and the weekly *Se7e* publish music, stage and screen listings and times of performances.

The **casinos** at Monte Gordo, Vilamoura and Praia da Rocha in the Algarve, and Estoril, Figueira da Foz, Espinho and Póvoa de Varzim offer dinner and a show (from 5,000 to 10,000 escudos) as well as gambling. To get into the gaming rooms and play roulette, baccarat, craps, blackjack or the slot machines, you need to be over 21, carry your passport and pay an entrance charge.

Bars and pubs are so varied that the only thing to do is take a look to see which suits your mood. **Discos** are popular and also vary widely in terms of atmosphere and age range. The entrance charge is usually in the region of 1,000 to 2,000 escudos, including the first drink.

*T*he fadista's *emotional song of lament is generally accompanied by two impassive guitarists dressed like businessmen.*

Fado

One theory says these songs of sadness may derive from the laments of African slaves, while another suggests Arabic origins. Whatever the history, this is now the most Portuguese of music and can be difficult for foreigners to fathom, although the drama and emotional power of a performance are clear from the start. In truth, the *fadistas* really need a Portuguese audience for their art to come alive. In Lisbon, that could be in a *Casa de Fado*, b ut some of those have been adapted for the tour group business. Whoever their patrons, they generally charge a high price for entry and serve dinner first (it may be possible to come in later just for a drink). The singing starts around 11pm and may continue on and off until 2 or 3 in the morning.

Accompaniment is usually provided by two guitarists, one with a round 12-string instrument probably descended from the Moorish *oudh*, who stroll in without ceremonial and play a couple of warm-up numbers. The lights dim, the audience goes quiet, and a spotlight picks out a woman in black who wails out her song of longing, regret, and nostalgia (summed up in the Portuguese word *saudade*). Most *fado* singers are women, but you may also hear a man perform the same sort of ballad.

The Coimbra *fado* is more light-hearted and may even extend to political satire. The *fado* itself is never danced, but folk dances may be part of the programme.

Portugal for Children

They'll probably love it, as long as you don't overdose them on museums and monasteries. The same applies to castles, but remember that exploring the remoter areas also means long drives along twisting roads, something to bear in mind if anyone suffers from motion sickness.

Most families will, of course, be heading for the beaches. They can be gorgeous, but many lack any shelter from the Atlantic waves (see p.320 for further guidance). To offer an alternative on days when the sea is too rough, a good-sized pool and garden should be a high priority when choosing your accommodation. The Algarve also has several waterparks with slides ranging from tame to terrifying, and there are others at Caparica south of Lisbon, Peniche to the north, and even far inland at Beja. Boat trips and fishing expeditions on the rivers, lakes and sea ought to appeal to all ages and older children can take sailing, windsurfing and tennis lessons at many resorts. Some of the big hotels run all-day, every day 'children's club' programmes so their parents can devote themselves entirely to golf.

Lisbon's attractions for smaller children are fairly limited, although they'll enjoy a ride on the antique trams and funiculars. In northern Portugal, the remaining narrow gauge railways have a similar appeal and the many fairs and festivals can also provide plenty of entertainment.

Festivals

There's some sort of fair or festival going on somewhere in Portugal at any time of year, but the high season is summer. That's when you'll find half the towns you visit strewn with flowers, or the streets roofed over by paper streamers for a **festa**. Check the timetables kept by tourist information offices when you plan your excursions. For the big events, expect traffic chaos and every room to be full – reservations are needed far in advance (see p.21).

The most colourful **religious processions** are in the north of the country, at Braga, Guimarães, Viana do Castelo and Ponte de Lima.

Almost anywhere, the local **Patron Saint's Day** (many of which are in June) may be celebrated both at church and on the streets – with dancing, fireworks and bullfights. **Carnival** throughout Portugal is relatively subdued, although some towns promote their processions as if they rivalled Rio's. Of these, only Loulé in the Algarve can realistically hope for weather to suit street festivities in February.

The Right Place at the Right Price

Selected Hotels

Hotel prices have risen in recent years and are comparable with most western European destinations, but even the most luxurious places offer special packages (such as summer or weekend reductions at hotels which normally rely on business people). It's always worth asking.

Our choice, listed alphabetically within each area, takes into account quality, location, price and character. The price indication given is for two people in a double room, with breakfast. Service and VAT (sales tax, currently 5% of room price) are both included.

I   below 12,000 esc. (£48/$72)

II   12,000-20,000 esc. (£48-80/$72-120)

III   20,000-35,000 esc. (£80-140/$120-210)

IIII over 35,000 esc. (£140/$210)

The rates quoted are for independent travellers. In Lisbon, Oporto and the beach resorts, you may find rooms in the same hotels offered as part of a package at much reduced prices. On the Algarve especially, winter prices can be much lower than quoted. *Pousadas* also offer considerably lower winter rates.

The list is not meant to be exclusive: don't forget that there are many value-for-money pensions (*pensões*, singular *pensão*) and room-only *residencials*, which cost about half the price of the lower priced hotels. (See also ACCOMMODATION on p.21)

Lisbon

Central

Altis   III
Rua Castilho 11
1200 Lisbon
Tel. 52 24 96; fax 54 86 96
307 rooms. Near Praça Marquês de Pombal. Modern and luxurious. Rooftop restaurant, fine views over city. Indoor swimming pool, sauna and health club.

Americano   I
Rua 1° de Dezembro 73
1200 Lisbon
Tel. 347 49 76; no fax
50 rooms. In busy heart of city, near Praça Rossio. No restaurant.

Capitol   II
Rua Eça de Queiroz 24
1000 Lisbon
Tel. 53 68 11; fax 352 61 65
58 rooms. Comfortable hotel in a side street near Edward VII park. Traditional Portuguese restaurant.

Da Lapa   IIII
Rua do Pau de Bandeira
1200 Lisbon
Tel. 395 00 05; fax 395 06 65
102 rooms. Luxurious conversion of palatial old mansion in the Lapa district, overlooking the Tagus. Outdoor and indoor swimming pools and beautiful garden.

Eduardo VII   III
Av. Fontes Pereira de Melo 5
1000 Lisbon
Tel. 53 01 41; fax 53 38 79
121 rooms. Stylish older hotel, close to the park of the same name. Rooftop restaurant and terrace. Good view over park.

Fénix   III
Praça Marquês de Pombal 8
1200 Lisbon
Tel. 386 21 21; fax 386 01 31
122 rooms. Comfortable older hotel, recently renovated, next to busy Pombal traffic circle. Good restaurant serving regional dishes.

Flamingo   II
Rua Castilho 41
1200 Lisbon
Tel. 386 21 91; fax 386 12 16
39 rooms. Comfortable hotel with bar and restaurant in busy area close to Praça Marquês de Pombal.

Insulana   I
Rua da Assunção 52-2°
1100 Lisbon
Tel. 342 76 25; no fax
32 rooms. Good location in the middle of downtown Baixa district. No restaurant.

Lisboa Plaza   **III**
Travessa do Salitre 7
1200 Lisbon
Tel. 346 39 22; fax 347 16 30
*112 rooms. Stylish, recently renov-
ated central hotel, near Avenida da
Liberdade. Noted restaurant serving
Portuguese specialities.*

Le Meridien Lisboa   **IIII**
Rua Castilho 149
1000 Lisbon
Tel. 69 09 00; fax 69 32 31
*331 rooms. Bright, modern luxury
hotel next to Edward VII park.
Health club and sauna.*

Miraparque   **II**
Av. Sidónio Pais 12
1000 Lisbon
Tel. 57 80 70; fax 57 89 20
*100 rooms. Facing Edward VII
park. Old-style building with
compact modern rooms.*

Mundial   **III**
Rua D. Duarte 4
1100 Lisbon
Tel. 886 31 01; fax 87 91 29
*147 rooms. Cylindrical 10-storey
block in busy central area. Rooftop
restaurant with fine views of old city.*

Nazareth   **I**
Av. António Augusto de Aguiar 25
1000 Lisbon
Tel. 54 20 16; fax 356 08 36
*32 rooms. Economical city centre
hotel situated near Edward VII
park. No restaurant.*

Principe Real   **III**
Rua da Alegria 53
1200 Lisbon
Tel. 346 01 16; fax 342 21 04
*24 rooms. Central, between Avenida
da Liberdade and Botanic Gardens.
Pleasant and elegant small hotel,
like a private club.*

Residencial Roma   **I**
Travessa da Glória 22A-1°
1200 Lisbon
Tel. 346 05 57; fax 346 05 57
*24 rooms. Friendly, central
residential, near Praça dos
Restauradores. No restaurant.*

Ritz Inter-Continental   **IIII**
Rua Rodrigo da Fonseca 88
1093 Lisbon
Tel. 69 20 20; fax 69 17 83
*310 rooms. Distinguished luxury
hotel, with unusually large rooms,
near Edward VII park. Outdoor
dining in summer.*

Tivoli Jardim   **III**
Rua Julio Cesar Machado 7
1200 Lisbon
Tel. 53 99 71; fax 355 65 66
*119 rooms. Near Praça Marquês de
Pombal. Heated pool. Tennis.*

Tivoli Lisboa   **IIII**
Av. da Liberdade 185
1200 Lisbon
Tel. 52 11 01; fax 57 94 61
*327 rooms. Central. Outdoor dining
in summer. Noted rooftop
restaurant. Heated outdoor
swimming pool. Tennis.*

York House   **III**
Rua das Janelas Verdes 32
1200 Lisbon
Tel. 396 25 44; fax 397 27 93
*35 rooms. Near the Museum of
Ancient Art, west of centre,
overlooking the Tagus. Adapted
from a 16th-century convent.
Outdoor dining in a garden
courtyard in summer.*

North Lisbon

Albergaria Pax   **I**
Rua José Estêvão 20
1100 Lisbon
Tel. 356 81 61; fax 315 57 55
*34 rooms. Pleasant smaller hotel
north of centre. No restaurant.*

Alfa Lisboa   **III**
Av. Columbano Bordalo Pinheiro
1000 Lisbon
Tel. 726 21 21; fax 726 30 31
*350 rooms. Modern tower block
northwest of city centre. Business-
oriented. Stylish. Good views.*

Dom João   **I**
Rua José Estêvão 43
1100 Lisbon
Tel. 54 30 64; fax 352 45 69
*18 rooms. Friendly small hotel
north of city centre. No restaurant.*

Dom Manuel I   **II**
Av. Duque d'Avila 189
1000 Lisbon
Tel. 57 61 60; fax 57 69 85
*64 rooms. North of Edward VII park
in quiet area near Gulbenkian
Museum. Pleasant decor and quite
spacious rooms. No restaurant.*

Lisboa Penta   **III**
Av. dos Combatentes
1600 Lisbon
Tel. 726 40 54; fax 726 42 81
*588 rooms. Large, business-oriented
hotel near Gulbenkian Museum.*

*Outdoor swimming pool, health
club, squash and sauna. Shuttle bus
to city centre.*

Lutécia   **III**
Av. Frei Miguel Contreiras 52
1700 Lisbon
Tel. 80 31 21; fax 80 78 18
*150 rooms. Modern block between
city centre and airport. Good view
over city and Campo Grande.*

Novotel Lisboa   **II**
Av. José Malhoa 1642
1000 Lisbon
Tel. 726 60 22; fax 726 64 96
*246 rooms. Modern block northwest
of Edward VII park. Good views of
city and Campo Grande. Outdoor
swimming pool.*

Roma   **II**
Av. de Roma 33
1700 Lisbon
Tel. 796 77 61; fax 793 29 81
*265 rooms. Informal hotel,
convenient for airport. Rooftop
restaurant. Indoor swimming pool.*

Sheraton Lisboa & Towers   **IIII**
Rua Latinho Coelho 1
1097 Lisbon
Tel. 57 57 57; fax 54 71 64
*384 rooms. Modern tower block,
one of the tallest buildings in the
city, east of Edward VII park. Lively
atmosphere. Heated outdoor
swimming pool, health club and
sauna.*

Costa de Lisboa

Estoril Coast
and Sintra

Albatroz   **IIII**
Rua Frederico Arouca 100
2750 Cascais
Tel. (01) 483 28 21;
fax (01) 284 48 27
*40 rooms. Elegant mansion which
has been extended to create an
exclusive luxury retreat above the
Praia da Rainha beach. Outdoor
pool, gardens.*

Casa da Pergola   **II**
Av. Valbom 13
2750 Cascais
Tel. (01) 484 00 40; no fax
*10 rooms. Beautifully furnished
guesthouse situated just a couple of
blocks from the beach. Closed
November to March.*

Central   II
Praça da Republica
Sintra
Tel. (01) 923 09 63; no fax
*14 rooms. Comfortable old-
fashioned hotel right opposite the
Palácio Nacional.*

Cidadela   III
Av. 25 de Abril
2750 Cascais
Tel. (01) 483 29 21;
fax (01) 483 72 26
*130 rooms. In residential area a few
blocks from the beach. Modern
resort hotel, outdoor pool, gardens.*

Estalagem Fundador   II
Rua D. Afonso Henriques 161
2765 Estoril
Tel. (01) 468 23 46;
fax (01) 468 87 79
*10 rooms. Pleasant small
guesthouse situated above the park.
Outdoor pool.*

Estoril Sol   III
Parque Palmela
2750 Cascais
Tel. (01) 483 2831;
fax (01) 483 22 80
*317 rooms. Towering over the bay
of Cascais, a luxurious resort hotel
by the beach. Freshwater and
seawater pools, sauna, squash.
Special rates at own golf course.*

Lido   II
Rua do Alentejo 12
2765 Estoril
Tel. (01) 268 41 23;
fax (01) 268 36 65
*60 rooms. Pleasant modern holiday
hotel in quiet area away from the
sea. Garden and outdoor pool.*

Palácio   IIII
Rua do Parque
2765 Estoril
Tel. (01) 468 04 00;
fax (01) 468 4867
*162 rooms. Long established luxury
grand hotel, that looks like a great
white cruise ship. Heated outdoor
pool, tennis, gardens. Special rates
offered at own golf course.*

Palácio de Seteais   IIII
Rua Barbosa do Bocage
2710 Sintra
Tel. (01) 923 32 00;
fax (01) 923 42 77
*30 rooms. Luxury hotel in historic
and beautiful 18th-century palace.
Antique furniture. Gardens, superb
views, heated outdoor pool, tennis.*

Quinta da Capela   II
Estrada de Monserrate
2710 Sintra
Tel. (01) 929 34 05;
fax (01) 929 34 25
*11 rooms. Offering attractive
accommodation in a rambling 16th-
century house on a country estate,
3km (2 miles) from Sintra. No
restaurant. Closed November to
February.*

Quinta das Sequóias   II
Casa da Tapada
Estrada de Monserrate
2710 Sintra
Tel. (01) 923 03 42;
fax (01) 923 03 42
*5 rooms. Modernized manor house,
4km (2.5 miles) from Sintra. Lovely
gardens, views. Meals on request.*

Vila das Rosas   II
Rua de António Cunha 2 & 4
2710 Sintra
Tel. (01) 923 42 16; no fax
*4 rooms. 19th-century house, lovely
garden. Tennis. Meals on request.*

Costa Azul

Albergaria Solaris   I
Praça Marquês de Pombal 12
2900 Setúbal
Tel. (065) 52 21 89;
fax (065) 52 20 70
*24 rooms. Fine old house on quiet
square. Modernized, well equipped
rooms. No restaurant.*

Esperença   I
Av. Luisa Todi 220
2900 Setúbal
Tel. (065) 52 51 51;
fax (065) 302 83
*76 rooms. Plain but comfortable
modern block. Business oriented.
Close to historic centre of town.*

Hotel do Mar   III
Rua General Humberto Delgado
2970 Sesimbra
Tel. (01) 223 33 26;
fax (01) 223 38 88
*168 rooms. Modern holiday hotel
with sea views, beautiful gardens,
outdoor and indoor pools. Tennis.*

Ibis   I
Vale da Rosa
2900 Setúbal
Tel. (065) 77 22 00;
fax (065) 77 24 47
*102 rooms. Comfortable, modern and
economical accommodation 5km (3
miles) south of the port. Outdoor pool.*

Pousada de Palmela   III
Castelo de Palmela
2950 Palmela
Tel. (01) 235 12 26;
fax (01) 233 04 40
*28 rooms. Luxury pousada installed
in a hilltop fortress-monastery
looking over Setúbal and the sea.
Notable restaurant serving local
dishes, especially seafood.*

Pousada de São Filipe   III
Castelo de São Filipe
2900 Setúbal
Tel. (065) 52 38 44;
fax (065) 53 25 38
*14 rooms. Luxury pousada inside
the walls of a fortress built in 1590,
just west of the port of Setúbal.
Some rooms are in former castle
dungeons. Close to the sea and the
Serra de Arrábida National Park.*

Quinta de Santo Amaro   II
Aldeia de Piedade
2925 Azeitão
Tel. (01) 218 92 30;
fax (01) 218 93 90
*8 rooms. 18th-century manor house
amid vineyards, 4km (2.5 miles)
west of Vila Nova de Azeitão.
Swimming pool, tennis.*

Quinta do César   II
Vila Fresca de Azetão
2925 Azeitão
Sétubal
Tel. (01) 208 03 87; no fax
*4 rooms. Delightful country
mansion with spacious rooms,
gardens, outdoor swimming pool
and hilltop setting.*

Residencial Espadarte   I
Av. 25 de Abril
2970 Sesimbra
Tel. (01) 223 31 89; no fax
*80 rooms. Modern, functional
holiday accommodation, right on
the seafront. No restaurant.*

Costa da Prata

Abrantes

Hotel de Turismo   II
Largo de Santo António
2200 Abrantes
Tel. (041) 212 61; fax (041) 252 18
*41 rooms. Situated on a hill at the
top of the town. Ugly modern
building, but comfortable, with a
good restaurant. Outdoor swimming
pool, tennis.*

Águeda

Pousada de Santo António II
Serem
3750 Águeda
Tel. (034) 52 32 30;
fax (034) 52 31 92
13 rooms. One of the first pousadas in the chain, recently renovated. Situated near the IP5, about 8km (5 miles) north of Águeda, overlooking the River Vouga. Swimming pool, gardens. Regional restaurant.

Alcobaça

Casa da Pedeira II
Estrada N8
Aljubarrota
2460 Alcobaça
Tel. (062) 50 82 72;
fax (062) 50 82 72
12 rooms. Family run inn, 6km (4 miles) from Alcobaça in the direction of Batalha. No restaurant, but dinner available if notice given in advance .

Aveiro

Imperial II
Rua Dr Nascimento Leitão
3800 Aveiro
Tel. (034) 22 141; fax (034) 24 148
107 rooms. Modern block situated on the edge of town, with views over canals and lagoon.

Pousada da Ria II
3870 Murtosa
Tel. (034) 48 332; fax (034) 48 333
19 rooms. Beside the calm waters of the Ria de Aveiro lagoon, 10km (6 miles) north of Aveiro. Close to sea. Swimming pool, tennis.

Batalha

Pousada do Mestre Afonso Domingues II
2440 Batalha
tel. (044) 96 260; fax (044) 96 247
21 rooms. A comfortable new pousada named after the architect of the great monastery which lies opposite. Notable restaurant serving regional specialities.

Quinta do Fidalgo II
2440 Batalha
Tel. (044) 96 114; fax (044) 96 114
5 rooms in family run manor house, opposite the monastery. Friendly, and with attractive gardens.

Buçaco

Palace III
Buçaco
3050 Mealhada
Tel. (031) 93 01 01;
fax (031) 93 05 09
60 rooms. A grand hotel in an opulent 19th-century royal palace, set in a national forest. Exotic decor, antique furniture, vast public rooms. Fine restaurant and notable wine cellar. Magnificent gardens, tennis.

Caldas da Rainha

Casa dos Plátanos I
Rua de Rafael Bordalo Pinheiro 24
2500 Caldas da Rainha
Tel. (062) 84 18 10; no fax
8 rooms. 18th-century town mansion near spa and park.

Coimbra

Astória II
Avenida Emídia Navarro 21
3000 Coimbra
Tel. (039) 22 055; fax (039) 22 057
64 rooms. Traditional comfort in a fine old hotel, recently renovated. Central, facing the Mondego river. Elegant restaurant serving local and international cuisine.

Ericeira

Pedro O Pescador I
Rua Dr Eduardo Burnay 22
2655 Ericeira
Tel. (061) 86 40 32;
fax (061) 623 21
25 rooms. Friendly, informal holiday hotel, a short walk from the beach. Closed January.

Vilazul I
Calçada de Baleia 10
2655 Ericeira
Tel. (061) 86 41 01;
fax (061) 62 927
21 rooms. Pleasant old house in town, well converted. Rooftop lounge and bar with views to sea. Noted restaurant.

Fátima

Estalagem Dom Gonçalo I
Rua Jacinta Marto 100
2495 Fátima
Tel. (049) 53 30 62;
fax (049) 53 20 88
45 rooms. Pleasant modern building with well equipped rooms. Situated close to the Sanctuary.

Hotel de Fátima I
Rua João Paulo II
2496 Fátima
Tel. (049) 53 33 51;
fax (049) 53 26 91
133 rooms. Modern, plain but comfortable hotel, centrally located near the Sanctuary.

Figueira da Foz

Casa da Azenha Velha II
Caceira de Cima
3080 Figueira da Foz
Tel. (033) 250 42; no fax
6 rooms. Modern country house on a large estate, situated 9km (6 miles) from town, with horses, geese and wild boar. Swimming pool, tennis.

Nazaré

Hotel da Nazaré II
Largo Afonso Zuquete 7
2450 Nazaré
Tel. (062) 56 13 11;
fax (062) 56 12 38
52 rooms. Established holiday hotel in the town, just off the esplanade, a short walk from the beach.

Pensão Ribamar I
Rua Gomes Freire 9
2450 Nazaré
Tel. (062) 55 11 58; no fax
23 rooms. Plain but comfortable, traditional boarding house situated very near the beach.

Quinta do Campo II
Valado dos Frades
2450 Nazaré
Tel. (062) 57 71 35;
fax (062) 57 75 55
10 rooms. A charming old manor house which was once part of a monastic estate, situated 5km (3 miles) from Nazaré on the road to Alcobaça. Swimming pool, tennis, gardens. Meals on request.

Óbidos

Albergaria Josefa D'Óbidos I
Rua D. João de Ornelas
2510 Óbidos
Tel. (062) 95 92 28;
fax (062) 95 95 33
38 rooms. Newly built but in traditional style, just outside the walls near the main gate. Named after the 17th-century artist: reproductions of some of her works are displayed on the walls.

Pousada do Castelo   **III**
2510 Óbidos
Tel. (062) 95 91 05;
fax (062) 95 91 48
9 rooms. Luxurious pousada set in part of the medieval castle, situated inside the beautiful walled town. Celebrated restaurant serving a selection of regional and national dishes.

Peniche
Hotel da Praia Norte   **II**
Praia Norte
2520 Peniche
Tel. (062) 78 11 66;
fax (062) 78 11 65
92 rooms. Modern holiday hotel located near a sandy beach north of the fishing port. Outdoor pool, tennis.

São Martinho do Porto
Parque   **II**
Avenida Marechal Carmona 3
2465 São Martinho do Porto
Tel. (062) 98 93 28;
fax (062) 98 91 05
36 rooms. Converted stately mansion, close to town centre and the sea. Gardens, tennis courts. No restaurant.

Tomar
Casa dos Pinheiros   **I**
Chão de Maças
Seiça
2300 Tomar
Tel. (01) 797 97 84 (reservations);
no fax
5 rooms. Traditional old farmhouse set in lovely gardens and vineyards, east of town. Swimming pool. Meals on request.

Estalagem de Santa Iria   **II**
Parque do Mouchão
2300 Tomar
Tel. (049) 31 33 26;
fax (049) 32 10 82
13 rooms. Attractive inn on a little island in the River Nabão. Good regional restaurant.

Hotel dos Templários   **II**
Largo Candido dos Reis
2300 Tomar
Tel. (049) 32 17 30;
fax (049) 32 21 91
84 rooms. Large modern block set right next to the river. Good restaurant with regional dishes. Swimming pool, tennis.

Pousada de São Pedro   **II**
Castelo do Bode
2300 Tomar
Tel. (049) 38 22 74;
fax (049) 38 11 76
25 rooms. On a hill 18km (11 miles) from Tomar above Portugal's largest artificial lake, with watersports available. Regional restaurant.

Costa Verde

Oporto
Ibis   **I**
Lugar das Chas-Afurada
Vila Nova de Gaia
4400 Porto
Tel. (02) 772 07 72;
fax (02) 772 07 88
108 rooms. New economy hotel close to autostrada on south side of Douro. Modern box-like building with bright interior, pleasant restaurant.

Infante de Sagres   **III**
Praça D. Filipa de Lencastre 62
4000 Porto
Tel. (02) 201 90 31;
fax (02) 31 49 37
74 rooms. Centrally located grand hotel with spacious public rooms. Guest rooms overlooking courtyard are quiet. Elegant restaurant, garden.

Sheraton Porto   **III**
Avenida da Boavista 1269
4100 Porto
Tel. (02) 606 88 22;
fax (02) 609 14 67
253 rooms including executive rooms and suites. Modern tower, west of city centre. Favoured by business people and groups. Indoor pool, health club, sauna, squash.

Tivoli Porto Atlantico   **III**
Rua Afonso Lopes Vieira 66
4100 Porto
Tel. (02) 609 49 41;
fax (02) 606 74 52
58 rooms. In a residential suburb west of the centre, off Avenida da Boavista. Compact but luxurious hotel. Indoor and outdoor pools, health club. No restaurant.

Vice Rei   **I**
Rua Júlio Dinis 779
4000 Porto
Tel. (02) 69 53 71;
fax (02) 69 26 97
27 rooms. Comfortable residencial west of city centre. No restaurant.

Amarante
Casa da Obra   **I**
Fregim
4600 Amarante
Tel. (055) 42 59 07; no fax
7 rooms. Early 20th-century manor house, 5km southwest of town. Quiet, with large garden. Meals on request.

Pousada de São Gonçalo   **II**
4600 Amarante
Tel. (055) 46 11 13;
fax (055) 46 13 53
15 rooms. Rustic mountain lodge, in the Serra do Marão, just off IP4 about 20km (12 miles) east of Amarante. Fine views and country cooking.

Barcelos
Casa de Abade do Neiva   **I**
Lugar da Igreja
4750 Abade do Neiva
Tel. (053) 81 15 53; no fax
4 rooms. Modern country house in woodlands, 3km northwest of Barcelos. Swimming pool, tennis.

Casa de Monte   **I**
Lugar do Barreiro
4750 Abade do Neiva
Tel. (053) 81 15 19; no fax
5 rooms. Modern manor house in beautiful gardens and woods, 3km (2 miles) from Barcelos. Swimming pool, tennis, meals on request.

Braga
Castelo do Bom Jesus   **II**
Bom Jesus
4700 Braga
Tel. (053) 67 65 66;
fax (053) 61 71 81
10 rooms. 18th-century manor house in spacious grounds near the famous staircase and sanctuary. Swimming pool, tennis. Meals on request.

Dos Terceiros   **I**
Rua do Capelistas 85
4700 Braga
Tel. (053) 704 66; fax (053) 757 67
21 rooms. Friendly central residencial. No restaurant.

Caniçada
Pousada de São Bento   **II**
4850 Caniçada
Tel. (053) 64 71 90;
fax (053) 64 78 67
29 rooms. Mountain retreat in a greatly expanded old hunting lodge, at the gateway to the Peneda-Gerês National Park. Pool, tennis.

Esposende

Casa do Matinho   I
Lugar do Matinho
4740 Forjães
Tel. (053) 87 11 67; no fax
2 rooms. Traditional country manor house, 12km (7 miles) northeast of Esposende. Swimming pool, gardens.

Guimarães

Casa de Sezim   II
Nespereira
4800 Guimarães
Tel. (053) 52 31 96; no fax
6 rooms. 18th-century manor house and vinho verde *winery near Santo Amaro. Swimming pool, tennis, meals available on request.*

**Pousada de Nossa Senhora
de Oliveira**   II
Largo da Oliveira
4801 Guimarães
Tel. (053) 51 41 57;
fax (053) 51 42 04
16 rooms. Beautifully adapted from 16th- and 17th-century mansions, in the heart of the old town. Notable restaurant in the old kitchens.

Pousada de Santa Marinha   III
Costa
4800 Guimarães
Tel. (053) 51 44 53;
fax (053) 51 44 59
51 rooms. Halfway up the Penha hill, 3km (2 miles) from the centre of Guimarães and high above it. In a magnificent, superbly converted 18th-century monastery. Gardens. Fine restaurant.

Ofir

Pinhal   II
Avenida da Praia
Ofir
4740 Esposende
Tel. (053) 98 14 73;
fax (053) 98 22 65
90 rooms. Modern resort hotel in pine woods close to sandy beach. Swimming pool, tennis, horse riding, fishing. Disco.

Ponte de Lima

Casa das Pereiras   I
Largo das Pereiras
4990 Ponte de Lima
Tel. (058) 94 29 39; no fax
3 rooms. 17th-century house and garden in historic area of town. Small swimming pool. Meals on request.

Póvoa do Varzim

Vermar   II
Rua de Martin Vaz N-O
4490 Póvoa de Varzim
Tel. (052) 61 55 66;
fax (052) 61 51 15
208 rooms. Modern white tower blocks situated near the beach. Outdoor pool, tennis, health club and sauna. Disco.

Valença do Minho

Pousada de São Teotonio   II
4930 Valença do Minho
Tel. (051) 82 40 20;
fax (051) 82 43 97
16 rooms. A modern but fitting building, within the massive walls of this fortified border town, overlooking the River Minho and 19th-century iron bridge to the Spanish town of Tuy.

Viana do Castelo

Albergaria Calatrava   II
Rua M. Fiúza Júnior 157
4900 Viana do Castelo
Tel. (058) 82 89 11;
fax (058) 82 86 37
15 rooms. Small, friendly hotel on the edge of town, a short walk from the historic centre. No restaurant.

Casa dos Costa Barros   II
Rua de São Pedro 22-28
4900 Viana do Castelo
Tel. (058) 82 37 05;
fax (058) 82 81 37
10 rooms. 16th-century mansion with Manueline windows, in historic town centre. Meals on request.

Pousada Santa Luzia   II
Santa Luzia
4900 Viana do Castelo
Tel. (058) 82 88 90;
fax (058) 82 88 92
55 rooms. Resort hotel managed by the Pousada chain. Set on a wooded hilltop high above Viana, next to a prehistoric citânia *site. Swimming pool, tennis, gardens.*

Viana Sol   I
Largo Vasco da Gama
4900 Viana do Castelo
Tel. (058) 82 89 95;
fax (058) 82 89 97
65 rooms. Traditional hotel situated near town centre and harbour. Indoor pool and sauna. Entertainment. No restaurant.

Vila do Conde

Quinta das Alfaias   I
Rua de António Azevedo dos
Santos 515
Fajozes
4480 Vila do Conde
Tel. (052) 66 21 46
5 rooms. 19th-century country mansion, on eastern outskirts of Vila do Conde. Swimming pool, gardens. Meals on request.

Vila Nova de Cerveira

Pousada de Dom Dinis   III
4920 Vila Nova de Cerveira
Tel. (051) 79 56 01;
fax (051) 79 56 04
29 rooms. Built within the walls of a 14th-century castle in the middle of this border town on the Minho. Views across the river to the Spanish bank from the ramparts and the glass-walled restaurant.

Vila Praia de Ancora

Quim Barreiros   II
Rua Dr Ramos Pereira
4915 Vila Praia de Ancora
Tel. (058) 95 12 18;
fax (058) 95 12 20
28 rooms. Modern four-storey hotel, situated on the seafront a few minutes' walk south of the centre of town. No restaurant.

Mountains

Alijó

Pousada Barão de Forrester   II
5070 Alijó
Tel. (059) 95 92 15;
fax (059) 95 93 04
11 rooms. In a charming house near the town square. Small pool, tennis, garden. Good restaurant. Convenient base for exploring the upper Douro valley.

Almeida

Pousada Senhora das Neves   II
6350 Almeida
Tel. (071) 54 283; fax (071) 54 320
21 rooms. New pousada which has been installed within the walls of a great border fortress. Good restaurant specializes in the dishes of the region.

Bragança

Pousada de São Bartolomeu II
5300 Bragança
Tel. (073) 33 14 93;
fax (073) 23 453
16 rooms. On a hill south east of Bragança, overlooking the castle and city. A good base for exploring the far north-eastern corner of Portugal. Local country cooking.

Tulipa I
Rua Dr Francisco Felgueiras 8-10
5300 Bragança
Tel. (073) 33 16 75;
fax (073) 33 17 48
33 rooms. Modern, friendly, functional residencial with good local restaurant.

Caramulo

Pousada de São Jerónimo II
3475 Caramulo
Tel. (032) 86 12 91;
fax (032) 86 16 40
6 rooms. Small modern pousada on the slopes of the Besteiros valley, below spa town of Caramulo. Swimming pool, garden, country cooking.

Castelo Branco

Rainha Dona Amélia II
Rua de Santiago 15
6000 Castelo Branco
Tel. (072) 32 63 15;
fax (072) 32 63 90
64 rooms. Attractive modern hotel in a quiet street, a short walk from the historic centre.

Chaves

Aquae Flaviae II
Praça do Brasil
5400 Chaves
Tel. (076) 26 711; fax (076) 26 497
176 rooms. Modern eight-storey block close to spa and historic centre. Tennis court.

Quinta da Mata I
Estrada de Valpaços
5400 Chaves
Tel. (076) 233 85; fax (076) 233 85
5 rooms. 17th-century manor house and farm, 3km (2 miles) south east of Chaves. Tennis. Meals on request.

Quinta do Lombo I
5400 Chaves
Tel. (076) 214 04; fax (076) 214 04
6 rooms. Traditional farmhouse situated 3km (2 miles) south of Chaves. Swimming pool, small private museum.

Covilha

Santa Eufêmia I
Sítio da Palmatória
6200 Covilha
Tel. (075) 31 33 08;
fax (075) 31 41 84
77 rooms. Comfortable base for exploring Serra da Estrela. No restaurant.

Guarda

Hotel de Turismo II
Avenida Coronel O. de Carvalho
6300 Guarda
Tel. (71) 21 22 05;
fax (071) 21 22 04
106 rooms. Modern hotel set in its own gardens on edge of city. Favoured by business people.

Quinta da Ponte I
Faia
6300 Guarda
Tel. (071) 961 26; fax (071) 961 26
10 rooms. 18th-century manor house in a pleasant setting of ornamental gardens by a Roman bridge over the Mondego, 12km (7 miles) west of Guarda. Swimming pool, fishing.

Residência Filipe I
Rua Vasco da Gama 9
6300 Guarda
Tel. (071) 21 26 58;
fax (071) 22 14 02
14 rooms. Comfortable, well maintained pensão in the city centre.

Lamego

Casa das Varais I
Cambres
5100 Lamego
Tel. (054) 232 51; no fax
3 rooms. 18th-century country house on Port wine estate 6km (4 miles) north of Lamego, with view of the Douro valley. Swimming pool, hunting. Meals on request.

Parque I
Nossa Senhora dos Remédios
5100 Lamego
Tel. (054) 621 05; fax (054) 652 03
38 rooms. At the sanctuary south of town. Good regional restaurant.

Quinta da Timpeira II
Lugar da Timpeira
5100 Lamego
Tel. (054) 628 11; no fax
5 rooms. Country house and wine-growing estate, 3km (2 miles) south of Lamego. Swimming pool, tennis. Meals available on request.

Mangualde

Casa da Mesquitela II
Mesquitela
3530 Mangualde
Tel. (032) 61 42 10; no fax
6 rooms. Extended 16th-century manor house in the Dão wine region, 4km (2.5 miles) from Mangualde. Meals on request.

Manteigas

Pousada de São Lourenço II
6260 Manteigas
Tel. (075) 98 24 50;
fax (075) 98 24 53
22 rooms. Mountain lodge in the Serra da Estrela National Park. Between Manteigas and Gouveia. A good base for walking.

Miranda do Douro

Pousada de Santa Catarina II
5210 Miranda do Douro
Tel. (073) 42 255; fax (073) 42 665
12 rooms. A plain, modern building 3km (2 miles) north east of the border town, on a hill overlooking a dam on the River Douro, which here forms the frontier with Spain.

Monsanto

Pousada em Monsanto II
Monsanto
6085 Medelim
Tel. (077) 34 471; fax (077) 34 481
10 rooms. Attractive new pousada, simply furnished, in the heart of one of Portugal's most ancient and intriguing hilltop villages.

Oliveira do Hospital

Pousada de Santa Bárbara II
Póvoa das Quartas
3400 Oliveira do Hospital
Tel. (038) 59 551; fax (038) 59 645
16 rooms. Attractive modern pousada set in pine woods, 5km (3 miles) north east of Oliveira do Hospital. Swimming pool, tennis.

Pinhão

Casa dos Pontes II
Quinta da Foz
5085 Pinhão
Tel. (054) 723 53; no fax
6 rooms. Family run manor house amid Port wine vineyards, part of Calem estate. Situated across River Pinhão from the town.

São Pedro do Sul

Hotel das Termas I
Termas São Pedro do Sul
3660 São Pedro do Sul
Tel. (032) 71 23 33;
fax (032) 71 10 11
*64 rooms. Modern hotel in a
riverside setting in an old spa
village. Regional restaurant serving
local dishes. Gardens.*

Quinta da Comenda I
São Pedro do Sul
Tel. (032) 71 11 01; no fax
*6 rooms. Farmhouse amid the
vineyards of a long-established wine
producer, 2km (1 mile) south of
town. Swimming pool.*

Vila Real

Mira Corgo I
Avenida 1 de Mayo 76
5000 Vila Real
Tel. (059) 32 50 01; no fax
*76 rooms. Modern block with fine
view of Corgo gorge. Indoor pool.
No restaurant.*

Viseu

Casa dos Gomes I
São João de Lourosa
3500 Viseu
Tel. (032) 46 13 41;
fax (032) 46 13 41
*7 rooms. 18th-century country
house and wine estate, situated 5km
(3 miles) south east of Viseu.
Swimming pool. Meals on request.*

Grão Vasco II
Rua Gaspar Barreiros
3500 Viseu
Tel. (032) 42 35 11;
fax (032) 27 047
*100 rooms. In garden setting but
close to the historic centre of town.
Good Portuguese restaurant.
Swimming pool.*

Alentejo

Alvito

Pousada Castelo de Alvito II
7920 Alvito
Tel. (084) 483 43; fax (084) 483 83
*20 rooms. New pousada set in
restored late-15th-century castle in
pleasant country town. Outdoor
pool, gardens.*

Beja

Monte da Diabrória I
Estrada N121
7800 Beringel
Beja
Tel. (084) 981 77; no fax
*9 rooms. Traditional Alentejo
farmhouse, 6km (4 miles) west of
Beja. Tennis, fishing.*

Santa Barbara I
Rua da Mértola 56
7800 Beja
Tel.(084) 32 20 28; no fax
*25 rooms. Modern, bright and
friendly pensão in centre of town.
No restaurant. Some distance
from parking.*

Castelo de Vide

Quinta da Bela Vista I
Póvoa e Meadas
7320 Castelo de Vide
Tel. (045) 981 25; no fax
*9 rooms. Fine modern country
house on farm estate, situated
14km (9 miles) north of Castelo de
Vide. Swimming pool. Meals on
request.*

Sol e Serra II
Estrada de São Vicente
7320 Castelo de Vide
Tel. (045) 91 301; fax (045) 91 337
*51 rooms. Pleasant modern hotel,
situated just outside the historic
area of town. Swimming pool,
garden. Good regional restaurant
serving local dishes.*

Crato

Palacete Flor da Rosa I
Rua da Cruz
Flor da Rosa
Crato
Tel. (045) 974 51; no fax
*5 rooms. Lovely 18th-century
manor house in picturesque village,
2km (1 mile) north of Crato. Meals
available on request.*

Elvas

Brasa I
Estrada de Badajoz
7350 Elvas
Tel. (068) 62 91 18;
fax (068) 62 91 43
*41 rooms. Modern functional
hotel, near the main road from the
Spanish border. Pleasant
restaurant offers simple local food.*

Dom Luis II
Avenida de Badajoz
7350 Elvas
Tel. (068) 62 27 56;
fax (068) 62 07 33
*46 rooms. Pleasant modern hotel
with a view of the massive walls of
the border fortress. Good regional
restaurant serving local dishes.*

Pousada de Santa Luzia II
Avenida de Badajoz
7350 Elvas
Tel. (068) 62 21 94;
fax (068) 62 21 27
*16 rooms. The first of the pousada
chain, opened in 1942 and since
modernized. It is located directly
opposite one of the mightiest
fortresses in Europe. Notable
restaurant.*

Estremoz

Hospedaria Dom Dinis II
Rua 31 de Janeiro 46
7100 Estremoz
Tel. (068) 33 27 17;
fax (068) 226 10
*15 rooms. Simple but highly
attractive accommodation in the
lower town.*

Pousada Rainha Santa Isabel III
Castelo de Estremoz
7100 Estremoz
Tel. (068) 33 20 75;
fax (068) 33 20 79
*33 rooms. Luxurious pousada set in
gorgeous palace-fortress within the
historic citadel. Swimming pool,
garden, superb views over
ramparts and city. Notable
restaurant.*

Évora

Dom Fernando II
Avenida Dr Barahona 2
7000 Évora
Tel. (066) 74 17 17;
fax (066) 74 17 16
*104 rooms. New, modern and
comfortable hotel on outskirts of
town. Outdoor pool.*

Estalagem Monte das Flores II
Monte das Flores
7000 Évora
Tel. (066) 254 90; fax (066) 275 64
*17 rooms. Traditional farmhouse,
6km (4 miles) south west of Évora.
Tennis, swimming pool, horse
riding, hunting. Meals on request.*

Planicie II
Rua Miguel Bombardo 40
7000 Évora
Tel. (066) 240 26; fax (066) 298 80
40 rooms. A fine, converted 18th-century mansion situated in the historic centre of the city. Good regional restaurant.

Pousada dos Lóios III
Largo Conde de Vila Flor
7000 Évora
Tel. (066) 240 51; fax (066) 272 48
33 rooms. Luxury pousada installed in beautiful 15th-century convent buildings opposite the Roman temple. Swimming pool, gardens. Notable restaurant specializing in Alentejo dishes.

Quinta da Nora I
Estrada dos Canaviais
7000 Évora
Tel. (066) 298 10; no fax
5 rooms. Modern farmhouse, gardens and vineyard 4km (2.5 miles) northeast of Évora. Swimming pool.

Marvão

Pensão Dom Dinis I
Rua Dr Matos Magalhães
7330 Marvão
Tel. (045) 93 236; no fax
15 rooms. Charmingly converted old house next to the ramparts. Superb views. Good local restaurant.

Pousada de Santa Maria III
7330 Marvão
Tel. (045) 93 201; fax (045) 93 440
29 rooms. Converted town houses within the walls of a dramatically sited mountaintop citadel. Notable restaurant serving local dishes.

Mértola

Casa das Janelas Verdes I
Rua Dr Manuel F. Gomes 38-40
7750 Mértola
Tel. (086) 621 45; no fax
3 rooms. In the heart of the ancient town, in an old house set round a courtyard filled with fruit trees.

Monsaraz

Estalagem de Monsaraz II
Largo de São Bartolomeu 5
7200 Monsaraz
Tel. (066) 551 12; fax (066) 551 01
8 rooms. Attractive inn just outside the walls of the old town. Small outdoor swimming pool.

Horta da Moura II
Monsaraz
7200 Reguengos de Monsaraz
Tel. (066) 552 06; fax (066) 552 41
14 rooms. Fine manor house on big farm estate south of Monsaraz. Swimming pool, horse riding, tennis. Meals on request.

Portalegre

Dom João III II
Avenida Liberdade
7300 Portalegre
Tel. (045) 211 92; fax (045) 244 44
62 rooms. Plain, modern but comfortable hotel. Outdoor pool.

Redondo

Convento de São Paulo III
Aldeia da Serra
7170 Redondo
Tel. (066) 99 91 00;
fax (066) 99 91 04
21 rooms. Magnificently restored convent dating from the 14th century. Superb rooms and public areas – chapels, marble fountains, azulejos. Outdoor swimming pool, lovely gardens, vast grounds. In forest setting between Estremoz and Redondo.

Santa Clara-a-Velha

Pousada Santa Clara II
7665 Santa Clara-a-Velha
Tel. (083) 98 250; fax (083) 98 402
32 rooms. Newly extended country house overlooking artificial lake. Watersports. Located in the mountains just north of the Algarve. Local cuisine.

Santiago do Caçem

Pousada da Quinta da Ortiga II
Quinta da Ortiga
7540 Santiago do Caçem
Tel. (069) 22 871; fax (069) 22 073
12 rooms. Quiet country estate 5km (3 miles) from town, off the Sines road. Swimming pool, gardens, and horse riding available.

Pousada de São Tiago II
7540 Santiago do Caçem
Tel. (069) 22 459; fax (069) 22 459
8 rooms. Small country-house-style pousada, a short way up the Lisbon road from the centre of town. Swimming pool, garden, outdoor dining in summer.

Serpa

Pousada de São Gens II
7830 Serpa
Tel. (084) 53 724; fax (084) 53 337
18 rooms. Modern Moorish-inspired pousada on a hill above the town. Swimming pool, garden. Local country cooking.

Sousel

Pousada de São Miguel III
São Miguel
7470 Sousel
Tel. (068) 55 11 60;
fax (068) 55 11 55
32 rooms. Ultra-modern version of a hunting lodge on a hill 3km (2 miles) from Sousel. Restaurant specializes in game in season.

Vila Viçosa

Casa de Peixinhos I
7160 Vila Viçosa
Tel. (068) 984 72; no fax
6 rooms. Beautiful 17th century manor house just east of town, set in orange groves. Closed August.

Algarve

Albufeira

California II
Rua Cândido dos Reis 10-16
8200 Albufeira
Tel. (089) 58 68 33;
fax (089) 58 68 50
56 rooms. On a hillside right in the middle of town. An old-established, friendly hotel. Rooftop pool, sauna.

Cerro Alagoa III
8200 Albufeira
Tel. (089) 58 82 61;
fax (089) 58 82 62
310 rooms. Stylish new resort hotel, with jungle theme swimming pool, indoor pool, health club and sauna. All rooms with balconies.

Estalagem do Cerro II
Rua Cerro da Piedade
8200 Albufeira
Tel. (089) 58 61 91;
fax (089) 58 61 93
89 rooms. Above the town and bay, 400m (440 yds) from beach. Comfortable, four-storey, modern informal hotel. All rooms with balconies or terrace. Swimming pool, garden, sauna.

Hotel da Aldeia III
Areias de São João
8200 Albufeira
Tel. (089) 58 88 61;
fax (089) 58 88 64
*125 rooms. Near Praia da Oura,
2km (1 mile) east of Albufeira.
Modern hotel with gardens, two
pools, tennis and mini-golf.*

Montechoro III
1200 Montechoro
Albufeira
Tel. (089) 58 94 23;
fax (089) 58 99 47
*410 rooms. Eleven-storey hotel and
sports complex on a hill 3km (2
miles) northeast of Albufeira. Pools,
tennis, squash, health club and
sauna. Noted grill restaurant. Free
shuttle bus to Albufeira town and
beach.*

Sheraton Algarve IIII
(Pine Cliffs)
Praia da Falésia
8200 Albufeira
Tel. (089) 50 19 99;
fax (089) 50 19 50
*215 rooms. New luxury resort hotel,
low-rise buildings beautifully
landscaped, on cliffs 10km (6 miles)
east of Albufeira. Indoor and
outdoor pools, 9-hole private golf
course, tennis, health club. Elevator
down the cliffs to beach.*

Almancil
*(see also Quinta do Lago,
Vale do Lobo)*
Quinta dos Rochas I
Estrada de Quarteira
8135 Almancil
Tel. (089) 39 31 65;
fax (089) 39 91 98
*6 rooms. Family house newly built
in traditional style. Rooms equipped
to luxury standard.*

Alvor – see Portimão

Armação de Pêra
Casa Bela Moura II
Alporchinhos
8365 Armação da Pêra
Tel. (082) 31 34 22;
fax (082) 31 30 25
*8 rooms. Modern house in
traditional style, near the sheltered
beaches of Nossa Senhora da
Rocha. Swimming pool, garden.
Meals on request.*

Do Garbe III
Avenida Marginal
8365 Armação de Pêra
Tel. (082) 31 21 94;
fax (082) 31 22 01
*108 rooms. Bright and modern hotel,
directly overlooking the beach.
Terraces and pool. Steps to beach.*

Viking III
Praia Nossa Senhora da Rocha
8635 Armação da Pêra
Tel. (082) 31 48 76;
fax (082) 31 48 52
*184 rooms. On cliffs close to beach,
2km (1 mile) west of town. Pools,
tennis, disco.*

Carvoeiro – see Lagoa

Faro
Eva II
Avenida da Republica
8000 Faro
Tel. (089) 80 33 54;
fax (089) 80 23 04
*150 rooms. Modern block overlooking
the town and harbour. Rooftop pool,
disco, free bus to beach. For those
who like to be right in town.*

Pensão O Farão I
Largo da Madalena 4
8000 Faro
Tel. (089) 82 33 56; no fax
*13 rooms. Old town house on small
square, with traditional furnishings
and decor, including azulejos.
Breakfast served on roof terrace. No
restaurant.*

Residencial Afonso III I
Rua Miguel Bombarda 64
8000 Faro
Tel. (089) 80 35 42;
fax (089) 80 51 85
*40 rooms. Simple and comfortable
accommodation near the centre of
town but 800m (0.5 mile) from
historic area. No restaurant.*

Lagoa
Almansor III
Vale Covo
Carvoeiro
8400 Lagoa
Tel. (082) 35 80 26;
fax (082) 35 87 70
*293 rooms. Futuristic looking
complex on the cliff above a pretty
cove. Swimming pool, sauna,
gardens, free bus to beach,
watersports. Entertainment.*

Lagos
Golfinho III
Praia Dona Ana
8600 Lagos
Tel. (082) 76 99 00;
fax (082) 76 99 20
*262 rooms. Modern eight-storey
block situated above the beach.
Indoor and outdoor pools, bowling
alley and disco.*

Hotel de Lagos III
Rua Nova da Aldeia
8600 Lagos
Tel. (082) 76 99 67;
fax (082) 76 99 20
*318 rooms. Attractive modern
complex not far from old town and
port. Outdoor and indoor pools,
health club. Free bus to Duna beach
club 1.5km (1 mile) away, with
watersports, tennis.*

Meia Praia III
Estrada de Meia Praia
8600 Lagos
Tel. (082) 76 20 01;
fax (082) 76 20 08
*65 rooms. Next to the beach, 3km
(2 miles) from Lagos. A three-storey
building, with its own gardens,
pools, tennis and mini-golf. Closed
November to March.*

Loulé
Loulé Jardim I
Praça Manuel de Arriaga
8100 Loulé
Tel. (089) 41 30 94;
fax (089) 63 177
*52 rooms. Comfortable older hotel,
in pretty town, 10km (6 miles) from
the sea. Terrace, swimming pool.
No restaurant.*

Monte Gordo – see Vila Real de Santo António

Portimão
Algarve IIII
Avenida Tomás Cabreira
Praia da Rocha
8500 Portimão
Tel. (082) 41 50 01;
fax (082) 41 59 99
*220 rooms. Modern seven-storey
luxury resort facing its own section
of the vast beach. Seawater pools,
health club, sauna, tennis, mini-golf,
watersports, disco.*

Bela Vista III
Avenida Tomás Cabreira
Praia da Rocha
8500 Portimão
Tel. (082) 24 055;
fax (082) 41 53 69
14 rooms. Something special – a century-old summer mansion in Moorish style with lovely interiors and azulejos. Also a more modern annexe. Close to the beach.

Casa Tres Palmeiras II
Praia de Vau
8501 Portimão
Tel. (082) 40 12 75;
fax (082) 40 10 29
5 rooms. Imaginative modern house on cliffs near Alvor. Swimming pool.

Dom João II III
Praia de Alvor
8500 Portimão
Tel. (082) 45 91 35;
fax (082) 45 93 63
219 rooms. Well established seven-storey resort hotel next to the beach. Gardens, seawater pool, children's pool, tennis, and watersports offered.

Penina III
Penina
Estrada N125
8502 Portimão
Tel. (082) 41 54 15;
fax (082) 41 50 00
192 rooms. Luxury golf and resort hotel with its own courses, situated west of Portimão. Beautiful grounds, large outdoor pool, horse riding, tennis, health club, and children's club. Notable restaurant.

Residencial Solar Penguin I
Avenida Tomás Cabreira
Praia da Rocha
8500 Portimão
Tel. (082) 24 308; no fax
13 rooms. Early 20th-century house with old-world atmosphere and a superb view of the nearby beach from its terraces. No restaurant.

Quarteira

Atis II
Avenida Francisco Sa Carneiro
8125 Quarteira
Tel. (089) 38 97 71;
fax (089) 38 97 74
73 rooms, plus apartments. Modern high-rise block overlooking the beach. With its own garden and small swimming pool.

Zodiaco II
Fonte Santa
8125 Quarteira
Tel. (089) 38 95 89;
fax (089) 38 81 58
60 rooms. Modern block set back from the noise and bustle of Quarteira's main strip, but still within a short walk of the beach and entertainment. Swimming pool and tennis available.

Quinta do Lago

Quinta do Lago IIII
8135 Almancil
Tel. (089) 39 66 66;
fax (089) 39 63 93
150 rooms. The Algarve's most exclusive development – a vast landscaped estate situated close to the sea. Private beach, watersports, pools, health club, sauna, tennis, squash, golf.

Sagres

Hotel da Baleeira II
8650 Sagres
Tel. (082) 642 12; fax (082) 644 25
120 rooms. On the cliff above the harbour. Seawater pool, tennis, garden, disco.

Navegante II
Sítio da Baleeira
8650 Sagres
Tel. (082) 643 54; fax (082) 643 60
56 apartments. Modern block on cliffs. Superb views of sea and fortress. Large outdoor pool, tennis and squash available.

Pousada do Infante III
Sítio da Baleeira
8650 Sagres
Tel. (082) 642 22; fax (082) 642 25
39 rooms. Modern white building with neo-Moorish touches, situated on the cliffs opposite the fortress. Swimming pool, tennis. Regional restaurant serving local dishes.

São Brás de Alportel

Pousada de São Brás II
Estrada de Lisboa
8150 São Brás de Alportel
Tel. (089) 84 23 05;
fax (089) 84 17 26
24 rooms. One of the first pousadas, built in 1942 and renovated several times since. Set above the inland town of São Brás. Swimming pool, regional restaurant.

Tavira

Quinta do Caracol I
São Pedro
8800 Tavira
Tel. (081) 224 75; no fax
7 apartments. Extended 17th-century house, situated 1 km (0.5 mile) west of the Algarve's most elegant town. Swimming pool, large gardens.

Vale do Lobo

Dona Filipa IIII
Vale do Lobo
8135 Almancil
Tel. (089) 39 41 41;
fax (089) 39 42 88
147 rooms. A beautifully landscaped, luxury resort hotel, the last word in facilities and comfort. Set in 182ha (450 acres) of grounds and gardens near the small, sandy beach. Swimming pools, tennis centre, squash and golf course nearby with green fees included. Gaming room.

Vilamoura

Golfe Country Club II
(Motel do Golfe)
Vilamoura
8125 Quarteira
Tel. (089) 30 29 75;
fax (089) 38 00 23
52 rooms. Quiet, low-rise motel next to Vilamoura 1 golf course, and with its own 9-hole pitch and putt course. Swimming pool, gardens, and free bus to marina and beach offered.

Marinotel III
Vilamoura
8125 Quarteira
Tel. (089) 38 99 88;
fax (089) 38 98 69
Imposing new twelve-storey luxury resort complex next to the huge marina and beach. Gardens, pools, health club, tennis, putting green.

Vila Real de Santo António

Alcazar II
Rua de Ceuta
8900 Monte Gordo
Tel. (081) 51 21 84;
fax (081) 51 22 42
95 rooms. Modern block situated near the beach. Outdoor pool, water sports. Disco.

Guadiana   **I**
Avenida da Republica 94
8900 Vila Real de Santo António
Tel. (081) 51 14 82;
fax (081) 51 14 78
*37 rooms. Comfortable hotel facing
the river and ferry to Spain. No
restaurant.*

Restaurants

The prices we quote are for a
meal consisting of starter, main
course and dessert, per person.
Service and VAT (sales tax) of
16% are included – as they generally are in the bill.

I   below 4,000 esc. (£16/$24)
II   4,000-5,500 esc (£16-
22/$24-33)
III   over 5,500 esc. (£22/$33)

We have not included bars with
snacks, fast food outlets, cafés and
coffee bars, where you can often
eat cheaper. Everything costs less
away from the main tourist areas.
Paradoxically, though the 'tourist
menu' in many restaurants, especially at lunchtime, is excellent
value at 1,200-2,500 esc., (£5-10/
$7.50-15) with wine, beer, min-
eral water or a soft drink
included.

Lisbon

Bairro Alto

Adega Machado   **III**
Rua do Norte 91
1200 Lisbon
Tel. 342 87 13
*Popular with visitors from abroad.
Dinner only, with fado and other
folk music and dance. Closed
Monday.*

A Quinta   **I**
Passarela do Elevador de
Santa Justa
1200 Lisbon
Tel. 346 55 88
*At the top of the elevator, with
superb views over the Baixa. Offers
international and local cooking.
Closed Sunday.*

Arcadas do Faia   **III**
Rua da Barroca 56
1200 Lisbon
Tel. 342 67 42
*Dinner only. Portuguese cuisine,
with fado and other folk music.
Closed Sunday.*

A Severa   **III**
Rua das Gáveas 51
1200 Lisbon
Tel. 342 83 14
*Traditional Portuguese food. Fado
and other folk music in the evening.
Closed Thursday.*

Bachus   **II**
Largo da Trindade 9
1200 Lisbon
Tel. 342 28 28
*Attractive and fashionable
restaurant, serving various regional
Portuguese dishes as well as an
international menu.*

Brasuca   **I**
Rua João Pereira da Rosa 7
1200 Lisbon
Tel. 342 85 42
*Informal restaurant serving
Brazilian and Portuguese dishes.
Closed Monday.*

Casa Faz Frio   **I**
Rua de Dom Pedro V 96
1200 Lisbon
Tel. 346 18 60
*Traditional Portuguese food is
served in a tiled restaurant like a
country wine cellar.*

Cervejeria da Trindade   **I**
Rua Nova da Trindade 20
1200 Lisbon
Tel. 342 35 06
*Big tiled beer hall and restaurant
with Portuguese cooking and
seafood specialities.*

Conventual   **II**
Praça das Flores 45
1200 Lisbon
Tel. 60 91 96
*West of Bairro Alto. Classic
Portuguese cuisine. Closed
Saturday lunchtime, Sunday and
throughout August.*

Delfim   **I**
Rua Nova de São Mamede 23
1200 Lisbon
Tel. 69 05 32
*On the northern edge of Bairro Alto.
Portuguese specialities and seafood.
Closed Saturday and late August.*

Mamma Rosa   **I**
Rua do Grémio Lusitano
1200 Lisbon
Tel. 346 53 50
*Informal restaurant serving pizzas
and other traditional Italian dishes.
Evenings only. Closed Sunday.*

Pap d'Açorda   **II**
Rua da Atalaia 57
1200 Lisbon
Tel. 346 48 11
*Alentejo and other Portuguese food
(açorda is the name of a traditional
shellfish stew). Closed Sunday and
Monday.*

Porta Branca   **II**
Rua do Teixeira 35
1200 Lisbon
Tel. 342 10 24
*For Portuguese regional cooking
and seafood. Well known for steaks
also. Closed Saturday lunchtime,
Sunday and throughout July.*

Tavares   **III**
Rua da Misericórdia 37
1200 Lisbon
Tel. 342 11 12
*Stylish traditional restaurant,
popular with business people,
serving classical French cuisine.
Closed Saturday and public
holidays.*

Central Lisbon

Aviz   **III**
Rua Serpa Pinto 12-B
1200 Lisbon
Tel. 342 83 91
*Stylish restaurant in Baixa district,
serving a mixture of Portuguese and
French cuisine. Closed Saturday
lunchtime, Sunday and throughout
August.*

Bom Jardim – Rei dos Frangos   **I**
Travessa de Santo Antão 11
1200 Lisbon
Tel. 32 43 89
*Central. Informal, busy place
specializing in grills, especailly spit-
roasted chicken.*

Casa da Comida   **III**
Travessa das Amoreiras 1
1200 Lisbon
Tel. 388 53 76
*Pleasant patio setting in an old
mansion near the aqueduct. Fine
French-Portuguese cuisine. Closed
Saturday lunch, Sunday and
throughout August.*

Gambrinus   III
Rua das Portas de Santo Antão 25
1100 Lisbon
Tel. 342 14 66
Central. Portuguese dishes;
especially noted for seafood
prepared in regional styles.

Pabe   III
Rua Duque de Palmela 27-A
1200 Lisbon
Tel. 53 74 84
Near Praça Marquês de Pombal
(Rotunda). English pub with good
international cooking.

Restaurante 33   II
Rua Alexandre Herculano 33A
1200 Lisbon
Tel. 54 60 79
Traditional Portuguese menu
accompanied by music in the
evenings. Closed Saturday
lunchtime and Sunday.

Ribadouro   I
Av. da Liberdade 155
1200 Lisbon
Tel. 54 94 11
Central. Informal seafood bar and
restaurant in basement.

Sancho   I
Travessa da Glória 14
1200 Lisbon
Tel. 346 97 80
Informal local restaurant near
Avenida da Liberdade. Closed
Sunday and public holidays.

São Caetano   III
Rua de São Caetano 27/31
1200 Lisbon
Tel. 397 47 92
Small, elegant restaurant in Lapa
district. Dinner only, fado
entertainment. Closed Saturday
lunch and Sunday.

Senhor Vinho   III
Rua do Meio à Lapa 18
1200 Lisbon
Tel. 397 74 56
In the Lapa district. Noted for
traditional Portuguese food. Dinner
only. Fado and other entertainment.
Closed Sunday.

Solmar   II
Rua das Portas de São Antão 108
1200 Lisbon
Tel. 346 00 10
Large and busy informal restaurant
in Baixa district, specializing in
seafood dishes.

Tágide   III
Largo da Academia Nacional de
Belas Artes 18
1200 Lisbon
Tel. 342 07 20
Elegant old house on the hillside just
west of Praça do Comércio, with a
good view of the waterfront. Regional
Portuguese cuisine. Closed Saturday,
Sunday and public holidays.

Xêlê Bananas   I
Praça das Flores 29
1200 Lisbon
Tel. 395 25 15
In Lapa district west of Bairro Alto.
Tropical decor. Closed Saturday
lunchtime and Sunday.

Old Lisbon

Casa do Leão   III
Castelo de São Jorge
1100 Lisbon
Tel. 888 01 54
Inside castle ramparts. Operated by
the Pousada chain. Noted for tradi-
tional Portuguese regional dishes, but
also serving an international menu.

Michel   III
Largo de Santa Cruz do Castelo 5
1100 Lisbon
Tel. 86 43 38
Next to St George's Castle. French,
international and Portuguese menu.
Folk music in the evening. Closed
Saturday lunchtime, Sunday and
public holidays.

O Faz Figura   II
Rua do Paraiso 15B
1100 Lisbon
Tel. 886 89 81
Near Santa Apolónia station. Local
and seafood dishes in a country-
style setting, outdoor dining in
summer. Closed Sunday.

North Lisbon

A Góndola   II
Av. de Berna 64
1000 Lisbon
Tel. 797 04 26
Outdoor dining in summer, in a house
near the Gulbenkian Museum. Italian
and local dishes. Closed Saturday
evening, Sunday and public holidays.

Antonio   II
Rua Tómas Ribeiro 63
1000 Lisbon
Tel. 53 87 80
Portuguese and international menu.
East side of Edward VII park.

Antonio Clara –   III
Clube de Empresários
Av. da República 38
1000 Lisbon
Tel. 796 63 80
In an art nouveau palace north of
the city centre. Formal restaurant
with French and international
dishes. Closed Sunday.

Celta   I
Rua Gomes Freire 148-C and D
1100 Lisbon
Tel. 57 30 69
North of city centre. Seafood and
other local dishes. Closed Sunday.

Chez Armand   I
Rua Carlos Mardel 38
1900 Lisbon
Tel. 52 07 70
East of centre. French cuisine.
Closed Saturday lunchtime, Sunday
and throughout August.

Clara   III
Campo dos Mártires da Patria 49
1100 Lisbon
Tel. 355 73 41
In an 18th-century mansion north of
the city centre. Portuguese-French
cuisine. Outdoor dining in summer
and music in the evening. Closed
Saturday lunch and Sunday.

Belém

Caseiro   I
Rua de Belém
1300 Lisbon
Tel. 363 88 03
Near the Mosteiro dos Jerónimos.
Informal local restaurant. Closed
Sunday and throughout August.

São Jerónimo   II
Rua dos Jerónimos 12
1400 Lisbon
Tel. 364 87 96
Stylish setting near the monastery.
Seafood and traditional Portuguese
dishes. Closed Sunday.

Costa de Lisboa

Cascais

João Padeiro   III
Rua Visconde da Luz 12
Tel. (01) 483 02 32
Town centre restaurant serving fish
and shellfish, pork and roast kid.
Closed Tuesday.

Lucullus   **II**
Rua da Palmeira 6/6a
2750 Cascais
Tel. (01) 284 47 09
Portuguese and international menu.
Outdoor dining around a pleasant
courtyard in summer.

O Batel   **II**
Travessa das Flores 4
2750 Cascais
Tel. (01) 483 02 15
Informal bistro specializing in
seafood. Closed Wednesday.

Estoril

A Choupana   **III**
Estrada Marginal
2765 São João do Estoril
Tel. (01) 468 30 99
Elegant dining and dancing with a
view of the sea. Portuguese and
international menu.

Furosato   **II**
Praia do Tamariz
2765 Estoril
Tel. (01) 468 44 30
Authentic Japanese cuisine. In a 19th-
century mansion, close to the sea.

Pak Yun   **II**
Centro Commercial Parque Loja 45
Rua de Lisboa 5
2765 Estoril
Tel. (01) 467 06 91
Chinese restaurant serving the dishes
of several regions. Closed Monday.

Queluz

Cozinha Velha   **II**
Palácio de Queluz
2745 Lisboa
Tel. (01) 435 02 32
Fine restaurant serving traditional
Portuguese cooking. Installed in the
spectacular old palace kitchen.
Operated by the Pousada chain.

Sesimbra

Angelus   **II**
Santana
2900 Sesimbra
Tel. (01) 223 13 40
Regional restaurant 3km (2 miles)
inland from the port.

Ribamar   **II**
Avenida dos Naufragos
2900 Sesimbra
Tel. (01) 223 48 53
On the seafront. Excellent fish,
shellfish and other Portuguese dishes.

Setúbal

O Capote   **II**
Largo do Carmo 6
2900 Setúbal
Tel. (065) 202 98
Just off the main avenue, near
Igreja de Jesus. Lively local
favourite serving excellent seafood.

Sintra

Adega do Saloio   **I**
Travessa Chão de Meninos
2710 São Pedro de Sintra
no tel reservations
Big, popular grill and tavern. Local
atmosphere and menu.

Solar de São Pedro   **II**
Praça Dom Fernando II, 12
2710 São Pedro de Sintra
Tel. (01) 923 18 60
Portuguese and French cuisine in
attractive dining room. Steaks are a
speciality: watch them being cooked
in the open kitchen. Closed
Wednesday.

Tópico   **I**
Rua Dr Alfredo Costa 8
2710 Sintra
Tel. (01) 923 48 25
Friendly and informal, family run
bistro. Local dishes.

Costa da Prata

Abrantes

O Pelicano   **I**
Rua Nossa Senhora da Conceição 1
2200 Abrantes
Tel. (041) 223 17
Informal restaurant, as well as a
bar and pastry shop. Friendly local
gathering place.

Aveiro

A Cozinha do Rei   **I**
Rua Dr Manuel dos Neves 65
3800 Aveiro
Tel. (034) 268 02
Attractive dining room and snack
bar, serving eels, shellfish and other
local dishes.

O Mercantel   **I**
Rua António dos Santos Le
3800 Aveiro
Tel. (034) 280 57
Excellent informal restaurant near
the fish market, specializing in
seafood dishes.

Coimbra

Trovador   **II**
Largo da Sé Velha 17
3000 Coimbra
Tel. (039) 254 75
Attractive bistro style restaurant.
Regional menu. Fado performances
on some evenings. Closed Sunday.

Zé Manuel   **I**
Beco do Forno 10
3000 Coimbra
Tel. (039) 237 90
Atmospheric, typical Portuguese
local restaurant. Closed Monday.

Fátima

Tia Alice   **I**
Rua do Adro
2495 Fátima
Tel. (049) 53 17 37
Small restaurant in an old house
near the sanctuary. Local cooking.
Closed Sunday evening, Monday.

Figueira da Foz

Teimoso   **II**
Estrada do Cabo Mondego
3080 Buarcos
Tel. (033) 227 85
Seafront restaurant 4km (2.5 miles)
north of Figueira da Foz. Varied
menu, noted for shellfish. 14
guestrooms are also available.

Nazaré

Arte Xavega   **II**
Calçada do Sítio
2450 Nazaré
Tel. (062) 55 21 36
Elegant restaurant in the clifftop
quarter. Portuguese and international
menu. Outdoor dining in summer.

Óbidos

Alcaide   **I**
Rua Direita
2510 Óbidos
Tel. (062) 95 92 20
Busy, lively bistro in the heart of the
walled town, serving local dishes.
Closed Monday and November.

Peniche

Abrigo do Pescador   **I**
Largo da Ribeira
2520 Peniche
Tel. (062) 78 34 36
Informal seafood restaurant next to
the harbour. Simple menu but
generous portions.

Beiramar　　　　　　　　I
Avenida do Mar 106-8
2520 Peniche
Tel. (062) 78 24 09
Lively, informal bistro near the
harbour. Popular for fish, shellfish
and other Portuguese dishes.

Santarém

O Mal Cozinhado　　　　I
Campo da Feira
2000 Santarém
Tel. (043) 235 84
Informal bistro-style restaurant on
the north side of the fairgrounds.
Regional dishes, including local beef.

Portas do Sol　　　　　I
Jardim das Portas do Sol
2000 Santarém
Tel. (043) 295 20
Regional restaurant in the gardens,
from where there are views of the
Tagus and Ribatejo. Outdoor dining
in summer. Closed Monday.

Tomar

Bela Vista　　　　　　I
Rua Fonte do Choupo 6
2300 Tomar
Tel. (049) 31 28 70
Attractive dining room next to the
old bridge. Outdoor dining in
summer. Closed Monday evening,
Tuesday, and November.

Nun' Alvares　　　　　I
Avenida Nuno Alvares Pereira 3
2300 Tomar
Tel. (049) 31 28 73
Big wood-panelled dining hall with
good traditional dishes of the region.

Costa Verde

Oporto

Degrau Chá　　　　　II
Rua Afonso Lopes Vieira 180
4100 Porto
Tel. (02) 69 87 64
Oporto and other Portuguese
dishes. Friendly local restaurant
situated in modern suburb off
Avenida Boavista.

Dom Tonho　　　　　II
13 Cais Ribeira
4000 Porto
Tel. (02) 200 43 07
Bistro for local and seafood dishes,
near the river.

Don Manoel　　　　　III
Avenida Montevideo 384
4100 Foz do Douro
Porto
Tel. (02) 617 01 79
Distinguished restaurant in palatial
old mansion situated in seaside
suburb. Serving excellent fish
dishes.

Esplanada Marisqueira Antiga II
Rua Roberto Ivens 628/38
4450 Matosinhos
Porto
Tel. (02) 93 06 60
Cheerful bistro with lots of
atmosphere, situated near the
container port. Noted for its soups
and fresh seafood specialities.

Green's　　　　　　　II
Rua Padre Luis Cabral
Foz do Douro
1086 Porto
Tel. (02) 618 57 04
Light, bright and informal
restaurant, also with a bar and
disco. Noted for its fish soups and
seafood. Closed Saturday lunchtime
and Sunday.

O Escondidinho　　　　II
Rua Passos Manuel 144
4000 Porto
Tel. (02) 200 10 79
Central, informal, family run
restaurant with a good reputation.
Portuguese menu.

O Macedo　　　　　　I
Passeio Alegra 552
4100 Foz do Douro
Porto
Tel. (02) 617 01 66
Popular eatery, good for fish and
local dishes. Lively bistro situated
in seaside suburb.

Vitorino　　　　　　II
Rua Canastreiros 44
4000 Porto
Tel. (02) 208 06 68
Good fish and shellfish restaurant
situated in Ribeira riverside district.
Closed Sunday.

Amarante

Adega Kilowatt　　　　I
Rua 31 de Janeiro
4600 Amarante
no tel. reservations
Atmospheric tasca for informal
meals and snacks: home cooking,
local hams, chourizo (smoked
sausage) and wines.

Zé da Calçada　　　　II
Rua 31 de Janeiro
4600 Amarante
Tel. (055) 42 20 23
Attractive dining room and terrace
overlooking the river. Well furnished
with antiques and rugs. Celebrated
for regional and national cuisine.
Guest rooms also available.

Barcelos

Bagoeira　　　　　　I
Avenida Sidónio Pais 57
4750 Barcelos
Tel. (053) 81 12 36
Picturesque and lively local
restaurant, packed on market day
(Thursday). A few guest rooms are
also available.

Braga

Inácio　　　　　　　II
Campo das Hortas 4
4700 Braga
Tel. (053) 61 32 25
Popular restaurant near the Porta
Nova serving traditional menu,
including bacalhau *and roast kid.*
Closed Tuesday.

Ponte de Lima

Encanada　　　　　　I
Praça Municipal
4990 Ponte de Lima
Tel. (058) 94 11 89
Simple restaurant near the river,
serving fresh food from the nearby
market. Closed Thursday.

Póvoa de Varzim

O Marinheiro　　　　II
Estrada N13
A Ver-o-Mar
4490 Póvoa de Varzim
Tel. (052) 68 21 51
Restaurant set up to look like a
beached fishing boat. Mainly
seafood dishes, with tanks of live
fish and shellfish to choose from.

Viana do Castelo

Galeão　　　　　　　I
Rua Grande 73
4900 Viana do Castelo
Tel. (058) 82 78 26
One of the many small informal and
reasonably priced restaurants
situated in the historic centre of
town. The menu is typically
Portuguese, with a heavy bias
towards seafood.

Os Tres Arcos   I/II
Largo João Tomas da Costa 25
4900 Viana do Castelo
Tel. (058) 240 14
*Restaurant and bar (with a lower
priced menu), facing the river.
Highly popular with locals and
visitors, especially for seafood.
Closed Monday.*

Os Tres Potes   II
Beco dos Fornos 7
4900 Viana do Castelo
Tel. (058) 82 99 28
*Good regional restaurant under the
stone arches of a converted bakery.
Folksong and dance performances
at weekends during the summer.
Closed Monday.*

Mountains

Bragança
Lá Em Casa   I
Rua Marquês de Pombal 7
5300 Bragança
Tel. (073) 221 11
*Rustic, informal restaurant. Good
regional and other Portuguese
dishes. Popular for fish and beef.
Closed Monday.*

Solar Bragançano   II
Praça da Sé 34
5300 Bragança
Tel. (073) 238 75
*Attractive restaurant on the first
floor of an old town house. Regional
menu emphasizes local meats –
veal, kid, hams, smoked and spicy
sausage.*

Castelo Branco
Praça Velha   I
Largo Luis de Camões 17
6000 Castelo Branco
Tel. (072) 32 86 40
*Attractive dining rooms in a 17th-
century stone house in the old part
of town. Regional menu.*

Chaves
O Pote   I
Estrada da Fronteira
5400 Chaves
Tel. (076) 212 26
*Situated just out of town on the
Bragança road, a lively regional
restaurant serving local produce –
trout and smoked ham are notable.
Closed Monday.*

Guarda
Belo Horizonte   I
Largo de São Vicente 2
6300 Guarda
Tel. (071) 214 54
*In historic centre, one of the limited
choice of restaurants in Guarda.
Regional dishes – lamb, rabbit,
trout – and Portuguese standards.*

Vila Real
Espadeiro   I
Avenida Almeida Lucena
5000 Vila Real
Tel. (059) 32 23 02
*Good informal restaurant serving
regional dishes, including beef,
hams, and sausage.*

O Aldeão   I
Rua Dom Pedro de Castro
5000 Vila Real
Tel. (059) 247 94
*Lively and popular local restaurant,
noted for its grills and generous
portions. Good value.*

Viseu
A Varanda da Sé   I
Rua Augusto Hilário 55
3500 Viseu
Tel. (032) 42 11 35
*Relaxed little local bistro in a
converted stone storehouse.
Portuguese, mainly meat-oriented
menu. Closed Tuesday.*

O Cortiço   II
Rua Augusto Hilário 43
3500 Viseu
Tel. (032) 42 38 53
*Small, informal restaurant in the
heart of the upper town. Local menu
includes trout, lamb, rabbit.*

Alentejo

Beja
Alcoforado   I
Largo de São João
7800 Beja
Tel. (084) 263 08
*Attractive dining room opposite
museum. Portuguese cooking.*

O Virgilio   I
Rua dos Infantes
7800 Beja
Tel. (084) 257 50
*One of many small local restaurants
along this street near the museum.*

*Cheerful service and Alentejo dishes.
Especially noted for soups and stews.*

Castelo de Vide
Dom Pedro V   II
Praça Dom Pedro V
7320 Castelo de Vide
Tel. (045) 912 36
*On the main square. Good
Portuguese restaurant with bar and
dance floor. Closed Monday.*

Elvas
Flor do Jardim   II
Jardim Municipal
7350 Elvas
Tel. (068) 62 31 74
*Outside the walls, near main
highway. Alentejo and other
Portuguese cooking. Pleasant
outdoor dining in summer.*

Estremoz
Adega do Isaías   I
Rua do Almeida 21
7100 Estremoz
Tel. (068) 223 18
*Authentic old wine cellar, bar and
prize-winning traditional Alentejo
restaurant. Much atmosphere,
wooden benches, and popular lamb
dishes.*

Casa Velha de Silves   I
Rua 25 de Abril
7100 Estremoz
Tel. (082) 44 54 91
*Traditional restaurant serving
Alentejo dishes, notably tasty stews.
In centre of lower town.*

Évora
Cozinha de Santo Humberto   I
Rua da Moeda 39
7000 Évora
Tel. (066) 242 51
*In an old house in the Judiaria
quarter, an informal restaurant
named after the patron saint of
hunting serving Alentejo dishes,
including soups and casseroles with
plenty of garlic and coriander.*

Fialho   II
Travessa das Mascarenhas 14
7000 Évora
Tel. (066) 230 79
*One of the best restaurants in
Portugal, specializing in Alentejo
dishes – rich soups and stews, pork
and game. West of city centre.
Closed Monday and September.*

Mértola

Migas   **I**
Mercado Municipal
7750 Mértola
Tel. (086) 628 11
Small, family run café-restaurant next to the covered market. Local dishes.

Portalegre

O Tarro   **I**
Avenida das Forças Armadas
7300 Portalegre
Tel. (045) 243 45
Good regional restaurant, bar and snack bar. Noted for its sweet desserts.

Redondo

Miga's   **II**
Rua Direita 28
Terena
7250 Alandroal
Tel. (068) 451 88
In a village near Redondo. Known far and wide for creative country cooking, including game in season. Outdoor dining in summer. 6 guest rooms are also available.

Santiago do Caçem

Martins   **I**
Largo de Santo André
7540 Santiago do Cacém
Tel. (069) 761 13
Busy bistro specializing in fresh local seafood – shellfish, caldeirada (fish stew), eels.

O Retiro   **I**
Rua Machado dos Santos 8
7540 Santiago do Cacém
Tel. (069) 226 59
Attractive regional restaurant in the town centre. Closed Sunday.

Algarve

Albufeira

A Ruina   **III**
Cais Herculano
Albufeira
Tel. (089) 51 20 94
Three-tiered típico famous for its fish. Basic dining room downstairs, rustic restaurant above and rooftop terrace with views over Praia dos Pescadores.

Atrium   **II**
Rua 5 de Outubro
Albufeira
Tel. (089) 51 57 55
Traditional Algarve dishes, including arroz marisco and cataplana, served in a century-old former theatre.

Casa da Avó   **III**
Rua do MFA 97
Albufeira
Tel. (089) 51 44 75
Stylish restaurant with a varied menu, including game and African- and Indian-inspired dishes.

Cave do Vinho do Porto   **II**
Rua da Liberdade 23
Albufeira
Tel. (089) 51 32 29
The tables are set in old vaults full of dust-encrusted bottles of Port. There's a chance to sample one or two, along with a short menu including Port-flavoured dishes.

Jardim d'Allah   **II**
Beco José Bernardino de Souza
Albufeira
Tel. (089) 51 22 96
Elegant Arabesque setting, with the choice of open air courtyard or mock palace settings. Portuguese and unusual North African and other exotic dishes.

O Cabaz da Praia   **II**
Praça Miguel Bombarda 7
Albufeira
Tel. (089) 51 21 37
French-Portuguese food on a terrace over the beach or in the restaurant's attractive dining room. Closed Thursday.

O Dias   **II**
Praça Miguel Bombarda
Albufeira
Tel. (089) 51 52 46
Charming little thatched and tiled restaurant with an open air terrace overlooking the beach. Grilled fish is the speciality. Closed Thursday.

O Fernando   **II**
Largo Eng. Duarte Pacheco
Albufeira
Tel. (089) 51 21 16
On the main square, serving traditional Portuguese cooking. Indoor and outdoor dining.

Os Arcos   **II**
Rua Alves Correira 25
Albufeira
Tel. (089) 51 34 60
Portuguese and international dishes, including good seafood. Shaded roof terrace for outdoor dining.

Tasco do Viegas   **II**
Rua Nova
Albufeira
No tel. bookings
Informal bar and restaurant, popular with locals. Open until late. Good selection of shellfish; also steak Portuguêsa.

Três Coroas   **II**
Rua Correio Valho 8
Albufeira
Tel. (089) 51 26 40
Award-winning restaurant with a Portuguese and international menu. Large outdoor terrace and traditional whitewashed dining room.

Near Albufeira

Adega do Zé   **II**
Olhos de Água to Albufeira road
Tel. (089) 50 16 17
Rustic local restaurant noted for grills and a great choice of fish dishes. Features regular folklore shows.

La Cigale   **III**
Praia de Olhos de Água
Tel. (089) 50 16 37
Attractive rustic beachside restaurant, informal by day, more elegant at night. Good for fondues, shellfish and regional specialities such as cataplana.

Pinhal do António   **II**
Roja Pé, Açoteias road
Pine Cliffs
Tel. (089) 50 387
Roadside terrace and traditional dining room, with local specialities, including fish and shellfish.

Três Palmeiras   **II**
Areias de São João,
road to Albufeira
Tel. (089) 51 54 23
Attractive indoor restaurant, popular with locals and visitors. Portuguese and international dishes, fish always prominent on the menu.

Almansil

Pequeno Mundo   III
off Quarteira Road
Almansil
Tel. (089) 39 98 66
*Charming renovated cottages are the
setting for fine international cuisine.
Notable for desserts. Closed Monday.*

Faro

Café Chelsea   I
Rua de Francisco Gomes 28
Faro
Tel. (089) 28 459
*A bright, modern downstairs room
is fine for daytime snacks and an
elegant blue-and-white upstairs
restaurant fits more formal
occasions. Theres's a wide ranging
menu, from pizzas to fresh fish and
shellfish specials.*

Cidade Velha   III
Rua Domingos Guieiro 19
Faro
Tel. (089) 27 145
*Lovely romantic setting in the old
town. Short Portuguese-
international menu – try the crab
cakes and* lombinho de porco, *pork
fillet stuffed with dates and walnuts.
Closed Sunday.*

Dois Irmãos   II
Largo do Terreiro do Bispo 18
Faro
Tel. (089) 23 337
*The 'Two Brothers' has been
famous for fish since 1925. Large
establishment with lots of local
specialities, including nine types of
cataplana alone.*

Green Steak House   II
Rua Pé da Cruz
Faro
Tel. (089) 82 13 03
*Small but smart. Specialities include
cataplana as well as steaks.*

Lagos

Dom Henrique   II
Rua 25 de Abril 75
Lagos
Tel. (082) 76 35 63
*In the heart of the old town. Classic
Portuguese and international
cuisine served in a formal setting.
Recommended for seafood
specialities.*

Dom Sebastião   III
Rua 25 de Abril 20-22
Lagos
Tel. (082) 76 27 95
*Popular rustic style restaurant
specializing in fresh seafood.*

Dos Reis   I
Rua António Barbosa Viana 21
Lagos
Tel. (082) 62 900
*A brightly lit informal restaurant
serving classic Portuguese and
international cuisine.*

Jotta 13   I
Rua 25 de Abril 58
Lagos
Tel. (082) 76 23 19
*Bright basic decor and standard, good
value Portuguese-international menu.*

O Alpenre   III
Rua Barbosa Viana
Lagos
Tel. (082) 76 27 05
*Established traditional restaurant
serving a wide range of Portuguese
and international dishes.*

O Galeão   II
Rua daLaranjeiro 1
Lagos
Tel. (082) 76 39 09
*Small traditional restaurant serving
fondues, cataplana and other
Algarve specialities. Closed Sunday.*

Piri-Piri   II
Rua Lima Leitão 15
Lagos
Tel. (082) 63 803
*Varied menu includes shellfish spe-
cialities and North African influenced
dishes such as turkey with raisins.*

Near Lagos

O Caseiro   I
Arão (on main road from EN125)
Tel. (082) 79 91 69
*Off the beaten track, large dining
room catering for locals but
welcoming to visitors. Simple fish,
shellfish and meat dishes.*

Vilalisa   I
Mexilheira Grande
on right of main road (off EN125)
No tel. bookings
*No sign outside so look for the low
house with bright blue and yellow
window panels, or ask in the village.
There may be a choice, or just the
dish of the day.*

Loulé

O Avenida   II
Avenida José da Costa Mealha 13
8100 Loulé
Tel. (089) 62 106
*Attractive traditional restaurant
situated in town centre. Closed
Sunday and November.*

Monchique-Fóia

Rampa   I
Monchique-Fóia road
Tel. (082) 92 620
*Roadside terrace enjoying a
panoramic view. Large portions.
Try frango piri-piri (spicy chicken),
grilled quail or eel dishes.*

Portimão

A Lanterna   II
Portimão Bridge (Ferragudo side)
Portimão
Tel. (082) 23 948
*Elegant dining in small,
traditionally furnished rooms.
Specialities include smoked fish and
various unusual desserts. Closed
Sunday.*

Avózinha   II
Rua do Capote 7
Portimão
Tel. (082) 22 922
*'Grandma's' has been serving
award-winning seafood for over 20
years. Cataplanas are a speciality.*

Bonjour Goodnight   II
Rua Serpa Pinto 22
by the bridge
Portimão
Tel. (082) 22 516
*Neon signs and brimming aquaria
give a lively feel to this small,
friendly restaurant. It claims to
serve the cheapest shellfish on the
Algarve.*

Carvi   II
Rua Direita 34A
Portimão
Tel. (082) 41 79 12
*Elegant dining room. Portuguese
menu, excellent fish and shellfish.
Closed Tuesday.*

Tipoia   II
Rua da Senhora da Tocha 10
Portimão
Tel. (082) 26 118
*Tucked away in a back street, a
small informal restaurant serving
the town's most varied menu,
including baked kid, a selection of*

curries, and Mozambican-influenced dishes. Closed Wednesday.

Praia da Rocha

Falésia II
Avenida Tomás Cabreira
Praia da Rocha
Tel. (082) 23 524
Elegant formal dining in an old mansion. Portuguese and international cuisine.

Fortaleza de Santa Caterina II
Avenida Tomás Cabreira
Praia da Rocha
Tel. (082) 22 066
In the courtyard of the 17th-century castle, a simple restaurant specializing in fish dishes. Fine views from the castle walls.

Safari II
Rua António Feu
Praia da Rocha
Tel. (082) 23 540
Decor and dishes from the former African colonies, as well as a standard menu.

The Penguin Terrace I
Avenida Tomás Cabreira
Praia da Rocha
Tel. (082) 24 308
Halfway down the steps to the beach, a pretty terrace for an informal lunch or dinner. Good chicken piri-piri and salads.

Titanic II
Edificio Columbia
Rua Eng. Francisco Bivar
Praia da Rocha
Tel. (082) 22 371
Good international cuisine, served in a formal restaurant, with a view of the open kitchen.

Near Praia da Rocha

Alvila III
Praia da Rocha-Alvor road
1km (0.5 mile) from Alvor
Tel. (082) 45 87 75
Small modern restaurant. Flambés are a speciality. Tuesday is fado night.

Ao Mar II
Rocha dos Castelos
Praia do Vau
Tel. (082) 41 39 83
Modern chalet on the beach with an attractive terrace. Portuguese and international dishes. Popular with local residents as well as visitors – can be crowded for lunch in summer.

Quarteira

Atlântico II
Avenida Infante de sagres 91
Quarteira
Tel. (089) 31 51 42
Informal beachside restaurant. Light lunch menu and more varied choice in the evening. Portuguese and international menu.

O Buzio I
just off fish market
Quarteira
Tel. (089) 31 57 25
Cheap and cheerful place serving excellent fish and shellfish, accompanied by live music.

Os Pescadores II
Largo Cortés Real
opposite fish market
Tel. (089) 31 47 55
Small modern restaurant with nautical decor. Good value fish and meat dishes.

Sagres

Restaurante Cabo de III
São Vicente
Fortaleza do Beliche
(5km/3miles north west of Sagres)
Tel. (082) 64 124
In the relics of a 17th-century fortress, operated by the Pousada do Infante. Serves traditional regional food. With 4 guest rooms also available. Closed November to March.

Vilamoura

The Mayflower II
The Marina
Vilamoura
Tel. (089) 31 46 90
Terrace for outdoor dining and interior restaurant. The menu is varied and good value.

344

Index

INDEX

INDEX

Discover the world

with **BERLITZ**®

Australia
Britain
Brittany
California
Egypt
Europe
Florida
France
Germany
Greece
Ireland
Israel
Italy
Kenya
Loire Valley
New England
Normandy
Portugal
Prague
Pyrenees
Rome
Singapore
Spain
Switzerland
Thailand
Tuscany

IN PREPARATION

Canada
Scandinavia
Turkey

BERLITZ DISCOVER GUIDES do more than just map out the sights – they entice you to travel with lush full-colour photography, vivid descriptions and intelligent advice on how to plan and enjoy your holiday or travel experience. Covering the world's most popular destinations, these full-colour travel guides reveal the spirit and flavour of each country or region. Use *DISCOVER* as a travel planner or as a practical reference guide. You'll find sightseeing information and suggested leisure routes, extensive full-colour maps and town plans, local hotel and restaurant listings plus special essays highlighting interesting local features. Colourful historical and cultural background is complemented by practical details such as what to visit and where to stay, where to eat and how much you should expect to pay.

No matter where you're going, make the most of your trip:

DISCOVER the world with BERLITZ.